Eurocommunism

Wolfgang Leonhard

Translated by Mark Vecchio

Eurocommunism

Challenge for East and West

Holt, Rinehart and Winston | *New York*

First published in the United States in 1979 by Holt,
Rinehart and Winston, 383 Madison Avenue, New York,
New York 10017.

Published simultaneously in Canada by Holt, Rinehart and
Winston of Canada, Limited.

Library of Congress Cataloging in Publication Data

Leonhard, Wolfgang.
Eurocommunism : challenge for East and West.

Translation of Eurokommunismus: Herausforderung
Ost und West.
Includes bibliographical references and index.
1. Communism—Europe. 2. Communist parties.
I. Title.
HX239.L46 1980   335.43′094   79-11290
ISBN 0-03-044951-0

Designer: Leon Bolognese

Printed in the United States of America

10 9 8 7 6 5 4 3 2 1

Contents

Preface to the American Edition

Eurocommunism can no longer be overlooked as an important trend in international politics. Since the coining of the term in 1975, Eurocommunism has attracted much attention among many of the world's political analysts and commentators. However, there have been conflicting appraisals of this new movement.

Many see in Eurocommunism a serious transformation and a true departure from Soviet Communism of the past. Adherents to the so-called "serious transformation theory" see certain Communist parties developing toward a new conception of democracy.

Others, however, view Eurocommunism as a large-scale tactical maneuver. Adherents to this "deception theory" fear that Eurocommunists are motivated solely by the desire to increase their own influence and to gain control of strategic positions in the governments of certain West European countries. Only after they succeed to power, claim these skeptics, will the Eurocommunists reveal their "true faces."

Within the last two years, certain commentators have made "intermediate" appraisals, integrating different aspects of the view of Eurocommunism as both a serious transformation and a tactical maneuver.

The wide spectrum of opinions is not surprising, for Eurocommunism does not fit into the mold of our usual conceptions of Communism and our previous, often tragic, experiences with Communist parties and Communist-ruled countries.

For the first time in the history of Communism, we are dealing with a movement which, in its official proclamations, has repeatedly taken issue with many of the fundamental aspects of Communism as it has manifested itself until now.

Eurocommunists continually assert their *independence from Moscow*. They reject the concept of a monolithic world Communist movement. They proclaim the need for Communists in each country to determine their own policies based on their particular traditions and on the economic, political, and cultural peculiarities of their own countries.

Eurocommunists state emphatically that Communist parties in industrialized countries with democratic traditions have not only the right but the duty to follow roads other than those followed by Russia, China, and the countries of Eastern Europe. Moreover, Eurocommunists continually criticize the repressive measures in the Soviet Union and East European countries. They condemn the occupation of Czechoslovakia, advocate reforms in the countries of the Soviet bloc, and support dissidents who are suppressed in their own countries.

Eurocommunists openly proclaim *new relationships between democracy and socialism*. They reject the theory of a violent revolution and the establishment of a dictatorship of the proletariat. They advocate instead a democratic road to socialism based on the will of the majority of the people and a majority in their respective parliaments. This majority, they insist, is to be supported by different parties and political forces. Eurocommunists reject the usual Communist conception of playing a "leading role" in political struggles. They strive, instead, for an equal alliance which includes not only Socialists and Social Democrats, but Christian Democrats and Liberals as well. In addition, Eurocommunists strongly reject atheism and seek broad-minded and long-term cooperation with religious forces.

Finally, in their official declarations, Eurocommunists continually advocate *new goals*. They are striving for a socialist society, which differs greatly from what is termed "socialism" in the Soviet Union and Eastern Europe. Instead of the bureaucratic and dictatorial systems of those countries, Eurocommunists proclaim as their goal a pluralistic socialism with all democratic rights and freedoms. They wish to establish a pluralistic socialist society which permits opposition parties to exist and to be active and which allows for the possibility of democratic changes from majority to minority and vice versa. Eurocommunists also vow to respect the decisions of the voters in a future democratic socialist society.

Despite the clarity of the programmatic declarations of the Eurocommunists, appraisals of this new movement are extremely diverse. Many skeptics are quick to point out the past negative experiences of Communism. After the war in 1945, for example, the Communists of Eastern Europe also promised to follow their own independent roads and to strive for an equal alliance with socialist, democratic, liberal, and Christian parties. Several years later, however, they established bureaucratic dictatorial satellite states and mercilessly persecuted their former alliance partners. Those who believe Eurocommunism is a tactical maneuver remind us of the violent suppression of the Hungarian revolution, the subordination of the East

European countries to the Soviet Union, and the erection of the Berlin Wall. They point to the Soviet missiles in Cuba in the early 1960s, the violent occupation of Czechoslovakia in August 1968, the repression of dissidents in the Soviet Union and Eastern Europe, and the Soviet Union's active intervention in distant areas of the world.

For skeptics, these and other events reflect the true nature of Communism. They have a difficult time reconciling Eurocommunism's clear commitment to democracy, pluralism, independence, and democratic freedoms with past experiences of Communism.

Adherents to the "serious transformation theory," on the other hand, point to the profound changes which Communism has undergone. Communism, they indicate, is no longer a monolithic world movement. It has split into several diverse trends. Defenders of the "serious transformation theory" assert that world Communism is now at the threshold of a schism similar to the Sino-Soviet conflict. It is time, they insist, to recognize Eurocommunism as a new and independent force, just as Chinese Communism is considered an independent trend.

This controversy is the main theme of the following book. It is my aim to discuss the development and the significance of Eurocommunism and to investigate critically the aims of the various Eurocommunist parties. Discussion, however, is not limited merely to the already well-known Communist parties of Italy, France, and Spain. Instead, the book attempts to portray Eurocommunism as an international trend. Eurocommunism is viewed not merely as a matter of Italian domestic politics but, rather, as a trend which several Communist parties are following.

The first part of the book deals with the aims of the Eurocommunists, while specifying which Communist parties can be considered Eurocommunist. The second part describes the origins and formation of Eurocommunism as an international tendency. The third part concentrates on the development of individual Eurocommunist parties. In this part, emphasis falls on the following questions: Under what circumstances can a pro-Soviet party transform itself into a Eurocommunist party? How can this change take place? And what are the difficulties, possibilities, and new perspectives resulting from such a change? In addition to the development of the Eurocommunist parties of Italy, France, and Spain, the third part undertakes an investigation of Eurocommunist tendencies in other Communist parties, including those of Denmark, Sweden, Norway, Iceland, Greece, Great Britain, and Finland as well as the non-European Communist parties of Japan, Australia, and Venezuela.

The fourth and last part of the book centers around the current debate over Eurocommunism, the different appraisals of the movement, and the possible effects which Eurocommunist participation in government might have on NATO and the process of European unification.

Unlike other commentators, I believe it is important not to limit oneself merely to the effects of Eurocommunism on the West and on the Western alliance system. Instead, one should consider, too, the effects which Eurocommunism has on the countries of the Soviet bloc and, in particular, the encouragement it gives to the reformist tendencies within those countries. For that reason, I think the subtitle "Challenge for East and West" is appropriate.

The German original, *Eurokommunismus: Herausforderung für Ost und West,* appeared in Germany in February 1978. During preparation of the American edition, I have tried to include the major events which have occurred since that time, thus bringing the book as up to date as possible. It is, however, not the aim of this book to focus on the current day-to-day events within the Eurocommunist movement but, rather, to present and analyze the historical process of the formation of Eurocommunism, to compare the development of different Eurocommunist parties, and to examine their goals in order to judge both the significance and the limits of this new trend.

New Haven, Connecticut **Wolfgang Leonhard**
March 10, 1979

Part I

The Present Status of Eurocommunism

The Concepts of Eurocommunism

1

A New Term Arises

The term "Eurocommunism" was coined in June 1975 by the non-Communist Italian journalist Frane Barbieri, an editor of the Milan daily newspaper *Il Giornale Nuovo*: "As far as I remember, I first used the expression in my article 'After Brezhnev,' which appeared in *Giornale* on June 26, 1975. I wrote: 'Meanwhile, Santiago Carrillo's concept of Eurocommunism, which has its stronghold in the Western European community and which has disengaged itself from strict adherence to Moscow's strategic policies, is gaining strength.' "[1]

Some consider Arrigo Levi, Editor-in-Chief of the Turin daily paper *La Stampa*, to be the originator of the term "Eurocommunism."[2] Still others claim that the Catholic philosopher Auguste della Noce was the inventor of the term.[3]

Almost as soon as it appeared, the term was adopted by the entire world press and employed in all discussions of the Communist movement. The widespread usage of the word "Eurocommunism" was clearly the result of the pressing need for a term that would characterize an important new movement in world Communism, a movement that was beginning to take definite shape, separating itself from Moscow, following new roads, and proclaiming new methods and goals of socialist society.

This movement, the beginnings of which were already visible in the fifties, was at that time labeled "Autonomism" or "Reform Communism" by western political experts. In the mid-fifties, Boris Meissner had coined the term "Reform Communism," indicating that, unlike national Communism, this movement sought not only autonomy and independence, but also a more liberal form of society.[4]

The term "Eurocommunism" that arose in the mid-seventies gained so much popularity that the Eurocommunists themselves accepted it, though at first somewhat hesitantly. It was first mentioned by leading representatives of the Italian and Spanish Communist parties and then later by the Swedish and Yugoslav Communists, who, nonetheless, were more reluctant, claiming that the new term implied certain fallacies.

Enrico Berlinguer, General Secretary of the Italian Communist Party, noted that the term "Eurocommunism" was not originated by the Italian Communists but insisted that the widespread adoption of the concept was in fact a result of the profound desire among Western European countries to effect new means of realizing the Socialist notion of societal transformation.[5]

Similarly, Santiago Carrillo, General Secretary of the Spanish Communist Party, claimed that the term "Eurocommunism," although actually a misnomer, had spread quickly because in a fundamental sense it characterized a new movement within Communism. "The policy and theoretical implications which justify Eurocommunism," according to Carrillo, "describe a tendency in the modern progressive and revolutionary movement that is endeavoring to come to grips with the realities of our continent—though in essence it is valid for all developed capitalist countries—and adapt to them the development of the world revolutionary process characteristic of our time." A "victory of the socialist forces in the countries of Western Europe" would neither "augment Soviet State power," nor "imply the spread of the Soviet model of a single party." It would mean the appearance of a "more evolved socialism that will have a positive influence on the democratic evolution of the kinds of socialism existing today."[6]

Stane Dolanc, Secretary of the League of Communists of Yugoslavia, contends that, among certain Communist parties, Eurocommunism is a form of emancipation from outdated concepts.[7] The goals of Yugoslav Communists are "almost identical to those of Eurocommunism."[8] Eduard Kardelj, a member of the Presidium of the League of Communists of Yugoslavia and for over thirty years Tito's closest adviser within the Yugoslav leadership, claims that the Communist parties of Western Europe have realized their ineffectiveness as mere instruments of the Soviet bloc and are now striving for autonomy within their respective countries. They therefore follow "independent roads" and reveal "new roads to Socialism in Western Europe." Although the Yugoslav Communists do not always agree completely with the individual views of these parties, there is no doubt that "Eurocommunism is a very significant, almost expedient phenomenon in the history of the Communist movement."[9]

Lars Werner, Chairman of the VPK (Left Party Communists, as they are known in Sweden), points out that the term "Eurocommunism" was not invented by the Communists, but that "we are not ashamed of it either." Eurocommunism is the result of the realization that some Communist parties in the capitalistic industrial countries of Europe, Australia, and Japan are in favor of a socialist society "within which democracy extends to all reaches of social life, where the trade unions remain an autonomous force with the right to strike, and where the opposition is guaranteed all democratic liberties."[10]

The term "Eurocommunism" is, indeed, somewhat of a misnomer. Although important for the definition of a new phenomenon within world Communism, it does not precisely communicate the true form and content of this new movement.

a) The term "Eurocommunism" seems to indicate that *all* European Communists adhere to its viewpoints. This is not the case. The term applies only to a few European Communist parties, while other parties continue to follow the Soviet line.

b) The term "Eurocommunism" refers to a purely European phenomenon. This, too, is incorrect, for the term also applies to some non-European Communist parties or movements (the Communist Party of Japan, for example).

c) The term "Eurocommunism" might imply a tightly knit organization with a center and a binding party line. This, however, is not the case either. Unlike the adherents of Soviet Communism, whose representatives meet regularly to work out a general party line, Eurocommunism observes no single party line. It denotes, rather, Communist parties whose theories are often very similar but which, at the same time, enjoy a great deal of autonomy.

Eurocommunism's representatives frequently meet on a bilateral level, issuing communiqués on common goals. These communiqués, however, can, and often do, outline varying courses of action and particular individual goals among the different parties. On domestic and foreign policy issues, each individual party invariably makes decisions based on the state of affairs within its own country.

The Goals of Eurocommunists

The common interests and goals recognized as such by all Eurocommunists of the late seventies can be summarized as follows:

Autonomy and Equality: All Eurocommunists deny the existence of a single center of the world Communist movement. They object to ideological and enforced general party lines, and to obligatory international ideological journals, reviews, and textbooks. Eurocommunists contend that these measures are no longer suitable for the different conditions of the various Communist parties today. They also reject the entire Soviet concept of "proletarian internationalism," which emphasizes unity and strict subordination to the Soviet Union. Rather, Eurocommunists advocate the principle of "unity in diversity" whereby each individual Communist Party has the right to determine its own policies independently and in accordance with the traditions and with the economic, political, and cultural peculiarities of its own country.

According to Eurocommunists, relations between the Communist parties—both ruling and nonruling—should proceed on the basis of absolute equality and on mutual nonintervention in domestic affairs. Instead of the "proletarian internationalism" of the Communists loyal to Moscow, Eurocommunists advocate the concept of "international solidarity," i.e., voluntary cooperation between the Communist parties of different countries on the basis of the equality, independence, and autonomy of each party. Eurocommunists, who proclaim the need for dialogue and open exchange of ideas, are critical of Moscow's world Communist conferences, which are invariably accompanied by attempts to establish a general party line and single ideology. In addition, Eurocommunists believe the Communists are isolated from other socialist and democratic forces because of the concept of a single party line. They advocate mutual interaction between Communists, Socialists, Social Democrats, and other progressive forces, and also place strong emphasis on cooperation with progressive Christian-Catholic and liberal forces.

Democratic Road to Socialism: Eurocommunists reject, although to different degrees, the Soviet concept of a violent revolution and the establishment of a dictatorship of the proletariat. They advocate a democratic road to socialism which relies solely on the consent of the majority of the population.

In the Eurocommunists' views, the October Revolution of 1917 in Russia is not the obligatory model for the transition to socialism and for all countries at all times, particularly not for developed capitalist nations with democratic traditions. The present conditions in the industrialized countries are completely different; consequently it is absolutely impossible to apply the Russian experiences of 1917 to other countries and other epochs. Different social relations, different class forces and parliamentary traditions necessitate different paths to socialism.

The concept of a democratic road to socialism includes, above all, the recognition of a pluralistic party system—in other words, unrestricted activities for all parties and all political groups as well as regularly held secret elections. The concept also entails a new interpretation of the role of the parliament. Parliamentary bodies cannot be used exclusively as tribunes for the denunciation of capitalism and propagation of socialism as Lenin had always proclaimed they should; they should be regarded as important instruments in political life, instruments which play a large role during both the period of transition to socialism and the future socialist society.

At the same time, however, the affirmation of a democratic road to socialism is not to be confused with Social Democratic conceptions. In the Eurocommunists' view, the Social Democrats limit themselves to doing away with many of the grievous problems of capitalism, and do not desire to alter society itself. The Eurocommunists explain that the democratic road to socialism implies a sweeping transformation of society, and that, therefore, one cannot expect a calm, uncomplicated evolutionary transition. In their opinion, democratic roads to socialism mean not only a definite renunciation of the earlier Communist conceptions of a violent revolution for the purpose of establishing a dictatorship of the proletariat, but also dissociation from the superficial reforms which are proclaimed and carried out by Social Democratic parties. The democratic road to socialism, as the Eurocommunists see it, is a transition period from capitalism to socialism dependent upon the consent of the majority of the population and carried out within a parliamentary framework.

This transition period, however, is interpreted differently by the individual Eurocommunist parties. The Italian Communist Party often considers it a period of "structural reforms." The French Communist Party talks about far-reaching changes in economic, political, and social life leading to an "advanced democracy." The Spanish Communist Party, in its party program published in 1975, considers the transition a "period of political and social democracy." In addition, the individual Communist parties suggest different measures. The main goal of most of these transition programs is to restrain and gradually overcome monopolistic ownership, i.e., large private banks, insurance agencies, and other monopolistic enterprises. The Eurocommunists, however, have no intention of achieving this through the establishment of state-owned enterprises directed by the government but, rather, through step-by-step nationalization. The nationalized enterprises are to be decentralized and directed by democratically elected bodies, in which the employees are to be well represented. Small private business and middle-sized enterprises are not to be affected by this economic change. Large land ownings and the practice of land speculation are to be controlled and eventually done away with, but farm property is to remain intact. It is interesting to note that some Eurocommunist parties foresee changes in other realms, including the control of the mass media and in the realm of culture, science, and education.

Broad Coalition Policy Without Claim for a Leading Role for the Communist Party: In the Eurocommunists' view, a democratic road to socialism can be realized only through a broad coalition with other social, political, and ideological forces and classes: a coalition based on dialogue, mutual tolerance, and the independence of each individual force.

In contrast, pro-Soviet parties advocate a coalition policy which is based on the leading role of the Communist parties. The pro-Soviet Communist parties proclaim that through their espousal of Marxism-Leninism, they command a deeper understanding and thus, through their activity and energy, should play a leading role in the implementation of the common program. The other partners of the coalition are, therefore, subordinate to the Communist Party. The Eurocommunists renounce a leading role and see their parties in such a coalition as equal partners with other political trends and organizations. "If we want a democratic road to socialism which is dependent upon a majority of the population which advocates it," declared Enrico Berlinguer, the leader of the Italian Communist Party, "the result is not only a new coalition policy but also a special system of political relations."

The Eurocommunists continually emphasize the desirability of a coalition, not only with those groups left of center, but also with groups in the middle of the political spectrum. Thus, the Italian

Communists strive for cooperation and agreement with the Christian Democrats, the Socialists, the republicans, and the Social Democrats. They emphasize the desire to offer not a leftist alternative but, rather, a democratic alternative, or a "historic compromise" between Communists and Christian Democrats. In addition, Italian Communists have no intention of estranging Catholic workers from their religion and church. On the contrary, they explicitly recognize the importance of the Catholic church and of Catholic political parties and organizations. The same is true, moreover, for Japan, where the Communist Party strives for a broad coalition of Communists, Socialists, Social Democrats, and the Komeito, a progressive middle-of-the-road group based on the Buddhist faith.

Opening Up of Marxism and the Necessity of Dialogue: A coalition policy among equals necessitates a new attitude toward Marxism. In fact, the Eurocommunists reject, with different emphasis and to different degrees, the Soviet form of Marxism-Leninism as a standard ideology. The Soviet ideology is based solely on the teachings of Marx, Engels, and Lenin and on Soviet interpretations of these works. Soviet ideologies claim Marxism-Leninism to be the only science of nature, society, and human thought which applies to all peoples of the past, the present, and the future. The Eurocommunists oppose such an absolute claim; they reject the term "Marxism-Leninism" and prefer the term "scientific socialism" (a term originally used by Marx and Engels). They do not attempt to justify all their activities with ideological references and do not insist upon the avowal of scientific socialism as a prerequisite for entrance into the party. They broaden the scope of Marxism with scores of other Marxist and socialist authors, forbidden in the Soviet Union and the Warsaw Pact countries. In addition, the Eurocommunists value free discussion about the different problems of scientific socialism, acknowledging divergent and even opposing views. Moreover a completely new attitude toward Christianity often appears in their numerous publications.

Eurocommunists reject the entire concept of an ideological struggle. They renounce obligatory atheism, which they see as a historical phenomenon of the past century. They advocate equal dialogue with partners of different ideologies, with the goal of mutual understanding. Dialogue partners are often different, however, depending upon the peculiarities of each individual country: For the Eurocommunists in Spain, Italy, and France, the Communist-Catholic dialogue is of prime importance; the Communist Party of Japan advocates similar dialogue with the Buddhists; and the Communist parties of Australia and Sweden with the Protestant church.

Critical Attitude Toward the Soviet Union and Eastern Europe: The Eurocommunists refuse to glorify indiscriminately all developments, actions, and declarations of the Soviet leadership and that of other Warsaw Pact countries, let alone make them the basis for their own policies. This is indeed one of the most important contrasts to Soviet Communism. The pro-Soviet parties consider the system in the Soviet Union and in satellite countries "real socialism," and thus see the Soviet model as an obligatory model for socialism. The Eurocommunists respect the October Revolution of 1917 as well as the Soviet Union as the first country to attempt to establish a socialist society. However, they do not regard Soviet evolution since then as exemplary and refuse to recognize the system established in Eastern Europe as the sole viable model of socialism. The Eurocommunists criticize the excessive centralization and bureaucratization of economic and political power in the East. They object to the inadequate analysis of Stalinism and incomplete de-Stalinization in the Soviet Union. They criticize the one-sided preoccupation with technological advancements, computers, and electronics prevalent in present-day policies of Warsaw Pact countries, where little consideration is given to necessary changes and reforms in the social, political, and cultural realms. They criticize the lack of legality and demand the development of a true socialist democracy. They criticize the Russification in the USSR, the lack of respect for the non-Russian nationalities, and anti-Semitism as well as the insufficient consideration given to new social and political problems by Soviet and Eastern European ideologues. As a logical consequence, the Eurocommunists have repeatedly protested against the repressive measures in the Soviet Union and the satellite countries. They criticized the Soviet occupation of Czechoslovakia as well as the repressive measures taken in compliance with the so-called normalization in Czechoslovakia. They protested against the suppression of the Polish workers' uprising in 1970 and the unrest in Poland in 1976. While pro-Soviet Communists consider even the most legitimate criticism of any event in Eastern Europe anti-Communist, the Eurocommunists explain that not every criticism of the Soviet Union is to be seen necessarily as anti-Communist. They clearly distinguish between reactionary, militant anti-Communism on the one hand, and legitimate criticism of the situation in the Warsaw Pact countries on the other.

In a declaration at the East Berlin Conference of European Communist parties at the end of June 1976, the Eurocommunists declared that "not all parties whose policies do not agree with those of the Soviet Union or which indulge in criticisms of its activities are necessarily to be considered anti-Communist."

The Eurocommunists base their criticism of the Soviet Union and the satellite countries on the following arguments: The socialist revolution was at first successful in countries where economic development was not at a very advanced level, in countries where the industrial working class made up only a small portion of the population. Industrialization had to be accomplished under particularly unfavorable conditions. This development led in the Soviet Union and in several Eastern European countries to authoritarianism, bureaucratization, centralization, amalgamation of party and state, the restriction and suppression of democratic freedoms, and a pronounced personality cult. After Stalin's death, particularly after the Twentieth Party Congress in February 1956, the hopes for complete de-Stalinization were frustrated as liberalization and democratization were halted in their early stages. Today in the Soviet Union economic modernization is promoted, but the social and political aspects of the transformation to a modern industrial society are not given any consideration. The present system in the Soviet Union and the satellite countries is commensurate with neither the potentialities nor the necessities of a developed socialist society.

Nevertheless, the Eurocommunists try to prevent a total break with the Soviet Union, apparently so as not to lose contact with the reform forces of that country and of Eastern Europe. They continually emphasize their "critical solidarity" with the Soviet Union—a solidarity with respect to all positive developments and with the right to criticize long-term negative developments which are not reconcilable with the aims of democratic socialism.

Pluralistic Democratic Model of Socialism: In the Eurocommunists' view, the present system in the USSR and the satellite countries is too monopolistic, too dictatorial, too centralized, and too bureaucratic. Therefore, such a system is clearly not suitable for an industrially developed nation with parliamentary democratic traditions. Consequently, the Eurocommunists advocate a model of socialism in which democratic freedom and participation by all citizens in national affairs are guaranteed. There is, however, considerable debate as to where the main emphasis of this socialist alternative model should rest. The majority of Eurocommunists, particularly in West European countries and in Japan, strive for a pluralistic and democratic model which guarantees all democratic rights and freedoms. This democratic model of socialism is based on the concept of rule of law, proclaims no state ideology, and distinguishes itself by a multiparty system whereby the popular vote is decisive. Finally, most Eurocommunists pledge that under socialism they would respect the vote even should they face defeat at the polls.

Other Eurocommunists, especially those in Yugoslavia, advocate socialist self-management. Under such a system, enterprises and the means of production are run by workers' councils or producers' councils and are interconnected by a national congress of delegates from all over the country. There are also Eurocommunists who desire to combine both the parliamentary multiparty system and the system of socialist self-management.

Rejection of the Leninist Party Structure: The Eurocommunists reject, although again to different degrees and with different emphases, both the present-day structure of the Communist Party of the Soviet Union and of the other satellite countries as well as the Leninist party principle of "democratic centralism." This democratic centralism is, in reality, bureaucratic centralism characterized by a chain of command from the top down, by the conception of a revolutionary elite party, and by tough party discipline. Moreover, under bureaucratic centralism, party members are required to make an avowal of Marxism-Leninism. In addition, a system of so-called "transmission belts" prevails whereby any other organization, such as trade unions, youth groups, cooperatives, and cultural associations, is completely subordinate to the leadership of the Communist Party and must profess unconditional acceptance of the Soviet pattern of Marxism-Leninism.

Instead, the Eurocommunists advocate reform of the party structure. As always, there is considerable disagreement about emphasis—particularly between the parties in which discussion and realization of the Eurocommunist trend have just recently begun, and those parties which have already begun making decisive changes in that direction. In general, the following principles form the basis for the desired goals, or in some cases, for reforms already introduced in the hope of changing the party's structure:

a) The Communist Party should not be open only to Marxists and Leninists, but also to people with completely different philosophical and ideological points of view. Party meetings should be open to the public and nonparty members should be allowed, even encouraged, to participate in them.

b) Leading party officials cannot simultaneously hold top-ranking positions in other organizations, such as trade unions. Moreover, party functionaries cannot hold office indefinitely; instead, there must be a rotation system—a regular change of party officers.

c) In the party press, at party meetings, and at party congresses, different opinions and interpretations should be freely expressed and openly discussed. Party members and party officials have the right to express individual opinions which do not correspond to the general party line by publishing them in interview or article form in newspapers and journals not belonging to the party or by having them printed in the form of brochures and books.

d) Commissions are not to be part of the bureaucratic party apparatus, but should instead represent the interests of the party members. In addition, representatives elected by the members, and not major party officials, are to serve on the committees.

e) In local, state, and national elections, Eurocommunist parties may also endorse nonmembers, who may then represent the Eurocommunists in the parliament.

f) Party members and functionaries cannot be expelled because of ideological differences or because of disagreement with certain aspects of the general party line. Members and functionaries who, in today's view, were expelled unjustly will be rehabilitated and will be returned, when possible, to their previous positions.

g) The party records should be accessible not only to a closed group of party officials, but to historians who are not even party members.

Several Eurocommunist parties have already realized many of these reforms, while others are still in the discussion stages. What is characteristic of all Eurocommunist parties, however, is that they no longer consider the Leninist party doctrine obligatory.

Independent Foreign Policy: The Eurocommunist parties express differing attitudes to the many aspects of Soviet foreign policy. They support certain aspects, criticize others, and at times even form their own policies. In contrast to the pro-Soviet Communists, the Eurocommunists refuse to be mere extensions of the Soviet and Warsaw Pact Communist parties. They identify themselves with their own foreign policy, which is independent of Moscow and the satellite countries. Moreover, they advocate new relationships with the

People's Republic of China, the European Economic Community, and NATO (North Atlantic Treaty Organization).

The foreign policy goals of the Eurocommunists differ from those of the Kremlin in the following ways:

a) The indiscriminate Soviet condemnation of the People's Republic of China and the campaign against the Chinese Communists are rejected by all Eurocommunist parties. They urge unbiased account of the events in the People's Republic of China and strive for an unbiased, objective understanding of the phenomenon of Maoism and post-Mao developments in China.

b) The Eurocommunists reject any one-sided portrayal of the Warsaw Pact as an alliance for freedom and socialism on the one hand, and of NATO as an alliance of capitalism and aggression on the other. The Italian and Spanish Communist parties are determined to overcome the division of the European continent into military blocs, to disband gradually the military strongholds, to reduce the number of foreign troops stationed in European nations, and to strive for a Europe which is capable of developing and enjoying relations based on equality with both the United States and the Soviet Union.

c) All Eurocommunists, although in different ways and with differing intensity, criticize the Soviet domination over the countries of Eastern Europe.

d) Besides the Eurocommunist goal of overcoming the bloc phenomenon in Europe, certain Eurocommunist parties, among them the Italian Communist Party and the Spanish Communist Party, are ready to support the process of European unification. They favor, however, the democratization of the bodies of the European Economic Community and the reduction of national and international monopolies. Other parties, such as the French Communist Party, advocate national freedom of action in their economic and social programs within the realm of the European Economic Community. On the other hand, the British Communist Party, as well as other leftist forces in Great Britain, are against England's entrance into the European Economic Community. Some Eurocommunists, like the Japan Communist Party, openly declare their opposition to Soviet territorial conquests during World War II and demand Soviet restitution of those occupied territories (the Kuril Islands, for example).

The attitude toward NATO has also changed. The Italian Communist Party declared that their final goal was indeed to overcome the blocs but that, nevertheless, one had to consider the present situation. As long as there was a military balance of power between the USA and the USSR in Europe and other parts of the world one would have to be realistic about it. A possible unilateral withdrawal of single countries from one or the other pact, according to the Italian Communists, would not be realistic at all. Italy's withdrawal from NATO would serve only to hinder or even endanger the stability of détente. The French Communist Party declared that it would not neglect France's obligation to NATO, but that at the same time it would strive for the utmost independence within the realm of the alliance.

Which Parties Are Eurocommunist?

The Italian, French, and Spanish Communist parties are regularly considered part of this new trend in world Communism. Both the Italian and the French Communist parties are important factors in the political arenas of their respective countries and their shared responsibility in governmental policies is an ever approaching reality. The Spanish Communist Party has attracted attention because many Eurocommunist ideas have been consistently realized in that party.

Occasionally one hears talk about a North-South division in European Communism, which implies that the three Communist parties of the Mediterranean countries represent the new ideas, while the Communist parties of Northern and Central Europe are pro-Soviet. Careful consideration, however, proves that this is a misconception, for Eurocommunist tendencies have become active in Northern Europe just as in the Mediterranean area, and, in some cases, even earlier than in some Latin nations. Despite the present interest in the Italian, French, and Spanish Communist parties, Eurocommunism deals with more than just the parties of those countries.

To begin with, six nonruling Communist parties of Europe may be considered part of the Eurocommunist trend:

a) The Italian Communist Party (PCI), with 1.8 million members and 34.4 percent of all votes cast during the elections of June 1976, is the strongest Communist Party outside the Soviet sphere of influence and has been involved in its own evolutionary process since 1956.

b) The Swedish Communist Party (CPS) began a new course in 1964, named itself Left Party Communists (VPK) in 1967, and received 4.8 percent of the vote in the Swedish election of September 1976.

c) The British Communist Party (CPGB) is not represented in the British Parliament, but does exercise influence over the trade unions and, to a lesser degree, over intellectuals.

d) The Communist Party of Spain (PCE), struggling against a pro-Soviet faction since 1968, has consistently followed a course of independence and new orientation, and during the national elections in Spain in March 1979 it received 10.7 percent of the vote.

e) The Greek Communist Party (KKE) in 1968, after an internal dispute during the illegal struggle against the military regime of the colonels, split into an exterior pro-Soviet group and an independent, interior group, which, however, received only 2.7 percent of the vote in the November 1977 election.

f) The French Communist Party (PCF), with 600,000 members, is the second strongest Communist Party outside the Soviet sphere of influence and in the national election of March 1978 received 20.5 percent of the vote. The French Communists only began to manifest Eurocommunist tendencies in 1972, and the ballast of the Stalinist past manifests itself more strongly in the PCF than in the other Eurocommunist parties.

In addition to these six Eurocommunist parties, two other Communist parties merit attention. The *People's Socialist Party* of Denmark, which came about as a result of a split among Danish Communists during 1957 −59, was the first party to espouse the idea of a democratic road to socialism and a democratic model of socialism. The Communists of Iceland, known since 1968 as the *People's Alliance*, received 23 percent of the vote in the election of June 1978 and were repeatedly represented in the Icelandic government.

Finally, there are two ruling Communist parties which continue to play extraordinarily large roles as supporters of nonruling Eurocommunist parties—*The League of Communists of Yugoslavia*, with 1.6 million members, and *The Romanian Communist Party* with 2.7 million members—which must be considered part of the Eurocommunist cause. Although the Yugoslav Communists sometimes expound their own ideas about socialist society (instead of a parliamentary model of socialism, they advocate a self-management socialism), they have actively supported all Eurocommunist movements.

A different situation prevails in the case of the Romanian Communist Party. The internal system of Romania can hardly be considered a realization of Eurocommunist ideals. There is no doubt, however, that for more than fifteen years all independent tendencies, especially the Eurocommunist movement, have been supported by the Romanian Communists.

Furthermore, three more Communist parties outside Europe (and this shows just how contradictory the term "Eurocommunism" is) can be mentioned. The *Japan Communist Party (CPJ)*, with almost 400,000 members, was able to muster 10.4 percent of the vote in the 1976 election and has consistently manifested Eurocommunistic attitudes. The relatively small but important *Australian Communist Party (CPA)* must also be mentioned in the context of Eurocommunism, as must the majority of the Communists in Venezuela, who broke away from the pro-Soviet Communist Party in 1971 and have since been known as the *Movement Toward Socialism (MAS)*.

Many humanist Marxists—individuals as well as large groups—of the countries of Eastern Europe and the Soviet Union profess views which fall well within the realm of Eurocommunism. Among them are the East German Robert Havemann, Wolf Biermann (expatriated in 1976), and Rudolf Bahro arrested in November 1977; the Polish historian Jacek Kuron, the economist Edward Lipinski, and the former Minister of Education, Wladyslaw Bienkowski; the Soviet historian Roy Medvedev, the former general Piotr Grigorenko, who was expelled from the Soviet Union in early 1978, and the mathematician Leonid Plyushch, who was expelled in 1976. Furthermore, many former leading representatives of the "Prague Spring" in Czechoslovakia, active today in the Human Rights movement of the "Charter 77," and several exponents of the so-called Budapest School in Hungary are also sympathetic to many Eurocommunist tenets.

Thus the Eurocommunist movement is not simply a phenomenon of Italian domestic politics. Rather, it is a synthesis of the ideas of several Western European Communist parties, several non-European Communist parties, and several Marxist opposition groups and movements within the Warsaw Pact countries. Eurocommunism, although articulated differently in individual countries, incorporates Communists from every continent and must, therefore, be treated as an international movement.

Eurocommunism is not merely a movement toward autonomy along the lines of national Communism. The movement away from Moscow is inseparably connected to a fundamental new course of policies. Eurocommunists strive not only for a new road—a democratic evolution to socialism—but for the completely new goal of a pluralistic democratic model of socialism. And finally, the new course of Eurocommunism involves fundamental questions of Marxist theory as well as the renunciation of many fundamental theories of Soviet Marxism-Leninism.

2

The Debate over Eurocommunism in the West

The Eurocommunism movement has become the subject of lively and increasingly intense public debate in the West. The many differences between Eurocommunist and traditional Communist concepts have made Eurocommunism a subject of much interest, and the possibility that in certain countries—Italy, France, and Spain in particular—the Eurocommunists might take a more active role in the government in the near future has enhanced this interest.

The discussion revolves mainly around the extent to which Eurocommunism is a true transition as opposed to a mere tactical maneuver that has as its goal the aggrandizement of power through democratic rhetoric.

Several main tendencies are already recognizable in discussions of Eurocommunism in the West. On the one hand, there are those who feel Eurocommunism is merely a high-scaled deceptive maneuver, a typically conceived Communist tactic. Others do not deny that there are positive aspects to the development of Eurocommunism, but tend to be more skeptical, believing that since this transformation is not yet complete, one has to consider the likelihood of opposing forces and setbacks and that any definitive conclusion is thus still premature. Finally, some see Eurocommunism as a welcome process of reform, which could lead to a viable solution to pressing social and economic problems and which represents a much greater danger to the bureaucratic regimes in the East than to the parliamentary systems in the West.

The view that Eurocommunism is a deceptive maneuver and that Eurocommunist participation in governments of Western Europe would have a dangerous, even catastrophic effect on NATO and the European Economic Community has been expressed most emphatically in the United States by former President Gerald Ford and former Secretary of State Henry Kissinger.

At the end of October 1977 Gerald Ford declared that Eurocommunism was not Communism with a human face or with democratic tendencies but, rather, "masked Stalinism and disguised tyranny." "If the victories of the Communists in Europe are not checked," he claimed, "the shroud of one-party rule will descend upon Europe."[1]

Similarly, Henry Kissinger emphasized the danger of Eurocommunism. If communist governments were elected in Western Europe, according to the former American Secretary of State in a statement made in April 1976, the Atlantic Alliance would collapse and the United States would be isolated. "An accession to power of Communist parties in Western Europe would result in a fundamental change in the established patterns of American policy."[2] The advent of Communists in the Italian government, Kissinger claimed, is likely to produce a sequence of events in which other European countries, particularly France, Portugal, Spain, and Greece, would follow suit. As a result European-American relations would be drastically changed. Mr. Kissinger's objections to a Communist role in government were threefold: Communist parties have Leninist, or authoritarian, organizations; they would inevitably decrease their countries' spending on defense against the Soviet bloc; and they would maintain political relations quite different from the pro-Western ones now practiced.[3]

Moreover, in major Washington addresses in April and June 1977, Mr. Kissinger warned that the traditional Communist strategy is seizure of power. He claimed that since democratic centralism was still evident within the Eurocommunist parties, they are not sincere in their liberal proclamations. Communist participation in European governments, he said, would have a decisive "effect on freedom throughout the world" because the "global balance" would "tip against the West."[4]

Similar views have been and are being voiced in Europe. The Christian Democratic Union (CDU) politician and President of the European Union of Christian Democrats (EUCD), Kai-Uwe von Hassel, for example, declared that Eurocommunism was "merely a slightly altered tactic, which doesn't change anything regarding the goals of the Communists." They want, simply, "to accede to power more easily and then immediately institute a well-enough known collective system from Eastern Europe."[5]

Senator Enzo Bettiza, a leading representative of the Liberal Party of Italy in the European Parliament, considers untrustworthy the Eurocommunists' declaration that they would accept a pluralistic social order with a multiparty system and surrender power if they lose an election. According to Bettiza, if one looks "behind the legalistic and faultless democratic façade," one sees that, in reality, "the Italian Communists are not striving for true cooperation with the other political forces but, rather, are planning to dominate, paralyze and undermine them. . . . One should not make the mistake of confusing the tactics with which the Eurocommunists hope to gain power with the methods they *could* employ if they were in power."[6]

Gaston Thorn, Prime Minister of Luxembourg and President of the Liberal World Union and the Federation of Liberal Parties of Europe, stated in May 1977: "What does Eurocommunism mean? I know only one Communism. Communists are Communists, they haven't abandoned their goals."[7]

He is "alarmed" by the possibility of a Eurocommunist participation in government. In European politics, "active Communist participation in government could result in drastic changes." Thorn claims it is not easy for him to believe the recent pro-European affirmations of many West European Communist parties, for they have always strongly opposed Europe. Should the Communists enter the governments of their respective countries as a result of electoral victory, would they respect the rules of democracy?[8]

In West Germany, similar and at times even harsher criticism of Eurocommunism is prevalent. Josef Strauss, Chairman of the Christian Social Union (CSU), declared: "Moscow allows the Eurocommunist to go as far as they see fit in order to establish a popular front with the Social Democrats, that is, with the socialists among the Social Democrats. It is ludicrous to think, however, that an independent Eurocommunist movement is developing in the West, for Communism and freedom are always incompatible."[9] And Helmut Kohl, Chairman of the Christian Democratic Union (CDU), defines Eurocommunism as "a part of the world Communist movement which should only be judged on its conduct after it is in power. Until then, everything else is simply verbal stalling."[10]

Moreover, Walter Laqueur, Director of the Institute of Contemporary History in London, insisted, "There is no denying that the Western European Communist parties have learned from past mistakes and that they have become more modern and more pragmatic in their approach. But they have to become more democratic, and it is difficult to imagine that parties which are still strictly authoritarian in their own internal structure could become guardians of liberty in the sphere of national politics."[11]

The views cited thus far are all based on a long-established conception of Communism. They reflect the tragic experiences which many have had with Communism, especially during the Stalin era: show trials and the Great Purge in the Soviet Union, the prison camps with millions of prisoners, the Hitler-Stalin Pact with the secret agreement between both dictators for the division of Poland and Eastern Europe into German and Soviet spheres of influence, the Stalinist usurpation of the countries of Eastern Europe after the war, with the arrest of hundreds of thousands of people (including many Social Democrats and Christian anti-Fascists), the Berlin Wall, the death camps, the command to fire upon those caught trying to cross the border between East and West Germany and finally the occupation of Czechoslovakia in 1968. Furthermore, the tactical methods of many Communist Party leaders in Eastern Europe after 1945 play a large role in the formation of such a rejectionist attitude. All too often the Communists lured coalition partners with promises of democracy, but as soon as their power permitted, began playing leading roles in the coalitions, subjugating and even completely eliminating the other coalition partners.

Clearly, the apprehension about Soviet Communists is understandable. It is questionable, however, whether *all* Communists can really be judged on the basis of the experiences mentioned above.

The history of Communism consists not only of tactical maneuvers, but also of numerous far-reaching transitions—Yugoslavia's break with Moscow and its independent policies since that time, the Sino-Soviet conflict, and the "Prague Spring" in Czechoslovakia.

Recognition of the serious changes within the Communist movement led a number of Western statesmen, politicians, and journalists to regard present-day Eurocommunism as a new movement and to avoid immediate condemnation of Eurocommunist concepts as diversionary tactics. A great number have already declared, although somewhat skeptically, a readiness to accept many Eurocommunist declarations as well intended.

Already at the end of November 1976, during the Ford and Kissinger administration, Zbigniew Brzezinski (later to become President Carter's adviser on national security affairs), declared that a new American administration would, of course, not advocate Communist participation in West European governments, but that "it has been perfectly ridiculous to agree to talk to Brezhnev and refuse any contact with Berlinguer."[12] The Carter administration refused to make threats of reprisals if Communists were to come to power. Such measures would do "more harm than good," it claimed, and one should not break off relations even if the Communists have a few seats in their respective parliaments.[13]

At the beginning of May 1977, in answer to a question about how the United States would react to a victory of the Eurocommunists in countries such as France and Italy, President Carter declared: "I believe the fundamental principle which we all should respect rests on the fact that the citizens of Europe are clearly in a position to make their own decisions about political affairs through free elections." The United States would like the governments in question to remain democratic. It disapproves of the increasing influence and domination of totalitarian elements and wishes to see the democratic parties maintain their ground in the future. The best way to prevent an increasing Communist influence in European politics is to ensure that democratic administrations are able to function openly and humanly and with true, lasting understanding of the needs and expectations of the people.[14] In September 1977 President Carter again declared that the United States should not succumb to the temptation of trying to influence the decisions of the voters in Italy, France, and Spain. According to the President, West European NATO countries in whose governments Communists participate would not necessarily have to withdraw from the alliance.[15]

Gregory F. Treverton, a close associate of National Security Adviser Zbigniew Brzezinski, is responsible for West European affairs at the White House. He indicated that Kissinger's apocalyptic warning about West European Communists' participation in government has since given way to a more cool-headed appraisal of the situation: "We are more at ease, but that is not to say indifferent, about leftist trends in Italy and France," said Treverton. "It is, however, important to characterize this movement according to its actual ideological orientations. Leftist governments in those countries will not necessarily result in a crisis for NATO, so long as they are loyal to the Atlantic alliance. This necessitates, of course, a critical separation from the Soviet Union."

In answer to a question about criteria upon which the Carter administration judges possible leftist governments in France and Italy, Treverton declared, "The general principle of the administration is not to oppose democratic processes. Openness and flexibility toward future developments are important. CIA manipulations are part of the past. The European countries have to decide their own futures."[16]

Similarly, in January 1978 Professor Stanley Hoffman, Chairman of the Center for European Studies at Harvard University, rejected Mr. Kissinger's cold-war attitude toward Eurocommunism, denouncing his failure to differentiate between the various Western European Communist parties and to realize that the parties' independent stance toward Moscow "was largely a response to the distaste of the electorate (including their own) for the Stalinist model." Hoffman also criticized Mr. Kissinger for advocating a "solemn U.S. warning against further Communist progress . . . bound to be interpreted, even by moderate Europeans, as an embarrassing call for intervention."[17]

Similar trends of thought have been expressed by several European statesmen and politicians. The Chairman of the Social Democratic Party of Germany, Willy Brandt, declared: "I am still very skeptical about all kinds of Communism after the experiences which we here in Germany have had with the SED [Socialist Unity Party of East Germany]. On the other hand, one must remember that the Communists in France and Italy were in the government soon after World War II. The Communists in France and even more so in Italy and Spain should not in the long run be excluded from the body politic. This does not imply, however, that we should be any less skeptical. If their development continues further, it is possible that in ten years people will still call themselves Communists but they will certainly be something other than what we mean by Communists."[18]

The long-time Swedish Prime Minister, Social Democrat Olof Palme, declared that he had trouble understanding "those who view the ideological revision within Communist parties with nothing but suspicion." One should consider it an advantage that these parties also affirm democratic freedoms and rights, want to protect human rights, and are beginning to understand the importance of reforms for social changes. Moreover, only further evolution can prove if the change of heart of the Communists is real.[19]

The Social Democratic Austrian Chancellor, Bruno Kreisky, has often referred to the transition process, though cautiously and skeptically. "We Social Democrats have no reason to consider it a defeat if the two largest Communist parties of democratic Europe completely dissociate themselves from political formulas which make up the basic requirements of Leninism," he declared in March 1976.[20]

Chancellor Kreisky added reservedly that he could accept Eurocommunism only conditionally, and that it was mainly a question of how much one could trust the Communists after all the many changes in their sixty-year history. The Italian Communists have had sufficient time to demonstrate their democratic reliability. For the French Communists, however, it would be much more difficult. If the Communists truly wish to become reliable democrats, they would have to eliminate more than just the dictatorship of the proletariat.[21]

Fundamental rejection of the dictatorial bureaucratic regimes of Eastern Europe as well as a cautious readiness to recognize Eurocommunist transformations were both reflected in the new party program of the Austrian Socialists published in the fall of 1977, which reads, ". . . the Socialists steadfastly support democracy and are opposed to any form of dictatorship." Consequently, the Socialists must be regarded as uncompromising opponents of both Fascism and Communism. It is a sign of the strength of Social Democratic ideas, that "in the last few years, large Communist parties of Europe are continually approaching democratic principles and at the same time striving to avoid Communist centralist dogmatism." In light of the many trends in Communism of the past, "we Social Democrats are observing this particular development very cautiously, in order to ascertain its degree of seriousness. In the event that Eurocommunism actually proves to be a genuine, far-reaching change, new perspectives for the development of social-democracy would result."[22]

Of particular interest are the views of Italian Christian Democrats and Socialists whose judgments are based on their own experiences with the Italian Communists. Luigi Granelle, the leading representative of the Italian Christian Democrats and a member of the European Parliament, declared that although there were still many unreconcilable differences, he recognized truly positive aspects of Eurocommunism. He referred, for example, to the Eurocommunists' constructive attitude toward the European Economic Community and the Western alliance. "It is the duty of all democratic parties of Europe to engage in a realistic appraisal of and to remain on good terms with Eurocommunism." In view of the crisis of Marxist-Leninist dogma and the Eurocommunists' search for new models different from those in Eastern Europe as well as for their own democratic pluralistic goals, a historic opportunity exists to "induce the Communist parties to redefine the relationship between power and freedom, between class and party, between centralism and pluralism, and between national independence and internationalism."[23]

Senator Gaetano Arfe, a member of the Executive Committee of the Socialist Party of Italy and a member of the European Parliament, expressed similar views. The problem of Eurocommunism cannot be put in such a way as to "doubt the sincerity of the leading Communists." Although the trial is not yet over, the Eurocommunists' position is supported by many facts of historical significance. According to Arfe, its further development will be decisively determined by the European socialists' ability "to have an active influence, to analyze unbiasedly and to begin debate with the same seriousness and emphasis as the Communists."[24]

Finally, two experts have considered the problem of Eurocommunism in particularly great detail. Horst Ehmke is convinced that it is important to differentiate between pro-Soviet and Eurocommunist parties. He claims that the incompatability of Social Democratic ideas with the concepts of the Social Unity Party of East Germany (SED) and its West German offshoot, the German Communist Party (DKP), has not changed, for the German Social Democrats have not forgotten the suppression of the Socialist Party of Germany (SPD) in the Soviet-occupied zone. It remains an indispensable part of democratic socialism to confront Soviet Communism with Eurocommunism's alternatives.

In view of the divergent trends of international Communism, there must be a corresponding diversity in the Social Democratic appraisals of the movement. A policy of mere separation from Eurocommunism is not sufficient. The new commitments of the Eurocommunists to overcome the traditional dogmatic positions of Communism, their refusal to support unconditionally Soviet foreign policy, and the fact that they accept ideological, political, and social pluralism may in many ways be tactics, but they are, nonetheless, of considerable importance and represent a critical point in the history of Communism. "Social Democrats have had enough experience with Communists to approach the new situation cautiously. It is too early to say whether the parties are engaged in tactical maneuvers or whether they have in fact opened their ranks to a free exchange of ideas. Certainly it will take more than proclamations to convince democratic socialists. On the other hand they are not likely to accept the conservative position which holds that the 'moderate' Communists are especially dangerous."[25]

Richard Löwenthal also declared that with the Communists in Italy, France, Spain, and Japan, one could distinguish a rejection of the "Leninist beliefs in violent revolutions and party dictatorship." Above all, since the changes in the development of the Italian Communist Party have taken place in open discussions and over a long period of time and have influenced other Communists, they cannot be regarded as having occurred either under direction from above or very suddenly. According to Löwenthal, there is a certain degree of validity in the belief that changes in Communism in Western Europe and Japan are underway which, as long as they succeed, will result in the parties no longer being Communist in today's meaning of the word.[26]

The diversity of interpretations of Eurocommunism demonstrates not only the degree to which it has been the center of attention in recent discussions, but also the difficulty in suppressing this increasingly important political trend. There is, of course, no one "right" or "wrong" answer, nor is there any infallible criterion on which to predict the future developments of Eurocommunism clearly. The question as to whether Eurocommunism is merely a tactical maneuver or a meaningful new trend will continue to be discussed. One thing is certain, however: a careful consideration of the historical development which has led to the appearance of Eurocommunism is essential for any accurate assessment of this phenomenon. I am of the opinion that not enough attention is given to this historical background in current discussions. A true evaluation, however, is hardly possible without a description of the origins and development of Eurocommunism.

There is much evidence that the current trends of Eurocommunism can be seen as a part of the ongoing split in world Communism which, in the course of several decades, has seen the end of monolithic world Communism under Soviet leadership. Through a difficult and turbulent process, three main streams have formed: Communism of the Soviet type, Maoism, and now nascent Eurocommunism. Eurocommunism appears as the result of far-reaching changes within the entire Communist world movement. It is a consequence of the transition from monolithic world Communism of the Stalin era to the diversified world Communism of today. The decisive split into different tendencies was mainly a result of the great schism—the break between Moscow and Peking—on the one hand, and the simultaneous appearance of Reform Communism, known since 1975 as Eurocommunism, on the other.

Such retrospect is by no means simply of historical interest. In recent years Eurocommunists have continually commented on the negative experiences during the Stalinist period. Communists in Yugoslavia, Romania, Japan, Italy, and Spain have not forgotten the twenties, thirties, and forties as the Communist movement in different countries suffered under the directives of Moscow. The experiences during the Stalin era played a decisive role in the origins of

Eurocommunism and are also very important to today's discussions of world Communism. The following remarks, therefore, are not abstractly historical but include consideration of what the Communists, both party members and party officials, thought of these events, what they learned from them, and how these events led to the appearance of Eurocommunism.

Part II

The Origins and Development of Eurocommunism

European Communism During the Stalin Era

3

The period between the mid-twenties and the mid-fifties was marked by the monolithic structure of world Communism under Soviet leadership. The interests of the Soviet leadership were the main priorities for Communists of all countries. When asked the same question, the Communists in different countries always gave identical responses. They glorified Stalin and obediently followed all of Moscow's directions. All declarations, resolutions, and orders of the Soviet leadership were accepted without criticism.

Communist parties included in their names at that time "Section of the Communist International." All declarations of the Executive Committee of the Communist International, the highest body for all Communists and referred to as the ECCI, were reprinted in their entirety. For three decades, the Communist Party newspapers of countries as different as Australia, Sweden, Venezuela, and Italy were hardly distinguishable.

The Origins of Monolithic World Communism

There are four main reasons for the monolithic Communism of that time:

1. The Psychological and Political Factor: All Communists had only one example—the Soviet Union. Only the Russians had carried out a successful revolution. All other revolutions led or supported by Communist parties in the twenties ended in defeat. The Bolsheviks, however, had reached their goal. Subordination to the Soviet leadership almost automatically ensued; though it sprang from sheer admiration, sincere fascination, and enthusiasm, it was later sustained by obligation, discipline, and obedience.

Stalin's declaration of August 1, 1927, was frequently cited in party newspapers and studied in party schools during the thirties and forties: "A *revolutionary* is one who is ready to protect, to defend the USSR without reservation, without qualification, openly and honestly, without secret military conferences; for the USSR is the first proletarian, revolutionary state in the world, a state which is building socialism. An *internationalist* is one who is ready to defend the USSR without reservation, without wavering, unconditionally; for the USSR is the base of the world-wide revolutionary movement. . . ."[1]

The Soviet Union was at that time considered the fatherland of the working class. Later it became known as the fatherland of all working people. Even the program adopted at the Sixth Congress of the Comintern (Communist International) in the summer of 1928, the organization's most important document, required the international workers' movement, in case of war against the Soviet Union, to organize mass action to overthrow the imperialist governments and to strive for an alliance with the USSR.[2]

Loyalty to the Soviet Union was expressed in the most distinct forms. Communist delegations, upon entering the Soviet Union, frequently kissed the holy earth of the Soviet ground. Communists in Germany at the end of the twenties greeted each other with "Hail to Moscow." The more critical Communists did recognize the deficiencies of the Soviet system, but they justified them with historical explanations: the Soviet Union was, after all, the first country to build socialism. A backward agrarian country was confronted with the technology of the twentieth century and threatened by capitalist encirclement. Most Communists were convinced that each Communist Party could be successful only if it relied upon the increasingly powerful Soviet Union.

2. The Common Party Training of Communist Functionaries: Although short-term courses of instruction were organized by the individual Communist parties of different countries, the principal ideological training of party functionaries of all Communist parties took place in the Soviet Union. Since the mid-twenties specially chosen Communists from different countries were instructed in the Soviet Union, where the most important school was the famous Lenin School. Although foreign Communists were also admitted as faculty members, the Soviet influence was, of course, decisive. Marxism-Leninism was taught solely according to Soviet interpretation, and the history of the Bolshevik Party was revered as the sole example. The policies of the Communist parties of other countries were, as a rule, regarded only as variations of the common goal—the establishment of an international Soviet republic. The Soviet pattern of the dictatorship of the proletariat was prescribed as obligatory for all countries after the planned revolution. All further stages of Soviet-Russian development were seen as universal and obligatory for every other party, and modification was allowed only in areas of lesser importance.

The Comintern School was founded in Kushnarenkovo, a small town about forty miles northwest of Ufa in the fall of 1941, replacing the Lenin School. The location seemed logical, since the most important leaders of the Communist International, including Dolores Ibarruri, Wilhelm Pieck, Walter Ulbricht, André Marty of the PCF (who had not yet fallen out of favor), Anna Pauker (at that time leader of the Romanian Communist Party), and Dmitri Manuilsky of the Soviet Communist Party, were living in Ufa at that time.

I attended the Comintern School from 1942 to 1943 and vividly remember my experiences as a student there. One-third of the approximately 150 students were old Communists, two-thirds were, like myself, children of foreign (non-Russian) Communists who had been brought up and were living in the Soviet Union. There were Germans, Austrians, Sudeten Germans, Spaniards, Czechs, Slovaks, Poles, Hungarians, Romanians, Bulgarians, French, and Italians, but no British or Americans at the Comintern School.

Since both instructors and trainees used pseudonyms, with the exception of two students—Amaya Ibarruri, the daughter of Dolores Ibarruri, Secretary General of the Spanish Communist Party, and Sharko, Tito's son—no one's real identity is known to me.

Completely isolated from the outside world, we students at the Comintern School studied the history of the German Communist Party, the history of the Soviet Communist Party, the Weimar Republic, Fascism, the character and course of World War II, political economy, dialectical and historical materialism, and the history of the Communist International. Although many lectures were given in Russian, translations were provided for the non-Russian-speaking students. The most important part of the instruction, however, was carried out in smaller national groups in the language of the particular group. In addition to political and ideological instruction, we also received military training, whereby all students were organized into three groups. One group consisted of Spaniards, French, and Italians, another of Germans, Austrians, and Sudeten Germans, and the third of Bulgarians, Romanians, Hungarians, Czechs, and Slovaks. In each group Soviet officers instructed us on how to engage in a partisan war. Moreover, Soviet Marxism-Leninism was preached as the sole ideology, and all other Marxist ideas were denounced as deviations.

The entire training process was conducted under the strictest conditions: one could not leave the school grounds for any reason; letters to the outside had to be handed in unsealed and the return address had to read "Agricultural Technical School No. 101." Complete subordination of the students was achieved through constant "self-criticism."

The sense of community and the realization that one belonged to a world party played an important role at the Comintern School. It was also obvious that one had an obligation to submit oneself to party discipline. All students acquired not only the same ideology, but the same way of thinking, the same manner of speech, and often even the same typical Soviet bureaucratic intonation. By this sort of pedagogical regimen, an absolute uniformity was established.

This was reinforced by uniform publications—the same newspapers for the Communists of all countries. The *Communist International* and the *International Press Correspondence* invariably repeated the Soviet interpretation of all international questions and events in every country. During the Stalin era, Communists as a rule did not read any "bourgeois" newspapers, but got their information exclusively from their own press.

3. The Organizational Component: The Communist parties were required not only to publish all resolutions and directives issued by the Executive Committee of the Communist International (ECCI) but to regard them as the "binding party line," and to communicate all decisions of the Comintern to the party leadership of the respective countries. After the October Revolution of 1917, the World Conferences, which were convened yearly and at which open and stimulating discussion took place, were the center of attention for all Communists. Since the late twenties, however, with the transition from revolutionary Leninism to bureaucratic Stalinism, the Comintern Congresses were seldom convened. Decision-making authority was gradually transferred to the ECCI, which grew in importance almost to the level of the Central Committee of the Communist Party of the Soviet Union (CPSU). During the thirties, the important decisions were made in the small centers of leadership, in the so-called Presidium of the ECCI (which corresponded to the Politburo of the CPSU), or in the Secretariat of the ECCI (which corresponded to the Secretariat of the Central Committee of the CPSU).

The so-called plenipotentiaries of the ECCI implemented the Comintern's policies in the Communist parties of all countries. In addition, there were so-called Comintern instructors for various fields of work. The plenipotentiaries as well as the instructors were seldom if ever members of the parties or citizens of the countries to which they were sent. The large organizational apparatus strengthened the influence of Moscow and furthered the centralized character of the Communist International. This centralization often led to serious misinterpretations, since the Communist parties had only a limited right of individual activity. Obviously, the Comintern not only made mistakes, but its centralized, monolithic character at that time undoubtedly harmed the Communist parties more than it helped them. Eurocommunists publicly admit this fact today.

4. Financial Dependence: Most Communist parties of the world were financially dependent upon the Soviet Union. Serious psychological effects followed as a result of this dependence. There were Communists who already questioned this development in the twenties, and several Communist leaders tried in vain to free themselves from this financial dependence. The most famous was Tito, who declared, "It is necessary to make the Party independent of foreign financial assistance. This is one of the basic conditions for success. If assistance is expected only from abroad, a man gets into the habit of never trying to find support in the surroundings in which he lives and works. During the whole period of the Communist Party's work from 1919 to 1937, the receipt of money from Moscow had had only a harmful effect. From the moment I took over as party head (1937), we discontinued the receipt of subsidies from abroad. We then had to rely on our resources, because the financial problem had become a political one. The support we received depended on the influence we had among the people. Furthermore, since our money was money that the workers had contributed from their salaries and the peasants from their small earnings, much greater attention was given to all our expenditures."[3]

This psychological and political glorification of the Soviet Union, the common ideological training, the centralized apparatus for direction and control, and the financial dependence upon the Soviet Union all helped to prolong the monolithic character of the world Communist movement well into the 1950s.

The World Communist Movement During the Depression and the Rise of Fascism: (1929–1934)

Many old-time Communists who still remember this period know that the obligatory political line changed constantly, often very suddenly, and usually in the interests of the Soviet Union and at the expense of the Communist influence in other countries.

From 1929 to 1934, during the period of the worldwide economic crisis and the continued ascent of Fascism, Communists, under the direction of Moscow, led a major struggle against the Social Democrats, known at the time as Social Fascists. Several prominent Eurocommunists today, including Tito, Santiago Carrillo, and Japanese Communist leaders, openly express their criticisms of the past policies of the Comintern.

The worldwide economic crisis afforded the Communists a great opportunity. Many workers became radical, anticapitalist feelings grew, and Communist parties began to flourish. But the most important aspect of political development at that time was the rapid ascent of fascism. If—as many Communists wanted—a united front against fascism had been possible at that time between Communists and Social Democrats, history might very well have taken another course. But, since Moscow's general party line required that Communists continue the struggle against the Social Democrats, any such unification was impossible. The long-winded declarations of the Communists from 1929 to 1933 invariably portrayed the Social Democrats as the main enemies of the political struggle: "Only by directing the main blow against Social Democracy, that social mainstay of the bourgeoisie, will it be possible to strike at and defeat the chief class enemy of the proletariat—the bourgeoisie" (Twelfth Plenary Session of the ECCI, September 1932). After Hitler's victory in January 1933, the Presidium of the ECCI declared with reference to the situation in Germany: "The establishment of the fascist dictatorship in Germany is the consequence of the Social Democratic policy of collaboration with the bourgeoisie throughout the entire life of the Weimar Republic. . . . The Communists were right when they called the Social Democrats 'Social Fascists.' "[4] At the same time, Social Democrats and Communists sat together in Hitler's prisons and concentration camps.

The Popular Front Period (1934–1939)

After many internal disputes, the political line finally began to change in the early summer of 1934. The French Communist Party, which had already concluded its first agreement with the socialists in July 1934, played an important role in the transformation. Maurice Thorez, Chairman of the PCF at that time, first introduced the idea of a Popular Front in October 1934. Other West European Communist parties, such as the Communist Party of Italy, quickly followed suit. Members of the Comintern in Moscow, however, argued back and forth until, at the famous Seventh Congress of the Communist International from July 25 through August 20, 1935, they officially proclaimed the change to a policy of a Popular Front.

Dimitrov of Bulgaria and Togliatti of Italy were the principal speakers at this decisive congress. The Communists renounced the theory of "social fascism" and resolved not to permit any attacks against the Social Democrats. All Communists were called upon to form a united front with the Social Democrats, and the long-term goal of a unified party of Social Democrats and Communists was proclaimed. All Communist trade-union factions were to be dissolved and were to join the large unions headed as a rule by Social Democrats. Moreover, the members of the Comintern proclaimed a Popular Front with all democratic forces in order to defend democracy against fascism. At the same time, they emphasized the importance of national traditions, gave up the atheistic campaign, and advocated alliance with Christian forces.

Most Communists welcomed this decisive change in the general line, which many thousands of Communists had been hoping for all along. The isolated nature of the Communist parties was finally overcome, and many Communist parties of Europe, particularly those of France and Spain, experienced a sudden surge in the struggle against fascism. In France, the Communists gained sixty-two seats in the Parliament in 1936, bringing the total up to seventy-two. Although the French Communists wanted to take an even greater part in the government, the Comintern forbade such a step, limiting the Communists' influence to the Parliament.

The Communists participated in a West European government for the first time after Franco's coup in Spain, when, during the Spanish Popular Front government from September 1936 to April 1939, they were appointed to the ministries of education and agriculture. During the civil war, the Communist Party experienced a tremendous increase in popularity and membership. Unfortunately, however, the self-sacrifice, the activity, and the fine organization of the Spanish Communists were undercut by the unjustifiable suppression of Trotskyites, anarchists, and many leftist socialists who were not willing to subordinate themselves to Moscow.

Nevertheless, the period of the Popular Front policy was for many Communists the happiest time in their political struggle. There was now a clear and definite enemy—fascism. The Communists fought together with socialists, Social Democrats, and other leftist forces, and, what is more, were successful in their endeavors. However, to maintain today that Eurocommunism is a continuation of the Popular Front policy is historically incorrect.

a) The Popular Front policy in no way changed the final goal of the dictatorship of the proletariat and the establishment of socialism according to the Soviet model.

b) There was no independence from the Soviet Union. At the same Seventh World Congress, which proclaimed the Popular Front policy, Stalin was portrayed as "leader, teacher, and friend of the proletariat and of the suppressed peoples of the entire world," and as "the beloved leader of international proletarianism." All Communists, in the event of war, were required "to assist in the triumph of the Red army over the imperialist armies by any means and at any price." The subordination to Soviet foreign policy was not questioned.

c) At the time of the Popular Front policy, a Great Purge, which decimated almost the entire apparatus of the Comintern, took place in the Soviet Union. Most functionaries who had played a leading role in the Comintern, including the famous Russian Communists Zinoviev and Bucharin, were arrested and executed. Radek died in a Soviet camp, and Trotsky was murdered in August 1940 while in exile in Mexico. There were thousands of victims among the foreign Communists in the Soviet Union, many of whom had fled there for their lives from European dictatorships and were now in Soviet prisons and camps. Few were spared. During the period of Popular Front, the entire Polish Communist Party was dissolved in the fall of 1938, and almost all Polish Communists living in the Soviet Union were arrested. Stalin also wanted to dissolve the Yugoslav Communist Party, and was dissuaded from this move at the last moment. All this proceeded without a single word of criticism from any Communist Party throughout the world.

d) Finally, Eurocommunism cannot be compared to the period of Popular Front, because this period lasted for just under four years. It ended in August 1939 with a sudden, unexpected change in the general line. No Eurocommunist Party today would submit itself to that kind of Moscow-dictated change in policy.

The European Communists During the Hitler–Stalin Pact (1939–1941)

The darkest chapter of European Communism followed the hopeful period of Popular Front. This chapter, originating with the Hitler-Stalin Pact, lasted from August 23, 1939 to June 1941. When today's Communists think back to those days, they either try to repress all memories, or they begin to construct elaborate rationalizations.

During those two difficult years, the Communists had to support a policy which meant literal or figurative suicide for most Communists in Europe. The Hitler-Stalin Pact was not, as described in the Soviet bloc, merely a nonaggression pact between the Soviet Union and Nazi Germany; rather, it was a tacit collaboration, documented in a secret additional agreement, dividing Eastern Europe between Nazi and Soviet spheres of influence. Of the independent Baltic states, Estonia and Latvia were included in the Soviet sphere of influence and Lithuania in the German sphere. Likewise, Poland was divided into spheres of influence, and Bessarabia, part of Romania, was promised to the Soviets. Moreover, Communists of all countries had to share in the responsibility for and even defend these annexations.

The European Communists found themselves in the impossible situation of practically having to give up the struggle against fascism. During these two years many European Communists left the party out of protest; the majority stayed, gritting its teeth while all the successes of the Popular Front period were nullified in a matter of months.

At first, the West European Communists, like Harry Pollitt, the Chairman of the British Communist Party, tried desperately to link the Hitler-Stalin Pact in some way with their own struggle against fascism. But when, on September 17, 1939, Soviet troops, with Hitler's obvious approval, invaded Eastern Poland (called Western Byelorussia and the Western Ukraine, according to Soviet terminology), West European Communists were placed in a quandary. They had to uphold the new line and treat the war between Nazi Germany and the Western powers as a struggle between imperialistic powers on both sides. But even that was not enough. At the end of October 1939, the Soviets attacked Finland—an event which resulted in catastrophe for the Scandinavian Communist parties, isolating them totally from the people of their countries. Finally, on October 31, 1939, Molotov declared that England and France, and not Hitler-Germany, were to be regarded as aggressors. When the Western powers maintained that they were fighting a war for the "destruction of Hitlerism," Molotov replied that there was "absolutely no justification for a war of this kind . . . for ideology cannot be destroyed by force." Hence "it was not only senseless, but criminal to wage a war for the destruction of Hitlerism camouflaged as a fight for 'democracy.' "[5] On November 6, 1939 the decimated Comintern officially declared that England and France were primarily to blame for the imperialistic war. As a result, Hitler's fascism was not to be seen as the main enemy.

European Communists suffered many setbacks in 1940. It has since been documented that the Soviet Secret Police (known at that time as the NKVD) handed German Communists over to the Gestapo, and that leading representatives of the Gestapo and NKVD met on the German-Soviet border in Poland to exchange prisoners.

After the occupation of Norway and Denmark by Hitler's military forces in April 1940, all socialist, liberal, and even conservative newspapers were forbidden. Only fascist (and Communist!) newspapers could appear urging people not to take part in the resistance movements. The same was true in May 1940, as a result of the German occupation of Belgium, Luxembourg, and Holland, and finally in June 1940, when Germany occupied France. In France, the German occupation forces permitted the Communist newspapers, such as *L'Humanité*, to appear, as long as they urged the people not to support the resistance movement and even to fight against it.

The Communist policies during the Hitler-Stalin Pact proved intolerable enough for many European Communists to break with the party. For others, however, that two-year period provided second thoughts about the ominous commitment to the foreign policy of the Soviet Union. They were, therefore, an important step along the road which later was to lead to Eurocommunism.

The Communists in the European Resistance Movement (1941–1945)

The general line changed drastically with the German invasion of the Soviet Union on June 22, 1941. Since Stalin had ignored all the warnings he had received, Hitler's attack came as a complete surprise. On June 14, 1941, just a few days before war broke out, the Soviet news agency TASS declared that all reports of the deterioration in German-Soviet relations were slanderous. On the weekend of June 21 to 22, the leaders of the Communist International were resting peacefully at a resort in Kunzevo near Moscow and were just as surprised as the Soviet leaders by the sudden attack by German troops.

Moscow immediately summoned the entire world Communist movement to mobilize all conceivable political and military forces in the fight against Hitler's fascism. Despite the difficult situation in which the Communists in countries occupied by the Germans found themselves, they, of course, welcomed the new line with enthusiasm and relief, and began the ardent struggle of resistance in which tens, if not hundreds of thousands, of today's Eurocommunists took part.

The Communists of all European countries participated actively in the antifascist resistance movement. This movement, depending on the country and the time, manifested itself in many different forms of struggle, e.g., passive resistance, production and distribution of illegal flyers, sabotage in arms factories, and later, armed warfare and the mustering of guerrilla troops, especially in Yugoslavia and Greece. In many countries resistance activity was clearly divided along pro-West and pro-Soviet lines. The European Communists themselves advocated the widest possible cooperation with all forces and experienced, as a result, a time of great sacrifice, much activity, strict organization, and heroic mission. The fact that toward the war's end Stalinist apparatchiks were occasionally harsh in settling accounts with non-Communists among the resistance movement only negligibly diminished the mutual war experience as a whole.

In this period, the Communist parties of Europe (and this is extremely important for their later development) were more independent than ever before. Faced with the imminent danger of the Nazi threat, the Soviet Union summoned the Communists of all countries to make tremendous concessions to possible allies in order to create the widest possible front in the fight against Hitler's fascism. The Communists in France and England were expected to work for the opening up of a second front in order to help reduce the burden of war on the Soviet Union. Sectarianism was always portrayed as the most serious political deviation. It was emphasized that it was not important to strive for one's own ultimate political goals, but rather, to mobilize all possible political and military forces in the fight against Hitler's fascism. Suddenly, in the middle of the war, toward the end of May 1943, the decision to dissolve the Comintern was announced. This decision came completely unexpectedly for most Communist parties and their leaders, as well as for many Comintern functionaries living in the Soviet Union. I myself recall that at the Comintern School near Ufa neither we students nor the instructors themselves received the slightest indication that the dissolution of the Comintern was forthcoming.

Originally, the course of study which I had begun at the Comintern School in August 1942 was to last two years. In May 1943 we were still praising the history of the Comintern. Then suddenly in late May 1943 a notice appeared on the main blackboard of the Comintern School announcing the dissolution of the Communist International. From that day on, all instruction in the school concentrated on a single issue—why it had been necessary to dissolve the Communist International.

The decree of May 23, 1943 announcing the dissolution of the Comintern declared: "The developments of the last quarter of a century have shown that the present form of the Comintern is obsolete. The Communist movement is growing far beyond the limits of its original dimensions. The differences in individual countries are becoming clearer and clearer, and a central Communist leadership in the form of the Comintern was already becoming an insurmountable obstacle for the further development of the Communist movement." Then followed the decisive sentence, upon which many Eurocommunists today rest their case and which is often cited by the Romanian Communist Party and its leader, Ceauşescu: "The profound differences in the historic development of various countries, the differences in their character and even contradictions in their social orders, the differences in the level and degree of their economic and political developments, the differences, finally, in the degree of consciousness and the organization of the workers necessitated the different solutions to the problems facing the working class of the various countries."[6]

Thus it was officially declared in May 1943 that differences in social orders, in political development, and in worker movements of the individual countries necessitated different solutions to the problems in each country. Finally, the Communists of all countries, "in decisions about each question, must proceed from the concrete situations and the specific conditions of each separate country."

The European Communists in 1945

At the end of World War II, the Communist parties of Western Europe had reached their zenith. Aside from the Italian Communist Party, which has since then been able to increase its influence, no other Communist Party has possessed as much authority as in the period directly following the end of World War II. This was true both in terms of membership and in terms of election results. In addition, the fact that in some West European countries the Communists actually participated in the government is often overlooked.

In *France*, the Communist Party received 26 percent of all votes and was the strongest party. From November 1945 until May 1947, the PCF participated in the government, and the party leader, Thorez, and four Communist functionaries took over such important ministries as those of Armaments, Industry, Economy, and Labor.

The Communists of *Finland*, part of the umbrella organization known as the Finnish People's Democratic League, were almost as strong as the French Communists, receiving 23.5 percent of the vote immediately after the war's end and provided ministers of Internal Affairs, of Social Welfare, and of Public Assistance.

In *Italy*, the Communist Party received just under 19 percent of the vote during the first election at the end of the war, and participated in the government until May 1947, with Togliatti as Minister of Justice.

In *Iceland*, under the name Socialist Unity Party, the Communists received 16 percent of all votes in the election in June 1944, and headed the ministries of Education and Labor.

In *Luxembourg*, the Communist Party was able to muster 14 percent of the vote in the first election after 1945; the party leader, Urbany, took over the Ministry of Health.

In *Belgium*, the Communist Party received 12.7 percent of the popular vote in February 1946 and took over the ministries of Reconstruction, Health, Labor, and Nutrition.

In *Denmark*, the Communist Party received 12.5 percent of all votes, and two party functionaries including Aksel Larsen, the party leader, took over the ministries.

In *Norway,* the Communist Party received 11.9 percent of the vote and two Communist ministers entered the government.

In *Sweden,* the Communists received 11.2 percent of the vote, the highest figure they had ever received. However, they were not represented in the government.

In the *Netherlands,* the Communist Party was able to win 10.5 percent of the vote. The party newspaper *De Waarheid* (Truth), with a circulation of 400,000, became one of the most important of the country, but the party did not take over any governmental positions.

In occupied *Austria,* the Communists temporarily belonged to a coalition government from April until the final elections in November 1945, and took over the ministries of Internal Affairs (Franz Honner) and of Education (Ernest Fischer).

The Communists were even represented in most governments of the three Western-occupied zones of Germany.

In the two years following World War II, Communist parties in at least eight countries outside the Soviet sphere of influence participated in responsible positions of government. The party leaderships advocated at that time widespread cooperation and unity among all antifascist forces for rapid reconstruction and publicly declared its strong commitment to democratic programs. The Communist parties appeared on the scene as the party for freedom, democracy, and progress. At that time there were many possibilities for future independent development and numerous Communists were already following their own road toward socialism.

Hopes for an Independent Road to Socialism (1945–1947)

Hopes for an independent road to socialism were not completely unfounded, since at that time Communist leaders, obviously with the tacit approval of Moscow, declared that they would tread their own roads to socialism and that the transition to socialism was possible in democratic ways, i.e., not as in the Soviet Union.

The first leading party functionary to profess this attitude was Anton Ackermann, a member of the top leadership of the German Communist Party in East Berlin responsible for agitation and propaganda. In 1945 Ackermann wrote a thought-provoking essay in the journal *Einheit* entitled "Is There a Separate German Road to Socialism?"[7] in which he declared that a peaceful transition to socialism was possible if the ruling capitalist classes did not have a military and bureaucratic state security apparatus at their disposal. He affirmed a peaceful road to socialism because "no one desires to prevent new struggles and increased bloodshed more sincerely than we do."

Even more important was Ackermann's emphatic declaration that the road to socialism in Germany would differ from the one in the Soviet Union. Defending his position, Ackermann explained that, economically, in 1917 Russia lagged behind the other European countries: productivity was extremely low, industry was poorly developed, and the labor force was rather small in number. In Germany, however, the high level of production could easily be restored and there was an incomparably greater number of qualified workers than in Russia in 1917. Even more important, in Germany, the working class represented the majority of the total population, which would also be of "great importance after the victory of the working class in Germany," claimed Ackermann, "since it will ease the internal political struggle, reduce the burden of sacrifices and hasten the development toward a socialist democracy."[8]

For many present-day Western readers, Ackermann's contentions may seem somewhat abstract and theoretical, but at that time they filled many Communists with hope. Many, myself included, then believed that following the withdrawal of the occupying forces, German Marxists, free from foreign control, would establish their own road to socialism, a road differing from the Soviet course of development and eventually leading to true socialist democracy.

Many other responsible Communist Party leaders voiced similar opinion at that time. On December 7, 1945 Wladyslaw Gomulka stated, "In a people's democracy . . . the transition to socialism can occur along the same evolutionary path as the social changes, and a people's democracy can be transformed into a socialist democracy by peaceful means."[9] The Bulgarian Communist Party leader, Georgi Dimitrov, went even further on February 27, 1946, when he declared that "Each country will accomplish its transition not along a predetermined road, following in the footsteps of the Soviet Union, but in its own way, according to the country's historical, national, social, and cultural conditions." It was important, therefore, "to find our own Bulgarian road to socialism."[10] In addition, both chairmen of the leading Communist parties of Western Europe expressed similar views. In an interview for the *Times* (London) in November 1946, Maurice Thorez of the Communist Party of France said, "The progress of democracy throughout the world, in spite of some exceptions which serve only to confirm the rule, permit the choice of other paths to socialism than the one taken by the Russian Communists. In any case, the path is necessarily different for each country."[11] And during a speech in Florence on January 10, 1947, Palmiro Togliatti of the PCI declared that "International experience has taught us . . . that in order to achieve socialism, that is, in order to develop democracy to its furthest frontiers, we must find new roads, different from those taken, for example, by the working class, by the working people of the Soviet Union. . . . It is our job . . . by developing democracy and by fighting for the most advanced democratic reforms and for socialism . . . to find our own road—the Italian road—that road which is indicated by the peculiarities, the traditions, and the conditions of our country."[12]

How serious were these declarations? That, of course, depends on which Communists one considers. For the Stalinist Party functionaries, this was the obligatory party line from Moscow. They followed it just as they had followed all other lines from Moscow. For the Communist honestly striving for independence and searching for the new road, however, this was a time of great hope.

The Stalinist leadership permitted proclamations of independent roads to socialism because Stalin, at least until spring 1947, was obviously interested in maintaining the wartime alliance with the Western powers. The Communist parties were not to go too far—not to "frighten" the Western allies. They were to appear to be truly independent democratic parties. Stalin clearly favored a wide coalition policy at first, through which the Communists could build their own party apparatus and gain control of the police, the military forces, and the administration—all of which would be necessary for later single-handed domination.

The majority of Communists who, in the early post-war years, had truly hoped for independent roads to socialism were therefore disappointed when, in 1947, a change in the general line was announced. The democratic coalition policy and the different roads to democratic socialism were mentioned less and less frequently. In autumn 1947 a harder line became obligatory for all Communist parties of the world. There are several reasons for this switch on the part of Stalin and his leaders:

a) The negotiations over Marshall Plan aid in June 1947 stirred Stalin's mistrust, especially since the Czechoslovak and Polish governments, including the Communists in these governments, faltered on this question. (The Czechoslovak government had originally even accepted the invitation of the Marshall Plan.) Only under pressure from Moscow did the governments of Eastern European countries finally agree to reject the Marshall Plan.

b) The removal of Communist ministers from the West European governments in spring 1947 was instrumental in increasing Stalin's distrust.

c) Relations between the Soviet Union and the Western powers became strained, and the wartime alliance of the anti-Hitler coalition was nearing its end. The cold war was beginning.

d) Despite the Soviet troops and a large number of Soviet advisers in the parties, state apparatuses, armies, and economic and state security services in East European countries, the growing tendencies toward independent development there unnerved Stalin, who witnessed with particular unease Tito's independent development and spreading power.

The Communist Information Bureau

The founding of the Communist Information Bureau (Cominform) in September 1947 was part of the harder line and the increased subordination to the Soviet Union. After secret preparations—many important functionaries of the Communist parties of Europe were not even informed—the Polish Communist Party leadership, under orders from the Communist Party of the Soviet Union and without any previous announcement, invited the ruling parties of Yugoslavia, Bulgaria, Romania, Hungary, and Czechoslovakia as well as the CPSU to meet in Poland. Among the nonruling Communist parties, the Italian and French parties were the only ones to receive invitations. Interestingly enough, the Chinese Communist Party was not present, nor was the Socialist Unity Party of East Germany, the Albanian Communist Party, and the important Finnish and Greek Communist parties.

The founding conference met from September 22 to 27, 1947, in a tightly guarded, isolated resort of the Polish Ministry of State Security in Sklarska Poreba. Each party was represented by two officials: Zhdanov and Malenkov from the Soviet Union, Kardelj and Djilas from Yugoslavia. From Italy, there was Luigi Longo (leader of the PCI after Togliatti's death) and Eugenio Reale (who after the Hungarian Revolution in 1956 broke with the Communist Party) and, from France, Jacques Duclos and Etienne Fajon, the two leaders upon whom the Soviet Union could most rely.

Zhdanov presented the new line: The world was divided into two camps, the camp of imperialism led by the USA and the camp of freedom and socialism led by the Soviet Union. This meant that the wartime alliance between the Soviet Union and the West European allies had ended and that the Communist parties of Western Europe could no longer continue their rather conciliatory policy and their cooperation with non-Communists but had to introduce a harder line immediately. Zhdanov's criticism of French and Italian Communists was particularly harsh. He reproached them for not having been militant enough after the war and for having displayed illusions about cooperation with non-Communists.

During their presentations, representatives of the French and Italian Communist parties, Duclos and Luigi Longo, were constantly interrupted by Zhdanov's shouts, "While you were fighting to remain in the government, you were being thrown out by the others."

After this introduction, Zhdanov suggested the founding of a Communist Information Bureau. The Polish Communist Party leader, Gomulka, expressed certain objections. He later yielded, but argued that there should be no official announcement about the meeting or about the organization. Everything should remain internal. Gomulka's recommendation, however, was rejected. Finally, the participants deliberated over the location of the seat of the new organization. Zhdanov and the others decided upon Prague. Then Zhdanov telephoned Stalin, who immediately declared Belgrade the seat.

In the official declaration it was maintained that the new organization was not a refounded Communist International, but rather, simply an information bureau with the task of assuring an exchange of information and experiences between the Communist parties and of establishing coordination of political activities on the basis of mutual agreement.

The Communist Information Bureau, soon known as the "Cominform," was to consist of two representatives from each participating Communist Party. At the same time, a Cominform weekly newspaper was to appear. On Stalin's recommendation it was entitled *For a Lasting Peace, for a People's Democracy.*

Henceforth, all tendencies toward autonomy or independence would be stifled by the Cominform. In addition, the Soviet leaders under Stalin planned to take action against Yugoslavia. It was for this reason that Belgrade had been made the seat of the Cominform, enabling the Soviets to have their own monitor right in the heart of the independence movement. Moreover, the newly founded weekly was to give the Soviet leadership the opportunity to pronounce policies and actions without having to sign its name to them.

The European Communists During Stalin's Last Years (1947–1953)

The period from the founding of the Cominform in autumn 1947 until the death of Stalin in March 1953 resembles in some aspects the period of the Hitler-Stalin Pact. Just as the Hitler-Stalin Pact crushed all hopes of success after the Popular Front period, history now repeated itself. After the optimistic period of antifascist resistance and a certain degree of autonomy in the postwar years—subordination and the hardening of the line meant the loss of important political terrain.

The impact of the founding of the Cominform became obvious in the following weeks and months. The Berlin blockade was being prepared, the complete takeover by the Communists in Prague was imminent (it followed in February 1948). After the spring of 1948, the Soviets applied more pressure to Finland and began the campaign against Yugoslavia, which was continually pushing toward independence. The result was Yugoslavia's expulsion from the Cominform in June 1948.

After 1948, any mention of an independent road to socialism was denounced as a subversive, antiparty deviation in the entire world Communist movement. The declaration of the leadership of the ruling party in East Germany in September 1948 was typical of the new line: "Any attempt at constructing a separate German road to socialism would result in disregard for the great Soviet example." Anton Ackermann, the founder of the theory of a separate German road to socialism was forced on September 24, 1948 to issue a self-criticism. In his self-critical declaration, "On the Only Possible Road to Socialism," Ackermann renounced his previous contention and explained that the theory of an independent road to socialism included a condemnable dissociation from the CPSU.

The merciless and persistent Stalinization of Eastern Europe followed this sharp turn in policy from September 1947 to summer 1948. West European Communists were directly affected, too. Now, according to the new party line, they had to defend everything which took place in Eastern Europe. They had to explain to the Western world why Soviet advisers with far-reaching authority were employed in the defense, the economy, and other public domains of the East European countries. The Soviet *Short Course on the History of the CPSU*, edited by Stalin, became the obligatory textbook in all countries of Eastern Europe. Moreover, the bureaucratic, centralized, state-planned economic system according to the Soviet pattern, forced collectivization of peasants, and the Soviet form of collective farming were introduced throughout Eastern Europe. All non-Communist parties in Eastern Europe lost their independence and became mere satellites of the Communist Party apparatus.

The Social Democrats were forced under pressure to "unite" with the Communist parties; in reality, they were being incorporated into the Communist Party. Within the newly formed unity parties, de facto Stalinist parties, members of the leadership were completely subordinated to the Soviets and a system of bureaucratic centralization was introduced, whereby the party apparatus monopolized all forms of public life. Intellectual and cultural life was also subordinated to the party's dictatorship, and, in accordance with the Soviet model, "socialist realism" was introduced in literature and art and "party-mindedness" prevailed in the sciences. The much feared and omnipotent secret police became the dominant instrument of power and the mainstay of the regime.

Tens of thousands of people, including Communists and former prominent Communist Party leaders, were arrested because it was thought they could possibly propagate independent goals. The European Communist also had to cover up the fact that just as in the Great Purge in the Soviet Union, show trials were being staged throughout Eastern Europe against high party officials, including many who were active in the illegal resistance or who had participated in the Spanish Civil War. And on December 21, 1949, the East European countries and all the Communist parties of the world celebrated Stalin's seventieth birthday just as it was celebrated in the Soviet Union—with all the characteristics of an immense personality cult. They were required to condemn the independent Yugoslav road to socialism and to brand the Yugoslav Communists as "Tito fascists."

These changes during late Stalinism were executed according to a carefully prepared plan. Stalin's long-range goal was obviously to incorporate the East European countries into the Soviet Union as Union Republics. Early in 1948, while I was living in the Soviet-occupied zone of Germany, Anton Ackermann once asked me during a private discussion if I ever noticed that the word "Russia" did not appear in the term "USSR." That was no coincidence, he claimed, because inherent in the term was the possibility that subsequent socialist states could become part of this Union. As soon as the people's democratic republics and later the Soviet zone of Germany had established the foundations of socialism, they would no longer exist as individual countries but would join the USSR as new republics. I was shocked at Ackermann's contention, but since that time, after close examination of many documents, the Yugoslav historian Vladimiv

Dedijer has confirmed Ackermann's view. According to Didijer, Stalin had clearly planned "to bring all the East European countries, including Yugoslavia, within Soviet borders."[13]

The events of that time, therefore, can be regarded as parts of a long-term plan which, by the time Stalin died in March 1953, had to a large extent already been accomplished. By complete subordination to the USSR in the realm of foreign policy and by a thorough adaptation of the Stalinist system on the domestic level, the countries of Eastern Europe had become inevitable satellites of the Soviet Union.

In the period of late Stalinism, the Communist parties of Western Europe also experienced purges of prominent party functionaries. Thousands of party members—particularly resistance fighters from World War II, Communists of Jewish origin, and former fighters in the Spanish Civil War—were disgraced and expelled from the party. One prominent Communist party leader who underwent such a "purge" was Pedre Furuboten, the long-time Secretary General of the Norwegian Communist Party and leader of the Communist resistance in Norway, once celebrated as "the Norwegian Tito," who was ousted in October 1949. A third of the members remained loyal to Furuboten and left the Communist Party. Several months later—and this event has played an important role in recent discussions—in January 1950, the Cominform newspaper *For a Lasting Peace, for a People's Democracy*, attacked the Japan Communist Party and its leader, Tokuda, for advocating a "centrist" line and a democratic road to socialism. Tokuda was forced to pronounce self-criticism and the Japanese Communists have not forgotten the harsh disciplinary punishment.

In February and March 1951, all West European Communist parties were required to make official declarations to the effect that in the event of war they would defend the Soviet invasion, whereupon many left the party and many more were purged. In December 1952, André Marty and Charles Tillon, two of the most prominent members of the Politburo of the French Communist Party who had also played decisive roles in both the Spanish Civil War and the resistance, were expelled from their party. Tillon had been the Minister of Armament Production from 1945 to 1947 in de Gaulle's first government.

The obligatory justification of Soviet actions, the developments in Eastern Europe, the glorification of Stalin, the proclaimed support of Soviet troops invading in the event of war—all this led finally to a tremendous loss of prestige and influence of the Communist parties. In Belgium, the Communist vote fell from 12.7 percent in 1945 to 3.5 percent in 1953; in the Netherlands, the Communists received only

6.2 percent in 1953, compared with 10.6 percent in 1945; in Denmark, the Communist vote fell from 12.5 to 4.3 percent over the same time span; in Norway, the vote fell from 11.9 to 5.1 percent; in Sweden, from 11.2 to 4.3 percent; in 1945 in Great Britain, 102,000 Britons voted for the Communist Party, in 1953 only 21,000 did so. Party membership in France fell from 800,000 at the end of the war to 200,000 at Stalin's death. Circulation of the party newspaper *L'Humanité* dropped from 600,000 in 1946 to 200,000 in 1951. Only the Italian Communist Party was spared this retrogression, mainly because it was the first Communist party to try, although somewhat cautiously at first, to realize an autonomous policy.

The entire Stalin era from the mid-twenties to the mid-fifties is not ancient history for the Communists of today. The three decades of Stalin's rule play a very important role in present-day discussions of Eurocommunism.

The subordination to the bureaucratic-centralized system of the USSR, the obligatory, unquestioning defense of Soviet interests and the suppression of all independent tendencies have greatly hindered the Communist movement in Europe. It was evident even at that time that successes were only possible when a certain level of autonomy was reached, as, for example, during the antifascist resistance movement in World War II. Although such thoughts could not be aired, many thoughtful Communists had already begun considering possible future independence and new orientation. The bitter experiences of the Stalin era laid the cornerstone for further development.

The First Signs of Diversity in World Communism

4

During Stalinism, especially during the period of late Stalinism from 1948 to 1953, the outward appearance of the world Communist movement did not correspond to reality. From the outside, things seemed completely unified. The Soviet Union enjoyed absolute authority over the satellite countries. Not only the Eastern European countries, but all Communist parties of the world as well exclusively proclaimed the Stalinist line, praised and glorified all events which took place within the Soviet sphere of influence, and loyally carried out all directions from Moscow.

But the monolithic unity of world Communism of 1953 was only a façade. Just as Stalin's domestic policies were in contradiction to the conditions of an emerging modern industrial society in the USSR, the monolithic unity under Moscow's direction no longer suited the changing world.

The centralized world Communist movement under Moscow's direction had been tailored to the existence of a single socialist country—the USSR. But the Soviet Union was no longer the only Communist-ruled country in the world. While immediately after the war it was still possible to retain the people's democracies of Eastern Europe in satellite status, after 1950 it became increasingly difficult for the Soviet Union to continue this subjugation. The East European countries, strengthened economically and politically, began to develop limited autonomy, and since 1948, a Marxist alternative to Stalinist Soviet Communism had appeared with the independent development of Yugoslavia. After the success of the Chinese Revolution in October 1949, a new force appeared in the Communist world, a force which later proved to be of tremendous significance.

However, contradictions developed not only in the relationships between Moscow and the other Communist parties, but within the Communist parties themselves as well. These contradictions were particularly pronounced in the parties of the West European indus trial countries which, with the atomic age, the second industrial revolution, and increased international economic integration, were confronted with a myriad of new problems. In the once strictly Stalinist and dogmatic Communist parties, new opinions were now being voiced.

Thus, not only did the relationship among the Communist parties have to be considered, but the political aims, the political strategy, the methods and the coalition policies of each individual Communist Party had to be revised. This, however, could not proceed without the appearance of different views and different conceptions both within the world movement in general and within individual Communist parties themselves.

The Differences Among the Communist Parties

At the end of the Stalin era, three trends emerged in the world Communist movement: the Stalinists, the centrists, and the autonomists.

The *Stalinists* favored (as they still do today) the closest possible cooperation under Soviet leadership. They insisted on subordination, and although the conditions had changed completely, on maintaining, as far as possible, the old form of the Communist International.

The *centrists* recognized the fact that the unity of the world Communist movement could no longer be accomplished through Stalin's harsh measures. They hoped that the acknowledgment of a similar ideology and similar aims would suffice to maintain the unity as long as common programmatic aims and principles were discussed at international conferences.

The *autonomists,* known today as Eurocommunists, comprised the third trend. This group continually proclaimed the independence of each individual Communist Party and strove for bilateral or multilateral cooperation solely on the basis of voluntary solidarity and mutual nonintervention.

More important than the different attitudes toward international

Communist cooperation, however, were the disagreements over general concepts and aims. Four groups illustrate the most pronounced Communist trends which developed since the end of the Stalin era:

1. The Stalinist Party Bureaucrats: The Stalinist Party functionaries are as much a part of the system today as in previous years. They get fulfillment out of power and organization and are not the least bit interested in theoretical discussions of Marxism. They ruthlessly and unscrupulously implement the directions of the leadership in Moscow. Ideological concepts and goals are of value only insofar as they serve to increase the functionaries' own power. They carry out even the most minute reforms and innovations reluctantly, at best, but become enthusiastic upon announcement of a hard line. Their favorite sayings come mostly from Stalin. They cherish Stalin's theory of "the intensification of class struggle," because it justifies "vigilance campaigns" and the removal of critical and independent Communists. The Stalinist Party bureaucrats are not afraid to speak of "socialist democracy" or even "socialist humanism" as long as they are certain that these terms are only epithets which do not endanger their own power or privileges.

They consider discussions about Stalin, Stalinism, and the system unnecessary, even harmful. As far as they are concerned, capitalist encirclement and foreign agents have made the system necessary. What is more, the "aberrations of socialist legality" (a reference to the fate of millions of Stalinism's victims) have long since been overcome.

Instead of expert economic and technological assistance, the Stalinist functionaries advocate medals, and "socialist emulations" to increase production. The priority of heavy industry is always emphasized, while a plea for an increase in consumer-goods production is looked upon as a sign of weakness. They consider economic and technical experts a necessary evil. Social scientists, writers, and artists are tolerable only when their activities are aimed at praising and glorifying the Stalinist bureaucrat, and at justifying the bureaucratic function ideologically. Any new interpretations and conceptions are automatically regarded as deviations not worthy of consideration and should be combated. For the Stalinist bureaucrat, hierarchical order with a clear chain of command from top to bottom is taken for granted. The masses of workers count only when they applaud their leaders and when, in organized demonstration, they flaunt banners proclaiming slogans prescribed by those very leaders. However, spontaneous actions, says the Stalinist, even if attended by hundreds of thousands of people, are always inspired and organized by "agents of the class enemy" and participants must be dispersed by the police.

The Stalinist bureaucrat always speaks in the name of the party, although as a rule, the bureaucratic type, as the development during the last decades has shown, comprises only a small minority of the Communist Party of any one country.

2. The Critical Reform Communists: On the other hand, there were, already during the Stalin era, critical Communists who valued the humanist concepts and goals of Marxism as well as liberation from exploitation and suppression. They were highly critical of Stalinism and sought alternatives to the Stalinist system. They joined the party out of protest against social repression, injustice, and national suppression—striving to belong to a movement fighting for the liberation of the working class, for a fraternal society, for the equality of all people, and for the abolition of social and national injustice.

Their criticism of Stalinism is understandable on the basis of these aims. They realized how far the Soviet Union has departed from these fundamental principles under Stalin and his successors. The privileges of the functionaries, the personality cult, the partially hidden, yet partially overt, nationalism, the limitations on freedom of opinion, the subjugation of the sciences, of art and of literature, the obligatory general line, the demeaning self-criticisms, the stupefying compliance with every change in the political line, the dogmatic fault-finding, the extended isolation from other leftist forces—all these things led the critical and reflective Communists to a gradual awareness that the system was not faced with temporary, local mistakes or abuses, but rather, with a fundamental departure from Socialist goals. In turn this led to the search for an alternative to Stalinist Communism, for new roads—for a new democratic model of socialism and a democratic road to this goal.

3. The Centrists: The centrists comprise the group between the Stalinist bureaucrats and the critical reform Communists. They are of the opinion that although one should search for new roads to socialism, one should not "go too far." One should discuss only the most obvious mistakes of Stalinism. Reforms, of course, have to be undertaken, but solely in the economic sphere and always under Party control.

4. The Idealists and Their Transformation: The most important role in the later disputes between the three trends in European Communism was the transformation of honest, sincere, and loyal Stalinists into critics of the system.

The loyal Stalinist was completely different from the already depicted, bureaucratic Stalinist party functionary. As an honest and involved Communist, the Stalinist believer thought that all the negative effects of Stalinist socialism resulted from slander and deformation on the part of capitalist propaganda. These faithful Communists represented an important force in Communism in each country. As long as they remained loyal to the Soviet Union and to Stalin, they provided the most important support for the Stalinist bureaucrats, although they differed in character from them immensely. The more these honest and true-to-Stalin Communists became critical and began to realize, however, that their belief did not correspond to reality—a process which was usually characterized by deep psychological turmoil—the more they dissociated themselves from the Stalinist bureaucrats. Frequently they became the most active champions of autonomy and a new course. Robert Havemann, Roger Garaudy, and Alexander Dubček, for example, along with hundreds of thousands of others, were all Stalinist Communists in the forties and fifties.

Since, for the most part, the Stalinist party bureaucrats, the centrists, and the reformers maintained their convictions, the transformation of loyal Stalinist Communists, which occurred at varying times and for varying reasons, played a particularly important role in the growing diversity in world Communism. The former faithful Stalinists who gradually became critical Communists were of great significance to the formation of Eurocommunism.

5

Yugoslavia – Cornerstone of Today's Eurocommunism

The beginnings of a Eurocommunist development date back to Yugoslavia's break with Moscow in the summer of 1948. "The Yugoslav Revolution is a great historical feat in Europe," wrote Santiago Carrillo, emphasizing its contribution "to the constructive work of rethinking the meaning of socialism."[1]

Yugoslavia was the first country to dissociate itself from Moscow and to tread an individual road to socialism. Many important Eurocommunist concepts, such as the equality of individual Communist parties and individual socialist countries, were first proclaimed in Yugoslavia after the break with Moscow. Yugoslavia not only broke with Moscow, but established its own model of self-management socialism, which differs greatly from the Soviet and Eastern European systems. Today Yugoslavia plays a decisive role in the Eurocommunist movement and supports the autonomy of the Western European Communist parties.

The Independent Character of the Yugoslav Revolution

When Tito first declined financial support from Moscow in 1937, and established a new, illegal leadership in the country in order to become independent from the "imported" foreign leadership, the Yugoslav Communists had thereby achieved a certain degree of autonomy.

By October 1940, party membership had already reached 12,000 (as compared with 1,500 in 1937) and membership in Communist youth leagues was up to 30,000.[2]

After Hitler's invasion in April 1941, the Yugoslav government collapsed in less than two weeks. German troops occupied Serbia, Italian troops occupied Montenegro and parts of Dalmatia, and Croatia became a fascist state. The government in exile in London, under the leadership of King Peter, could do little to influence further developments. From then on, Tito's Communist Party would be the decisive force in the resistance movement against foreign occupation. From the very beginning, Tito emphasized not only the national, but the revolutionary nature of the struggle for liberation. Proletarian brigades were formed within the framework of the partisan movement, and people's liberation committees were elected as the new bodies of power in the liberated areas.

In the beginning of 1942 Stalin, who was taking all possible measures to keep the independent Yugoslav socialist revolution in check, started meeting with considerable difficulty. Stalin obviously feared that a successful, independent revolutionary movement in Yugoslavia would mean that the country would slip from his control. Stalin withdrew the help he had promised, repeatedly complaining about the revolutionary socialist character of the Yugoslav partisan movement. The disagreements were so pronounced that the Soviet press did not even publish the communiqués issued by the Yugoslav guerrilla leadership during the war.

In autumn 1942, the Yugoslav partisan troops already numbered 150,000. In November 1942, the "Anti-fascist Council of the People's Liberation of Yugoslavia" was convened. Moscow, however, ruled against the original intention of establishing a provisional government. One year later, in November 1943, at its second session—this day is now the Yugoslav national holiday—a national committee was formed, which was to become the core of the new government. Again the Soviet Union failed to publish the important resolutions of this second session. Only in February 1944, when the Yugoslav Army for People's Liberation had on its own already freed more than two-thirds of the country, did a Soviet military mission enter Yugoslavia.

The Yugoslav revolution had a powerful effect on many Communist parties of the world.

By the end of World War II, the Yugoslav Communists alone had liberated their country. There was no imposed Sovietization as in other East European countries; rather, Yugoslavia experienced its own successful revolution, which soon came into conflict with the bureaucratic, dictatorial Communism which Stalin had established in Russia—a conflict between the Yugoslavs who had won national independence and the Soviet leaders who wanted to incorporate Yugoslavia within the Soviet sphere of influence.

Disagreements with Moscow Between 1945 and 1948

After 1945 the Soviet leadership sent its advisers to occupy the key political, economic, and military positions and supplied the Yugoslav government with Soviet officials, almost as though they were colonial lords in an overseas possession. The Soviet advisers received salaries four times as high as Yugoslav army commanders and three times as high as members of the Yugoslav government.

The Yugoslavs had to stand by as the Soviet secret police began to organize its informants, recruiting Yugoslav citizens, including party members and high officials.

On the economic scene, the Yugoslavs were required to accept joint (Soviet-Yugoslav) companies whose obvious goal was to subordinate the Yugoslav economy to that of the Soviet Union. After long negotiations, a joint company for aviation and for shipping was established. The Yugoslav share was determined according to 1938 prices, whereas the Soviet share was determined according to completely different 1946/47 prices. There were no board meetings, no bookkeeping audits. The Soviet director decided everything and the prices were determined in accordance with Soviet regulation: the lowest rates for the Soviet Union, slightly higher ones for other countries on the Danube, and the highest rates for Yugoslavia. In 1946 and 1947, the Soviet Union insisted upon joint companies for petroleum, coal, lead and zinc, aluminum, and even for iron and steel.

More and more the Yugoslavs realized that the Soviet Union was opposed to the development of basic industries for the industrialization which Yugoslavia so needed for its economic independence. As representatives of the Soviet Union continued to oppose economic plans and industrialization programs, it became all too clear that Yugoslavia was to serve as a supplier of raw materials and agricultural products for the USSR.

Finally, the Yugoslavs were compelled to accept increasing Soviet intervention in the cultural realm and in the mass media. They were required to publish Soviet newspaper articles, to show Soviet films, and to present Soviet plays. In this way they were expected to make their cultural life more and more Russian.

The Yugoslavs realized that Stalin was not treating them as an equal socialist country, but, rather, as another satellite country in his sphere of influence. It was against this backdrop that the dramatic events between February and June 1948 took place.

Stalin's Campaign Against Yugoslavia (February to June 1948)

The methods which Moscow used against the Yugoslav Communist Party in 1948 were characteristic of the methods used in later conflicts with the Communists of the "Prague Spring" and with the Communists of Japan, Spain, and other parties.

The Soviet leaders' first task was to force a kind of recognition of guilt from the Yugoslavs. On February 10, 1948, Stalin invited the highest-ranking Yugoslav and Bulgarian officials to an urgent meeting in Moscow. During a discussion, Stalin harshly reproached the Yugoslavs for making a habit of never conferring with the Soviet government on questions of foreign policy. Such actions were not to be repeated, warned Stalin. An agreement whereby the Soviet Union was to review all Yugoslav foreign policy decisions was prepared for the same evening.

The signing of this agreement was carried out in a degrading and humiliating fashion. The leading Yugoslav Communist Kardelj was awakened late at night and urgently directed to appear before Molotov, where he had to sign a treaty consisting of two typed pages. Molotov summoned him rudely, shouting, "Sign this!" Kardelj later described how furious he was and what humiliation, resentment, and embarrassment he felt as he realized that it was more a matter of a giant power dictating to a smaller, weaker state, than a real treaty between socialist countries. At first he did not want to sign, but he decided to do so in order not to exacerbate the situation unnecessarily. It is psychologically interesting that in his excitement, Kardelj signed his name where Molotov was to sign. Molotov angrily tore up the paper, the last page was retyped and then signed by both parties.[3]

With this treaty, Stalin now had a tool with which to control even the smallest foreign policy steps of Yugoslavia. But the Soviet Union did not think it sufficient and decided to put additional pressure on Yugoslavia. Ten days later the Yugoslav representatives in Moscow were informed that the Soviet Union would no longer continue trade negotiations with the Yugoslavs and that the delivery of raw materials important to Yugoslavia would be temporarily interrupted. This was the beginning of an economic blockade which was clearly intended to force Yugoslavia to yield. Simultaneously, the rumor spread among the high East European functionaries that "there is something wrong in Yugoslavia." In mid-February 1948, the first portraits of Tito were removed from important buildings in East European capitals. In this way, the functionaries of the East European countries were psychologically prepared for the conflict with Yugoslavia.

On March 18 and 19, 1948, the Soviet Union withdrew all its advisers from Yugoslavia in the hope that Yugoslavia, because of its tremendous economic difficulties, could be forced to yield—a method which Moscow later used against China and Albania. On March 20, the Yugoslav party leadership sent a letter to the Soviet leadership requesting an explanation of its behavior. In the letter, the Yugoslavs politely criticized the underhanded Soviet methods of gathering information and declared their readiness to forward all desired information directly from the central authorities.

A week later, on March 27, the answer came from Moscow. With this reply a new phase was introduced, for the letter was strongly worded and was definitely threatening. The Yugoslav Communists were reproached for hindering the activity of Soviet advisers, for spreading anti-Soviet rumors, for charging the Soviet Union with great power chauvinism, for claiming that the Soviet Union wanted to subordinate Yugoslavia economically and that socialism was no longer revolutionary in the Soviet Union. The strange thing about these accusations was that the Yugoslav Communists had not even made those criticisms—had probably not even thought so harshly of the Soviets—but that Stalin assumed they *could* think along those lines. The Soviet attacks were mainly leveled against the four leaders who occupied the four key positions in which the Soviets wanted to exercise influence: the economy (Kidrić), the military (Vukmanović), internal affairs (Ranković), and propaganda and the press (Djilas). Stalin hoped that Tito would dismiss the leaders in question and thus concede the first step, making it possible to demand further concessions from him later. At the same time, however, other Yugoslav leaders were supposed to be intimidated, for the letter from Moscow accused them of being serious enemies of the party and compared them to Trotsky. Then the threatening sentence followed: "We consider Trotsky's political career highly instructive." Trotsky was assassinated in 1940—there was thus no question about the allusion. The letter was signed by Stalin and Molotov.

The letter prompted a decisive meeting on April 1, 1948, of the Yugoslav Central Committee in the library of the former king's palace of Dedinje. The meeting was secret; not even a stenographer was allowed to enter. Tito read the text of the Soviet letter as well as a draft of his answer. In his answer, Tito emphasized that the relationship with the Soviet Union could be based only on the principle of independence and mutual trust. In the subsequent discussion, seventeen members of the Central Committee advocated this rebuff to Stalin. Only one member, Zujović, at that time Secretary of the Popular Front, who favored a close relationship with the Soviet Union, was opposed to the response. According to Zujović, even the Soviet Union's and Stalin's most negligible and irrelevant utterance should be "a warning to us to review everything before we take any further steps." A participant in this secret conference at Dedinje later wrote that the conference had opened a new era in the relationships between the socialist countries and the Communist parties.[4] This is not an exaggeration. The conference of April 1, 1948 can clearly be regarded as the beginning of the development which was to lead to Eurocommunism.

Yugoslavia's answer put Stalin for the first time in the position of having to face the opposition of an entire Communist party.

It was clear to him that through neither economic threats nor political pressure had he been able to prompt a split in the Yugoslav party leadership. Now he tried to engage other Communist parties to apply pressure on Yugoslavia. The Hungarian Communist Party leadership was the first (on April 8) to try to influence the Yugoslav Communists. But there were also other more welcome reactions for Yugoslavia. A Bulgarian governmental delegation under the leadership of Georgi Dimitrov made a stop in Belgrade on the way to Prague on April 19, 1948. During the stop at the Belgrade train station, Dimitrov conversed briefly with Djilas. He gripped Djilas by the hand and whispered to him, "Be firm!" but broke off as soon as other Bulgarians approached.[5]

Two weeks later, in a letter dated May 4, 1948—signed by Stalin and Molotov—the Kremlin leaders declared that the Yugoslav affair was put before the Communist Information Bureau and that the next session of the Cominform would take place in the Ukraine. On May 22, in a second letter from Moscow, the Yugoslav Communist Party leaders were again requested to attend the session, and it was announced that the Cominform meeting had been postponed until late June so that the Yugoslavs could participate.

By June 19, 1948, Stalin had still not yet abandoned hope that the Yugoslavs would attend the Cominform meeting. In a telegram, the Yugoslavs were informed that the Cominform meeting would take place on June 21 in Bucharest and that their presence was of utmost importance. The Yugoslav Central Committee again rejected the invitation, and suggested that the Soviet leadership instead send a delegation to Yugoslavia to explore the problem on the spot before convening a Cominform meeting. But the meeting was finally held in the last week of June 1948 without Yugoslavia. A total of twenty-one Communist Party leaders participated in the session held at the former royal palace in Bucharest. Zhdanov, Malenkov, and Suslov represented the Soviet Union, two top officials came from Bulgaria and Poland, three from Romania and Hungary, and four representatives were present from Czechoslovakia. The Stalinists Duclos and Fajon represented the French Communist Party, and Palmiro Togliatti and Pietro Secchia represented Italy. Both Gomulka, the Polish Communist Party leader and George Dimitrov, the Bulgarian Communist Party leader and former General Secretary of the Communist International, were conspicuously absent from the conference.

The Break with Moscow

Through a resolution prepared in Moscow and substantiated in Bucharest by Zhdanov, the Soviets demanded the expulsion of the Yugoslav Communist Party from the Cominform. According to the Yugoslav sources, several party leaders had carefully opposed the resolution, especially the Romanian Communist Party leader, Gheorghiu-Dej, who later played an important role in attempting to increase the autonomy of Romania. He supposedly posed several "disturbing" questions, but the well-coordinated apparatus could not be hindered, especially after Zhdanov declared, "We are in possession of certain information which indicates that Tito is an imperialist spy." Thereupon, the Cominform resolution was adopted. For the first time in the history of Communism, a ruling Communist Party was banned.

The contents of the resolution of the Cominform are insignificant. They consist of unfounded, often contradictory accusations, such as bourgeois nationalism, false agrarian policy, defense of capitalist elements in villages and anti-Soviet attitudes, and charged the Yugoslavs with "leftist deviation," as well as "opportunistic attitude." Clearly, the resolution was intended to discredit Yugoslavia and to force the Yugoslavs to engage in self-criticism. In this context, the Communist Information Bureau's statement at the end of the document, expressing its hope that within the Communist Party of Yugoslavia there were also some "healthy forces," is important. These forces were openly summoned to overthrow the Yugoslav leadership: "Their task is to compel their present leaders to recognize and rectify their mistakes openly and honestly. . . . Should the present leaders of the Yugoslav Communist Party prove incapable of doing this, they must be replaced and a new internationalist leadership for the Yugoslav Communist Party must be set up."[6]

The Cominform resolution of 1948 was widely discussed in all Communist parties. The Communists desirous of independence hoped that the Yugoslavs would not yield; many, myself included, even expected that other Communist parties would join the Yugoslavs. But for the time being, Yugoslavia stood alone. Two days later on June 30, in a long letter, the Yugoslavs rejected the Cominform resolution. They claimed that the resolution was based on inaccurate and unfounded assertions, and that it represented an attempt to destroy the prestige of the Yugoslav Communist Party and to arouse confusion in the international workers' movement. One by one, each accusation was calmly and objectively refuted, but the Yugoslavs at the same time aired their own critical objections. They protested against the Soviet secret police's attempts to infiltrate a fraternal Communist Party with their agents and claimed that such an attitude toward a country developing socialism was forbidden. Unmistakably, the Yugoslav Communists closed with the declaration that they would not recognize the accusations of the Cominform resolution, but would "continue to work even more persistently on the building of socialism."[7]

Yugoslavia's Independent Road

Yugoslavia was now an independent socialist state. The break with Moscow was at the beginning misinterpreted in both East and West. The most important newspapers of the Western world, including the *Times* (London), the *Manchester Guardian*, and *The New York Times*, were of the opinion that the Yugoslav government would not be able to remain in power. Western papers assumed that Tito and the other leaders would be arrested and tried at any time. In Moscow, Stalin declared that all he had to do was wave his little finger and there would be no more Tito. Moreover, upon leaving Belgrade, Pavel Judin, the head of the Cominform newspaper, declared, "You won't hold out three weeks."[8]

Stalin's leaders immediately started a violent campaign against Yugoslavia. All Communist parties of the world were required to condemn Yugoslavia. Moscow increased the pressure on Yugoslavia through a unilateral breach of treaties and agreements, an economic blockade, border provocations, slander and false reports, mass arrests of real and supposed "Titoists" in the countries of Eastern Europe, and radio propaganda surpassing anything anyone had ever heard. The Soviet and East European stations broadcast more at that time in Serbo-Croatian than in all other languages combined.

Under these most difficult conditions, the Communists in Yugoslavia tried in both theory and practice to follow a new road to socialism, a road which tens of thousands of Communists of all countries had long awaited, a road which offered an alternative to Stalinism. This new road affected the entire international Communist movement. In Communist parties of Europe, many party members and officials were secretly on the side of the Yugoslav Communists. Even several Communist Party leaders indicated their discontent. Dimitrov, who had since become ill and broken, unwillingly signed the Cominform resolution. Gomulka also supposedly expressed criticism of the resolution. During the vote in the sixteen-member Central Secretariat of the Socialist Unity Party of Germany in East Berlin, two members opposed the acceptance of the anti-Yugoslav resolution. One of them was Erich W. Gniffke, who was forced to leave the Soviet zone of Germany in September 1948.[9]

The Yugoslav newspapers published both the Cominform resolution and the Yugoslav Communists' reply. For the first time since Lenin's era, one could read two opposing viewpoints in a Communist newspaper. Needless to say, the other Communist parties of the world published only the Cominform resolution, and not the Yugoslav answer. The letter was not even reprinted in excerpts. As a result, the Yugoslav Communists did something which the reformers of the "Prague Spring" twenty years later unfortunately did not do: they immediately convened a party congress. Just three weeks after the break with Moscow, from July 21 to 27, the Fifth Party Congress of the Yugoslav Communist Party took place. Over two thousand delegates represented 470,000 Yugoslav party members. All the speeches at the Congress were broadcast by Yugoslav radio. After Tito's report and declarations about the Cominform conflict, all those who spoke condemned the resolution. No one defended the Cominform resolution—and all this transpired in the presence of Soviet and East European correspondents. On the last day the election for party leaders was held. It was conducted by a secret ballot. Everyone knew it was a vote for or against the Cominform resolution. Tito received 2,318 out of 2,323 votes. A roar of cheers broke out; everyone knew that there were five Cominform supporters in the crowd.[10]

In the months following the Cominform resolution, the Soviet Union was repeatedly invited to send a delegation to Yugoslavia in order to convince itself of the falseness of the accusations. Moscow gave no reply. Until late spring 1949—and I can attest to this since I was living there at the time—Soviet films were shown, and Soviet books and newspapers were openly sold at newsstands all over Yugoslavia. The Yugoslavs took pains to rectify the slander and defamation. In the party newspaper *Borba,* a column appeared daily (often taking up a whole page) under the title "Against Slander and Disinformation," and the false accusations of the East European countries made within the last twenty-four hours were refuted. In late summer 1949, this column was finally discontinued, for it was simply impossible to refute all that the Soviet leaders, the leaders of East European countries, and the leaders of almost every Communist Party of the entire world alleged in the course of twenty-four hours. At the beginning the Yugoslav Communists were accused of "nationalistic deviations," but soon the term "Tito-fascism" was adopted, without explaining how the leader of an antifascist resistance movement could himself be a fascist. In Yugoslavia, this propaganda had little effect. The discussions were dedicated to reviewing and discussing the fundamental political problems of an independent road to Socialism.[11]

Three decisive concepts were proclaimed in Yugoslavia after 1948, which today comprise the essential elements of Eurocommunism: *(a)* equality between Communist parties within the world movement and the rejection of a single leading center; *(b)* economic and political equality of all socialist countries; and *(c)* the right to an independent road to socialism in accordance with a country's own traditions and its cultural, political, and economic conditions.

Of the numerous publications of that time, one sentence from the writings of Milovan Djilas (summer 1949) reads: "To imagine that all people will advance toward socialism in one and the same way, according to one and the same pattern, would be just as senseless as to imagine socialism like some barracks where all people are lined up 'equally' and uniformly."[12] Eduard Kardelj pointed out that even after a successful socialist revolution, continual development toward socialism was not necessarily guaranteed. There was great danger of a bureaucratic deformity, he said, and of the growth of a bureaucratic apparatus. A bureaucratic development would lead to the suppression of the creative initiative of the population, to the creation of a class of sycophants, and to intellectual stagnation. In order to prevent a bureaucratic deterioration, Kardelj demanded the extension of democracy to all areas of social life. The goal was self-government in which the public participated in the administration of the state on every level and, as actual producers, in the direction of the economy. As the first step in this direction, Kardelj in May 1949 recommended the formation of workers' councils.[13]

From Bureaucratic Centralism to Worker Self-Management

In 1949, the responsibilities of the central authority were handed over to individual republics, districts, and communities. Factories and small enterprises received greater independence and, in autumn 1949, the first workers' councils were tentatively introduced in some factories.

However, it was not the ideal situation for the transformation of society. In August 1949, the Soviet leaders issued an ultimatum, concentrated troops on the Yugoslav border and, in September 1949, abrogated all treaties and sent a threatening letter to the Yugoslavs, signed by Acting Foreign Minister Gromyko. There was danger of a military invasion. Nevertheless, the internal reforms were implemented. After many months of experimentation, the most decisive change—the introduction of elected workers' councils in all Yugoslav enterprises—was executed. This was the first step in converting state ownership to social ownership and in replacing the bureaucratic, centralized planned economy with socialist self-management.

In his speech before the Yugoslav Parliament on June 26, 1950, Tito endorsed the introduction of workers' councils in Yugoslavia by pointing out the negative aspects of bureaucratic centralization in the Soviet Union. He declared that bureaucratic development was the most dangerous threat to socialist development, since it obstructed the development of socialism acting as it did, like an octopus with a thousand tentacles. Bureaucratic centralization was especially dangerous, however, because it wormed its way unnoticed into the pores of all social activity. Tito further stated that the state ownership was not, as the leaders of the Soviet Union claimed, the highest, but rather, the lowest form of social ownership. He alluded to the Marxist formula of the "association of free producers." According to Tito, social production must be managed by the producers themselves. Management of factories by elected workers' councils was "the only right road as regards the withering away of state functions in the economy."[14]

In the course of 1951, the transition from centralized *detailed* planning, which still prevails today in the Eastern European countries, to general economic coordination was accomplished. In June 1951, the Yugoslav Central Committee resolved that only party resolutions and not declarations by individual members of the party leadership were binding for all party members, thereby formulating open debate over fundamental questions.[15] There followed, finally, the gradual withdrawal of the Yugoslav Communist Party control from many realms of the state life, specifically from cultural life, literature, and art. "Socialist realism" and party-mindedness—obligatory principles in the Soviet Union and Eastern Europe—were considered obsolete. In foreign policy, the concept of "nonalignment" was defined as the fundamental line.

At the Sixth Congress of Yugoslav Communists, held from November 2 to 7, 1952, the reforms which were realized after the break with Moscow were analyzed and extended. The Yugoslav Communist Party changed its name to League of Communists, partly in order to differentiate itself from the Stalin-type Communist parties and partly to recall the original concepts of Marx whereby the Communists were not a specific party leading the working class but, rather, a part of the working class itself. The apparatus of the high-ranking officials was drastically reduced in size, and the autonomy and independence of lesser party bodies were increased considerably. The League of Communists, it was explained, did not issue directions in either economic or political life, but rather concentrated on political and ideological work and on the power of persuasion. The Party Congress decided to continue workers' management of the factories, i.e., producers' self-management, and to increase the rights of the actual producers and to restrain bureaucratic centralism.[16]

The Effects on European Communists

The Yugoslav Communists frequently dealt with the conditions of other Communist parties in detail. Many Yugoslav publications appeared in foreign languages and were secretly read and discussed in the countries of the Soviet bloc. The Yugoslav Communists pointed to the fact that the pro-Soviet parties were stagnating and had become an obstacle to further development. Forced into Stalin's mold, the pro-Soviet Communist parties of other countries had become politically and ideologically unable to continue to lead the progressive forces struggling for socialism.[17]

In his speech at the Sixth Congress of the League of Communists in 1952, Tito prophesied that the Yugoslav development would stimulate change in other Communist parties. "The Yugoslav example," declared Tito in 1952, "will lead to critical attitudes toward the measures and the policies of the Soviet Union on the part of the entire world Communist movement." In many Communist parties, particularly those in West European countries, criticism of pro-Moscow policies was intensified: "The Communist parties of individual countries must strive to consider the interests of the working population of their own country and not foreign interests."[18]

From 1948 until late 1952, over 8,500 people, often in danger for their lives, fled from the Stalinist countries of Eastern Europe to Yugoslavia.[19] In several West European countries, Communist Party members who either left or were expelled from the party formed groups and organizations which, inspired by Yugoslav publications, discussed similar problems and arrived at similar conclusions. The Acción Socialista was one such group, which was made up of Spanish Communists expelled from the party, including the editor-in-chief of the party's newspaper *Mundo Obrero*, Felix Montiel, and an important party leader from Catalonia, José del Barrio. The former Politburo member of the Spanish Communist Party, Jesús Hernández, visited Yugoslavia in 1950, where he spoke at the party university. In Italy, the Unione Socialista Independente, led by the two Italian Communist Party representatives in Parliament, Aldo Cucchi and Valdo Magnani, was founded. In West Germany the Unabhängige Arbeiterpartei (UAP), was established in Worms in the spring of 1951 by former functionaries of the West German Communist Party.

The Belgrade Declaration of June 1955

Stalin died in March 1953. Shortly thereafter, the Soviet leaders began a partial reconciliation with Yugoslavia. In November 1954, Moscow declared that the Soviet government was ready to promote complete normalization of Soviet-Yugoslav relations.[20] Normalization, however, was not accomplished for some time, for there were serious disputes among the Kremlin leaders; Molotov particularly opposed an improvement of relations with Yugoslavia.[21] On May 25, 1955, though, a Soviet delegation headed by Khrushchev, along with Prime Minister Bulganin and his deputy, Mikoyan, arrived in Belgrade. It was a unique occurrence. For the first time ever, the top leaders of the USSR traveled to an independent socialist country in order to apologize for previous Soviet policies. Upon arriving at the airport, Khrushchev drew some papers from his pocket and proceeded to make the sensational declaration that he deeply regretted the anti-Yugoslav campaign. To be sure, he blamed the conflict on the long-time Soviet chief of state security, Beria, claiming, "We studied assiduously the materials on which were based the serious accusations and offenses directed at that time against the leaders of Yugoslavia. The facts show that these materials were fabricated by enemies of the people, detestable agents of imperialism, who, by deceptive measures, pushed their way into the ranks of our Party. We are wholeheartedly convinced that this period of the deterioration of our relations has been left behind."[22]

Ten days later, on June 3, 1955, after long and hard discussion and debate between the Yugoslav Communists and the Soviet leaders, the Belgrade Declaration was issued. Since then Yugoslav Communists have frequently referred to this declaration which is also important for the Eurocommunist movement. The Declaration of Belgrade recognized not only different roads to socialism, but also the existence of different models. It was clearly stated that "differences in the concrete forms of socialism are exclusively affairs of individual countries."

Both the contents as well as the methods of the Soviet-Yugoslav dispute are extremely significant for Eurocommunism. Between 1948 and 1955, neither Tito nor any other member of the Yugoslav leadership went to a single East European capital to justify themselves or to apologize, as was unfortunately the case during the "Prague Spring" of 1968. The Yugoslavs were not afraid to defend openly their independent road to socialism and to criticize the Soviet system. They were not intimidated by threats from Moscow—not even the threat of Soviet invasion. And in the first mutual Soviet-Yugoslav declaration after the rapprochement, they insisted on clearly expressing their own point of view.

6

The Effects of the Twentieth Party Congress of the CPSU on European Communism

At the Twentieth Soviet Party Congress in February 1956, the Khrushchev leadership officially sanctioned the de-Stalinization measures already underway, clearing the way for further departure from Stalinism through controlled reforms from above. With de-Stalinization, the Khrushchev leadership intended to mold the system inherited from Stalin to the new conditions of Soviet society. In addition, the Khrushchev leadership set out to develop new relations with the countries of Eastern Europe. The leading role of the Soviet Union was to be maintained, but in more modern and more flexible terms.

Amazing Confessions

In the official published report, Khrushchev declared that under Stalin an "atmosphere of lawlessness and arbitrariness" had reigned, and that the secret police had "fabricated false charges against leading officials and rank-and-file Soviet citizens." He also claimed that the activities of party members were suppressed and that the Soviet Union was responsible for the deterioration of relations with several foreign countries. Khrushchev continued, admitting that facts had been falsified in historical works and that many honest party officials had unjustly been labeled "enemies of the people."

These criticisms were coupled with proclamations for socialist legality, for a more realistic interpretation of Soviet history, for the rehabilitation of innocently condemned people, for stronger control over the state security service (secret police) and for the revision of many of Stalin's "guiding principles" as well as for a new version of the history of the party.

These declarations alone would have sufficed to highlight the Twentieth Party Congress as an important event not only for the Soviet Union but also for the history of international Communism.

At the same congress new political concepts were announced, acknowledging, at least partially, the new conditions in the Soviet Union and in the world Communist movement. Instead of Lenin's thesis of the inevitability of wars—which Stalin had also adopted—Khrushchev now declared that due to these new conditions wars could and must be prevented. The new concept of noninevitability of wars formed the cornerstone of the doctrine of peaceful coexistence, which was officially proclaimed as the general line for Soviet foreign policy. Even more important for the formation of Eurocommunism, however, was the proclamation of different roads to socialism. Important Soviet leaders, including Khrushchev and Suslov, declared that the forms of the transition to socialism were becoming more and more varied, that henceforth the transition to socialism in the capitalist countries would occur under different circumstances, and that new forms of the transition to socialism would always appear. The report of the congress even declared that "it is completely lawful that in the future the forms of the transition to socialism will become more and more varied."[1] It was the first and last time that a Soviet Party Congress openly announced the concept of different roads to socialism in different countries.

In this connection the Twentieth Party Congress stressed the possibility of peaceful socialist transformation. Khrushchev now declared that, although the Soviet Communists continued to be convinced of the need for a revolutionary process, the transition to socialism did not necessarily have to be associated with civil war under all circumstances. In a number of capitalist countries there existed the realistic possibility of a peaceful transformation to socialism.

The new concepts of different roads to socialism and the possibility of the peaceful transformation to socialism obviously came completely unexpectedly to the fifty-five foreign Communist Party delegations present at the Twentieth Party Congress. They had not been informed at all about the new policies, or the fact that Stalin was to be criticized.

Among all the foreign Communist Party delegations, only two referred to the theory of different roads to socialism. The French

Communist Party leader, Thorez, recalled an interview given November 18, 1946 in which a representative of the French Communist Party had declared that the French road to socialism might be different from that of the Soviet Union. He did not mention, however, that he himself had given this interview. Thorez promised that the French Communist Party would always be faithful to the great ideas of Marx, Engels, Lenin, and Stalin—a peculiar declaration, since the Soviet leadership had just criticized Stalin.

Only the Italian Communist Party leader, Togliatti, immediately took advantage of the situation. In his speech, he declared that the Soviet road could not be compulsory in every respect for other countries, drawing a far-reaching conclusion for standards at that time: "The Italian Communists are faced with the task of finding an Italian road to socialism. This road must take into account the historical development of the country, its social structure, the mentality and aims of the broad masses of workers and must make it possible to find the forms which are suitable to Italy so that the majority of the people can be won over to a socialist reorganization of society." This declaration, which was reprinted in *Pravda* and in all East European countries, provided the first hint to an attentive observer that the Italian Communist Party would proceed the furthest in these new developments.[2]

Khrushchev's Secret Speech

On the last day of the Party Congress, February 25, Khrushchev gave his famous secret speech. For a long time the political background of the occurrence was unclear. We have since learned from Khrushchev's memoirs that there had been vehement arguments about the secret speech among the Soviet leaders. The final decision to give the speech was made, according to Khrushchev, during a break in the congress, when only the members of the Politburo (then called the Party Presidium) were present in the room. Khrushchev was against ending the congress without having completely settled with Stalin. Voroshilov and Kaganovich disagreed with Khrushchev, fearing that such action would diminish the prestige of both the Communist Party and the Soviet Union. "They'll all point their fingers at us," they claimed, realizing that they would have to explain their own behavior under Stalin. But Khrushchev remained firm. He claimed it was futile to try to cover everything up, since sooner or later people would return from the prisons and the camps and explain everything anyway. Now, at the first Party Congress after Stalin's death, he insisted, it was necessary to review openly with the delegates all that had happened. After some discussion over who should give the speech, it was decided that Khrushchev himself should do it.[3]

In his sensational secret speech, Khrushchev quoted for the first time from Lenin's famous "Testament" and disclosed Lenin's decision to break with Stalin. Until then, Lenin's "Testament" had been kept strictly secret, and any mention of it was punished—as has since been documented—with several years imprisonment. Khrushchev claimed that Lenin's fears as expressed in his "Testament" were justified. He emphasized Stalin's despotic character and concentrated mainly on the Great Purge of 1936–1938, on the mass repression, on the meaning of the term "enemies of the people," and on the fact that "confessions" were acquired through physical pressure against the accused. The most loyal and devoted Communists, who were never enemies or spies, were branded as "enemies of the people" and often accused themselves when they were no longer able to bear the barbaric torture. Of the 139 members and candidates of the party's Central Committee who were elected at the Seventeenth Congress in 1934, ninety-eight persons, i.e., 70 percent, were arrested and shot during the Great Purge. In the entire country, uncertainty, suspicion, and mistrust prevailed while all sorts of slanderers and careerists preyed on Soviet society. Purges in the Red Army, beginning literally at the company and battalion commander level and extending to the higher military centers, had weakened the Soviet armed forces: all military leaders who had been active in Spain or in China were liquidated. The mass arrests in the army, according to Khrushchev, had been a decisive cause of the Soviet defeats at the beginning of the war in 1941.

Particularly surprising for those present was Khrushchev's criticism of Stalin's behavior during World War II. He mentioned the fact that Stalin had ignored all warnings, both from Western and from Soviet sources, about Hitler's impending attack on June 22, 1941; that when war broke out he lost his nerve and feared immediate defeat; that Stalin had not taken part in any military operations during the first few months of the war, that he had been "demoralized," had shown "symptoms of nervousness and hysteria," and throughout the entire war had never visited any section of the front.

Khrushchev further criticized Stalin for having deported entire nationalities in the Caucasus for no good military reason, and (news to the delegates present as well as to all Soviet experts) for wanting to deport the Ukrainians also. They escaped this fate only because there were too many of them and there was no place to which Stalin could deport them.

Khrushchev, from his own experience, described how after the war Stalin had become even more capricious, irritable, and brutal. His suspicion and persecution mania reached unbelievable dimensions, and he staged imaginary conspiracies in order to hurl the Soviet Union into another Great Purge.

As for foreign policy, Khrushchev only mentioned that Stalin had been responsible for the Soviet-Yugoslav conflict; he had underestimated Tito, which was a sign of his megalomania.[4]

Although Khrushchev's criticism dealt too much with Stalin's person and too little with the Stalinist system, this secret speech was of great significance. It became a symbol of de-Stalinization. Particularly important was the fact that this criticism had been made by the First Secretary of the Central Committee of the CPSU himself. One has to put oneself in the place of both the Soviet and (even more so) the European Communists of that time: for three decades they were raised in the spirit not only of respect and admiration, but of love for Stalin—now they had to learn the truth about their idol.[5]

The Effects on the European Communists

For the Communists searching for new roads, de-Stalinization was a confirmation of all their previous claims, and it gave fresh impetus to their desires for reform. For the faithful Stalinists, on the other hand, it was the deepest shock imaginable. They were now confronted with the truth about Stalin by their own party leadership. The West German author Ralph Giordano, at that time still a young Communist in Leipzig, East Germany, had this to say concerning the revelations about Stalin:

> Khrushchev's so-called secret speech of February 25 has never been printed in East Germany, but what comes to us by way of rumor was later confirmed in written reports. The first shock occurred in the town-hall restaurant. A few of us were sitting around together, and what we had just learned made our blood curdle. Everything sounded hushed, whispered, like something unbelievable, inconceivable; it would have been unbearable if repeated aloud. In *his* time, a contradiction, even a single glimpse, was enough to have someone disappear and never be seen again—the guards of the old Bolsheviks destroyed by *him*—the

numerous delegates and candidates of the Seventeenth Party Congress killed or arrested—Kirov assassinated with *his* knowledge—*his* threat to the Minister of State Security of having him beheaded if the Kremlin doctors made no confession—the camps—the mass displacement—the uprooting of entire races—the reading of letters of despairing Communists from prison, into which *he* had thrown them—the people's fear for their very lives which lasted at least two decades. It couldn't be! Stalin, embodiment of our strength, symbol, friend, protector, remote father, personification of the Revolution, omniscient, kind, and just—Stalin now a violent monomaniac possessed by a persecution mania, a vain, evil, mean dictator? It couldn't be! We rose, wandered through the streets, as in a dream. . . ."[6]

Khrushchev's secret speech, published first in excerpts, then in its entirety, profoundly shook the thinking of all Communists. Finally freed from Stalinist fetters, they were no longer corraled into a predetermined course. Different tendencies and currents now openly revealed themselves. Most East European party leaders succeeded in warding off the shock and were content with the renaming of a few streets or the removal of several politically incriminated officials. Show trials which had occurred in various countries had now to be considered. Only in Poland in March 1956 did more traumatic events immediately result. Even the official party newspaper reported the serious internal disputes. During discussions at party assemblies, Communists discussed not only Stalin's personality cult but all the characteristics of Stalinist corruption: the deterioration of party life, the results of Stalinist discipline and force, the unanimity enforced from above, and the transformation of the governmental apparatus into a terrorist organ of autocracy.

Not only were the East Europeans bewildered, but so too the West European Communists. Each party took a completely different position. In the decisive days of March 1956, the French Communist Party emphasized Stalin's achievements exclusively and tried desperately to play down the controversy over Stalinism. The Italian Communist Party, on the other hand, reacted differently. Togliatti wasted no time, declaring on March 15 that the Twentieth Party Congress of the CPSU created a new situation, which differed not only quantitatively, but qualitatively from the old. Under Stalin, the desperate perspective of endless persecution prevailed. Stalin's distrust, he said, led to unjust measures of suppression and to breaches of socialist legality, in which the prosecutors relied solely on confessions and not on proof. It was now time, claimed Togliatti, to make precise criticism and to draw new conclusions based on new studies of Soviet development.[7] The British Communist Party also engaged in much freer speech. For days, letters to the editor included statements[8] which would earlier have been considered antiparty and which expressed the deep-rooted conflict of conscience suffered by Communists, particularly those who had believed and trusted Stalin.

The Dissolution of the Communist Information Bureau (Cominform)

In the middle of the first discussions of de-Stalinization in April 1956, the Communist Information Bureau (Cominform) was dissolved. On April 18, 1956, all Communist newspapers issued a short "Informatory Announcement about the dissolution of the information bureau of Communist and workers' parties" declaring that the Cominform Bureau had fulfilled its function. Moreover, it was emphasized that the Cominform Bureau had "contributed to the strengthening of proletarian internationalism," but that it no longer corresponded to the new conditions.[9] The next day *Pravda* formulated the idea of the independence of each Communist Party more clearly than ever before: it was now of utmost importance to consider carefully the national conditions within different countries. *Pravda* called upon the Communist parties "to pay careful attention to the characteristics and special conditions of their countries . . . and to develop a policy that would be most suitable to the special characteristics and circumstances of the people in question."[10]

The dissolution of the Cominform Bureau was welcomed by all Communist parties, but not without some criticism. The Yugoslav Communists criticized the wording of the dissolution, particularly the reference to the supposed positive role which the Cominform had played. According to the Yugoslav Communists, the Cominform had in no way played a positive role or contributed to the strengthening of internationalism; it had in fact done internationalism considerable harm. The Yugoslav theoretician Mosha Pijade declared that "a future serious historical analysis of the Cominform would show that it played no constructive role."[11]

In addition, the Italian Communist Party leader, Togliatti, unexpectedly declared that it had been a mistake to have interfered in the affairs of the Yugoslav Party in 1948 and 1949, that the composition of the Cominform leadership had been much too heterogeneous, and that the activity of the Cominform had proved "increasingly unproductive." Togliatti expressed the hope that the dissolution of the Cominform would result in greater autonomy for critical evaluations and a greater tendency to adapt the activities of the Communist parties to the conditions of each particular country."[12] Now all Communists saw that Yugoslavia no longer stood alone. The Italian Communist Party, the largest mass party of Europe, began to approach Yugoslavia's views—a further if only small step on the road to Eurocommunism.

In early summer 1956, Tito finally visited the Soviet Union for the first time since 1948. Immediately before Tito's arrival in Moscow, Lenin's "Testament" of 1922 was finally published, after thirty-four years. The previously well-protected document was now available to all. On June 20, 1956, the official Soviet-Yugoslav declaration was proclaimed. Both parties asserted that the roads of socialist development were different in different countries, that the "abundance of roads to socialism added to its very strength," and, finally, that "it is wrong for any trend to force its own conceptions about the forms and road to socialist development on any other trend." Since then, the Yugoslavs have continually referred to the declaration of June 1956, as have, more recently, Eurocommunists of other countries.

Togliatti's Concept of Polycentrism

During Tito's visit to Moscow, the Italian Communist Party leader, Palmiro Togliatti, gave a detailed interview, which was later published in the Party newspaper *Unità*. The text of this interview is another milestone in the formation of Eurocommunism.

In this interview, Togliatti was the first European after the Yugoslavs to offer an independent, critical analysis of the Soviet Union. While he welcomed Khrushchev's disclosures about Stalin, he criticized the Soviet comrades for having so far failed "to tackle the thorny subject of an over-all political and historical judgment." The Soviet thesis that Stalin's personal characteristics were the cause of the Soviet development could not, according to Togliatti, be considered satisfactory, since such a judgment was not based on Marxist criteria. The real problem was how and why Soviet society "was able to deviate to the point of degeneration and in fact did so degenerate." That was the first time that the word "degeneration" was used by a foreign Communist Party leader while referring to the Soviet Union. Togliatti spoke openly about bureaucratization and referred to the party in particular. "We do not doubt that Stalin's errors were closely linked with an excessive growth of the bureaucratic apparatus in the Soviet Union's economic and political life, and it would not be incorrect to maintain that the Party was the starting point for the noxious restraint of democracy and the gradual spreading of bureaucratic forms of organization."

It was against this backdrop, Togliatti declared, that Stalin's role must be seen. Stalin had proved an "organizer and conductor of the bureaucratic apparatus" from the moment that apparatus had begun to "displace the forms of democratic life." That had been the basis of the "one-man rule which eventually declined to the point of degeneration"—a situation which persisted to his death and which "may possibly still linger to a certain extent." A continuation of Stalinist policies, Togliatti said, might "possibly have led to a violent change" in the Soviet Union.

Togliatti concluded that the criticism of Stalin had raised the general problem of the danger of bureaucratic degeneration and the stifling of democratic life. The Soviet Union must now "define precisely the extent of the old mistakes," and the rectification must be carried out with courage and without hesitation. Only in that way could the socialist society recover its impetus and develop "on a broad healthy democratic basis, rich in lively new impulses."

For the world Communist movement, continued Togliatti, the criticism of Stalin had given rise to "a wish for an ever-increasing autonomy and this could only be of advantage to our movement." The situation had changed so extensively that the Soviet model "can and must no longer be obligatory." Within the international labor movement a "polycentric" system was emerging, and even within the world Communist movement one could "no longer speak of a single leadership."[13]

This was the most significant declaration in the world Communist movement since the Yugoslav Communists broke with Moscow, and it immediately affected the European Communists. Even the French Communist Party now declared, although more cautiously, that one could not consider the Soviet explanations satisfactory.[14] The British Communist Party expressed itself more clearly, demanding a complete Marxist analysis of the causes of the degeneration and the operations of Soviet democracy. It was inadequate, it claimed, to attribute this development exclusively to the character of Stalin.[15] Similar declarations were made by the Communist parties of Norway and Belgium.[16] Thus several Communist parties had for the first time dealt critically with the Soviet Union.

Moscow responded promptly. On June 30, 1956, the Soviet Central Committee, in a detailed declaration, announced the Soviet leadership's position on the Stalin problem, rejecting Togliatti's ideas about "certain forms of degeneration in the Soviet system."[17] No Western European Communist Party, however, retracted its criticism. Thus, although hardly visible, the first signs of a split between Moscow and the Western European Communist parties appeared in June 1956.

The "Polish October" – 1956

Autumn 1956 witnessed both the Polish October and the Hungarian Revolution. Since the backgrounds and issues are well known, I limit myself here to a discussion of several points significant for the development of Eurocommunism.

In Poland, confrontations between new social forces on the one hand, and an obsolete bureaucratic apparatus on the other, became especially sharp. At the end of June 1956, Poland was shaken by a workers' uprising in the city of Poznan, prompted by embitterment over petty patronization and neglect of grievances. The small strike soon escalated to a large political event, resulting in armed conflict with the police and military forces. The Stalinists among the party leaders considered the strike a "provocation by imperialist agents" and a "counter-revolution." But the more moderate and open-minded wing of the party recognized the discontent of the workers as the cause and advocated improvements in the social realm and certain liberalization. In the course of the summer, many political prisoners were released and rehabilitated. Among them were Gomulka and many of his fellow combatants who, after their rehabilitation, have risen to the important positions of the party leadership. From these positions of power, Gomulka and his associates aggravated the disputes between the Stalinists and the liberal reformers, who were supported by large parts of the population.

On October 19, 1956, the Eighth Plenum of the Polish Central Committee was convened, electing Gomulka First Party Secretary and deciding on measures for democratization. The Soviet troops stationed in Poland, under the direction of Marshal Rokossovsky, began marching toward Warsaw. The majority of the Communist Party organizations in Warsaw mobilized the workers in the factories, who demonstrated with the students in the streets, shouting for arms which they then received. On that same morning, a delegation of the Soviet leadership headed by Nikita Khrushchev landed in Warsaw. Threatening to deploy military forces, the Soviets commanded the Polish Communist Party leaders to prevent the election of Gomulka and to retain all pro-Soviet functionaries in their offices. Only after an unusually violent exchange of opinions did the Soviet delegation agree to stop the Soviet troops from moving toward Warsaw and other large Polish cities. Gomulka, nevertheless, was still named First Party Secretary and the liberal reform wing won a majority in the Polish Politburo. Many Stalinists, including Marshal Rokossovsky, were dismissed from the party leadership. Rokossovsky returned to the Soviet Union with thirty-five other high-ranking Soviet officials.

At the end of the Eighth Plenum, the Polish Central Committee limited the authority of the secret police, relaxed censorship, legalized the spontaneously formed workers' councils, proclaimed a more moderate policy toward the peasantry and the Catholic church, and reassessed the importance of the Parliament. Throughout Poland a hope arose that the bureaucratic system might be transformed into a true socialist democracy. For several months, from late autumn 1956 until the summer of 1957, there was unrestricted discussion about many issues, which have since come to concern all Eurocommunists. The sociologist Zygmunt Baumann, for example, demanded departure from the Leninist Party doctrine, and Wladyslaw Bienkowski, the Polish Minister of Education at that time, who is very active in the Human Rights movement in Poland today, advocated a new democratic structure within the party. Edward Lipinski, a Polish economist and active in the Human Rights movement today, demanded the transition of the centralized economic system into a system of social self-management; and Leszek Kolakowski, the Polish philosopher, advocated the independent development of an open Marxism. There was also much discussion of the relationships among different forces in the world Communist movement and the assertion that they be based on equal rights. All these discussions and disagreements in Poland in the autumn of 1956 represented an important step in the theoretical development of Eurocommunism.

In May 1957, however, the reaction set in. The "revisionists" of the reform wing were slowly driven back, and Gomulka and other "centrists," out of fear that the status quo of the party apparatus might be endangered, opposed any further domestic reforms. During 1958, the bureaucratic apparatus again took hold, all measures for democratization were ended, intellectual life was again subjugated, and the Polish Communist Party leaders gradually oriented themselves back toward the Soviet Union.

The Concepts and Aims of the Hungarian Revolution

In addition to the "Polish October," many aspects of the Hungarian Revolution of late October/early November 1956 are important to the development of Eurocommunism. After the Twentieth Party Congress, the Hungarian reformers, though still engaged in fierce arguments with the Stalinists, gradually regained the dominant position. The Hungarian Reform Communists of the Petöfi Circle, which began its work in March 1956, can be considered true Eurocommunists. Their original intent was to hold meetings to discuss the lessons of the Twentieth Party Congress for Hungary. Very soon, however, the meetings organized by the Petöfi Circle, marked as they were by free discussion, went far beyond the limits desired by the party leadership. Demands were made for economic reforms, release and rehabilitation of innocently arrested people, and explanations of the show trials. On July 27, 1956, when the Petöfi Circle had the topic "Freedom of the Press" on the agenda, six thousand people showed up at the meeting. The discussion lasted all night and loudspeakers carried the proceedings into the streets.

Among the Hungarian Party leaders the Stalinists Rákosi and Gerö vehemently opposed the reformers and centrists led by Imre Nagy. While Poland's Gomulka was clearly a centrist, Hungary's Imre Nagy must be considered a true reformer, and according to today's terminology, even a pioneer of Eurocommunism.

Like Tito, Imre Nagy (1896–1958) had served in the Austro-Hungarian Army and was a prisoner of war in Russia, where he witnessed the Russian Revolution of 1917. In 1918, Nagy joined the Russian Communists and took part in the civil war on the side of the Red Army. In 1921, he returned to Hungary, where he at first joined the left wing of the Hungarian Social Democrats and then the Communist Party. Nagy was later arrested and exiled to Austria, from where he ran the Hungarian Communist Party. He then moved to the Soviet Union where he lived from 1930 until 1944. During his fourteen-year stay in the Soviet Union, he worked at the International Agricultural Institute, represented the Hungarian Communist Party at the Seventh World Congress of the Comintern, was demoted during the Great Purge, worked on a collective farm in Siberia, and directed the Hungarian-language radio station during World War II. Returning to Hungary in late 1944, Nagy became Minister of Agriculture, and in September 1947 was named President of the Hungarian Parliament. During Stalin's last days, however, he was removed from all important positions.

In July 1953, shortly after Stalin's death, as Hungarian Premier, Imre Nagy proclaimed a far-reaching program of reforms, including abolition of prison camps, protection of personal freedom and safety, development of the consumer-goods industry, freedom for farmers to leave collective farms, and a tolerant policy toward the intelligentsia.[18] However, the opposition of the Stalinist bureaucrats was so strong that, in March 1955, Imre Nagy was deposed and subsequently expelled from the Politburo, and his program of reforms was halted. Shortly thereafter, Nagy also lost his seat in the Parliament and his chair at the Hungarian University. Rákosi even demanded a public self-criticism, but Nagy refused. Instead, he spent the time from the summer of 1955 to the beginning of 1956 drafting a detailed memorandum to the Central Committee, which he hoped to have discussed by the party membership before the Twentieth Party Congress of the CPSU. This, however, never occurred. In his memorandum—clearly an important document for the development of Eurocommunism— Imre Nagy defined two possible roads for the development of socialism. The development up to now, declared Nagy, had been dictatorial. "The power was not obtained from the spirit of socialism or democracy, but from the spirit of dictatorship of the minority, or Bonapartism. Its goals are not based on Marxism, the doctrine of scientific socialism, but are set, rather, with the sole purpose of maintaining the system of one-man rule at all costs and by all means."

As an alternative, Nagy demanded a socialism based on a "constitutional legal system, administration of justice and democratization of our entire political and social life." Thus Nagy was the first Communist leader to have set forth the ideas of order and legality as the fundamental conditions of a socialist society.[19]

News of the successful Eighth Plenum of the Polish Central Committee, which seemed to mark the liquidation of Stalinism and the breakthrough to a socialist democracy, swept through Hungary. On October 22, spontaneous demonstrations for Poland were held in many Hungarian towns. On October 23, several hundred thousand people from all segments of the population demonstrated in Budapest, demanding independence, democratization, freedom of the press, equality with the Soviet Union, the condemnation of

Rákosi, and the reappointment of Imre Nagy. During the Hungarian Revolution, the demand for independence was inseparably connected to the demand for far-reaching internal reforms. Between October 26 and 30, the revolution spread from Budapest throughout the entire country. Workers' councils and self-elected people's councils were formed all over, and the collective farms were disbanded. More important, however, was the collapse of the Stalinist party structure. On October 30, 1956, the revolution in Hungary had almost been successful. Imre Nagy announced the end of the one-party system as well as the formation of a socialist government on the basis of cooperation between several parties. Thus, in 1956, Hungary achieved a goal which is important to present-day Eurocommunism.

At the same time, János Kádár, a member of the Imre Nagy government, declared that the Communist Party had been dissolved and that the founding of a new party had been planned for November 1. This new party, according to Kádár. would "break away from the crimes of the past once and for all . . . and build socialism, not through servile imitation of foreign examples, but by reliance on the doctrines of Marxism-Leninism free of Stalinism. This socialism would be developed in a democratic way which would correspond to the economic and historical character of our country."[20] Today this reads like the declaration of a Eurocommunist party.

The Effects of the Events in Poland and Hungary

The tragedy of Soviet military intervention and the bloody suppression of the Hungarian Revolution—termed "counter-revolution" by the Stalinists—were heavy blows for thousands of Communists, especially as they occurred only months after the optimistic, initial phase of the Twentieth Party Congress of the CPSU. But Soviet intervention was not taken lightly by many European Communists. In the French and Italian Communist parties, hundreds of members, including many long-time officials, left the party in protest. In Poland, where at the end of 1956 one could still speak relatively freely, many critical views were expressed. "Tell me what you think about Hungary and I will tell you who you are," wrote a leading Polish newspaper at the time. Another wrote that the Hungarian tragedy had proved that "Stalinism was the death of Communism."[21]

On November 11, 1956, Tito expressed the hope that the terrible sacrifice that the Hungarian people had suffered would have a positive effect; namely, that "the comrades in the Soviet Union, even the Stalinists, would gradually realize that it cannot be done that way any longer. It just cannot be done that way any longer."[22]

On the same day, the Danish Communist Party appealed to Moscow to let the working Hungarian people pursue the reconstruction of their own country independently. On November 12, 1956, the Norwegian Communist Party declared that "all people have the right of self-determination." Internal problems could not be solved with the help of foreign troops.[23]

At its Eighth Party Congress in mid-December 1956, the Italian Communist Party stated that the Soviet intervention was an "evil necessity which could not and should not have been avoided." In a resolution of the Congress, however, it declared that "the development in Hungary has shown that there are still misconceptions, namely the insufficient attempt at a national form of the development of socialism as well as the servile imitation of the Soviet model, which caused a wide gap between the party and the government on the one hand and the people on the other." The events in Poland and Hungary proved that a socialist system can proceed only from the principle of different roads to socialism. Moreover, the sovereignty of small countries should not be violated by "intervention and pressure" by stronger nations.[24]

The Italian Communist Party did not clearly express its objection to Soviet intervention in Hungary until 1976, on the occasion of the twentieth anniversary of the revolution. Nevertheless, the Italian Party made clear the fact that, as the largest European Communist Party of Europe, it did not side with the Soviets on this important issue.

The World Communist Conference (1957)

In order to resist the trends toward independence and to restore Moscow's role in the world Communist movement, especially in Europe, the Soviet leadership decided to convene a world Communist conference. It was the intention of the Kremlin to convene such meetings regularly in order to limit the independence of individual parties, to restrict them to a single obligatory general party line, and to restore the shaken unity of the world Communist movement.

The Soviet Communist Party ideologue, Michail Suslov, demanded on November 6, 1956 that the unity of the world Communist movement be restored.

It is interesting to note that the world conference was first suggested by other Communist parties so as to give the impression that the Soviet Union was later merely agreeing to it.[25] The first suggestion came from the Socialist Unity Party of Germany (SED) in East Germany, the Austrian Communist Party, and the French[26] and Czechoslovak Communist parties. Moscow was surprised to see, however, that there was opposition also. At its Eighth Party Congress in December 1956, the Italian Communist Party explicitly declared that "the return to a central organization of Communist parties would be opposed." International meetings should not adopt obligatory resolutions but should serve only to "clarify present positions."[27] In addition, the British Communist Party, supporting the Italian suggestions, protested against the formation of a new central organization. The commentary of the British Communists[28] went so far that the SED newspaper in East Germany, *Aus der Internationalen Arbeiterbewegung*, censured them.[29] After almost a year's preparation, the official Soviet Communist Party periodical, *Kommunist*, declared that international conferences were necessary for the success of the world Communist movement.[30]

The First World Conference took place in Moscow between November 14 and 19, 1956. Delegates from sixty-four Communist parties participated. Yugoslavia was not represented. Interestingly enough, the conference was divided into two sections. First, the twelve ruling Communist parties of Eastern Europe met, adopting a prepared political and ideological declaration proclaiming the general party line. Then from November 16 to 19, all sixty-four Communist Party delegates (twelve ruling and fifty-two nonruling) met, agreeing only on a colorless peace manifesto. Among the twelve points of the declaration adopted by the twelve ruling parties, the most important were:

a) Restoration of the unity of the socialist camp (i.e. the Warsaw Pact countries) "against all intrigues of enemies."

b) Establishment of eight universal laws based on Soviet development, including the proletarian revolution, the establishment of the dictatorship of the proletariat under the leadership of a Marxist-Leninist party, and the protection of the "achievements of socialism."

c) Consideration of national characteristics and traditions and of the actual conditions in individual countries. (At the same time, however, the warning was issued about the dangerous exaggeration of national characteristics and about deviation from the "universal truths of Marxism-Leninism about the socialist revolution and the building of socialism.")

d) The obligation of all Communist parties to fight against "dogmatism" as well as "revisionism," whereby dogmatism (adherence to the Stalinist model) was only condemned and revisionism (any reforms toward independence and a new course) was declared the "main danger."

e) Recognition of the leading role of the party and the principles of "proletarian internationalism" (i.e., subordination to the Soviet Union).[31]

The First World Conference was to a great degree a success for Moscow. The Soviet leadership had regained authority and control—just a few months after the Twentieth Party Congress, Khrushchev's secret speech, the Polish October, and the Hungarian Revolution.

At the same time, however, the Soviet leadership did have to make the following concessions to the "autonomists," the forerunners of modern Eurocommunism:

a) Under pressure from the Italian and Scandinavian Communist parties, which were not ready to sign the far-reaching declaration and would support only the peace manifesto, it was necessary to hold two separate conferences—one for the ruling parties and one for the non-ruling parties.[32]

b) As a result of opposition from other ruling Communist parties (Poland and Hungary in particular), Moscow was unable, as it had wanted, to include a passage in the political declaration making periodic world conferences mandatory.

c) Moscow's intention to announce the founding of an international Communist periodical in the declaration was not realized. The international periodical was decided upon four months later at a conference in Prague in March 1958, and not even all Communist parties agreed to it. The first copy of this periodical, *World Marxist Review,* did not appear until September 1958.

d) Moscow's intention to proclaim "revisionism" as the main danger for all parties was weakened by the addition that each Communist Party could decide for itself what constituted the main danger.

Even if these concessions seem relatively unimportant today, it was indeed significant that as early as November 1957 there was no general consensus in West European Communism on questions of the structure of the world Communist movement, on the extent of centralized direction, on the obligatory general party line, and on strategy (the struggle against revisionism). For the first time, the

Soviet leadership had to make concessions to autonomous forces. From then on, autonomous forces within both East European (Polish and Hungarian) and West European Communist parties began to appear despite all Soviet attempts to establish a monolithic centralized world movement. After his return from the Moscow World Conference, the Italian Communist Party delegate declared openly: "It is not a question of a return to either the Comintern or the Cominform. Such forms of organization of the world Communist movement no longer comply with present situations and needs."[33]

The events of 1956 represent the second step along the development of Eurocommunism after Yugoslavia's break with Moscow. The Polish October and the Hungarian Revolution demonstrated the fragility of, and the inconsistencies within the Stalinist system. Togliatti's famous declaration of polycentrism in June 1956 was the first official proclamation outside Yugoslavia that the Soviet model was no longer obligatory. The violent suppression of the Hungarian Revolution was no longer accepted without criticism. Besides Yugoslavia, the Italian, British, and Scandinavian Communist parties expressed more and more critical observations. Even at the First Communist World Conference concessions had to be made to the autonomists, the forerunners of Eurocommunism.

7

European Communism in the Shadow of the Emerging Sino-Soviet Conflict (1957-1967)

The decade from 1957 to 1967, during which European Communism stood in the shadow of the emerging Sino-Soviet conflict, can be considered the third step in the formation of Eurocommunism.

The Sino-Soviet conflict deeply shook all of world Communism and led to the formation of two centers of the world Communist movement—Moscow and Peking. At the head of these centers stood the two largest ruling parties with completely different, even opposing aims. The existence of two centers enabled the European Communists to discuss their strategy and aims more freely and to increase the scope of their autonomy and new orientation.

Romania's Road to Independence

Until the beginning of the sixties, Romania appeared to be the one country of Eastern Europe most fully subordinated to the Soviet Union. No one would have guessed that Romania would become an important factor in the Eurocommunist movement.

The fascist Antonescu regime was toppled in August 1944 by antifascist Romanian forces as well as by the invasion of Soviet troops. At that time, August 1944, the Romanian Communist Party numbered about 1,000 and it wielded only a small influence over the population. But the party, which at the end of 1945 already numbered 700,000, soon became the leading force of the country. At the head of the party stood the Romanian resistance fighter Gheorghe Gheorghiu-Dej, a member of the party since 1929 who had spent the eleven years from 1933 to 1944 in prison in Romania. It was not Gheorghiu-Dej, however, but the Communists returning from the Soviet Union, particularly Anna Pauker, who at first played most important roles after 1945. In no other country of Eastern Europe was the Soviet influence, particularly in the economy, so strong as it was in Romania. From July 1945 until August 1952, sixteen Soviet-Romanian companies ("Sovroms") were founded in Romania as compared with seven in Bulgaria, six in Hungary, and one in Czecho-slovakia. With the help of these Sovroms, which enjoyed extraterritorial rights and which were completely removed from Romanian economic planning, the Soviets controlled the most important branches of the Romanian economy—including petroleum, banks, the chemical industry, heavy industry, coal, wood and lumber, river and sea transportation.

This "Sovietization" was also expressed in the Romanian Constitution of September 1952. It was practically a verbatim copy of the Stalin Constitution of 1936 and included, in addition, a hymn of praise to the Soviet Union in the preamble. In the realm of culture, Romanian traditions were repressed in favor of the Slavic influences and Russification took place even in the Romanian language.

Only gradually and with the utmost caution was Gheorghiu-Dej able to limit the influence of Anna Pauker and other pro-Soviet Communists in Romania. Finally, in 1952, he removed them from the Politburo entirely. At the same time, he succeeded in placing in high positions those loyal to him, including Nicolae Ceauşescu, who played a dominant role in later developments.

The decisive changes did not occur, however, until after Stalin's death in March 1953. Between 1954 and 1956 the Soviet Union sold its share of the Sovroms to Romania, thus permitting the Romanian Communist Party to control its own economy for the first time. The Romanians were still somewhat constrained, however, by the presence of Soviet troops. Under these circumstances, the Romanian leaders decided on an unusual, indeed a unique step in the history of the world Communist movement, a step which did not become known until many years later. During one of Khrushchev's visits to Bucharest, the Romanian Communist Party leaders, including Minister of Defense Bodnaras, proposed to the Soviet guest that he arrange nothing less than the complete withdrawal of Soviet troops from Romania. Khrushchev himself recalled the unusual incident in his memoirs:

Not long after Stalin's death I was in Romania and had a talk with the Romanian Minister of War, Comrade Bodnaras. He was a good friend of the Soviet Union, an Old Bolshevik who had spent some time in prison in Romania and who enjoyed our absolute confidence and respect. Without warning he brought up the question, "What would you think about pulling your troops out of Romania?"

I must confess that my first reaction to his suggestion wasn't very intelligent. I would even go so far as to say I lost my temper. "What are you saying? How can you ask such a question?"

"Well," he explained, "Romania shares borders with other socialist countries and there's nobody across the Black Sea from us except the Turks."

"And what about the Turks?" I asked.

"Well, we have you right next door. If it were necessary, you could always come to our assistance."

"It's not just the Turks I'm thinking about. They control the Bosporus and the Dardanelles. So the enemy could always invade Romania by bringing landing forces into the Black Sea."

The Romanians exchanged glances. Obviously they had already talked this matter over among themselves. "Well, all right," they said, "if that's how you feel we'll withdraw the question. We just didn't want you to think that we were standing firm on socialist positions because your troops are stationed on our territory. We're standing firm because we believe in building socialism and in following Marxist-Leninist policies, and because our people recognize us as their leaders and support us completely." I was more than satisfied with this elucidation of their reason for proposing the removal of Soviet troops from their territory. I believed that the Romanian comrades were sincere in reaffirming their dedication to the building of socialism.

A few years later we did start reducing the size of the Soviet Army, cutting it to almost half of what it had been under Stalin.[1]

But the new mood went further than just the reduction of troops mentioned by Khrushchev. By the summer of 1958 the last Soviet troops had been withdrawn from Romania. In November 1958 at a Plenum of the Central Committee of the Romanian Communist Party, it was decided that Romania would undertake its own rapid industrialization. This course was stressed even more clearly in the new six-year plan at the Third Party Congress of the Romanian Communist Party in June 1960. The new plan included construction of new steel works in Galati (Galaz), which was obviously against the will of the Soviet leadership. The Soviet Union had wanted to restrict Romania exclusively to oil refining, products of light industry, and agriculture, which would have increased that country's economic backwardness and dependence on the Soviet Union. The Romanian leadership under Gheorghiu-Dej, however, insisted on continuing Romania's industrialization in accordance with its supply of raw materials and energy, and saw the large steel works under construction in Galaz as very important to that goal. The Soviet Union refused the technical assistance for the steel workers that Romania was hoping for, and the first controversy resulted.

A further controversy broke out when Romanians opposed the Soviet Union's plan to increase the strength of the Council for Mutual Economic Assistance (COMECON) by giving it the right to dictate obligatory economic plans for all members and to make all COMECON resolutions legally binding for all member states. The Romanian Party leadership decisively rejected these Soviet plans. This rejection was confirmed and made public in March 1963 at a session of the Central Committee of the Romanian Communist Party, where it was also declared that the economic cooperation with COMECON countries could only proceed on the basis of national independence and complete equality. Central planning for all COMECON countries would mean the economic subordination of Romania, and Romania refused to play the role of agrarian producer and oil supplier. The Romanian opposition was so strong that the COMECON conference in July 1963 deemed it necessary to abandon the thought of an international planning commission.

But the Kremlin leadership did not give up. In a Moscow University periodical, it suggested setting aside the Danube region of Romania, Bulgaria, and part of the Soviet Union and establishing an international economic area, to which Romania was to contribute almost 40 percent of its land, Bulgaria 30 percent, and the Soviet Union .05 percent. The Romanians also rejected this attempt so forcefully that the Soviet Union never went back to that plan. That was the third controversy with the Soviet Union.

Romania's road to independence, however, was not limited to conflicts over Soviet-Romanian economic relations, although they did play a very important role. In early 1963, Romania began trading with Western countries as well as concluding economic agreements with Yugoslavia and China. Mutual visits by Romanian and Chinese leaders became more frequent. At the end of June 1963, Romania was the only Soviet bloc country to publish important declarations of the Chinese Communist Party on the subject of the Sino-Soviet conflict without negative commentary, declaring itself neutral in the conflict.

In 1963 the Romanian edition of the Soviet foreign policy periodical *Novaya Vremya* (New Times) ceased to be published, and instead the Romanian Communists began to publish their own foreign policy journal, *Lumea* (The World), which expressed the Romanian point of view, particularly on the struggle for sovereignty, equality, and independence. In the same year, Russia lost its monopoly in Romanian schools, and the attempts to render the Romanian language more Slavic were openly criticized and even partially overcome.

On April 26, 1964, after a session of the Central Committee of the Romanian Communisty Party which lasted from April 15 to 22, the Romanian Communists announced the famous "Declaration of Independence" in which the economic equality of socialist countries as well as the independence of the Communist Party was emphasized.

As far as the economic relations among socialist countries were concerned, the Romanian Communists demanded that the COMECON organization be transformed from a rigid instrument of integration into a loose economic association. A central COMECON planning commission was rejected because it would limit the sovereignty of the member states. Economic planning, according to the Romanians, must remain in the hands of each individual country. "The state plan is an indivisible entity. One cannot simply detach parts or sectors and move them somewhere outside. Thus, one has to reject multilateral associations of producers or enterprises managed by several Communist countries together."

The Romanians also demanded that the COMECON become more democratic. Every member state should have a veto right and the COMECON authorities should not have the right to impose economic sanctions against a member state which does not obey the majority decision. The clear demands for complete equality of all Communist parties was most important for later Eurocommunism: "There are and can be no father-son parties and no first or second class parties. There exists solely the large family of equal Communist and workers' parties. No party has or can claim precedence, nor can one party force its political line or ideas on any other." As justification, Gheorghiu-Dej referred to the Communist International. He criticized the Comintern's "unsuccessful methods of intervening in the internal affairs of other Communist parties," which went so far that "important leaders and even entire Central Committees were removed, leaders were forced in from the outside, useful functionaries were removed from different parties and some Communist parties were even dissolved." This had to stop. "It is the responsibility of each Marxist-Leninist party and the sovereign right of each socialist state to formulate, elect, or alter the forms and methods of the construction of socialism."[2]

After Gheorghiu-Dej's death in March 1965, the leadership of Romania fell into the hands of Nicolae Ceauşescu, who strengthened its independent course even further. Ceauşescu was first active in the Communist youth movement. He had belonged to the Central Committee since 1948, was Deputy Minister of Defense in 1950, candidate member of the Politburo in 1952, and already in 1955, at the age of thirty-seven, a full member of the Politburo. As second Party Secretary, Ceauşescu had clearly been designated Gheorghiu-Dej's successor since 1957.

In June 1965, in a new statute of the Romanian Communisty Party, all previous references to the Soviet model were stricken and no mention at all was even made of the Soviet Union. In May 1966, at the twenty-fifth anniversary of the founding of the Romanian Communist Party, Ceauşescu stressed the different forms and methods in the development of any new social order. The struggle for socialism, claimed Ceauşescu, proceeded under different conditions in each country of the capitalist world. Experience proved the Communist parties to be successful only "when they work out their own strategic and tactical lines which correspond to the particular conditions and characteristics of their country." Such diversity would therefore necessarily exclude an international center. A monolithic center within the international movement had in the past only harmed the Communist parties.[3]

Romania has been playing an important role in the development of Eurocommunism for more than a decade—although, of course, the internal political situation of that country by no means corresponds to the Eurocommunists' conceptions of a democratic and pluralistic socialism. In any case a second ruling Communist party has consistently given active support to autonomous tendencies in nonruling European Communist parties.

More Nonruling Communist Parties Become Autonomous

In the decade from 1957 to 1967 six nonruling Communist parties achieved autonomy in different ways and with different goals.

Denmark: Between 1956 and 1958 there were serious disputes about the Twentieth Party Congress of the CPSU and the subsequent de-Stalinization. After long internal debate between an independent reform wing under the leadership of Aksel Larsen on the one hand, and pro-Soviet forces on the other, the Danish Communist Party split in the autumn of 1958, resulting in the formation, in early 1959, of a new Socialist People's Party of Denmark with Eurocommunist goals. In the elections in November 1960, the new Socialist People's Party received 6 percent of the vote, while the pro-Soviet Communist Party fell to 1.1 percent and was no longer represented in the Parliament.

Sweden: After long internal discussions at the decisive Twentieth Party Congress of the Swedish Communist Party in January 1964, the Stalinists fell into the minority. The newly elected chairman, Carl Henrik Hermansson, advocated a democratic road to socialism and was the first European Communist to advocate a democratic model of socialism.

The Netherlands: The Dutch Communist Party exercised restraint in the Sino-Soviet conflict and declined to support either side in this dispute. In March 1964, Paul de Groot, Chairman of the party, announced the "new orientation" at the Twenty-first Party Congress. Thereafter, the party was to concentrate on internal development and was to refuse to follow Soviet directives. As a result, the Dutch Communists did not participate in any world or regional conferences from 1964 to 1976, but they also did not develop in any Eurocommunist direction.

Norway: The Sino-Soviet conflict also influenced the Norwegian Communist Party. Small groups within the party had wanted to support either Moscow or Peking. The majority, however, pleaded to stay out of the dispute. At the Thirteenth Party Congress in March 1965, a change in leadership—Reider T. Larsen was elected to replace the Stalinist Lövlien as party chairman—led to increasing independence, and the Norwegian Communist Party declared it would not take any more instructions from the outside.

Japan: The Japan Communist Party was more strongly influenced by the Sino-Soviet conflict than were the European Communists. Since 1963/64, the Japan Communist Party sided more and more with the Chinese Communists without identifying themselves completely with Peking. Several pro-Soviet functionaries, including Shiga, formed their own splinter party with Soviet support. Breaking away from China in 1967, the Japan Communist Party has since strengthened its independent policies. Since 1968 the Japanese

Communists have been following a road to a new course in line with Eurocommunism.

Australia: The Australian Communist Party was also strongly affected by the Sino-Soviet conflict. After the Australian Maoists left the party, an important change in leadership occurred. Laurence Aarons, a reformer, replaced the Stalinist Laurence Sharkey. Since 1965, the Australians have followed an independent course, especially after the Twenty-first Party Congress in June 1967. A new political course was advocated; the leadership proclaimed a far-reaching democratization of the party structure, the renunciation of the party's leading role in coalitions, freedom of thought and expression within the party, respect and tolerance among different groups and parties, and support for a democratic model of socialism.

Thus the autonomous forces in world Communism gained considerable strength during this decade. The methods of transformation were appreciably different in individual countries. Of greatest importance was the fact that since the mid-sixties not only Yugoslavia and the Italian Communists but several nonruling Communist parties in industrialized countries as well were following new roads.

The Togliatti Memorandum

The Italian Communist Party, however, was still the indisputable forerunner of Eurocommunism. Togliatti's memorandum of August 1964, "On the Question of the International Workers' Movement and Its Unity," was of particular importance. Togliatti had finished his draft during his stay in the Crimea, just one day before his death. This document has since come to be known as the Togliatti memorandum or the Togliatti testament. Togliatti's main theses were:

a) The unity of the world Communist movement should be based on exchanges of experience between the parties of different countries and not by the re-creation of a centralized organization. It is now impossible to proclaim universally valid formulas for the international Communist movement because the forms and concrete conditions differ from country to country. Therefore, each party has to know how to act in an autonomous manner.

b) The Communist parties of capitalist countries must not confine themselves to propaganda but should try to have a real effect on the political life of their countries. Thus the Communists had to "develop a great deal of political courage, overcome every form of dogmatism and tackle and solve problems in new and innovative ways." The Communists could not remain indifferent to the Common Market, but had to provide constructive suggestions for reforming the economic structure and offering an alternative to capitalist programs. A peaceful road to socialism required careful study, the imperative of increasing democratic freedoms, and effective means of enabling the workers to participate actively in economic and political life.

c) The Communists, according to Togliatti, should not confront other forces with their own ideologies in an abstract manner but, rather, should initiate discussion with those forces. A definite shift to the left had occurred in organized Catholicism, creating a suitable condition for cooperation. The old atheistic propaganda was completely useless. The problem of religious conscience had to be handled differently from the past if the Communists seriously wanted to gain access to the Catholics. Otherwise, "our out-stretched hand would be conceived as simply an expedient gesture, or even hypocrisy." A different attitude toward culture was also necessary. The Communists, claimed Togliatti, had to become pioneers of the spirit and of free artistic creation: "Not all those who are strangers to us in the realm of culture, philosophy, and social science are our enemies or stooges of our enemies."

d) Finally, declared Togliatti, it was not right to assume that other socialist countries, including the Soviet Union, were above criticism. One had to portray openly the difficulties and inconsistencies within socialist countries. "The worst thing we can do is to give the impression that everything is going smoothly and then suddenly be faced with difficult situations and have to explain them." Political arguments and disputes should be possible in socialist countries, and it would be helpful if the political leadership in socialist countries would be willing to discuss the most controversial topics openly. "The political developments which have led to Stalinism must be carefully examined. The problem that claims greatest attention today is that of overcoming the regime, introduced by Stalin, of restricting and suppressing democratic and personal freedoms." Movement toward democratization was obviously occurring slowly and with great resistance. In addition, a nationalist revival was becoming noticeable in socialist countries. Thus it was necessary, even in the socialist camp, "to protect oneself from forced outward uniformity and to establish unity in diversity with the complete autonomy of each country." Socialism, Togliatti stressed in conclusion, had to be understood as an order "which guarantees the workers the greatest possible freedom and in which the workers actually participate in an organized manner in the direction of all social life."[4]

Since Togliatti's manuscript was immediately sent to the PCI's central headquarters in Rome and published by his successor, Luigi Longo, even *Pravda* and the Socialist Unity Party of Germany's organ, *Neues Deutschland*, had to publish the memorandum. Thus, for the first time, many Communists heard about the new thoughts which were being discussed among Communists outside their own countries. The Togliatti memorandum was important in the development of Eurocommunism not only because of its contents, but also because of the extent of its circulation.

European Communist Parties and Khrushchev's Downfall

Togliatti was not able to share the ideas contained in his memorandum with Khrushchev. Six weeks after Togliatti's death in mid-October 1964, Khrushchev was overthrown. For the first time in the history of Soviet Communism the highest leader, who had simultaneously been both First Party Secretary and Premier, was relieved of his duties. But no political explanation, no justification, and no sign of gratitude for what he had accomplished followed his downfall. Immediately thereafter, Leonid Brezhnev was named First Party Secretary and Alexei Kosygin was named Premier. Khrushchev's name disappeared from the Soviet press. It soon became clear that his de-Stalinization reforms were being slowed down, then discontinued altogether, and finally, that a harder line was being introduced in Soviet politics.

Until then, the Communist parties of the world had always simply accepted a change of leadership in the Kremlin. This time, however, it was different. The Yugoslavs contended that the Soviet explanations for Khrushchev's downfall were not satisfactory and claimed that, for Yugoslavia, Khrushchev continued to be the great fighter "who paved a road through the Stalinist jungle." The Italian Communist Party declared that, as a result of the change of leadership, the Italian Communists were "wary and critical." The party sent a delegation to Moscow to find out what was happening at the Kremlin. But after the delegation returned, the Italian Communists were still not satisfied. Khrushchev had been praised for opening up new roads for the Communist workers' movement and his services could not simply be forgotten. The PCI officially declared that it regretted the fact that there had been no satisfactory explanation for Comrade Khrushchev's displacement.[5]

Even the French Communist Party demanded clarification of the events which had led to Khrushchev's downfall and similarly sent a delegation to the Soviet capital. The Dutch Communist Party declared that it would continue to exercise its right to criticize the CPSU. The Dutch Communist Party newspaper advised the new Kremlin leaders to dedicate most of their attention to the standard of living in the Soviet Union, which left much to be desired.[6]

The comments of the Swedish Communist Party were the most far-reaching: "If the only reason [for Khrushchev's downfall] was sickness and old age, it would not have been unusual in light of his seventy years. But why then wasn't his resignation announcement published verbatim? Why weren't there any medical reports as is usually the case? Why no word of thanks to Khrushchev, who has spent the greater part of his life serving the Soviet State in positions of responsibility and authority, almost for as long as the party itself has existed? Why wasn't he himself given the opportunity to announce the decision of his resignation?" The Swedish Communists claimed that according to the constitution, the Supreme Soviet should have been convened but that the Presidium of the Supreme Soviet alone had decided on Khrushchev's removal and that not a single member of this Presidium had taken a stand. "The way in which Khrushchev resigned or was forced to resign left a bitter after-taste," they claimed.[7]

The first criticism of events within the Soviet Union set an important precedent. From October 1964 on, the Eurocommunist parties commented more and more independently on developments within the Soviet Union. Thus when, at the beginning of 1966, the two Russian authors Sinyavsky and Daniel were sentenced to five and seven years of hard labor respectively, the Italian and British Communists protested profusely. In addition, Carl Henrik Hermansson, leader of the Swedish Communist Party, declared: "I am completely opposed to the sentences brought against the two Soviet writers. My conception of democracy does not include the right of political institutions or parties to decide which opinions are admissible and which are not."[8]

Critical Discussions, New Ideas

The sixties were most important for later Eurocommunism. The decade witnessed the beginning of open discussions among European

Communists. Until then, discussions of many political questions had been taboo among both the West European and the East European Communists. Now detailed discussions about the many important problems which the Communists of the industrialized nations were facing in a world which had changed completely were made public. These discussions were extremely important for the intellectual and theoretical preparation of Eurocommunism. The program of the League of Communists of Yugoslavia in March 1958 marked the beginning of such discussions. Then, at the Plenum of the Central Committee of the Italian Communist Party in November 1961, the concept of "unity in diversity" emerged. Moreover, the conferences in the Liblice Castle near Prague in May 1963 on the occasion of Kafka's eightieth birthday proved that not only political, but also profound ideological questions were being considered. At that conference, participants examined the problem of alienation in socialism. Shortly thereafter, in his lectures of 1963/64 at Humboldt University in East Berlin, Robert Havemann addressed himself to this problem.

In 1964, the philosophical Marxist journal *Praxis* was founded in Yugoslavia. The ideas of the Yugoslav Marxists Svetozar Stoyanvić, Rudi Supek, Gajo Petrović, Mihailo Marković, and Predrag Vranicki which appeared in *Praxis* received much attention in Europe. European Communist intellectuals met with Catholics on several occasions. The conferences of the Society of Saint Paul in Salzburg in 1965 and at Herrenchiemsee in April 1966, as well as the one in Marianske Laszne (Marienbad) in April 1967, aroused particular attention. The participants of the conferences, including Roger Garaudy (at that time a Politburo member of the PCF), Luciano Gruppi (a leading theoretician of the PCI), and the Italian Communist Party Professors, Lucio Lombardo Radice and Cesare Luporini, redefined the relationship between Marxism and Christianity and stressed the pluralistic aspects of a socialist society. A conference of intellectual Social Democrats and critical Communists in Vienna, in May 1967, featured the Marxist theoretician Franz Marek (who has since been expelled from the Austrian Communist Party) and the sociologist Andreas Hegedüs, Director at that time of the Institute of Sociology at the Hungarian Academy of Sciences. Besides West European Communists, more and more East European Communist Party theoreticians (including Edward Goldstücker, Ota Šik, and Julius Strinka from Czechoslovakia and George Lukács from Hungary) participated in these conferences and/or contributed to the discussion in periodicals.

The problems of a changing social structure, the different role of the working class, the integration of the economy, and the resulting responsibilities for the state in the capitalist world were thoroughly analyzed. In these discussions it was indicated that Lenin's theory of the state was outdated. The state could no longer be regarded solely as the suppressive apparatus of a ruling class. This implied the renunciation of the dictatorship of the proletariat.

In the discussions about the democratic road to socialism, several European Communists rejected the old theses that only the Communist parties lead the struggle for socialism. They recognized the fact that other forces could play equal roles and that the Communist Party should thus act as a partner in a coalition with other forces.

Discussions also centered around development of Marxist theory. The representatives of several Communist parties openly declared that Marxism had fallen behind social development. Psychology and the whole realm of anthropology had been neglected and the problem of alienation had not been dealt with adequately, they claimed. The discussion also dealt with new attitudes toward religion.

The debate over a new model of socialism was of particular importance for today's Eurocommunism. It became increasingly clear that there could be no uniform socialism throughout the world and that the present socialist systems could be considered, at best, initial forms or first attempts which had to be further developed. Several Communists advocated a self-management model of socialism and the gradual withering away of all parties and all state organs, but the majority, particularly the West European Communists, preferred a multiparty system. In the course of these discussions, in early 1962, several emigrants from Hungary who had been followers of Imre Nagy started publishing in Belgium a new periodical entitled *Pluralistic Socialism*. Soon many Communists, particularly the Italians, began advocating the idea of a pluralistic socialism, developing proposals for a socialist multiparty system and rejecting a state ideology. They favored free development of different ideologies and acknowledged the role of the parliaments and the rule of law.

The theoretical discussions between 1957 and 1967 were an important background to the "Prague Spring" of 1968. Moreover, the intellectual debates of that time prepared the ground for many programmatic declarations and documents of Eurocommunism.

European Communism and the "Prague Spring" 8

The significance of the "Prague Spring" of 1968 extends far beyond the realm of the history of Czechoslovakia. The "socialism with a human face" in 1968, had a great impact on West European Communists, many of whom felt this development corresponded to their own conceptions. Indeed, many Eurocommunists could easily identify with the party which developed the model of socialism of the "Prague Spring."

Czechoslovakia Before the "Prague Spring"

The ossified bureaucratic and dictatorial system of the Novotný regime in Czechoslovakia was in sharp conflict with the requirements of the country and its people. Economic policy had been enforced through administrative methods that no longer corresponded to the economic possibilities of the country. A hasty buildup of heavy industry, unfulfillable production aims, illusory promises and inadequate initiative in individual enterprises—all had thrown Czechoslovakia into an economic crisis and had effected a marked reduction in the standard of living.

All political and economic decisions were concentrated in the hands of the party apparatus. The party organs had taken over the duties of federal and economic bodies and were interfering in the economic process. This led to the undermining of whatever little initiative remained and to a general indifference at all levels. A policy of pro-Czech nationalism had increased tension between the Czechs and the Slovaks, and the discontent of the minority nationalities—German and Hungarian—had grown continuously. In the social realm, the trade unions did not represent the interests of the workers, but functioned, rather, as "transmission belts" for the party and the economic bureaucracy. These political, social, and national problems reached such intensity that the country could no longer be ruled by the old methods The call for reforms became louder and louder. Writers and poets, as well as a group of outstanding economists, technologists, sociologists, and philosophers, had stressed the need for far-reaching reforms since the early sixties.

The struggle for "socialism with a human face" began in February 1963 when Professor Eduard Goldstücker of Karls University in Prague published an article in the periodical *Literární noviny* in which he denounced the assumption "that a new higher social order can be achieved without humanity and legality and that great human accomplishments can be championed in theory but trampled upon in practice." Then, at the Fourth Writers' Congress in Czechoslovakia in June 1967, reformers battled furiously with Stalinists. Pavel Kohout, Alexander Kliment, Milan Kundera, Ludvík Vaculík, and Jan Prohazka—all of whom played an important role in the "Prague Spring"—courageously advocated democratization. Several were subsequently expelled from the party and others were admonished, but the supporters of democratization were already so strong that the party apparatus had to reckon with them. This became clear at the Thirteenth Congress of the Czechoslovak Communist Party in 1966, where a program of economic reforms was adopted. During his speech at the Congress, Ota Šik declared that the adoption of this program was a "great step on the road to the democratization of our society," but admitted that it was only a modest beginning. It was now a matter, declared Šik, of preparing the way for democratization both within the party and within the entire political sphere of state management.

Although the intellectuals from the cultural, sociological, and economic spheres had taken the initiative, these forces would not have been able to succeed alone. But with the support of many Slovak Communists and functionaries who opposed Novotný's pro-Czech policies, as well as the limited help of officials of the state apparatus and the party who longed for an end to dogmatism and for modern working methods, the reform forces wielded considerable power.

Many factory directors and economic planners demanded systematic economic reforms and also supported the reformers. Thus the party apparatus was now clearly divided between the bureaucratic Stalinist forces on the one hand, and a progressive wing on the other.

The First Stages of the "Prague Spring"

As a result of these developments, a serious dispute broke out during a meeting of the Central Committee of the Czechoslovak Communist Party at the end of October 1967. Alexander Dubček, Secretary of the Slovak Communist Party since 1963, demanded the transformation of party structure, the transition to new methods, and the separation of party and state. However, that meant an attack on Novotný who, at that time, was both First Party Secretary and President. At a later meeting of the Central Committee in December 1967, the dispute between the reformists and their opponents grew harsher. Within the Presidium, as the Politburo was called in Czechoslovakia, Novotný's supporters were as strong as his opponents, so neither side dominated. The decisive change did not occur until the Central Committee meeting of January 1968. After stormy discussions (a total of 150 speeches were made), Novotný's opponents finally gained the upper hand. They forced Novotný to resign as First Secretary (although for the time being he remained in the party Presidium and retained the office of State President) and Alexander Dubček, the spokesman for the reformers, was elected to the post.

Consequently, there was great hope for liberalization and democratization. The situation in Czechoslovakia changed virtually overnight. Censorship suddenly disappeared. Now, under the direction of reformers Jiří Pelikan (television) and Zdeněk Hejzlar (radio), the mass media, which until then had been a propaganda instrument of the ruling bureaucracy, expressed the ideas, hopes, and needs of the public. Apathy and lack of political interest were abruptly replaced by an almost unknown interest in all political issues. The periodical *Literární listy* played an important role, and already in mid-February Zdeněk Mlynář, one of the most consistent reformers, was able to present his thesis in the party newspaper, *Rudé Právo*. According to Mlynář, the task was not to improve the existing political system, as the centrists wanted, but rather, to achieve a "qualitative transformation." Mlynář declared that the rights and freedoms of every citizen had to be guaranteed by the legal order and that a political system had to be set up which did not aim at the implementation of obligatory directives but fostered the formation of opinion and decision-making and expressed the objective requirements of the entire society. In the party, Mlynář emphasized, the minority had to be guaranteed the opportunity to voice its opinions. This process would undoubtedly lead to conflict, "but there is no other way unless we wish to stifle the inner dynamics of socialism."[1] And the Marxist philosopher Ivan Sviták summed up the aims of the "Prague Spring" most precisely: "Replacement of totalitarianism dictatorship by socialist democracy, in other words, a change in the manner of the exercise of power without giving up our socialist achievements—in particular, the public ownership of the means of production—that is the basic problem of today.[2]

The democratization which was instituted so suddenly benefited from the general disillusionment with the Stalinist past and the crimes of the Novotný era. In early February, Josef Smrkovský, one of the top leaders of the reform movement (and himself a victim of the Novotný regime), described the rehabilitation of Communists and non-Communists as an important aspect of socialist morality: "We Communists must be able to look everyone, including ourselves straight in the face, and that is why we must support full rehabilitation of all innocent victims."[3]

The critical analysis of the past nurtured a conviction that this state of affairs must never again be permitted in Czechoslovakia. It also led inevitably to further steps in the direction of socialist democracy. The more the reformist forces crystallized within the party, increasing their importance, the more the relations between the party and the public began to change. The party, until recently isolated as an instrument of bureaucratic power, was now regaining public support. And the more positive the public's judgment was of the party and the more interest it showed in the party's problems, the more the new ideas of the reformist faction within the party gained strength.

When, on March 1, 1968, the Stalinist Major General Sejna, who was under investigation for embezzlement, fled to the United States with a diplomatic passport, the moral degradation of the Novotný regime was complete. Sejna had been party Secretary in the Ministry of Defense. Soon after his escape, it was discovered that, in December 1967, Sejna had assisted Novotný in planning a military coup to eliminate the reformers. After a Stalinist, of all people, who had continually called for increased vigilance against the class enemy, had fled to the United States, the demand for Novotný's resignation from the presidency became more persistent. Novotný finally yielded on March 21, and a wave of resignation of Stalinist officials followed. It was still uncertain who would succeed Novotný as President.

In the meantime, other Soviet bloc countries became involved. On March 23, a meeting of the leaders of the Soviet bloc (with the exception of Romania) was convened in Dresden. At this meeting, Alexander Dubček was to justify the "Prague Spring." In contrast to the Yugoslav leaders, who, in early 1948, refused to take part in such conferences outside their own country, Dubček obviously hoped to be able to convince Brezhnev, Ulbricht, and Gomulka of the sincerity of his intentions and the necessity of democratization in Czechoslovakia. According to Jiří Pelikan's report, Dubček continually tried to convince the other leaders of the Soviet bloc countries that his party possessed the widest support of the population, that the changes were in the interest of socialism in Czechoslovakia, and that the Czechoslovak example could assist the Communist parties of the West European countries. Gomulka interrupted him rudely: "We are not interested in a socialist revolution in the Western countries. We are solely interested in protecting what we already have. Therefore, we cannot allow any experiments." Dubček later confessed his "astonishment" at the response. Unfortunately, he had not taken the advice of the Romanian leader Ceauşescu, who had warned him: "Don't ever agree to a discussion of internal affairs on any level or at any time."[4] The earnest, yet unrealistic attempt by the Dubček leadership to introduce "socialism with a human face" in Czechoslovakia without conflict with the leaders of the Soviet bloc, let alone with their approval, led to concessions which were to have negative effects.

This was already obvious during the election of the new president. For the first time in a Communist-ruled country, several candidates were put forward: Ludvík Svoboda (the former commander of the Czechoslovak Brigade in the Soviet Union), the reformers Josef Smrkovský and Laco Novomeský (the Slovak resistance fighter and poet), both of whom had been in prison under Novotný, and Cěstmír Císař, the former Minister of Education demoted under Novotný, were all candidates. In order to appeal to the Soviet bloc parties, Dubček spoke out in the Central Committee meeting for General Svoboda. He knew that Svoboda was the most acceptable candidate to the Kremlin leaders. At a meeting of the National Assembly on March 30, General Svoboda, the least outspoken reformer, was elected President of the Republic. Smrkovský, the most active reformer, was elected President of the National Assembly. "The National Assembly is faced with the task of establishing a socialist parliamentarianism by its entire legislative practice," Smrkovský declared in his inaugural speech. "Parliament must create safeguards to ensure that the Czechoslovak Socialist Republic becomes a law-abiding state in the purest sense of the word."[5]

At the April Plenum of the Central Committee, the reformers scored a further victory. Novotný and six of his followers lost their seats in the party Presidium. Important reformers, including Josef Smrkovský and František Kriegel, Chairman of the National Front, took over their posts. Furthermore, Zdeněk Mlynář was elected to the Secretariat of the Central Committee.

The April Plenum of the Central Committee was of great significance, for it was at that meeting that the "Action Program of the Czechoslovak Communist Party" was published. Moreover, a communiqué was issued, claiming that "The Central Committee emphatically supports the development of socialist democracy and will not allow the road it has now chosen to lead us back to the state of affairs that prevailed before January."[6] This Action Program, one of the most important documents in the history of Eurocommunism, was published on April 10, 1968.

The Czechoslovak Action Program

The detailed Action Program began with a strong criticism of the ruling system which had prevailed until January 1968. (The description of the state of affairs at the beginning of this chapter is taken to a great extent from the original texts of the Action Program.) It continued with suggestions for reform which affected all realms of society. The program is of such great significance to the development of Eurocommunism that it is essential to cite several key sections here:

Main Goal: "It is important to reform the whole political system so that it permits the dynamic development of socialist social relations and combines broad democracy with scientific, highly qualified management . . . the basic structure of the political system must at the same time provide firm guarantees against return to the old methods of subjection and high-handed tyranny."

The Role of the Communist Party: "The Communist Party depends on the voluntary support of the people. It cannot carry out its leading role by ruling over society, but by faithfully serving free and progressive socialist development. The Party cannot impel its authority, but must constantly acquire it by its actions. It cannot force its line by command, but by the work of its members and the truth of its ideals."

Freedom of Discussion within the Party: "Each member of the Party and Party bodies has not only the right but the duty to act according to his conscience, expressing initiative, criticism, and different views on the matter in question, and to oppose any functionary. . . . It is not permissible to restrict Communists in these rights, to create an atmosphere of distrust and suspicion of those who voice different opinions, and to persecute the minority under any pretext—as has happened in the past."

The Party and the State: "Substitution and interchanging of federal agencies with agencies of economic leadership and social organization by Party agents must be stopped. Party resolutions are binding for Communists working in these agencies, but the policy, managerial activities, and responsibility of the federal, economic and social organizations are independent."

The Communist Party and the National Front: "The political parties of the National Front are partners. . . . Possible differences in the viewpoints of individual component parts of the National Front or divergence of views as to a state policy are to be settled on the basis of the common socialist conception of National Front policy by way of political agreement and unification of all component parts of the National Front."

Against the Monopolization of State Power: "Socialist state power cannot be monopolized either by a single party or by a coalition of parties. It must be open to all political organizations of the people. The Communist Party of Czechoslovakia will use every means at its disposal to develop such forms of political life that will ensure the expression of the direct voice and will of the working class and all working people in political decision-making in our country."

Freedom of Association: "The implementation of the constitutional freedoms of assembly and association must be ensured this year so that the possibility of setting up voluntary organizations, special-interest associations, societies, etc., is guaranteed by law. . . . Freedoms guaranteed by law and in compliance with the constitution also apply fully to citizens of various creeds and religious denominations."

Freedom of Opinion and of Information: "The working people, who are no longer ordered about by a class of exploiters, can no longer be dictated to by any arbitrary edict from a position of power as to what information they may or may not be given, which of their opinions can or cannot be expressed publicly, where public opinion may play a role and where it may not."

Freedom of the Press and the Elimination of Censorship: "The Central Committee of the Communist Party of Czechoslovakia considers it urgently necessary to define in a press law and more exactly than heretofore when a state body can forbid the propagation of certain information (in the press, radio, television, etc.) in order to preclude the possibility of preliminary censorship. It is necessary to overcome the delay, distortion, and incompleteness of information and to remove the unwarranted secrecy of political and economic facts."

Freedom of Opinion and the Party Press: "The Party press especially must express the Party's life and development along with criticism of various opinions among the Communists, etc., and cannot be made to coincide fully with the official viewpoints of the state."

Freedom of Mobility: "The constitutional freedom of mobility, particularly that of travel abroad for our citizens, must be precisely guaranteed by law. In particular, this means that a citizen should have the legal right to long-term or permanent sojourn abroad and that people should not be placed in the position of emigrants without reason."

Rehabilitation: "The Party realizes that people unlawfully condemned or persecuted cannot regain the lost years of their lives. It will, however, do its best to remove any shadow of the mistrust and humiliation to which the families and relatives of those affected were often subjected and will resolutely ensure that such persecuted people have every opportunity of showing their worth in work, in public life, and in political activities."

Democratic Electoral Systems: "It is therefore necessary to work out an electoral system that will take the changes in our political life into account. An electoral law must lay down exactly and clearly the democratic principles for the preparation of elections, the proposal of candidates and the method of their election."

The Parliament (The National Assembly): "The Party regards the National Assembly as a socialist parliament with all the functions the parliament of a democratic republic must have . . . which actually decides on laws and important political issues, and does not just approve proposals submitted."

Prevention of Concentration of Power: "The party policy is based on the principle that no undue concentration of power must occur, throughout the state machinery, in one sector, one body, or in a single individual. It is necessary to provide for such a division of power and a system of mutual supervision that the faults or encroachments of any of its members can be corrected on time through the activity of another member."

Reforms of the State Security: "The State Security Service must have the status, organizational structure, staff, equipment, methods, and qualifications which are in keeping with its work of defending the state against the activities of enemy centers abroad. Every citizen who has nothing to hide must know with certainty that his political convictions, his opinions, personal beliefs and activities, cannot be the object of attention of the bodies of the State Security service. The Party declares clearly that this apparatus should not be directed toward or used to solve internal political questions and controversies in socialist society."

Attitude toward Science: "Socialism originates, combats and dominates by combining the working movement with science. . . . The more resolute and impartial the advancement of science, the more it is in harmony with the interests of socialism; the greater the achievements of the working people, the larger the scope opened to science."

Freedom of Cultural and Artistic Creation: "We reject administrative and bureaucratic methods of implementing cultural policy, we dissociate ourselves from them, and we shall oppose them. Artistic work must not be subjected to censorship.

Art and Culture under Socialism: "It is necessary to overcome the narrow understanding of the social and humane function of culture and art, the overestimation of their ideological and political role and the underestimation of their basic cultural and aesthetic task in the transformation of man and his world."

Foreign Policy: "Our foreign policy has not taken advantage of all opportunities for active work; it did not take the initiative in advancing its own views on many important international problems. The Central Committee of the Communist Party of Czechoslovakia, the National Assembly, the government and appropriate ministers must overcome these shortcomings without delay and consistently ensure that our foreign policy expresses fully both the national and international interests of socialist Czechoslovakia. . . . This is linked with the necessity of making prompt and detailed information available to the public on international problems and on the course of our foreign policy thereby creating conditions for the active participation of Czechoslovak citizens in the shaping of foreign political attitudes."

The World Communist Movement: "The Czechoslovak Communist Party will take every opportunity to establish contacts with the socialist, peace favoring and democratic forces in the capitalist and developing countries."

New Model of Socialism: "We want to start building up a new intensely democratic model of a socialist society which will fully correspond to Czechoslovak conditions. . . . We cannot squeeze life into patterns, no matter how well-intended. It is up to us to make our way through unknown conditions, to experiment, to give socialist development a new character. . . ."

International Significance: "We want to set in motion penetrating new forces of socialist life in this country to give them the possibility of a much more efficient confrontation between social systems and world outlooks, allowing a fuller application of the advantages of socialism."[7]

In the economic sphere, individual enterprises were to be allowed greater freedom in the decision-making process and factory management was to be democratized. This was to be accomplished through electing committees in the enterprises consisting, on the one hand, of representatives of the labor collectives and, on the other, of representatives from outside the enterprise, thereby ensuring the influence of the entire society's interests as well as an expert and qualified level of decision-making. The trade unions were to retain the right of protecting the interests of the working people and, at the same time, cooperate in the shaping of the economy. Moreover, the agricultural cooperatives were to become more independent; they were to be freed from excessive supervision and centralization.

Foreign Communists on the "Prague Spring"

Following the publication of the Action Program, Communists throughout Europe engaged in heated debate over the "Prague Spring." The bureaucratic dictatorial wings condemned the Action Program sharply and the new Czechoslovak development. On April 12, during the April Plenum of the Czechoslovak Communist Party, *Pravda* declared that the "influence of non-Marxist and non-socialist ideas had been expressed." A shortened, totally distorted version of the Czechoslovak Action Program was published in *Pravda*; all new points were omitted, and not a single line of the excerpts cited above appeared in the Soviet newspaper.[8] At the end of April, *Pravda* reported that a wave of "anti-Communist hysteria" had swept through Czechoslovakia. The East German press expressed similar ideas.

On the other hand, parties which today are considered Eurocommunist supported the development of the "Prague Spring" and declared openly that it set an example for their own individual paths. On April 12, Luigi Longo, at that time Secretary General of the Italian Communist Party, declared: "The realization of a more advanced socialist democracy is not only a great contribution to the struggle of the working class and of left-wing forces in capitalist countries, but also represents a stimulus for all socialist countries to overcome more boldly the obstacles standing in the way of full development of socialist democracy."[9]

At the beginning of May, on the occasion of his visit to Czechoslovakia, Longo promised the Czechoslovak Communist Party "the full support and solidarity of the Italian Communists."[10] After his return, he reported on the Czechoslovak Communist Party at the Gramsci Institute in Rome, claiming, "We assess their course of action positively, not only for their country but for all socialist countries and for the entire international workers' movement."[11]

Bernard Taft, a leading member of the Australian Communist Party, who was also in Czechoslovakia in April 1968, claimed that the world was an "eye-witness to a tremendous transition period which must be regarded as a sign of future socialism."[12] Among the Spanish Communists, Santiago Alvarez, one of the most important leaders of the Spanish Communist Party next to Dolores Ibarruri and Santiago Carrillo, spoke of the "Prague Spring" already at the beginning of May and described the development in Czechoslovakia as a model for the future of Spain.[13] Santiago Carrillo later concurred with this view. The Austrian Communist Party, which for a short span between 1966 and 1969 was one of the most progressive Communist parties in Europe, also expressed a positive point of view. Franz Muhri, Chairman of the Austrian Communist Party, said in an interview at that time: "We Austrian Communists sincerely wish our Czechoslovakian friends success in the realization of new goals not only because it's good for the Czechoslovak Socialist Republic, but because it's also the best help in the struggle for democracy and socialism in Austria."[14]

The French Communist Party, however, took a "middle position" similar to the centrists. At a Plenum of the Central Committee of the French Communist Party in mid-April 1968, Emile Waldeck-Rochet declared: "The announcements pouring in from Czechoslovakia have confirmed the fact that the Czechoslovak Communists are ensuring that the foundations of socialist society are in no way being endangered."[15] The French Communists neither approved nor disapproved.

In addition to the European Communist parties, various reform forces within the Soviet Union also welcomed the "Prague Spring." In spring 1968, Andrei Sakharov, a member of the Soviet Academy of Sciences, composed his memorandum, "Progress, Coexistence and Intellectual Freedom": "Today the key to a progressive restructuring of the system of government in the interests of mankind lies in intellectual freedom. This has been understood, in particular, by the Czechoslovaks, and there can be no doubt that we should support their bold initiative, which is so valuable for the future of socialism and all mankind. That support should be political and, in the early stages, should include increased economic aid."[16]

In East Germany, Robert Havemann saw the "Prague Spring" as a promising example and model. In a statement which he was not allowed to publish in East Berlin, he declared: "Socialists and Communists throughout the world today follow the political developments in Czechoslovakia with the warmest sympathy and with great hopes. What is happening there will be of decisive importance not only for the future of that country but will have worldwide repercussions and indeed is already doing so. For the first time the attempt is here being made to harmonize socialism and democracy. There have indeed been a number of attempts in the socialist countries to break through the diabolical circle of Stalinism by some kind of creeping democratization. But the lead weight of the party bureaucracy has time and again paralyzed and halted the few hopeful attempts. In Czechoslovakia we are witnessing today the magnificent attempt of a radical and uncompromising breakthrough toward socialist democracy. If this attempt succeeds, then it will be of great historical significance, comparable only to the Russian Revolution of October 1917."[17]

The Dramatic Months from May to August 1968

The developments from May until the end of July proceeded on two levels: within Czechoslovakia, the development of "socialism with a human face" continued; at the same time, pressure on Czechoslovakia from the Soviet bloc grew stronger.

The freedoms enumerated in the April Action Program were realized step by step in Czechoslovakia; discussions about the new forms of socialist democracy took place openly everywhere. In those weeks, many concepts were developed which later were to comprise the essential ideas of Eurocommunism. Many prominent philosophers, including the Marxist theoretician Karel Kosik, Professor of Philosophy at Charles University in Prague, and Robert Kalivoda, member of the Philosophical Institute of the Academy of Science, discussed the interrelation of self-management in socialism with political democracy.[18]

The leaders of the "Prague Spring" emphasized the fact that Marxism was not to assume an ideological monopoly in a socialist society. Cestmír Císař, the Central Committee Secretary for Education and Culture, declared that although Czechoslovakia is socialist, Marxism-Leninism would not be a state ideology. One had to realize that along with Marxism, non-Marxist views also existed in society. Moreover, Císař said it was "also important to stress that Marxism is not a party monopoly."[19]

From April until June, the Stalinists in Czechoslovakia continually lost ground, while the reform policies received increasing approval from the population. The rally for the May 1 celebration in 1968 became a spontaneous and enthusiastic demonstration for Dubček and the "Prague Spring." Unfortunately, the Czechoslovak leadership did not take full advantage of the situation. A more rapid removal of Stalinists from the high party offices, the immediate convening of a party congress (which would have confirmed the reforms and endorsed the Action Program), an increased contact with Yugoslavia and Romania (possibly even with China), and invitations to the progressive Communist parties which supported the "Prague Spring"—all these measures would clearly have had positive effects. Instead, however, much time was lost in Prague as leading officials tried to justify their positions at conferences of the Soviet bloc. A new summit conference was convened in Moscow on May 8, 1968, and was attended by Brezhnev from the Soviet Union, Gomulka from Poland, Ulbricht from East Germany, Zhivkov from Bulgaria, and Kádár from Hungary, but there was no representative from Romania. From Czechoslovakia, Dubček, Prime Minister Černik and the Stalinist Secretary of the Slovak Communist Party, Bilak, took part. But the Czechoslovaks made a serious mistake by participating in such a summit conference. They did not even protest against the fact that Romania had not been invited. During the conference, the leaders of the Soviet bloc countries demanded that the Czechoslovak leaders agree to the field training of Soviet troops in Czechoslovakia. Thereafter, the Soviet press campaign against the "Prague Spring" was abruptly stepped up. Several days after the meeting in Moscow, *Pravda* declared that the whole Czechoslovak concept of socialist democracy was wrong and unscientific, since it had been proved that the dictatorship of the proletariat was the "highest form of democracy."[20] Shortly thereafter, the well-known Soviet ideologist Konstantinov accused the Czechoslovak Central Committee Secretary Císař of being a revisionist and compared him with Bernstein, Kautsky, and rightist Social Democrats.[21] The Soviet press labeled the Czechoslovak Marxist philosopher Ivan Sviták "mad."[22] The Ukrainian Party Secretary and Politburo member Piotr Shelest indicated the real reasons for the campaign when he objected to "continued and non-viable models of socialism which could not be permitted."[23]

But Soviet actions did not stop at press polemics. On May 17, a military delegation arrived in Prague under Marshal Grechko's leadership. A few days later military exercises began in Czechoslovakia. The intention was to provide political support for Stalinists in the country. The editorial office of the pro-Soviet publication *World Marxist Review*, located in Prague, served as the base for propaganda. There flyers were printed and distributed and connections were made with forces opposed to the "Prague Spring." Already in May 1968, the East German State Security Service had approached Czechoslovak specialists and even students working in East Germany with offers to work for a radio station which was not yet completed. The East Germans promised them large sums of money and said they would "later" receive prestigious jobs in Czechoslovakia.[24] In addition, the East German press promptly featured a false report about the alleged presence of American tanks in Prague.

Under growing pressure from the Soviet Union, a Plenary Meeting of the Central Committee of the Czechoslovak Communist Party (the May Plenum) was held from May 19 to 20. At this meeting, the issues were discussed in a more reserved and cautious manner. Dubček requested members of the press, radio, and television not to carry criticism of the past too far and not to jeopardize Czechoslovakia's state interests in their reports about socialist countries. At the same time, Antonín Novotný and six of his prominent followers, who had been involved in the political show trials of the 1950s, were suspended from party membership. And finally, the Central Committee decided to convene the Fourteenth Party Congress on September 9, at which time the "Prague Spring" was to be officially sanctioned.[25]

Large segments of the public regarded the May Plenum as a setback and feared that democratization might be halted. These fears were reflected in the manifesto by Ludvík Vaculík, entitled *Two Thousand Words*, which was signed by sixty-seven prominent public figures.[26] The Vaculík manifesto opposing any decrease in democratization was met with tremendous positive response. By the end of June, spontaneously founded committees for the protection of freedom of the press had sprung up in Czechoslovak factories and other institutions. The workers in Czechoslovak factories also threatened a general strike in the event that the reform process was halted or reversed. In late June, the National Assembly adopted the Rehabilitation Law for persons innocently sentenced, and the new Press Law, involving the abolition of censorship. Moreover, it was officially announced that any citizen of Czechoslovakia enjoyed the right to travel abroad without a special visa. The elections for the delegates to the forthcoming Fourteenth Party Congress took place in the midst of these reforms; almost all of those elected were progressive reformers and the Stalinists suffered a crushing defeat.

The dispute reached a high point in mid-July. While the Prague reformers were receiving the support of the Yugoslavs, the Warsaw Conference of the party chiefs of the Soviet Union, Poland, East Germany, Hungary, and Bulgaria took place (Romania was again missing). There the Soviet bloc leaders drew up the so-called "Warsaw Letter," in which they blamed the Czechoslovak Communists for jeopardizing the vital interests of the rest of the socialist countries. They demanded an immediate halt to democratization, the revocation of democratic freedom (especially the freedom of assembly and of the press), and the reintroduction of the centralized, bureaucratic principle of subordination to the party. In the "Warsaw Letter," the leaders addressed themselves to certain "forces" inside Czechoslovakia, assuring them that, provided they took the "necessary measures," they could always count on "the solidarity and all-around help of the brother socialist countries."[27] This was a new and unmistakable threat of intervention. The leadership of the Czechoslovak Communist Party politely but firmly responded that the transitional difficulties were due mainly to the fact that "for many long years the old party leadership governed according to the principle of bureaucratic centralism and suppressed internal party democracy." They rejected the assertion that socialism was jeopardized in Czechoslovakia and stressed that the leading role of the Communist Party was stronger than ever before because it had the voluntary support of the people. "Any attempt to revert to the old methods would evoke the resistance of the overwhelming majority of party members, the resistance of the entire working class."[28]

At this time the "middle-of-the-roaders," the centrists, advocated a so-called "political solution," i.e., an attempt to stop the "Prague Spring" by means of political pressure. The French Communist Party immediately adopted this approach. On July 15 and 16 the General Secretary of the PCF, Emile Waldeck-Rochet, discussed such a solution with Suslov in Moscow. Immediately after his return on July 17, Waldeck-Rochet proposed a meeting of all European Communist parties within the next several days in order to deal with the Czechoslovak problem. The goal was obviously to apply more pressure on the Prague leadership but also to advise against military action. On July 18 and 19, Waldeck-Rochet went to Prague where he conducted talks with Alexander Dubček and other Prague leaders. After the return from Prague on July 22, the PCF withdrew its invitation of July 17 and now declared that a Conference of European Communist parties was not advisable.

The French Communists obviously saw no chance of arriving at a compromise. As a matter of fact, the pressure had increased. On July 19, 1968, *Pravda* and other pro-Soviet newspapers spread the false report that a cache of weapons of American origin had been discovered within Czechoslovakia near the West German border; these were to have served the preparation of an armed coup.[29]

Furthermore, it was claimed that the CIA had worked out a secret operational plan to "undermine the unity of the socialist countries." This was supposedly a plan under which American forces would effect the liberation of East Germany and Czechoslovakia. In addition, it was claimed that a coup d'état in Czechoslovakia would soon follow.[30] *Pravda* also carried reports about the alleged involvement of West Germany.[31] After the Prague leadership investigated the allegations, they discovered that the American weapons had been left over from World War II. Thanks to an excellent preservative that the Soviet Army had used, the weapons were still in good condition. The bags in which the weapons were found carried the trademark GUM in Cyrillic letters.[32]

While ideological polemics from Moscow became more and more threatening and the military maneuvers in the entire Western part of the Soviet Union across the border from Czechoslovakia added to the war of nerves, Soviet-Czechoslovak negotiations finally took place at Čierna from July 29 to 31, 1968. There followed a conference of the leaders of the Soviet bloc countries (again with the exception of Romania) in Bratislava on August 3, 1968.[33] Both conferences represented the attempt to commit the Czechoslovak party and state leaders to the Soviet line.

Following the negotiations in Čierna and Bratislava, most Czechoslovak Communists believed that they could now continue and further consolidate their reform activities. Many Communists in other countries had this impression. The Italian Communist Party expressed its satisfaction over the negotiations and declarations of Čierna and Bratislava and now declared that it was only a matter of "implementing our line of the democratic road to socialism and our ideas of a socialist society, which is open, modern, and democratic." The Italian Communist Party was to continue along this road "with full consideration of the Czechoslovak experiences."[34] Both the British and the Austrian Communist parties made similar statements.

European Communists and the Occupation of Czechoslovakia

In this period of pacification and even hope, the Warsaw Pact countries were undertaking the military preparations for the occupation by Soviet troops, supported by troops from East Germany, Poland, Hungary, and Bulgaria, which was to come during the night of August 20–21, 1968. Never before had the Soviet leadership undertaken anything which met with such widespread disapproval. In many countries even the Communists faithful to Moscow became suspicious and distrustful, for several reasons:

a) The justification for the occupation, according to which there were "anti-socialist forces" repeatedly at work in Czechoslovakia, proved to be a lie. In fact, there was not the slightest sign of antisocialist or counter-revolutionary forces in Czechoslovakia. Nobody in Czechoslovakia had pleaded for the return to capitalism either in word or in deed. On the contrary, the goals of socialism were more strongly supported by the population than ever before.

b) The occupation troops were not welcomed, much less called for, by anyone in Czechoslovakia. Even after the occupation, the Soviet troops did not receive any cooperation. The Czechoslovak National Assembly, the Central Committee of the Communist Party of Czechoslovakia, and the Fourteenth Congress, which took place illegally on August 26, 1969, all unanimously opposed the occupation of their country.

c) It was obvious to everyone that all Soviet declarations of equality, nonintervention, and sovereignty are conveniently ignored when the vested interests of bureaucracy are or might be jeopardized.

Thus it became obvious within the Communist movement of Europe that the only reason for the occupation of socialist Czechoslovakia was the fear of the dynamic and widespread power that a new democratic and humanist model of Socialism would have, the fear that the Czechoslovak example might find followers in other Eastern European countries or even in the Soviet Union. The Soviet invasion and occupation of Czechoslovakia on August 21, 1968, suddenly widened and deepened the chasm between the bureaucratic, dogmatic forces, on the one hand, and the Communist forces striving for independence and a new course, on the other.

Outside the Soviet sphere of influence in Europe only the Socialist Unity Party of West Berlin, the West German Communist Party, the Communist Party of Luxembourg, the Turkish and Portuguese Communist parties, and the Progressive Party of the working people of Cyprus (AKEL) approved of the Soviet occupation of Czechoslovakia. According to the Italian Communist Party newspaper *Unità*, however, the Cypriot Communist Party leadership met with considerable opposition and resistance from local Communist groups.

Eighteen Communist parties, including the ruling parties of Yugoslavia, Romania, and Albania, condemned the Soviet occupation. The official position of the League of Communists of Yugoslavia is typical of the declarations of the European Communist parties at that time. In summary, it was:

a) The League of Communists of Yugoslavia (LCY) does not accord any nation the right to intervene arbitrarily in the internal affairs and development of an independent country, whether it be through military or by any other means.

b) The LCY rejects all arguments presented by the government of the five Warsaw Pact countries as justification for the invasion of Czechoslovakia. The LCY offers the Communist Party, the working class, and the people of Czechoslovakia its full support in their struggle for independence and the socialist development of their country.

c) The LCY demands the immediate end to the occupation of Czechoslovakia and the release of all democratically elected representatives and officials of the Communist Party of Czechoslovakia. It also demands the establishment of conditions which protect the socialist development against foreign intervention.[35]

The Romanian, Italian, Swedish, Spanish, and Norwegian Communist parties, the People's Alliance of Iceland, and the Japan and Australian Communist parties—i.e., today's Eurocommunist parties—all severely condemned the occupation of Czechoslovakia. The Italian Communist Party declared: "The Politburo of the Italian Communist Party considers the decision [to occupy Czechoslovakia] unjustified because it is not compatible either with the principle of autonomy and independence of all Communist parties and each socialist state or with the requirements for the defense of the unity of the international Communist and workers' movement."[36] Carl Henrik Hermansson, Chairman of the Swedish Communist Party, even called upon the Swedish government to break off relations with the governments of the occupying forces and recommended that a European conference of independent Communist parties be convened in order to condemn officially the invasion of Czechoslovakia.

Of particular importance was the fact that after August 21, 1968, two Communist parties which had previously been pro-Soviet—the Spanish and Greek Communist parties—introduced an independent course. During the occupation of Czechoslovakia in August 1968, the leaders of the Spanish Communist Party, Santiago Carrillo and Dolores Ibarruri, were in Moscow. In the name of their party, both protested to the Soviet leadership and received an interesting response from Suslov: "Don't forget that you're just a small party." In early 1968, during the "Prague Spring," the Greek Communist Party had split into an independent "interior" and a pro-Soviet "exterior" wing. The leader of the exterior, pro-Soviet party hailed the occupation; however, the majority of Greek Communist Party leaders, including Mitsas Partsalides, declared their profound discontent over the intervention in internal affairs of a socialist country.

The Communist Party of Finland, which was to celebrate the long-awaited fiftieth anniversary of its founding on August 23, 1968, found itself in a particularly difficult situation. Under the pressure of the occupation, the atmosphere was so tense that the jubilee celebration was canceled. Like the Greek Communist Party, the Finnish Communist Party was divided into an independent reform wing and a dogmatic Stalinist wing. The independent trend under Saarinen proclaimed a mild but (under the circumstances) distinct criticism of the occupation of Czechoslovakia, while the pro-Soviet Stalinist faction approved of the occupation. After *Pravda* published only the pro-Soviet declaration, the Finnish Communist Party proclaimed that the failure of *Pravda* to express the view of the majority of the Finnish Party was tactless and deplorable.

Several Communist parties, including the Austrian and Belgian parties, at first strongly condemned the occupation, but later, for varying reasons, did not continue that course. The French Communist Party, as usual, took its "centrist" course, expressing its "disagreement." Finally, two parties that expressed especially interesting positions should be mentioned: the ruling Communist Party of Albania and the nonruling Communist Party of the Netherlands. Both parties were extremely critical of the "Prague Spring," but later also protested against the occupation. Moreover, the Albanian Communist Party urged the Czechoslovak population to offer active resistance to the foreign occupation.

Although the different Communist parties expressed their protest and criticism in various ways, one thing is certain—for the first time in the history of Communism, more than two-thirds of all Communist parties of Europe openly opposed an action by the Kremlin leadership. Furthermore, none of the declarations of the eighteen Communist parties which opposed the occupation was published by the Soviet Union or any Soviet bloc country. Instead, *Pravda* and other Soviet bloc newspapers gave front-page headlines to declarations from individual isolated groups which approved of the occupation or from Stalinist officials who had been dismissed from their position and who no longer represented anyone.

Luigi Longo's Memorandum "Unity in Diversity"

Immediately after the occupation of Czechoslovakia, the Soviet Union again tried to control the independent tendencies by convening a world Communist conference. The Italian Communist Party seized the opportunity to express its own attitudes toward the relations in the world Communist movement. In several essays, Luigi Longo announced the Italian Communist Party's readiness to participate in the

Moscow world conference but only under certain conditions. According to Longo, there could no longer be a return to the monolithic structure of Communism. It was now more important to develop new relations among Communist parties, ensuring the autonomy of each party.

Longo demanded that at future world conferences *(a)* no Communist party could be excluded; all must be allowed to participate; *(b)* other progressive forces besides Communists also participate; *(c)* every attempt to force one's own opinion on others be prevented; *(d)* only current issues and not theoretical problems of Marxism-Leninism be discussed. According to Longo, the theories of Marxism-Leninism should be dealt with on a more academic level at smaller meetings, seminars, and panel discussions.

Furthermore, Longo demanded that world Communist conferences be less ceremonial, more open and more concrete, and that they take on the character of an advisory committee and not a congress or ecumenical council. He also maintained that it should not be necessary to accept prepared documents or theses and international gatherings should not be secret, but open to the public in order that party members as well as the general public might become familiar with all discussions.[37]

Longo's suggestions have since become fundamental concepts of all Eurocommunists and were in fact realized to a great extent at the East Berlin Conference in June 1976.

Building on Longo's theses about "unity in diversity," in December 1968, Enrico Berlinguer announced the "politics of presence" (*politica di presenza*) for the Italian Communist Party. It was the task of the "politics of presence" to provide for continuous discussion and new solutions within the world Communist movement. The PCI thus advocated a politics of presence and not of rupture in order to make one's own autonomous contribution to the international movement. The Italian Communists, declared Berlinguer, are against all forms of excommunication and against all imitation of other models, since to date no experience is transferable to Italy.[38]

The Third World Communist Conference

The Third World Conference was originally scheduled for autumn 1964, but after numerous preparatory meetings and consultations, the date was pushed further and further ahead. Finally, from February 26 to March 5, 1968, a consultation conference was convened in Budapest, where the different opinions became clear. At a later preparatory meeting, from April 24 to 28, 1968, it was decided to convene a Communist World Conference on November 25, 1968, in Moscow. In June of that year, a working group had already produced a draft for the main document of the forthcoming Third World Communist Conference. As a result of the occupation of Czechoslovakia, however, all previous planning had to be completely revised. At the end of August 1968, Luigi Longo of the Italian Communist Party declared that the World Conference should be postponed until the Warsaw Pact troops were withdrawn from Czechoslovakia. Not until a satisfactory settlement of the crisis had been reached could a world conference even be considered, Longo said. In September, the French Communist Party also spoke out in favor of postponing the Conference scheduled for November 25, 1968, but they still did not take a clear position on the occupation of Czechoslovakia. Afterward, the British and Austrian Communist parties also supported postponement.

After more than six years of preparation, the Third World Communist Conference at which delegations from seventy-five Communist and workers' parties were present, finally took place from June 5 to 17, 1969, in Moscow. Seventeen Communist parties, including some of the largest and most important ones, boycotted the conference: the ruling Chinese and Albanian Communist parties, the Indonesian Communist Party, the Communist party of Laos, the Communist Party of Nepal, the Communist Party of the Philippines, the Communist Party of Singapore, the Malaysian Communist Party, the North and South Vietnamese Communist parties, the North Korean party, and the Communist Party of Cambodia (now Kampuchea). For the future Eurocommunist development it was especially important that the League of Communists of Yugoslavia, the Japan Communist Party, and the People's Alliance of Iceland, as well as the Communist Party of the Netherlands, did not attend the congress. The Swedish and Cuban Communist parties only sent an observer. Thus from the outset, the Third World Communist Conference was clearly not representative of all Communists of the world.

The Third World Communist Conference adopted a document under the long-winded title, "Tasks of the Struggle against Imperialism at the Present Stage and the United Action of the Communist and Workers' Parties and of All Anti-imperialist Forces." The document was divided into four parts.

The first part of the document dealt with an analysis of imperialism indicating that the present epoch was undergoing a transition from capitalism to socialism. This development was marked by the struggle between the aggressive policies of imperialism under the leadership of the United States and the peace-loving policies of the socialistic camp under the leadership of the Soviet Union. The Communist parties were called upon to unite with all democratic and revolutionary forces in order to combat imperialism.

The second part of the document dealt with the "world socialist system," considered the decisive force in the anti-imperialist struggle. The "world socialist system" included the fourteen countries ruled by Communist parties and with particular emphasis on the Soviet Union. "The world socialist system," it was maintained, had opened new perspectives for advancement along the road to socialism throughout the entire world. After an optimistic portrayal of the situation in the Soviet bloc countries, it was admitted that the building of a new society was a long and complicated process.

The third part of the document involved the policy of coexistence and the anti-imperialist struggle. It dealt with what is commonly called East-West relations. In this section, it was declared that the struggle for peace was closely connected to the policy of peaceful coexistence with states of different social orders. One sentence is of particular interest: "Peaceful coexistence demands observance of the principles of sovereignty, equality, territorial inviolability of every state, big and small, and noninterference in the internal affairs of other countries, respect for the rights of every people to decide their social, economic, and political system and the settlement of outstanding international issues by political means through negotiation." Appearing ten months after the occupation of Czechoslovakia, this statement seemed almost oppositional.

The fourth and last part of the document of the Third World Communist Conference dealt with relations within the world Communist movement. Reflected in a myriad of contradictory explications, the disputes between the pro-Soviet and autonomous groups became quite clear. It was not uncommon that one clause of a sentence expressed the opinion of one group, and the following clause that of the other. The "principles of proletarian internationalism" (i.e., ideological subordination to the Soviet Union) as well as solidarity and mutual support, respect for independence and equality, and nonintervention in internal affairs were to form the basis of the relations between the Communist parties of different countries. In accordance with the compromise, either bilateral consultations (the autonomists' suggestion) or international conferences (the Soviet suggestion) would be acceptable forms of cooperation. Following this came the most important sentence of the entire document of the Third

World Communist Conference: "All parties have equal rights. As there is no leading center of the international Communist movement, voluntary coordination of the actions of these parties in order to carry out effectively the tasks before them acquires increased importance." After this sentence, clearly included by the autonomist forces, it was declared that cooperation between Communist parties was based on the "principles of Marxism-Leninism"—a phrase obviously insisted upon by the Soviets.

Despite the concessions and compromises in this document, three of today's Eurocommunist parties, the Italian, San Marino, and Australian Communist parties, rejected all important parts of the resolution and signed only the third part, dealing with East-West relations. The British and the Norwegian Communist Party delegates did not sign the resolution at all, declaring that the decision would be made by the Central Committees of their respective parties. The British Communist Party later rejected the resolution, declaring that it was not satisfied with the principles upon which the relations between Communist parties and socialist countries were based.[39] The Norwegian Communist Party declared that not a single problem could be solved on the basis of a feigned unity.[40] Five other parties, including three from Europe (the ruling Romanian Communist Party, the Spanish and Swiss Communist Parties) signed with explicit reservations.

Eurocommunism Becomes an Independent Force (1970-1976)

9

During the seventies, the Communist parties freed themselves from Moscow's leadership and assumed independent policies which, in the mid-seventies, became known as Eurocommunism.

The tendencies of European Communist parties to dissociate themselves from the Soviet Union (which before had been the exception) now became the rule. In addition, cooperation among the future Eurocommunist parties increased through bilateral declarations. This cooperation was especially important during preparation for the European Communist conference in East Berlin in June 1976.

Moreover, in the seventies, several parties drew up and published programmatic documents, such as the program of the Spanish Communist Party and the historical compromise of the Italian Communist Party announced in October 1973. During the seventies, along with their inclination toward independence on a domestic and ideological level, many Communist parties also pronounced their own positions on foreign-policy issues such as relations with China, the European Economic Community, and NATO. Many of these positions differed greatly from the Soviet line.

Criticism of the USSR

Since the end of the sixties, Eurocommunists have made their criticism of Soviet development increasingly clear. This open protest was reinforced within the Soviet Union itself, where a number of dissident Marxist groups emerged. The most important political representatives who headed these groups were former Major General Piotr Grigorenko the historian Roy A. Medvedev, the journalist Ivan Dzyuba, and the Soviet-Ukrainian mathematician Leonid Plyushch.

The critical independent Marxists within the Soviet Union, who can almost be considered the Eurocommunists of the East, advocate democratization of the Communist Party and of society, a drastic restriction of the State Security Service and the guarantee of individual rights, freedom of the press, of speech, of assembly, of artistic creation and of scientific research, the restoration of Marxism and the end to Russification in the nationalities policy. In the economic and social spheres, the critical Marxists advocate the abolition of excessive centralization and call for economic reforms which are not limited solely to technological renovation but which guarantee worker participation in production management.[1]

The one-party system, according to the independent Marxists in the Soviet Union, is not essential to socialism but serves only to maintain the privileged bureaucratic apparatus. A democratization of the bureaucratic system is impossible without the presence of legal opposition, that is to say, the establishment of a multiparty system.[2]

The critical Marxists in the Soviet Union were encouraged by the increased interest on the part of Western Communists in problems of the Soviet Union. This became clear for the first time during the Leningrad trial at the end of December 1970.

The trial against some Soviet citizens who had supposedly attempted to hijack a plane to escape from the Soviet Union took place behind closed doors in Leningrad from December 25 to 29, 1970. The accused were sentenced to death. The Italian, French, Spanish, Swedish, and British Communist parties immediately criticized the death sentence. They objected to the secret nature of the trial and to the fact that the death sentence was pronounced even though the hijacking had never been carried out.[3] The Spanish and Swedish Communist parties called for a repeal of the death sentence "in accordance with the principles which had to be observed by authorities of justice in a socialist country." The French Communist Party declared that true friends of the Soviet Union were enraged, and rightly so, over the sentencing in Leningrad.[4]

A particularly clear manifestation of the independence of the future Eurocommunists occurred at the Twenty-fourth Party Congress of the CPSU in March 1971. For the first time, delegates of foreign

Communist parties put forth their own ideas and later submitted their own evaluation of the party congress.

Nicolae Ceauşescu declared in the name of the Romanian Communist Party that all Communist parties act under different conditions, and for that reason relations among them should proceed on the basis of trust and mutual respect. Thus any foreign intervention in the internal affairs of Communist parties is completely objectionable.[5]

Similarly, Miyalko Todorović, a representative of the League of Communists of Yugoslavia, stressed the importance of the principles of equality, mutual respect, and nonintervention and especially emphasized the different forms of socialist transformation in the world. Socialism must solve not only contradictions inherited from the past but new problems and contradictions as well, claimed Todorović, and cooperation to that end could only proceed on the basis of "democratic exchange of ideas."[6]

In addition, much to the surprise of Soviet listeners who were used to hearing the names Marx, Engels, and Lenin, Berlinguer acclaimed the Marxists Gramsci and Togliatti of the Italian Communist Party as forerunners of the theory of a new road to socialism. Furthermore, Dolores Ibarruri, representing the Spanish Communist Party at the conference, referred to the existence of different conditions in different countries and therefore rejected the idea of intervention.[7] The delegates of the Japan, British, and Belgian Communist parties also emphasized the need for independent development, open criticism, and the rejection of all forms of foreign intervention.[8]

After the Soviet Party Congress the Italian, Yugoslav, Romanian, and even French Communist parties published reports in which they politely but clearly pointed out the shortcomings and limitations of the Soviet party. Their main criticism was that public debate in the Soviet Union centered almost exclusively around economic matters. They stressed that exchange of information in the economic and scientific spheres had improved but that there were still many restrictions in the cultural and literary spheres, and that the intellectual climate in the Soviet Union did not differ much from that of a besieged fortress.[9]

When Khrushchev died on September 11, 1971, the differences between Eurocommunism and Soviet Communism again became evident. The Soviet leadership issued the short casual statement: "The former First Secretary of the Central Committee of the CPSU and Chairman of the Council of Ministers of the USSR, the retired Nikita Sergeyevich Khrushchev, died at age 78."[10]

In contrast to this brief announcement, the newspapers of the Italian and French Communist parties, as well as that of the League of Communists of Yugoslavia, published, although not without criticism, detailed and fair appraisals of the important effect Khrushchev had had on the process of de-Stalinization. The Yugoslav paper commended Khrushchev for having signed the Declaration of Belgrade in June 1955.[11] The Italian and French Communist press praised Khrushchev's speech at the Twentieth Party Congress. Moreover, the Italian Communist Politburo member Gian Carlo Pajetta said that to remember Khrushchev did not mean to forget his mistakes and to disregard his drawbacks: "He was a unique human being, an unusual comrade."[12] The difference between the Italian and Yugoslav appreciation on the one hand, and the Soviet disregard for Khrushchev's accomplishments on the other, was so great that Khrushchev's widow, Nina Khrushchev, wrote a letter to Luigi Longo expressing her thanks for the moving obituary in *Unità*.[13]

The Polish Workers' Uprising (December 1970 to January 1971)

The workers' uprising in Poland (especially in the Polish ports on the Baltic Sea) was declared by the Soviet bloc to be the work of "counter-revolutionaries" or hoodlums; but the Western European Communist parties interpreted it differently. The PCF declared that the workers' uprising had not been directed against socialism and was not anti-Soviet. The workers' demonstrations, according to the French Communists, were directed, rather, against an unsuccessful economic policy and an administration which did not consider the needs of the people.[14]

In a round table of discussions published in *Rinascità*, the PCI journal devoted to theoretical issues, some writers declared that the Polish unrest was not a crisis of socialism but a crisis of Stalinist concepts. Construction of the state in the shape of a pyramid with a system of "transmission belts" that worked in only one direction could have nothing but disruptive effects on the economy and the political order of a country. An apparatus, formed at first in accordance with the needs of the country, began expanding on its own, grew enormous, and began to employ administrative, repressive, and authoritarian means. It began divorcing itself from society, and even started working against it. The complete unification of party and state led to restrictions against the working class organizations. In addition, the trade unions fused with this bureaucratic apparatus. The social and political system lacked the most important guiding principle. Moreover, the party lacked all forms of democracy, and the events in Poland illustrated the most important need of the Communists—that of internal democracy.[15] The Yugoslav press also noted that the workers' uprising was a reaction to the system. Many letters to the editor in Polish newspapers raised the question of socialist democracy—"which neither Gomulka nor Gierek could create."[16] The Spanish Communist Party claimed that the measures of suppression against Polish workers were bureaucratic deformations of socialism which ruined socialism's reputation and lessened its appeal.[17]

An Independent Attitude Toward China

In addition to the increasing critical dissociation from events within the Soviet bloc countries, the Eurocommunists' own attitudes toward the People's Republic of China became increasingly clear from 1970 on. At the end of October 1970, several representatives of the PCI, including the Director of the Foreign Affairs Bureau of *Unità,* Alberto Jacovielli, visited the People's Republic of China. In mid-November 1970, Enrico Berlinguer declared that, despite certain differences of opinion, the PCI expressed its readiness to reestablish relations with the Chinese Communist Party. Travel reports stressed the significance of the Cultural Revolution and China's endeavors to establish a decentralized model of development which would differ from Stalin's system.[18] However, they also criticized China's praise of Stalin and the fact that in Chinese political life the "struggle between two lines" is continually marked by defamatory accusations. On October 1, 1971, the twenty-first anniversary of the founding of the People's Republic of China, the Italian Communist Party sent a congratulatory note to the Chinese Communist Party.

In October 1971, a Spanish Communist Party delegation under the direction of Santiago Carrillo visited China, announcing that therewith the first contacts between the Spanish and Chinese Communist parties had been established. In a detailed report, Carrillo analyzed the internal development of China, including the Cultural Revolution and the People's Communes, and indicated that, in China, forms of socialism had been developed which would correspond to the reality of that country. Carrillo also pointed out that the Chinese Communist Party was a large revolutionary party which had successfully accomplished the most important revolution since the Russian Revolution of 1917.[19]

The Eurocommunists and the "Normalization" in Czechoslovakia

The Eurocommunists continued consistently to oppose the restoration of bureaucratic dictatorial conditions in Czechoslovakia, undertaken by the Husak leadership under the deceptive term "normalization." After Dubček was dismissed and Husak named First Party Secretary in March 1969, the reformers had to bury their hopes of trying, despite the occupation, to prevent the worst and to save something from the "Prague Spring."

Husak soon broke his promise not to make any reprisals against the supporters and representatives of the "Prague Spring." A Socialist Movement of Czechoslovak Citizens spoke out against this "normalization." Its Manifesto of October 28, 1970, announced the goal of a socialist, democratic, and free Czechoslovakia, the realization of civil liberties, and guaranteed rights and a political and social system within which citizens could formulate their own ideas. In this first Manifesto of October 1970, the socialist opposition in Czechoslovakia hailed the Communist parties of Western Europe because they too rejected a monopolistic dictatorship and advocated a pluralistic socialism.[20]

In the second half of 1970, the pressure increased. The Husak regime ordered mass expulsions from the party and purges of representatives of the "Prague Spring." Toward the end of 1970, a detailed resolution of the Plenum of the Central Committee of the Czechoslovak Communist Party dealt with the evaluation of the "Prague Spring" and the occupation of Czechoslovakia, declaring that the "Prague Spring" had led to a counter-revolution in Czechoslovakia. However, the Italian,[21] French,[22] and British[23] Communist parties rejected and even harshly criticized the Prague bosses' attempt to justify their actions.

The position of the future Eurocommunists was also clearly expressed during the preparatory stages of the Fourteenth Party Congress of the Czechoslovak Communist Party in May 1971. At a huge meeting in Paris, on May 18, 1971, just two weeks before the conference, five prominent representatives of the "Prague Spring" who had left Czechoslovakia—Eduard Goldstücker, Zdeněk Hejzlar, Jiří Pelikan, Ota Šik, and the journalist Josef Pukstefl—urged the Communist parties of Europe to condemn the occupation of Czechoslovakia. They also called for withdrawal of Soviet troops from Czechoslovakia, the restoration of democratic freedoms, and the suspension of political persecution.

Several Communist parties criticized the forthcoming congress of the Czechoslovak Communist Party. The Czechoslovak Communist Party was in such a state of crisis that since the occupation 500,000 members had either left or been expelled from the party. With the exception of Lenart, none of the thirteen members of the Party Presidium (Politburo) during the "Prague Spring" was in office; of the eight members of the Secretariat, only the former Prime Minister, Lobumir Štrougal, remained; and of the 110 members of the Central Committee during the "Prague Spring," over forty had left. [24]

The British Communist Party did not participate at the Congress since the Prague leaders forbade the British representative to give the speech he had prepared on the "Prague Spring." The Spanish Communist Party refused to participate "since the conditions for sending a delegation were not given." At the congress the delegates from Romania, Japan, France, Belgium, and the League of Communists of Yugoslavia refused to use the term "counter-revolution" of 1968 as prescribed by the Husak leadership.

The Eurocommunists voiced their criticism in protests, quiet diplomacy, and above all by publishing declarations, letters, and memoranda of former representatives of the "Prague Spring."

Of particular importance was the detailed interview with the former Czechoslovak President of the Parliament, Josef Smrkovský, in which he discussed the attitude of the world Communist movement to the suppression in Czechoslovakia. When asked what Communists and progressive forces in Europe could do, Smrkovský answered: "Above all, they must not allow a curtain to drop around our country, and they must always know what is happening in our country. What one can do behind a curtain one cannot do on an open stage—that is a very important point." He also urged the Communist parties to act and to search for a solution. "Suppression should concern all our brother parties, for it is not only our affair." [25]

At the beginning of 1972, suppression in Czechoslovakia suddenly became harsher. Leading party officials of the "Prague Spring," including Karel Kaplan and Milan Huebl, were arrested, and proceedings were held against former officials and members of the Central Committee, against district party secretaries and against students and youth leaders. All this was happening despite Husak's promise to foreign Communist Party leaders, especially leaders of the French

Communist Party, that there would be no persecutions similar to those in Czechoslovakia during the fifties.

The mass arrests of the representatives of the "Prague Spring" and the show trials met with protest from the Italian, French, Swedish, Dutch, Belgian, Norwegian, Spanish, Australian, and Icelandic Communist parties. These parties claimed that freedom of opinion was no longer being respected, that administrative measures and terror were taking the place of political debate, and that the form of the proceedings and the methods of justice were not in accordance with a system of justice based on socialist principles. Several Communist parties, including the Australian party, even demanded the immediate release of all prisoners, the nullification of sentences, and the cessation of all further proceedings.[26]

The actions of the Eurocommunists were considered of great assistance to the socialist opposition in Czechoslovakia. In August 1972, the Socialist Movement of Czechoslovak Citizens expressed its appreciation that the Italian, French, British, Swedish, Belgian, and Australian Communist parties and the Swiss Labor Party had condemned the proceedings of the Soviets in Czechoslovakia. The movement announced its decision to continue its struggle for a socialist society in Czechoslovakia which would "provide its citizens with more rights than the most developed capitalist countries, including freedom of speech, of the press, of assembly and of organization."[27]

On August 21, 1973, the fifth anniversary of the occupation of Czechoslovakia, several Communist parties, including the PCI, recalled how correct their attitude toward the occupation had been. The military intervention in Czechoslovakia had not solved the problems of the country. The occupation and present situation in the country made it difficult for the Communist movement to promote détente policy and the East-West dialogue. The Czechoslovak authorities continually refused to allow the Italian Communists to enter the country, and a representative of the Communist Party newspaper *Unità*, who wanted to enter Czechoslovakia during German Chancellor Willy Brandt's visit in December 1973, was denied entry even though he had a visa.[28]

The Eurocommunists and Solzhenitsyn

In early 1974, the Russian author Alexander Solzhenitsyn was arrested in the Soviet Union and exiled to West Germany in the custody of Soviet officials. The Eurocommunist parties condemned this measure. In mid-January 1974, after a conference of West European Communist parties in Geneva, the Italian, Spanish, and French Communist parties and the Swiss Labor Party declared that, although they did not share Solzhenitsyn's views, they opposed the administrative measures, insisting that Solzhenitsyn's works be published in the Soviet Union and that they be freely discussed and criticized. Referring to Solzhenitsyn, the Italian, British, Swedish, Australian, and Japan parties and—although in a somewhat softer tone—even the French Communist Party[29] declared that a government should argue politically with dissidents and not punish them. Even reactionary opinions had to be discussed openly and not subjected to censorship and police repression.[30]

The Japan Communist Party dealt with the Solzhenitsyn case in greater detail. The Communist Party newspaper *Akahata* declared that creating works such as *The Gulag Archipelago* was the right way of dealing with the Stalin era; it also spoke favorably of Solzhenitsyn's *The First Circle* and *Cancer Ward*. At the same time, however, the Japan Communist Party regretted the fact that in depicting the Stalin terror, Solzhenitsyn lost sight of the historical context and did not see Stalinism as a deviation from the ideas of scientific socialism but, rather, as an inevitable consequence of socialism.[31]

Similarly, the French Communist Party historian Jean Ellenstein said it was wrong to regard Stalinism as the natural progeny of the socialism of Marx and Lenin. Solzhenitsyn, claimed Ellenstein, had cited Lenin completely out of historical context—that is to say, the context of the bitter and merciless civil war: "It is not the facts which Solzhenitsyn cites which are questionable but, rather, the conclusions he draws from them." For Solzhenitsyn, the entire history of the USSR was a history of mass persecutions. He hates Communism so much that he is blind to the economic and cultural development in the USSR. It was therefore no coincidence that Solzhenitsyn never mentioned the Twentieth Party Congress of the CPSU—the Congress at which Stalinism was condemned. Finally, according to Ellenstein, one could not compare the USSR of 1975 with that of 1953 and could therefore only reject Solzhenitsyn's one-sided and negative presentation of the facts.[32]

The Sarodov Article (August 1975)

In summer 1975, the critical declarations of the parties which have since come to be known as Eurocommunist had reached such a pronounced level that the Soviet leadership entered the ideological debate. The impetus had been provided by an article by Konstantin Sarodov, the editor-in-chief of the international pro-Soviet publication *World Marxist Review*. On August 6, 1975, he wrote an article for *Pravda* entitled "Lenin's Strategy of the Revolutionary Struggle."[33] In the article, Sarodov cited a number of political arguments from Lenin's publication of August 1905, *Two Tactics of Social Democracy*, arbitrarily using them against the Eurocommunists. According to Sarodov, it was essential for revolutionary strategy and tactic to rely on the majority of the population, but this majority was for Leninists "not an arithmetical, but a political term." It was important, according to Lenin, to form coalitions, but the Communist Party was to assert its own position in the entire democratic movement. A Marxist party, claimed Sarodov, was determined by its ability to lead other social forces. Thus the old concept of the leading role of the Communist Party was again stressed and, in addition, the disregard for the democratic principles of the majority was justified.

Sarodov did not succeed in his attempt to sway the West European Communists. Not only the Italian Communists, but this time the French Communists as well rejected Sarodov's concepts in detailed, ideological articles. The Italian and French Communists particularly opposed Sarodov's attempt to reduce all of Lenin's thinking to a single concept based solely on a few quotations and short statements. They also criticized his attempt to establish dogmatic general rules and thus restore the monolithic system which had long since been overcome. The relationship between socialism and democracy was seen by the Eurocommunists as something different from the doctrinaire model outlined by Sarodov. It was necessary to consider the experiences of the labor movements of other countries which did not fit into this model. The world had changed drastically since the turn of the century and the Western Europe of 1975 was not the czarist and feudalist Russia of 1905. Therefore, one could not simply reduce Lenin's thought to "dull formulas applicable at all times and in all places."[34]

The Eurocommunists and the Twenty-fifth Party Congress of the CPSU

In his report to the Twenty-fifth Party Congress of the CPSU (from February 24 to March 5, 1976), Brezhnev warned against rightist and leftist revisionism and maintained that there were universal laws in the development of the revolution and the building of socialism. Only on the basis of these laws could Marxist-Leninists consider the actual conditions of each country: "When a compromise with opportunism is made by any party for reasons of expediency, even if that compromise proves temporarily advantageous, the result in the end is damage to the party." He argued against certain "people" who wanted to free themselves of proletarian internationalism, insisting that this would rob the Communist parties of "a powerful and reliable weapon."[35] Other party leaders, such as the Ukrainian Schcherbitsky and the Byelorussian Masherov, complained of the dangerous penetration of "revisionist influence" and warned against the "revision of the principles of proletarian internationalism."[36]

The Eurocommunist delegations voiced their own opinions at the Twenty-fifth Congress in Moscow despite these warnings. In his speech, Nicolae Ceauşescu emphasized the importance of new relations, the equality of all nations, respect for national sovereignty, nonintervention in internal affairs, and especially the renunciation of violence as well as the threat of violence in international life. He confirmed the right of each party to work out its own line, strategy, and tactics.[37] In addition, Stane Dolanc, in the name of the Yugoslav Communists, stressed the principles of nonalignment and socialist self-management which were being expanded in the new Yugoslav Constitution.[38] Enrico Berlinguer went so far in his speech that *Pravda* censored several passages. He did not limit himself to proclaiming the necessity of an independent Italian road to socialism, but advocated a socialist society "which should be the epitome of the development of all democratic achievements and should guarantee the respect for all individual and collective freedoms, for religious freedom and for cultural, artistic and scientific freedom." The future socialist society must be established by cooperation among different political forces, organizations and parties. The labor movement could "fulfill its historical duty only in a pluralistic and democratic system."[39]

The Soviet Party Congress was the scene of several interesting incidents which had never before occurred at a Communist conference. For example, while at the conference the Italian Communist Party delegation called on the Italian Ambassador in Moscow. In addition, on Sunday, February 25, when no sessions were being held, but when speeches were expected to be made in factories, Berlinguer and his delegation went to visit the Sagorsk Monastery.[40]

While the Spanish Communist Party was represented at the congress by Dolores Ibarruri ("La Pasionaria"), Secretary General Santiago Carrillo went to Rome, declaring that he would rather go to

Rome with a delegation of Spanish opposition than to Moscow because "In Rome, our trip has a direct connection to the problems of
Spanish democracy."[41] In Rome on February 26, 1976, Carrillo said
about the "real socialism" of the Soviet Union: "It is still burdened by
the quasi-feudal system which it overthrew and whose stigma it still
carries. In the West, we can have socialism if the democratic pluralistic system is respected, if it is implemented with the approval of the
majority and if it is ready to surrender power in the event that it no
longer has the approval of that majority." In answer to the question if
he feared condemnation by Moscow, Carrillo claimed, "What right do
they have to condemn us? They can criticize us just as we criticize
them. Condemnation, however, is excommunication from a church.
The Communist movement was once like a church but it no longer
is." Moreover, Communist participation in the democratic governments of the West would also assist the democratization of socialist
countries in Eastern Europe.[42] In an interview with the western press
after the Twenty-fifth Party Congress, Andrei Sakharov defended
Carrillo's claim. Moreover, the ideas of the Italian Communist Party
were "very close" to his own, declared Sakharov. In Berlinguer's
speech, Sakharov saw criticism of the Soviet system as well as support, although indirect, of the ideas and concepts of the dissidents in
the USSR, who, like Berlinguer, had for years complained that Soviet
society was neither pluralistic nor democratic.[43]

In all probability, Sakharov was not the only critical Soviet citizen
who saw support for the oppositional reform currents in the USSR in
the speeches of the Eurocommunists at the Twenty-fifth Party Congress.

Suslov and Midtsev Against the Eurocommunists

On March 17, 1976, just two weeks after the Twenty-fifth Party Congress ended, Suslov gave a speech at the yearly meeting of the
Academy of Sciences of the USSR entitled "Our Epoch—The Epoch
of the Triumph of Marxism-Leninism," in which he continued the
polemics against the Eurocommunists. He spoke of "enemies of
Marxism" who had begun "disguising themselves as Marxists" and
who would attempt "to undermine the revolutionary essence of
Marxism-Leninism." Therefore, Suslov claimed, "What the oppor-
tunists see as some regional or national versions of Marxism has
nothing in common with the revolutionary theory and only hurts the
cause of the working class."[44]

The French Communist Party General Secretary, Georges Mar-

chais, claimed that, since he had already repeatedly said that proletarian internationalism must be reciprocal, he was not affected by
Suslov's declarations. Moreover, declared Marchais, the French
Communists will build a socialist society which "will be neither Russian nor Chinese nor Cuban: it will be French."[45] The Italian Communist Party argued that it was wrong to restrict the concept of internationalism by use of the adjective "proletarian," for in the world
today there are those who advocate international cooperation in
which not only Communists, but other forces also play important
roles. A term such as "proletarian internationalism" excluded cooperation with other important powers. "It is clear to us that the road to
socialism and the development of socialism in our country (and the
rest of Western Europe) are inseparably connected to the extension of
democracy."[46]

At the same time that Suslov gave his speech, the Soviet ideologue Venyamin Midtsev's booklet entitled *Revisionism in the Service of
Anti-Communism* was being distributed. Midtsev fought "revisionist
attitudes" about the plurality and diversity of the models of socialism.
In his booklet, Midtsev tried to refute the ex-Communist officials
Roger Garaudy, Ernst Fischer, Alexander Dubček, and Franz Marek,
as well as Luciano Gruppi, a member of the Central Committee of the
Italian Communist Party. The Italian Communists declared that it was
indeed unfortunate that the author should brand as revisionists those
who believe that the road of the Soviet people is not suitable for their
own country. Midtsev would call anyone a "falsifier of Marxism-
Leninism" simply for maintaining that realization of democracy in the
USSR had not yet reached the necessary degree of maturation.[47]
Midtsev's booklet was also sharply criticized in Yugoslavia. Accord-
ing to Radio Belgrade, it would not have been necessary to take
Midtsev's thesis seriously if he had written it for himself alone, but
behind his booklet stood the Soviet demand for subordination to the
Soviet Union, and Yugoslavia could never accept that.[48]

Sarodov's warnings in August 1975, and the Suslov speech and
Midtsev booklet in March 1976 showed that Soviet leadership was
gradually realizing the significance of Eurocommunism and was determined to combat this movement ideologically.

Increasing Eurocommunist Cooperation

The seventies were also marked by the fact that it was no longer just
single Communist parties which opposed Moscow, but that Euro-

communist parties were joining together in a common purpose, thus increasing their activity and improving their effectiveness. Several important events should be mentioned in this context.

In March 1971, a delegation of Spanish Communists visited Carl Henrik Hermansson, Chairman of the Swedish Left Party Communists. The meeting ended in "a declaration of general agreement of the ideas of both parties."[49]

In September 1971, a delegation of the Japan Communist Party under the direction of Chairman Kenyi Miyamoto visited the Romanian Communist Party and its Secretary General, Ceauşescu. The leaders of both parties later declared that they supported the right of each party to determine its political line independently.

After a delegation of the Spanish Communist Party under the leadership of its Secretary General, Santiago Carrillo, visited Romania in September 1971, both parties declared in a communiqué that there was no need for a leading center of the Communist movement anywhere in the world. Communist parties were to develop their policies in accordance with the characteristics of their own countries.

Ceauşescu welcomed a delegation from the Greek Communist Party (interior) in November 1971, expressing genuine concern over the arrest of Drakopolous and Partsalides, two leaders of the Greek Communist Party (interior).

In August 1972, a delegation of the Spanish Communist Party under Santiago Carrillo and Dolores Ibarruri again met with Secretary General Ceauşescu and other representatives of the Romanian Communist Party and issued a communiqué declaring that the two parties had agreed on all matters discussed.

In March 1973, Enrico Berlinguer, Secretary General of the Italian Communist Party, met with both Labour Party and British Communist Party leaders in London. Then in May 1973, Georges Marchais, Secretary General of the PCF, and Enrico Berlinguer appeared for the first time together in Bologna in front of 100,000 people. This occurred after both parties had taken positions which had still been controversial until the beginning of 1970.

At the beginning of July 1973, a Communist faction formed at the European Parliament in Strassburg. Besides eight Italian and three French Communists, the Communist faction of the European Parliament, called "Communists and Sympathizers," included a representative of the Socialist People's Party of Denmark, an independent Italian leftist, and a representative of the Dutch Communist Party.

The cooperation of the Eurocommunists soon spread to other

countries. During a stay in Venezuela in September 1973, the Romanian Party leader, Nicolae Ceauşescu, visited Pompeyo Marquez, the Secretary General of the Movement toward Socialism (MAS).

Finally, a meeting of a delegation of the Italian Communist Party under the direction of Secretary General Berlinguer with President Tito in April 1975 was especially important. The Italian Politburo member Gian Carlo Pajetta later declared that the Italian Communists were convinced that the stability and strengthening of Yugoslavia should be protected against external intervention. There was no doubt as to whom Pajetta was referring.

In July 1975, the famous meeting between Carrillo's Spanish Communist Party delegation and leaders of the Italian Communist Party took place. Instead of a communiqué, which is usually issued after such meetings, the "Spanish and Italian Communist Party Declaration" was published in July 1975. Both parties agreed on all points; and it was after this declaration that the name "Eurocommunism" was coined.

In November 1975, the French and Italian Communist parties held a summit meeting that ended in a declaration in which the two strongest Eurocommunist parties confirmed their recognition of a democratic road to socialism. Thus, although somewhat belatedly, the French Communist Party also professed the principles of Eurocommunism.

The development from 1970 to the beginning of 1976 was to be considered the emancipation process of Eurocommunist parties. This emancipation, including the ever growing cooperation among Eurocommunists, explains why it was possible to promote many of these attitudes at the European Communist Party Conference in July 1976 in East Berlin.

10

Recent Developments of Eurocommunism

As the Eurocommunist parties dissociated themselves from the Soviet Union and the repressive measures in several Soviet bloc countries and strengthened their cooperation, the Conference of European Communist Parties was in preparation. The difficulties and obstacles and the many concessions that the Soviet leaders had to make in order to hold the conference exceeded the demands of their role in the history of world Communism. It is also important to realize that, originally, the Soviets had no intention of holding a *European* Communist Party Conference but wanted to convene a new Communist *World* Conference.

The Preparations for the European Communist Party Conference in East Berlin

Unable to reach a consensus within the world Communist movement for a world conference in 1973 and 1974, the Soviet leadership decided to concentrate on preparations for a European Communist Party Conference. The first step of the preparation was the consultative meeting of delegations of twenty-eight European Communist parties in Warsaw from October 10 to 18, 1974. For the first time (since 1948), the League of Communists of Yugoslavia also took part in the multilateral meeting. At the meeting, however, the confrontation between the pro-Soviet Communist and Eurocommunist parties (of

Yugoslavia, Romania, Italy, Spain, Sweden, and Great Britain) prevented the adoption of a common resolution. After long and hard debate, it was decided that a conference of all the Communist parties of Europe would be held in mid-1975 in East Berlin. The theme would be "The struggle for peace, security, cooperation and social progress in Europe." The conference was to follow and thus highlight the Helsinki Conference on European Security and Cooperation. The responsibility for the preparation of the conference was given to the Polish and Italian Communist parties—an interesting concession to the Eurocommunist parties. [1]

A second preparatory meeting took place from December 19 to 21, 1974, in Budapest. Once again, the Eurocommunists rejected all attempts to proclaim a new general line at the Berlin Conference and they demanded a guarantee of autonomy, equal rights, and nonintervention. At this second meeting, it was decided to hold an editorial conference which would prepare the documents. Finally, the practical work was assigned to a working group meeting regularly in East Berlin. At the first working group meeting (January 17 to 19, 1975), no communiqué was issued, and at the second meeting (April 8 to 10, 1975), the leadership of the SED (East Germany), the host party, offered suggestions for a resolution which the Eurocommunists rejected.

In mid-July 1975, the SED delegation in charge of the working group drafted a detailed ideological platform, which the Eurocommunist parties, supported since May 1975 by even the PCF, also rejected.

New Problems and Difficulties (1975–1976)

As mentioned above, publication of the Sarodov article in the autumn of 1975 led to a heated controversy. As a result, the Soviet and other East European leaders came to the conclusion that certain concessions were necessary. This became evident at a new meeting in East Berlin, held from October 9 to 10, 1975, in which delegates of twenty-seven European Communist parties participated. At this conference, the SED leaders presented a third draft of their document which, for the first time, did not include a general ideological line. The Eurocommunists accepted it as the foundation for the future conference. The final draft was to be prepared in November 1975.

But by the time participants met again, from November 17 to 19, 1975, new problems had arisen. The SED (the ruling Communist

Party of East Germany) had since proposed a fourth draft, again trying to force a general ideological and political line upon all Communist parties. The Eurocommunists rejected this fourth draft, and the delegations left without setting a new date for the European Communist Conference. With no other alternative, the Soviet leadership began to yield. Boris Ponomaryov and Konstantin Katushev, who had until then represented the Soviet Communist Party during the preparations for the conference, were replaced by the more conciliatory Vadim Sagladin. In Rome, he agreed to strike the more controversial matters from the SED's draft.

After the Soviet Union yielded, two more editorial conferences took place in East Berlin, one from December 16 to 19, 1975, and one from January 13 to 22, 1976. The SED now proposed its fifth and last draft, which very much accommodated the Eurocommunists. There were, however, still some unanswered questions, but at least a starting point for the document was finally reached.[2] Moreover, the position of the Eurocommunists had been strengthened, thanks to the recent changes in direction of the French Communist Party. At the Twenty-second Party Congress of the French Communist Party in Nanterre (February 4 to 8, 1976), Georges Marchais rejected the notion of a unified center of world Communism more strongly than ever before, renouncing the "dictatorship of the proletariat" and emphatically pronouncing a French road to socialism.

Despite the optimistic attitude of the Eurocommunists at the beginning of May 1976, the Yugoslav weekly *NIN* warned against illusions. *NIN* complained of the recurrent effort in the Soviet bloc to create a monolithic structure, and to make Communist Party conferences a permanent institutionalized procedure. The Yugoslav Party organ warned that such attempts were still being made. The article appeared under the headline "Establishing a Center Indirectly?"[3]

Under the circumstances, the only way the Soviet leadership could ensure a European Communist Party Conference was through concessions. At another meeting of the editorial committee, this time with twenty-eight Communist party delegations participating, the differing points of view finally began to merge. At the beginning of June 1976, the Soviet Union accepted Yugoslavia's suggested modification, and the controversial term "proletarian internationalism" was stricken. On June 3, 1976, at a rally in Paris, Georges Marchais and Enrico Berlinguer reemphasized their parties' cooperation, promising to remain on an independent course and to reject any unified center. Several days later, Stane Dolanc, the Secretary of the Central Committee of the League of Communists of Yugoslavia, met Berlinguer in

Rome for discussions of the European Communist Conference. The last two editorial meetings were held in East Berlin, first on June 10 and 11 and then again on June 24, 1976. The European Communist Party Conference was finally scheduled for June 29 to 30, 1976. In all, the working groups and editorial conferences, as well as the Plenum of all twenty-eight delegations, had met *twelve times* in preparation for the European Communist Conference.[4]

The European Communist Party Conference in East Berlin (June 29–30, 1976)

The European Communist Party Conference in East Berlin differed greatly from any previous conferences of a similar kind. First of all, more than a hundred foreign correspondents were allowed to attend the fifteen-minute opening ceremonies. Furthermore, the city was not decorated with stately banners welcoming the different delegations, as was usually the case. Moreover, each delegate found a printed copy of the conference document at his seat bound in red and embossed in gold—a finished document that could not and would not be altered.

The Berlin conference was more like a working meeting, just as the Eurocommunists had desired. Of special significance was also the fact that the speeches of all participating delegations were published in full in East Berlin by the host party, the SED. Consequently, the 3.4 million readers of the SED central organ, *Neues Deutschland*, were presented with ideas and attitudes which normally would have been considered injurious to the party.

Every European Communist Party, with the exception of the Albanian Labor Party and the Icelandic People's Alliance, participated in the conference in East Berlin. At first, the Dutch Communist Party refused to attend, but then reversed its decision and arrived late; it was the first time in a long while that the Dutch Communist Party had taken part in any multilateral Communist conference. Counting the tiny SEW of West Berlin as an individual delegation, the Soviet bloc announced that twenty-eight Communist parties had participated in the conference. From the Greek Communist Party, only the leader of the pro-Soviet (exterior) faction, Florakis, attended; the Eurocommunist (internal) faction was not represented. During the conference, speaking time was limited to thirty minutes per speaker, a rule which was to be observed by everybody. Only Brezhnev did not comply, speaking for over an hour. Moreover, it had been previously decided not to discuss the problem of China, but both Brezhnev and the Bulgarian Communist Party leader, Zhivkov, ignored this agreement and in their speeches condemned the Maoist leaders.

Although *Neues Deutschland* published all speeches in full, all other Soviet bloc newspapers censored the texts. Important excerpts and explanations such as Berlinguer's critical reference to Eastern European developments and his remarks about the lagging behind of Marxist analysis and his positive statements on European unity were deleted. In addition, all critical references of the Eurocommunists to the occupation of Czechoslovakia were missing from the Soviet bloc publications.

Three main points of view were clearly recognizable in the speeches, reflecting the main currents existing in European Communism:

1. The Pro-Soviet Group: The views of the pro-Soviet group in East Berlin were presented by Leonid Brezhnev of the USSR, Todor Zhivkov of Bulgaria, Gustav Husak of Czechoslovakia, and Erich Honecker of East Germany; the delegations from the Austrian, Turkish, West German, Luxembourg, Portuguese, and Danish Communist parties; the Socialist Unity Party of West Berlin (SEW); as well as by what remained of the Norwegian Communist Party (after its leader Reidar Larsen and a third of its members and officials joined the left Socialist Party) and one wing (the exterior faction) of the Greek Communist Party. Edward Gierek of Poland and Janos Kádár of Hungary also supported the pro-Soviet group, although they were less outspoken and emphasized certain individual nuances.

Though with different emphases, the pro-Soviet Communists continually stressed (a) the unity of the world Communist movement; (b) the importance of "proletarian internationalism" as the most important weapon and source of strength for Communists of all countries; (c) the solidarity of all Communist parties with socialist countries, but first of all with the Soviet Union; and (d) the leading role of the Soviet Union, because the Soviet Union was the strongest socialist country and the CPSU was the strongest and most experienced party in the world Communist movement.

Proceeding from these views, the representatives of the pro-Soviet direction demanded the intensification of the struggle against anti-Communism and especially against anti-Sovietism and the strengthening of the unity of the world Communist movement through multilateral meetings, i.e., world conferences. It was obvious that Gierek from Poland and Kádár from Hungary did not make all these demands, or at least did so less emphatically. There were also differences in the emphasis of these ideas among the pro-Soviet non-ruling Communist parties.

2. The Middle Group: The "middle group" of the European Communist Party Conference consisted of, among others, the Belgian, Cypriot (AKEL), and Dutch Communist parties, as well as the small Irish Communist Party and the Swiss Labor Party. Representatives of this group reported on the situation within their own countries without taking sides with either the pro-Soviet group or the Eurocommunist group.

3. The Eurocommunist Group: The Eurocommunist conceptions were proclaimed by Josip Broz Tito of Yugoslavia, Nicolae Ceauşescu of Romania, Santiago Carrillo of Spain, Enrico Berlinguer of Italy, Georges Marchais of France, Gordon McLennan of Great Britain, Lars Werner of the Left Party Communists of Sweden, Ermenegildo Gasperoni of San Marino, and, at least in part, by Aarne Saarinen of Finland.

All supporters of Eurocommunism opposed the notion of any center of the world Communist movement and all attempts to bind the participants in the East Berlin Conference to an obligatory ideological document.

Tito welcomed the free exchange of ideas at the conference and emphasized the principles of independence, equal rights, and nonintervention in internal affairs. Ceauşescu repeated those points and demanded, in addition, the end to all threats of violence. Moreover, the Eurocommunists rejected the term "proletarian internationalism" and advocated, instead, "international solidarity" which, as Ceauşescu claimed, implies the struggle for the interests of the working class in each individual country. Berlinguer spoke of a free movement of independent and equal partners and emphasized the open spirit of the conference. He demanded an end to obsolete methods, made it clear that the earlier days of the Communist International were long gone, and insisted that completely new forms of international relations were prevalent.

Santiago Carrillo emphasized the dissociation from the Communist International with the following words: "The suffering to which our parties were exposed—and which they must still endure—and the time that we spent in the catacombs brought about within our ranks a connection between scientific socialism and a kind of sacrificial mysticism and predestination. We became a sort of new church with our own martyrs and prophets. For years Moscow, where our dreams became reality, was our Rome. We spoke of the great October Socialist Revolution as if it were our Christmas. That was the period of our infancy. Today we have grown up. The Communists rule in many countries. In others, we are already a noticeable force. The example of the victory of the Communist Party in the elections in Italy is the most recent and significant proof. We are continually losing the church-like character. The scientific values of our theories are taking the place of the belief in and the mysticism of predestination."

All Eurocommunists advocated new roads to socialism. Tito declared that socialism offered no ready solutions applicable to all times and all conditions. Ceauşescu addressed himself to new forms of the struggle for socialism, which differ from country to country. Berlinguer saw the transition to the new social order as a process which extended far beyond the Communist parties and which required new forms of interconnections among the political, social, and theological forces. It is important, according to Berlinguer, not only to think about the experiences of the past, but also to search for new roads to socialism in the West European countries.

Georges Marchais declared that the French Communists would carefully consider the realities of French life, the peculiarities and traditions of their country.

The Eurocommunists' remarks about the future of socialist society were particularly significant. All Eurocommunist speakers made it clear that what they understood as socialist society was something far different from what the Soviet bloc countries called "real socialism."

Tito described socialism as a synonym for democracy, sovereignty, independence, human justice, and freedom. Berlinguer declared that the Italian Communists were fighting "for a socialist society that has as its foundation the affirmation and guarantee of the value of individual and collective freedoms." Gordon McLennan, the British Communist Party representative, saw socialist society as a society with freedom of the press, freedom of assembly, freedom of demonstration, freedom of religion, of culture, of art and of science, freedom to travel, freedom to form trade unions, and freedom of activity for all democratic political parties, including all opposition parties.

Carrillo admitted that previously Communists had been guilty of underestimating democracy and speaking about "formal freedoms." Georges Marchais said: "The socialism for which we are fighting will be a profoundly democratic socialism . . . not only because it will guarantee the working people the necessary conditions for freedom by doing away with exploitation but also because it will guarantee, develop and increase all the freedoms for which our people have struggled." The Swede, Lars Werner, was the only Eurocommunist who called for complete dissociation from the Stalin era and demanded democratization in Eastern Europe. The restrictions of democracy and the inadequacy of democratic rights in the countries of "real socialism" should be discussed self-critically, he said. Such criticism, he claimed, was not negative but, rather, simply the expression of one's concern for the fate of socialism.

Finally, the Eurocommunists proclaimed their own ideas about the aspects of foreign policy and East-West relations. Tito made clear his hope that détente would extend beyond the realm of the blocs and the regional frontiers and emphasized the importance of nonalignment for the world. Ceaușescu spoke of the two military blocs in Europe "whose existence increased mistrust along with the danger of another war." He advocated abolition of the two blocs, NATO and the Warsaw Pact. Berlinguer, McLennan, and Tito also supported a future simultaneous dissolution of NATO and the Warsaw Pact.

In reference to the new name "Eurocommunism," Berlinguer remarked: "We, of course, did not coin the term, but its popular usage is evidence of the depth and breadth of the desire of the countries of Western Europe to carry out and pursue new solutions in the socialist transformation of society."

Santiago Carrillo spoke of an "unfortunately chosen term," but added that "it is obvious, however, that we, the Communist parties of developed and highly developed capitalist countries, are faced with a particular problem. The specific demands of the development of the class struggle within our own area lead us along roads to socialism which cannot possibly be the same as in other countries. This is an objective fact which we must consider."[5]

The Document of the European Communist Conference

The document adopted at the conference, "The Struggle for Peace, Security, Cooperation, and Social Progress in Europe," was completely different from the document of the Third World Conference held in Moscow in June 1969. It clearly reflected the changes within the Communist movement as a whole and especially the growing significance of Eurocommunism as an independent force.

What induced the Soviet Union to hold a conference at all under the conditions described above? First, the Kremlin leaders were able to get several points into the final document:

1. The document, although sometimes vaguely, supported the general foreign policy of the Soviet Union. Particularly important for Moscow was the assertion that the policy of coexistence facilitated a democratic and socialist transformation in the European countries, providing it with more favorable conditions for the struggle.

2. The declaration complied at least partially with Soviet interests in that the Communist parties would develop their international, friendly, voluntary cooperation and solidarity on the basis of the main ideas of Marx, Engels, and Lenin; of course the Soviet leadership would have preferred a more unequivocal acknowledgment of Marxism-Leninism.

3. In the document, it was clearly stated that "anti-Communism is and remains an instrument which imperialist and reactionary forces use not only against the Communists but against other democrats and democratic freedoms as well." The final document condemned all campaigns directed against socialist countries, including the Soviet Union. The goal of these campaigns was supposedly to discredit the Communists in the eyes of the people. The document lacked, however, the clear rebuff to "anti-Sovietism" which the pro-Soviet groups demanded.

4. Finally, the claim that the socialist countries had played a "prominent role" in securing peace and pursuing détente was also important to the Soviet Union. Nevertheless, the Soviet Union did not succeed in including a specific reference to its particular role, as it had hoped to do.

The Kremlin leadership had to make considerable concessions to the Eurocommunists for the declarations it wanted. The new aspects of Eurocommunism in the final document were:

1. The European Communist Party Conference was not mentioned as the first stage of a world conference. No world Communist conference was even mentioned. As a result, the Soviet leaders will have greater difficulties in convening a Fourth World Conference in the near future.

2. The Berlin document did not contain any condemnation of Maoism, as the Soviet leadership had so desired.

3. The Soviet leaders for the first time had to agree to the principle that each participating party actually had a veto right when formulating joint resolutions.

4. The Soviet leaders also had to agree to the protection of the

equality and the sovereign independence of each party, and to nonintervention in internal affairs; and they had to agree to respect free elections and different roads in the struggle for the transformation to socialism.

5. Moreover, Soviet leaders and their supporters were unable to force through a binding political ideological line, for the document of the East Berlin Conference was solely a declaration of intent regarding current problems.

6. Furthermore, condemnation of "anti-Sovietism," which the Kremlin so desired, was not included either. The term "anti-Communism" was newly defined by the following passage: "The Communist parties do not consider all those who do not agree with their policies or who are critical of their actions, anti-Communists." In my opinion, this distinction between "enemies" and "critics" mentioned here for the first time was one of the most important results of the conference.

7. Instead of the coalition with other political parties and forces led by a Marxist-Leninist Party, as was usually the case in the Soviet Union and in pro-Soviet groups, the East Berlin document advocated contact, understanding, and cooperation among all political and social forces in the form of a dialogue between Communists and other democratic forces in which no partner takes the leading role, and it reiterated the Communists' readiness to "cooperate on an equal basis with all democratic forces of society."

8. In the realm of foreign policy, the document of the European Communist Party Conference advocated not only increased commerce between East and West and cooperation in the areas of culture, science, and technology, but also cooperation in the area "of information and human contact in order to promote mutual understanding and increased trust as well as enrichment of intellectual life—all on an equal basis."

9. In addition, clearly at Yugoslavia's request, the role of the nonaligned nations of the world was considered especially important.

10. The term "proletarian internationalism," which is so important for the ideological justification of much of the Soviet Union's actions and attitudes, was not mentioned in the document.

11. Despite Soviet objection, "Marxist-Leninism" was not referred to.

12. Democratic rights and political freedoms were emphasized more than in any other previous document of the world Communist movement.

The Polemics after the European Communist Conference

All Western experts on Communism, although to different degrees, have stressed the growing importance of the Eurocommunist movement, pointing out the many concessions made by the Soviet Union. [6]

Botho Kirsch, Director of the East European division of Deutsche Welle, international radio service of the Federal Republic of Germany, declared that at the conference in East Berlin the unity of world Communism was as shattered as the unity of the Roman Catholic Church has been at the Diet of Worms. [7]

Victor Zorza, the well-known British expert on Soviet and Eastern European affairs, was more skeptical. The Communist Party Conference in East Berlin was not as great a defeat for the Kremlin as it may have appeared at first. Zorza declared that the European Conference had been only a prelude to a world conference at which the independent forces were to have much greater difficulty. One should not forget, insisted Zorza, that the Kremlin leadership worked slowly and methodically and pushed toward its goals step by step. [8]

Professor Robert Havemann, a Eurocommunist living under constant surveillance in East Germany, appraised the conference most optimistically. He wrote that after this conference, the CPSU could no longer play the leading role in the world Communist movement. Brezhnev's doctrine of limited sovereignty, which was supposed to justify the invasion of Czechoslovakia, was, according to Havemann, abandoned at this conference. The great significance of the Berlin Conference lay in the fact that all attempts at hegemony on the part of a single party were ended. The hegemony of the Soviet Communist Party, Havemann contended, had ended not only vis-à-vis Western Communist parties, but vis-à-vis all the parties of Europe, including those of the Soviet bloc countries. [9]

Immediately after the East Berlin Conference of June 1976, the pro-Soviet forces tried to interpret the conference resolutions in their own way. It was continually stated that the conference had stressed the general laws of socialism, had raised high the banner of Communist unity, had strongly condemned anti-Communism and especially anti-Sovietism, had worked out a program of common actions, and had confirmed the CPSU as vanguard of the world Communist movement. [10] The pro-Soviet forces declared that since the Soviet Union was the first country to accomplish a socialist revolution, it possessed the greatest experience in the building of a new society and as a world power could make the greatest contribution to the change of the balance of forces in favor of socialism. No Communist party should underestimate the experiences of the Soviet Communist Party, and unity under Soviet direction was a definite necessity.[11]

On the other hand, in their reports, the Eurocommunists declared that the conference clarified the differences among Communist parties and stressed the independence of all Communist parties. It was unfortunate, according to the Eurocommunists, that the Soviets were now trying to include in their interpretations the very points which were *not* adopted at the conference. The Eurocommunists protested against the declarations of Soviet ideologues, that all new perceptions were nothing more than "refined forms of bourgeois infiltration."[12]

After the East Berlin Conference the rift between the pro-Soviet Communists and the Eurocommunists grew more intense, especially when, in autumn 1976, Benito Corghi, a member of the Italian Communist Party, was shot and killed on the East German border and when, not long afterward, the poet Wolf Biermann was expatriated from East Germany. The Italian, French, and Spanish Communists were particularly opposed to Biermann's expatriation and declared that he was only exercising his legitimate right to criticize; he had always supported socialism. An author and artist in a socialist democracy, claimed the Eurocommunists, had to have the right of expressing himself freely, even if his views and his work did not comply with those of the government.[13] Biermann was later invited to Italy and to Spain where he appeared at electoral assemblies of Italian and Spanish Communists. Finally, after a long discussion with Carrillo, Biermann joined the Spanish Communist Party.[14] Moreover, the East German authorities' attacks on Robert Havemann also exacerbated the situation. In an interview, Lucio Lombardo Radice, a member of the Central Committee of the Italian Communist Party, declared that Biermann and Havemann had to be regarded as Eurocommunists.[15]

The Eurocommunists and the Human Rights Movement in Eastern Europe

In the spring of 1977, the Eurocommunists again grew concerned about events in Eastern Europe. In Czechoslovakia and Poland, the dissident movement had entered a new phase. Since 1976, different oppositional forces have begun uniting in a common struggle for the realization of human rights. The documents of the Helsinki Conference helped considerably, since they were confirmed and published by the respective governments. In October 1976, the Czechoslovak government ratified and published a number of treatises dealing with civil and human rights. Respect for these rights became the key issue for the forces striving for liberalization and democratization. This was the background for the origin of the new movement "Charter 77." This movement is made up of people of different religions and different occupations who insist on the respect for civil and human rights in Czechoslovakia.

The first declaration of Charter 77 proclaimed that since the Czechoslovak government had ratified the Helsinki agreement, in Czechoslovakia, too, every citizen had the right to be governed by this agreement.

The signers of the Charter welcomed the fact that the government of Czechoslovakia had concurred on the agreement, but, at the same time, they objected to the abuses, listed below, within that country:

a) Hundreds of thousands of citizens in Czechoslovakia cannot enjoy the freedom from fear, which is explicitly described in the agreement, because they live in the continual danger of losing their jobs if they express their opinions.

b) Young people are denied the right to study simply because their parents express opinions which are considered unacceptable by the regime.

c) Freedom of opinion, in contradiction to the signed agreement, is suppressed. No political, philosophical, or scientific opinion, no artistic expression which deviates the slightest bit from the framework of the official ideology, can be published.

d) Public criticism of social injustices is impossible.

e) There is no opportunity for public defense against untrue or insulting assertions.

f) Religious freedom is suppressed.

g) Freedom of opinion is impossible because all institutions and organizations are subordinate to the political directives of the apparatus of the ruling party.

h) The most important rights, to which the Czechoslovak government signed its name, namely freedom of association, the prohibition of any sort of restriction, the equality of rights, the right to participate in public affairs, equality under the law as well as the right to strike, are all suppressed.

i) Despite the fact that they are forbidden to interfere in private life, the Ministry of the Interior controls the lives of the citizens in many ways—for example, by eavesdropping on telephone conversations and in apartments, by opening mail, by personal surveillance, by searches of private homes, by sustaining a net of informants, and often by threats or promises. [16]

Charter 77 was signed by a large number of well-known representatives of Czechoslovakian cultural life (authors, professors, philosophers, theologians) as well as leading representatives of the "Prague Spring." Among the signers were Milan Huebl, Jiří Hájek, Zdeněk Mlynář, František Kriegel, Ludvíć Vaculik, Alexander Kliment, Jiří Kolar, Václav Havel, Jaroslav Seifert, Zdeněk Urbanek, Pavel Kohout, Vladimir Kadlec, Jiří Lederer, Ladislav Hejdanek, Erika Kadlecova, and others. [17]

Charter 77 provided a wide platform upon which different Czechoslovak oppositional groups and tendencies could unite in a common goal: the defense of human rights and freedoms which were guaranteed by international conventions, including the Helsinki accord, as well as by the Czechoslovak Constitution and by Czechoslovak laws.

Several days later, however, citizens on their way to personally deliver the document to the highest organ of the State of Czechoslovakia were arrested. The document was confiscated and a huge campaign against Charter 77 was introduced. Numerous signers of the Charter were harassed by the police, home searches began, several well-known signers, including the author Václav Havel, were arrested, and professors were dismissed solely because they had signed Charter 77.

The suppressive measures of the Czechoslovak authorities met with strongest protest from European Communist parties since the occupation of Czechoslovakia on August 21, 1968. The Italian and Spanish Communists even protested repeatedly. Other parties which protested were the Belgian Communist Party, the British Communist Party, the Communist Party of Greece (interior), the Swedish Communist Party, the Swiss Labor Party, and finally even the Communist Party of Denmark which, until then, had been part of the pro-Soviet camp. All these parties expressed their profound discontent with the intimidation methods used by the police and protested against the attitude that Charter 77 was subversive, since it demanded only the human rights guaranteed in the Helsinki accord. They supported the signers of Charter 77 and reproached the government of Czechoslovakia for being anti-socialist. [18]

The supporters of Charter 77 also expressed their solidarity with the Eurocommunists. Harassed reformers in Czechoslovakia, including the Secretary of the Central Committee of the Czechoslovak Communist Party during the "Prague Spring," Zdeněk Mlynář (also a signer of Charter 77), and seventeen former members of the Central Committee of the Czechoslovak Communist Party, turned to Eurocommunists in the West. They requested assistance against the suppressive measures of the Prague authorities, and suggested that Eurocommunists demand that the Czechoslovak leaders deal with them in accordance with the spirit of the East Berlin Conference. The former Foreign Minister Jiří Hájek, as well as four former members of the Secretariat of the Central Committee: Zdeněk Mlynář, Václav Slavek, Bohumil Simon, Josef Spaček, as well as František Kriegel, a former member of the Party Presidium and President of the Czechoslovak National Front, all signed the letter to the Eurocommunists.[19] The Italian Communist Party published the appeal and added that the campaign against the signers in Czechoslovakia discredited socialism not only in that country, but all over Europe.

Upon arriving in Rome, once he had finally received permission to leave Czechoslovakia, Zdeněk Mlynář thanked the Italian Communist Party for having insisted that the Czechoslovak matter not be stricken from the agenda.[20]

The Eurocommunists also supported the civil rights movement in Poland. The publication of a new Polish Constitution which stressed the leading role of the party and the close connection to the Soviet Union led, at the end of December 1975, to an open letter from fifty-nine leading Polish intellectuals who appealed to the Helsinki accord and who demanded the restoration of democratic freedoms in Poland. The subsequent controversy included open letters from the well-known Marxist economist, Edward Lipinski, and the former Minister of Education, Wladislaw Bienkowski. The considerable rise in food prices in June 1976 led to unrest and to workers' strikes. Although the price increase was repealed, striking workers were soon arrested and given severe sentences. Letters of protest against the actions of the police and the courts were signed by hundreds of workers. Soon afterward, the Committee for the Defense of the Workers (KOR) was founded. Its members included leading intellectuals, among whom were the well-known Polish author Jerzy Andrzejewski, the economist Edward Lipinski, and the critical Marxist historian Jacek Kuron. This committee represented the first meaningful attempt to build a bridge between intellectuals and workers in Poland. The movement received, although to a minimal extent, the moral and political support of the Eurocommunists in the West.

The Madrid Conference of Eurocommunists (March 1977)

The meeting between Santiago Carrillo, Enrico Berlinguer, and Georges Marchais in Madrid was of great significance to the further development of Eurocommunism. Santiago Carrillo had initiated the meeting. At the end of the three-way talks, in a mutual declaration, the Italian, French, and Spanish Communists confirmed the need for broad cooperation of different political forces for far-reaching democratic reforms. The three parties advocated a pluralistic model of socialism, declaring, in sentences which were omitted from the reprint of the declaration in *Pravda* and other Soviet bloc newspapers, that "the Communists of Spain, France and Italy see the building of a new society as a result of the plurality of different political and social forces. The new society will respect, guarantee and develop all collective and individual freedoms—freedom of thought and of speech, of the press and of assembly, the freedom to join organizations, the freedom to hold demonstrations, freedom of mobility within one's own country and abroad, the freedom to form independent trade unions and the right to strike, the inviolability of private life, respect for universal voting rights and the possibility of the democratic change of majorities, religious and cultural freedom and the freedom of different trends and opinions on a philosophical, cultural and artistic level. The concepts which we three completely independent parties have formulated are imbued with the profound desire to achieve a democratic and free socialism."

Finally, the three parties proclaimed the importance of a free Spain for all of Europe. The dialogue and understanding among Communist, socialist, and Christian forces, they claimed, were necessary for the development of democracy and for progress.[21]

The East German Communist Party organ *Neues Deutschland* was the only newspaper of the Soviet bloc to publish the unabridged communiqué of the Madrid Conference of the Eurocommunists, including the reference to a pluralistic free model of socialism. Since the summer of 1976, the SED has limited itself to publishing Soviet attacks against Eurocommunism, without adding any of its own.[22]

The Eurocommunist Summit Conference in Madrid echoed so much throughout the world that the pro-Soviet ruling parties decided to take countermeasures. An ordinary editorial meeting of the pro-Soviet international publication *World Marxist Review* in Prague at the end of April 1977 was suddenly played up by the Soviets. The pro-Soviet parties sent their top outfits, Politburo members, and Central

Committee secretaries, and on May 9, 1977, in a three-column article, *Pravda* reported on an "important political meeting of Communists."

The pro-Soviet speakers now emphasized everything that they had not achieved at the European Conference in Berlin. They stressed the importance of "proletarian internationalism," the rejection of the campaign for human rights, the warning against "rightist revisionism," the importance of "real socialism," and the rejection of all independent tendencies.

The Eurocommunists reacted immediately. The Communists of Italy, France, Spain, and other countries announced that the Prague Conference was simply an editorial meeting at which the usual examination of the publication's work and future topics was to be undertaken, and not a meeting to discuss questions which had nothing to do with the journal.[23] At the conference itself, the representatives of the Italian Communist Party and other Eurocommunist parties complained that the publication had dealt in a biased manner with the subject of Eurocommunism. The Italian Communists demanded that the publication be "an organ of objective information about the policies and attitudes of every party."[24]

Carrillo's Book *Eurocommunism and the State*

In April 1977, during the Madrid Summit Conference of the Eurocommunists and the counterconference of the pro-Soviet group in Prague, Santiago Carrillo's book, *Eurocommunism and the State*, was published in Spain. German and Italian translations were soon published, and later an English translation followed.

In his book, Carrillo attempted to develop a Marxist state theory which would correspond to current conditions in the industrialized countries. After a detailed analysis of the role of the state in Western industrial countries, Carrillo demonstrated why the Leninist theses of 1917 no longer apply to the developed capitalist countries of Western Europe. In his books *State and Revolution* (1917) and *The Proletarian Revolution and the Renegade Kautsky* (1918), Lenin, according to Carrillo, had underestimated the importance of democracy and declared the dictatorship of the proletariat to be the only way to socialism. After the painful experiences with fascism and Stalinism, democracy must be seen, Carrillo claims, not only as the decisive component along the road to socialism, but as the fundamental principle of a socialist society.

The development in the Soviet Union has to be considered in the context of the backwardness of Russia in 1917. Industrialization had to be accomplished in the shortest possible time. This led to the formation of a bureaucratic apparatus with its own interests which was soon in control of an unlimited and virtually unchecked political power on all levels. The present Soviet state, insisted Carrillo, is not capitalist, but neither is it the workers' democracy that Lenin had envisaged. The Soviet state structure, according to Carrillo, has become a serious obstacle for the further development of socialism. Consequently, the Soviet Union has to be transformed into a true workers' democracy; this can be accomplished only through profound changes. [25]

Carrillo's significant theoretical work would probably not have received so much attention if it were not for a sudden massive attack by the Soviet weekly magazine *New Times* against the Secretary General of the Spanish Communist Party in June 1977. Not a single one of the issues Carrillo had raised in his book was even mentioned in this long-winded attack; rather, the Soviet publication warned against refined and insidious actions of the enemy who are trying to "drive a wedge" in order to "split and destroy the movement." The term "Eurocommunism," declared the *New Times*, was erroneous because the was only *one* Communism. Moreover, the term only served to defame real socialism and the Soviet Union. Carrillo was reproached for advocating that Spain join NATO, "the aggressive bloc whose main goal it is to wage war against the Soviet Union and other socialist nations." (In his book, Carrillo had *not* advocated Spain's joining NATO.) According to the Soviet publication, the aim of Carrillo's book was to split the Communist movement and "to place the West European Communist movement on a dubious third or middle road somewhere between capitalism and socialism." Carrillo's plea for democratization of the Soviet system was characterized by *New Times* as an attempt "to weaken the Soviet Union" and to interfere in the internal affairs of another party. Finally, the Soviet journal condemned his advocacy of Eurocommunism as being "solely in the interest of imperialism and of aggressive and reactionary forces." [26]

Clearly, the *New Times* attack on Carrillo at the end of June 1977 had nothing to do with his book; its goal was rather to discredit the Secretary General of the Spanish Communist Party. Shortly before, the first free elections since the Spanish Civil War had been held, and the Communist Party received only 9.4 percent of the vote. Dolores Ibarruri had returned to her native country from the Soviet Union. The Soviet leaders apparently thought that the relatively poor showing of the Spanish Communist Party at the election was an indication of dissatisfaction with the party leadership. They believed they could discharge Carrillo and thus bring the Spanish Communist Party closer to the Soviet line.

After the polemics of the Soviet press against Carrillo, a storm of protest broke out among the European Communists. The Belgian Communist Party organ *Le Drapeau Rouge* claimed that the *New Times* accusations, "made in a tone which was not at all conducive to calm discussion, do not at all correspond to the repeated positions and actions of the Spanish Communists nor to those of other Communist parties classified as 'Eurocommunist.' "[27] The Spanish Communist Party immediately declared that Carrillo's book had only served as a pretense and that the Soviets' attack was really directed against the entire Spanish Communist Party and its fundamental concepts of a democratic road to socialism. It was about time, the Spanish Communists proclaimed, to stop replacing scientific analysis of current problems with banishment and excommunication.[28]

The Soviet leadership's hopes of splitting the Spanish Communist Party were not fulfilled. At a Plenum of the Central Committee of the Spanish Communist Party, attended by 130 Central Committee members and 180 other officials, not only Carrillo, but Dolores Ibarruri and a host of other functionaries who had previously served in the Soviet Army and had fought for the Soviet Union behind German lines during World War II, signed the Spanish Communist Party's sharp response to Moscow.[29] The entire world press now took up the polemics, and Carrillo seized the opportunity to clarify his point of view in interviews with the press. In one such interview, Carrillo denied ever having advocated Spain's entrance into NATO, claiming, "I have always said that Spain should not join NATO and my book clearly demonstrates what I think of the organization. What we did say is that we are not against having American military bases in Spain." To journalists in Madrid, Carrillo declared that he would like to have an open debate with Moscow over the theses of his book and the problems of socialism. One of the subjects of this debate could be about clearly defining the state the Soviet Union represents today.[30]

All Eurocommunist parties supported the Spanish Communist Party's position. The Italian Communist Party, the League of Communists of Yugoslavia, the Belgian Communist Party, the Swiss Labor Party, and the Romanian Communist Party leader Ceauşescu rejected the Soviet accusations, declaring that instead of discussing the matter the Soviet Union had accused the Spanish Communists of revisionist sins. Several Eurocommunists even charged that the attack against Carrillo was, in reality, an attack against all Eurocommunist parties.[31]

Several days after the attack by *New Times*, Pajetta and a delegation of the Italian Communist Party visited the Soviet leadership in Moscow. After their return, Pajetta declared that the talk in Moscow had been helpful and open, that there were still differences of opinion on several matters, and that he and his colleagues had expressed their own opinions about the *New Times* polemics against Carrillo, an opinion which differed considerably from that of Moscow.[32]

Moreover, the French Communist Party declared that one could certainly disagree with and criticize several chapters of Carrillo's book, but that one should not resort to affronts and insults. Such action, it insisted, did nothing to further the necessary discussion within the world Communist movement.[33]

The declaration of one Yugoslav publication, comparing the *New Times* attack on Carrillo with Stalin's attack on Yugoslavia in the spring of 1948, was especially interesting:

> Is infamous history really repeating itself? . . . Instead of the confidential correspondence of 1948, an editorial has appeared. . . . Instead of an official meeting of a party organization (the Communist Information Bureau in 1948), the orthodox individual parties issue their own declarations. . . . Nevertheless, things are not happening as had been expected. . . . The Spanish Communist Party is no longer alone, as was the Yugoslav Party in its time. And the resistance is also much wider and more articulate. There is no Stalin, no possibility of a blockade or military pressure, and finally, unanimity does not prevail among all other countries as it did back then. So far, only three parties have expressed their allegiance to the Soviet position—the Czechoslovak Communist Party and the Bulgarian Communist Party, while the third, the SED, limited itself to repeating Moscow's viewpoint without a commentary of its own. One cannot speak of a Soviet-Spanish conflict. In essence, it is a struggle between two different viewpoints about the relations between the parties and the future of the Communist movement—a struggle to which no one may remain indifferent.[34]

Part III

The Eurocommunist Parties: Models of Independence and New Orientation

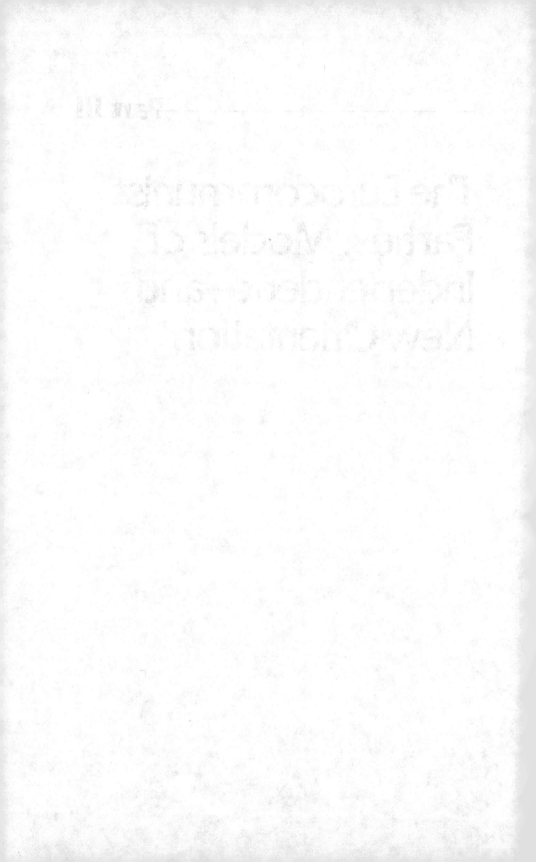

The Italian Communist Party (PCI): A Twenty-Year Period of Transition

11

An evaluation of the Italian Communist Party reveals three charac-teristic features: the PCI is the strongest mass party outside the Communist-ruled countries; the process of separation from Moscow and the development of today's Eurocommunism has been going on for over twenty years without dramatic change in leadership; finally, significant rifts, evident in other Eurocommunist parties, have been avoided.

The PCI from 1945 to the Death of Stalin in 1953

Postwar development began for the PCI with the downfall of Musso-lini and the signing of an armistice with the Allied powers by the Badoglio government at the beginning of September 1943. Im-mediately thereafter, the PCI took an active part in the development of democratic life in southern Italy, while in the north, which was still occupied by Germans and followers of Mussolini, the PCI was the most important force in the resistance movement. At that time, the PCI was under the leadership of Palmiro Togliatti, who had returned to Italy from Moscow early in 1944.

Born in Genoa in March 1893, Togliatti participated in the socialist movement from the time he was a youth. By 1920, he had already become Secretary of the Turin Committee of the Socialist Party. After the Italian Socialists split up at the party congress in Leghorn in January 1921, Togliatti helped found the Italian Communist Party, and in May 1922 he became a member of the Central Committee. In 1924, he visited the Soviet Union for the first time and, in the summer of the same year, participated in the Fifth Congress of the Comintern. After returning from Moscow in 1925, he was arrested and imprisoned for several months. He took part in the most important congress of the PCI in Lyon in 1926, and for many years thereafter was the PCI's representative to Moscow. He also represented the PCI at the Comintern Congress in the summer of 1935. For many years, under the pseudonym Ercoli, Togliatti was a member of the Presidium and of the Secretariat of the Executive Committee of the Communist International. He experienced the beginning of the Great Purge in Moscow and, in June 1937, was sent to Spain as a representative of the Comintern. During the Spanish Civil War, Ercoli was the most important plenipotentiary of the Comintern. Beginning in March 1939, he directed all PCI operations from Paris. Togliatti was arrested in the summer of 1939 but was released again in February 1940. He then went to Moscow by way of Belgium, directed the Italian-language radio programs in the Soviet Union and, in May 1943, was one of the leading Communist officials to sign the act dissolving the Comintern.

After his return to Italy in spring 1944, Togliatti, in the 180-degree change in policy known as the "Svolta di Salerno," summoned all Italians to struggle against fascism, deflecting attention from the then controversial debate over monarchism and republicanism. The PCI was ready, he said, to support the Badoglio government. Togliatti wanted to transform the PCI into a mass party without antireligious or anticlerical goals, a party whose members would not be obliged to espouse Marxism. As temporary Minister of Justice, Togliatti himself cooperated with the Badoglio government.

When the PCI held its Fifth Party Congress in January 1946, it already had a membership of 1.7 million. In the national elections of June 1946, it received 18.9 percent of the votes cast. Thereafter, with 140 deputies, the PCI was the third largest party in the Parliament, following the Christian Democrats and Socialists. The Italian Communists took an active part in collaborating on the Italian Constitution. As a result, from the very beginning it was one of the "parties within the framework of the Constitution." At the same time, the PCI, contrary to the Socialists, advocated the reintroduction into the Constitution of the treaties signed between the Vatican and the Italian state (the Lateran Treaties). Only with the onset of the cold war in

May 1947 was the PCI excluded from the Italian government.

From 1948 on, the PCI, as far as domestic politics was concerned, was an opposition party. During the period of the cold war, it was subjected to increased pressure from the Soviet leadership. Nonetheless, Togliatti endeavored to pursue a realistic domestic course as far as possible. Moscow, however, required that he link this domestic course with praise for the Soviet Union and support of Soviet foreign policy.

At the second meeting of the Cominforn, in Budapest in November 1949, Togliatti addressed himself to the need for a broad coalition policy but also declared that the Italian Communists would "follow the great example of the Soviet Union." He referred to a "revolutionary vigilance" against "Tito's band of spies" and added that all deviations should be mercilessly eliminated.[1] Although Togliatti at that time seemed to satisfy the desires of the Kremlin, toward the end of 1950 Stalin tried to draw him out of Italy and make him Director of the Cominform Bureau.[2]

The pro-Soviet line did not proceed without opposition within the Italian Communist Party. At the beginning of 1951, two former resistance fighters and parliamentary deputies, Aldo Cucchi and Valdo Magnani, the latter Secretary of the PCI party organization in the province of Reggio Emilia, withdrew from the party, explaining that they would still support socialism but that they no longer wished to belong to a party which subjugated itself to the foreign-policy interests of a foreign power. Hundreds of party members and officials joined with Cucchi and Magnani.[3] Both "deviants" were branded as "two-faced servants of the enemy" and "agents of Tito."[4] Valdo Magnani has since rejoined the party and is presently in an important position.

At the Nineteenth Party Congress of the CPSU in October 1952, the last congress of the Stalin era, Luigi Longo still extolled Stalin as the "builder of Communist society" and as "teacher and leader." Nevertheless, the PCI was able to prevent many of the considerable setbacks which other Communist parties suffered during the postwar years. In June 1953, the PCI received 22.7 percent of the vote and was represented by 153 deputies in the Parliament. This increase in their popularity is explained by the fact that, in Italy, East-West relations and fear of the Soviet Union played a much smaller role than in most other European countries. Furthermore, the PCI, by concentrating on domestic politics and by actively cooperating on reconstruction, managed not only to secure, but to further strengthen its position.

The PCI after the Death of Stalin (1953–1956)

Shortly after the death of Stalin, Togliatti cautiously began to change certain emphases within the party. In the fall of 1953, he advocated a new united front of all democratic forces in order to limit the predominance of the privileged capitalist classes in industry and agriculture. Italy's republican constitution provided the political foundation for a "far-reaching agreement among all democratic forces." According to Togliatti, "democratic forces" should include not only the middle classes, but the propertied classes as well, as long as they were "not reactionary," and did not oppose "the necessary reforms and the revival of our political life."[5] However, there was still a definite orientation toward the Soviet Union.

At the Twentieth Party Congress of the CPSU, in February 1956, Togliatti finally had the opportunity to introduce the concept of an "Italian road to Socialism." After returning from Moscow, he declared before the Central Committee, in March 1956, that the PCI had already demonstrated a "certain courage." In addition, the search for their "own road of development to Socialism," according to Togliatti, had always been the object of the unremitting efforts of the Italian Communists.[6]

At the end of May 1956, Togliatti was the first European Communist Party leader to meet with Tito in Belgrade. After returning from his talks with the Yugoslav leader, he gave an interview, in June 1956, in which he far exceeded Khrushchev's criticism of Stalin at the Twentieth Party Congress in Moscow. Togliatti rejected the Soviet thesis blaming everything on Stalin's personal characteristics and perceived Stalinism as a "bureaucratic degeneration of Soviet society." Togliatti called upon the Soviet leadership to undertake the necessary changes courageously and without hesitation. He further contended that strict adherence to the Soviet model could and must no longer be obligatory. Communists of all countries had to proceed from their own national traditions and conditions. The situation demanded a continually growing autonomy, which could only be advantageous for the Communist movement, for within the movement itself a "polycentric system" was developing. Togliatti also declared that one could no longer justifiably speak of a single unified leadership within the world Communist movement.[7]

Togliatti's claims were rejected by the Soviet Central Committee. The subsequent events of 1956—the Polish October and the tragedy of the Hungarian Revolution—led many trusted party members and even officials, such as Eugenio Reale, who had represented the PCI at the congress at which the Cominform was founded, and Antonio Giolitti, who later joined the Socialists and was to play an important role in the Italian government, to withdraw from the party.[8] The PCI had at that time not condemned the Soviet intervention in Hungary.

However, the first real independence appeared at the Eighth Party Congress of the PCI in December 1956. This congress was an important turning point in the development of the present-day PCI.

At its Eighth Party Congress, the PCI declared that the events in Poland and Hungary had revealed problems, weaknesses, and even serious faults in both the economic development and the realization of socialist democracy. The events in Poland and Hungary, claimed the PCI, made it clear that the development of socialist countries had to be based on the recognition of the principle of different roads to socialism. The sovereignty of smaller countries could not be limited or challenged; consequently, each individual Communist Party had to be allowed to follow its own road to socialism.

In addition, the Italian Communists opposed the return to a central organization of world Communism. They advocated bilateral relations between Communist parties based on mutual respect and constructive criticism whereby current problems could be openly discussed. According to the Italian Communists, any kind of intervention in the internal affairs of the Communist parties of other countries was out of the question. Communists as well as non-Communists were to participate in international conferences. These international conferences were not to adopt obligatory resolutions. Italian Communists at the Eighth Party Congress cautiously spoke of a change of goals. For the first time ever, they spoke of a "new democratic and socialist society" in which "other forces" would also play "a useful and progressive role." Clearly, the development of a model for democratic socialism as evidenced by the "Prague Spring," for example, dates back to the Eighth Party Congress of the PCI.[9]

The French Communist Party, in particular, criticized the Italian Communists.[10] In a detailed response to the French accusations, the PCI supported its view of the Italian road to socialism as a "fundamental goal" and declared that "along the road to socialism the conditions of our country would always be carefully considered." Moreover, the PCI declared that even a Communist government in Italy would not set out to nationalize thousands of handicraft factories and small enterprises, for, they declared, "We saw what happened in Hungary and Poland when such foolish mistakes were made."[11]

The Revival of Gramsci and the Further Development of the PCI

With the Togliatti interview in June 1956, and the Eighth Party Congress of the PCI shortly thereafter, the tables had clearly turned. From then on, the revival of Antonio Gramsci's theories played an increasingly important role in the development of the PCI.

Antonio Gramsci (1891 –1937) was a brilliant Italian Marxist. He had been a member of the Central Committee since the founding of the PCI and had lived in Moscow from 1922 to 1924, where he often had occasion to speak with Lenin. From January 1926 until November 1926 when he was arrested and sentenced to twenty years' imprisonment, Gramsci shared the leadership of the PCI with Togliatti. In prison, he wrote over 4,000 printed pages, which for a long time went unnoticed and were only rediscovered after World War II. These writings are marked by an unusual diversity of ideas, consisting of philosophical treatises, reflections on Machiavelli's theory of the state, analyses of Italian literature, and essays on the role of the church. Gramsci's so-called *Prison Notebooks* was published in 1947. Later, an anthology of Gramsci's letters from prison appeared. Gramsci tried to root Marxism more deeply into European intellectual history. The practical political conclusions which Gramsci drew from his reflections were important for the new course of the PCI.

Gramsci's main theses can be summarized as follows:

a) In the countries of Central and Western Europe a different strategy is necessary from the one which prevailed in Russia during the October Revolution. The political superstructure of Western Europe is so different from that of the czarist Russia of Lenin's time, that this fact necessitates this different strategy.

b) Marx, Engels, and especially Lenin saw the state solely as an instrument of repression. Indeed, the state claims a monopoly on power. But the state is not only power; and it relies on more than just the instruments of force of the executive branch and the bureaucracy. In Western European countries, the state also relies on a multitude of institutions, ideas, judgments, and prejudices which ensure at least the passive consent of a large segment of the population.

As a result the capitalist system in Western Europe, according to Gramsci, is much more complicated than the economic and political system of the Russian state of 1917. Instead of a frontal attack, which occurred in Russia in 1917, "trench war" would be necessary in the West European countries. Only step by step can the complete transformation of the masses through a new ideology, a new mentality, be accomplished.

c) In addition to the transformation of the social structure, an intellectual and moral transformation would be necessary. Under the given conditions, the role of the intelligentsia is of particular importance. Moreover, instead of proclaiming the leading role of the working class and the dictatorship of the proletariat, it would be important in the Western European countries to create a "hegemony" of the labor movement based on a "historical bloc."

d) This "hegemony" of the workers in a "historical bloc" would necessitate a new attitude toward the party. The party should function as a form of "intellectual collective." In this context, Gramsci also criticizes a one-party system following a successful revolution.

e) In contrast to Stalin, who saw the trade unions as "transmission belts" of the party, Gramsci emphasized the importance of trade-union autonomy. He also recognized the importance of workers' councils and self-management in a socialist society and the necessity of developing democracy further.

f) Finally, Gramsci stressed the fact that the majority of the Italian population is religious. For that reason, even a socialist Italy must reach some sort of agreement with the Vatican. He rejected strict anticlericalism, stating that if one were to concentrate solely on atheists, one would always remain in the minority in Italy.[12]

Since the beginning of the sixties, the Italian Communists have increasingly relied on Gramsci's theses. Gradually, the ritualized trinity of Marx-Engels-Lenin common among the Communists began to give way to an independent intellectual attitude which enabled the Italian Communists to develop their own ideas on fundamental issues. Inspired by Gramsci, the Italian Communists began to recognize the possibilities of a Communist-Christian dialogue after the death of Pope Pius XII. The Ninth Party Congress of the PCI (January 30 to February 5, 1960) advocated steps to an understanding with the Catholic world, indicating that such steps were one of the preconditions for the Italian road to socialism.[13]

In November 1961, it was again the Italian Communists who made the most advantageous use of the anti-Stalinist declarations of the Twenty-second Party Congress of the CPSU (October 1961) in their own policies. Togliatti advocated a complete exposure of all crimes committed under Stalin's leadership.

He proclaimed that the "Stalin problem" went far beyond its inhuman deeds, and posed fundamental problems for the entire world

Communist movement. For the Italian Communists, the only guarantee against any similar future development was a democratic road to socialism which corresponded to the particular conditions and traditions of the individual country. For the world movement, this meant that there could no longer be any states or parties which prescribed what had to be accepted by everyone.[14]

This new course, which included criticism by the Italian Communists of their own mistakes in the past, led to harsh attacks by pro-Soviet parties. In December 1961, leading representatives of the French Communist Party spoke of "certain opportunist and revisionist elements within the Italian Party." The thesis of polycentrism, they declared, denied the universal validity of Marxist-Leninist theories. Instead of proclaiming polycentrism, according to the French Communists, one should rely on the "rich experiences of the Soviet Union."[15] The East German party official Hermann Axen emphatically declared that the thesis of polycentrism negated the leading role of the Soviet Union.[16]

In the course of 1962, the Italian Communists' position regarding the European Economic Community was the center of attention of all political discussions. The EEC had become so important that it could no longer be overlooked by the Communists in East and West. While a majority of Communist economists from twenty-three countries, meeting in late August and early September 1962, limited themselves to a denunciation of the EEC,[17] the Italian Communists advocated that the existence of the European Economic Community be recognized as a fact of life and that a democratic alternative to monopolistic integration be developed. Thus the Italian Communists were among the first to demand democratization of the European institutions.[18]

Luciano Gruppi, the Director of the ideology department of the Central Committee of the PCI, played a particularly important role in establishing a new course for the Italian Communists. In the summer of 1964, he was the first theoretician of a European Communist Party to review critically several of Lenin's concepts. One could not view all of Lenin's concepts of the state and the dictatorship of the proletariat as sacrosanct and universal, argued Gruppi. When Lenin wrote his *State and Revolution* in 1917, Gruppi wrote, it was in light of the Russian state at that time. Consequently, Lenin's analysis of the state was necessarily one-sided. Gruppi recalled Gramsci's definition of the state as an instrument of hegemony and emphasized the importance of popular consent. Under the existing conditions, national and regional parliaments as well as community and provincial administrations could clearly be used to renovate the social and state order. In this way, the transition to socialism could be accomplished without interrupting constitutional continuity and without abrogating democratic legality and its institutions.[19]

Togliatti's memorandum of August 1964 affected the Communists of Europe even more strongly. In this memorandum, Togliatti expressed his goals: the autonomy of the individual Communist parties, continuous dialogue with dissidents, a free model of socialism, and greater participation by workers in the leadership of social life. Togliatti was again criticized by the pro-Soviet French Communist Party.[20]

Enrico Berlinguer, at that time the party's spokesman for international affairs, responded in the name of the PCI. Concerning the demand for unity in the world movement, Berlinguer declared: "It must not be a unity which regards the Communist movement as a sect or a church and which is concerned exclusively with protecting its ideological purity against this or that 'deviation,' but a unity which is regarded rather as a great political movement which must be more closely tied with the progressive forces."[21]

PCI under Luigi Longo (1964–1969)

Togliatti died immediately after having finished his memorandum. Luigi Longo, his deputy, became the new Secretary General of the Italian Communist Party.

Longo had already taken part in the founding congress of the PCI in Leghorn, in January 1921. When Mussolini came to power in 1923, Longo was arrested and spent one year in prison. In 1926, he became a Central Committee member and, five years later, in 1931, a member of the Politburo. He was active in the Italian Communist resistance against Mussolini and, from 1933 to 1934, represented the PCI at the Communist International in Moscow. From 1936 to 1939, under the name Gallo, Longo was General Inspector of the International Brigade in Spain. In spring 1939, he emigrated to France where he was detained by the French and finally handed over to the Italian authorities, who subsequently deported him. After Mussolini's downfall in 1943, Longo played a key role in the leadership of the resistance movement in northern Italy. In 1945, he became deputy Secretary General of the PCI and from 1946 on was a deputy of the PCI in the Italian Parliament.[22]

On October 18, 1964, shortly after his accession to the secretary generalship, while in Milan, Longo declared in a speech that Togliatti's course would be continued, emphasizing the importance of the Togliatti memorandum.[23] Moreover, the Eleventh Party Congress of the PCI in Rome, from January 25 to 31, 1966, confirmed the continuation of Togliatti's course. The Congress demanded structural reforms, including a land and school reform, new real estate regulations, the autonomy of regions, and economic planning. According to pronouncements made at the congress, such reforms could only be realized with a new political alliance. For the first time, it was also made clear that the Italian Communists were not only advocating a new road but were setting a new goal. The new socialist society "will not be only what the Communists want but what all others who are willing to help build it want also."[24]

The Gramsci-Congress in Cagliari on the thirtieth anniversary of the Italian Marxist's death in April 1967 also played an important role in the theoretical formation of the new line. In contrast to similar ideological congresses of the Soviet bloc countries, the Gramsci-Congress offered a completely open academic discussion in which 250 historians, sociologists, and philosophers from ten countries participated, including professors from Oxford, London, Edinburgh, the Sorbonne, Grenoble, and Frankfurt. The political scientist, Professor Dr. Iring Fetscher came from West Germany, George Lukács came from Budapest, and Adam Schaff from Warsaw. In critical commentaries, the Italian Communists noted that the East German leadership had refused to allow several invited guests, including Professor Havemann, to leave the country. The entire Italian press reported in detail on all aspects of the congress.[25]

In autumn 1967, Luigi Longo published his memorandum, "Unity in diversity," in which he proclaimed the willingness of the Italian Communists to attend a world conference while making precise suggestions concerning the change of the character of the world movement.[26]

For the Italian Communists, the most important event of 1968 was the "Prague Spring." On January 12, 1968, even before the January Plenum of the Czechoslovak Communist Party, the PCI had already welcomed the first signs of change in Czechoslovakia.[27] At a press conference in April 1968, Luigi Longo declared: "We are for a pluralistic state which is the product of cooperation among all democratic forces that are willing to help build socialism. . . . Socialism in Italy will develop just as those forces which participate in its establishment want it to develop. . . . We are for the broadest democracy and also for those parties which, during the building of socialism, disagree not only with one measure or another, but with the basic principles." In his speech before the Central Committee of the PCI on August 27, 1968, Longo harshly condemned the Soviet occupation in the name of the entire PCI. Several days later, a Soviet Russian publication called the Italian Communist concept of polycentrism a "bourgeois concept," whose main goal was to "cause a split in the socialist camp."[28] The pro-Soviet groups in other countries did not limit themselves to press polemics but intervened directly. Pro-Soviet brochures, written in Italian but printed in Dresden (East Germany), which justified the military intervention in Czechoslovakia were sent to Italian Communist officials and local branches of the PCI.[29]

The Congress in Bologna (February 1969)

The Twelfth Party Congress in Bologna, from February 8 to 15, 1969, was of particular importance to the further development of the PCI. Luigi Longo was reelected Secretary General, and Enrico Berlinguer became his deputy. The PCI had become an important force within Italy—in a time of deep social, economic, and political crisis.

In his report to the congress, Luigi Longo emphasized more clearly than ever before the PCI's desire for equality in the world Communist movement: "It is our right and our duty to criticize and to reject opinions which we do not share." Differing views were expressions of the diversity of the movement. Recognition of the different contributions as well as the autonomy of individual movements within a political coalition, claimed Longo, was in no way a tactical maneuver. He declared: "We want a broader development of inner-party democracy." Longo claimed that the present inner-party democracy in the period of the struggle for socialism would guarantee the democratic character of the future socialist society.

Foreign-policy aspects also received much attention at the congress. The PCI repeated its negative attitude toward NATO but at the same time rejected the Soviet theory of "limited sovereignty," claiming: "The strength of a socialist country as well as of the community as a whole cannot be based solely on military power." It must depend above all on the consent of the population and on the development of socialist democracy. Members of the congress repeated their condemnation of the military intervention in Czechoslovakia and demanded the restoration of Czechoslovak sovereignty. Berlinguer advocated a "critical and objective historical review" of the development within the socialist countries. In this review, claimed Berlinguer, one should consider both the positive and the negative aspects of the system. One had to understand the development in the socialist countries objectively, "seizing on contradictory as well as dynamic elements." It would be truly strange, claimed Berlinguer, if Marxism, which arose a hundred years ago just as utopian conceptions were being overcome, should now, in the judgment of socialist society, revert to a utopian attitude: "Belief in socialism is founded on the truth and on serious and critical historical analysis."[30]

In 1970, the PCI issued a number of declarations against the repressive measures within Czechoslovakia, resulting in repeated controversy between the Husak leadership and the PCI. The PCI also analyzed and criticized the events in Poland in December 1970—the workers' uprising and the change in leadership (Gomulka was replaced by Gierek). At the Twenty-fourth Party Congress of the CPSU in spring 1971, Enrico Berlinguer stressed that international solidarity did not necessarily entail identification with all measures of every socialist state.[31]

Since 1971, the PCI has made clear its new attitude toward developments in China. It has refused to participate in Moscow's general campaign of condemnation, and has proclaimed its desire to "reestablish relations with the Chinese Communist Party."[32]

The PCI and the "Historic Compromise"

In January 1972, as a result of the increasing economic difficulties in Italy, the center-left coalition of Christian Democrats, Social Democrats, Republicans, and Socialists gave way to the formation of a Christian Democratic minority government which, however, did not obtain the consent of the Parliament. New elections, therefore, had to be held in May 1972. Behind this backdrop, the Thirteenth Party Congress of the PCI took place in Milan from March 13 to 17, 1972. At this congress, Enrico Berlinguer was elected Secretary General, while Luigi Longo received the newly created position of President of the party.

At the congress, a "democratic change" was announced, the main goal of which was to afford Italy a new political perspective through cooperation among the three main popular groups: the Communists, the Socialists, and the Catholics. Communist participation in the Italian government, according to Berlinguer, was conceivable only under two conditions: either to counteract a reactionary attack which threatened democracy, or in the presence of conditions which permitted the realization of a program of renewal based on the active support of the majority of the population. After this congress, the possibility of PCI participation in the Italian government was frequently discussed. At the Thirteenth Party Congress, Berlinguer also expressed a new attitude toward NATO: the position on NATO could "today no longer be considered in the static frame of reference of the cold war." This problem could no longer "be reduced to a position for or against the military pact."[33]

At the subsequent elections, in May 1972, the PCI exceeded its election victory of 1968, receiving over nine million votes, i.e., 27.2 percent of all votes cast. The PCI now had 179 deputies in Parliament, and the coming greater. For that reason, in the course of 1972 and especially 1973, the PCI made several concrete suggestions for governmental policy. In July 1973, Berlinguer declared that the PCI was striving for a positive solution of the most pressing economic and political problems. The Italian Communists suggested a decentralization of the state apparatus, delegation of authority to the regions and districts, a reform of the state administration in order to overcome incompetence and bureaucracy, and educational reform as well as democratic public control over the mass media.

The increased emphasis of a nearly de facto government party was also reflected in foreign policy, especially in its positive position toward the EEC. In a resolution concerning the European Economic Community published in February 1973, the Central Committee of the PCI declared its willingness to cooperate in the unification of Europe and at the same time advocated a far-reaching democratic transformation of the EEC. The goal, according to the PCI, was an autonomous Europe, neither anti-Soviet nor anti-American, which would enjoy friendly relations with the Soviet Union and the socialist countries as well as with the United States and, what is more, would establish a new relationship with the developing countries. The PCI strove for cooperation and democratization within the framework of the EEC. In addition, it aimed at cooperation and dialogue with socialist and social democratic and other democratic progressive forces of Europe, including the Catholic church.

The military coup d'état in Chile in autumn 1973 had important effects on the PCI. After the reactionary coup against the popular unity government under Allende in September 1973, in his articles "Reflections on the Recent Events in Chile," "Democratic Road and Reactionary Violence," and "Social Alliances and Political Groups,"[34] Berlinguer outlined the concept of "historic compromise."

The main points of the "historic compromise," as seen by Berlinguer, may be summarized thus:

The events in Chile should induce the Italian Communists more than ever to try to prevent a vertical split in the country. As a result, it is important to isolate the reactionary groups with greater determination, intelligence, and patience and to seek understanding and cooperation with all progressive forces. But the decision to carry on a political struggle based on democratic legality does not mean indulging in a kind of legalistic illusion. Rather, one should continually develop initiatives in order to reform the laws, structures, and state apparatus democratically. After the tragic experience in Chile, it is important for Italy to pursue a policy which can unite the social and political forces in support of thorough democratic renewal. "Even if the left-wing parties and forces succeeded in gaining fifty-one percent of the vote and seats in Parliament (something which would in itself mark a big step forward in the relative strength among the parties in Italy), it would be completely illusory to think that this fact alone would guarantee the survival of a leftist government representing this fifty-one percent." Democratic renewal could only be accomplished when the government and the Parliament have the support of a large majority strong enough to defend the country against any reactionary adventure.[35]

The policy of "historic compromise" is clearly more than just a new formula for government. It implies that the leadership of Italy must have the support of the large democratic components of Italian society. Only this sort of policy could open a road to socialism in Italy.

Discussion of the "historic compromise" stood in the foreground of the Fourteenth Party Congress of the PCI in Rome from March 18 to 23, 1975. In his report, Berlinguer declared that the "historic compromise" was more than a parliamentary majority with the inclusion of the Communist Party. Italy's economic crisis, according to Berlinguer, urgently necessitated the solidarity of all democratic forces. The PCI's participation in the government would be, of course, a decisive factor, but the main emphasis, Berlinguer stated, was not on acquiring ministerial positions but, rather, on forming a new orientation in order to solve the pressing problems of the country, and on agreeing upon a new strategy for overcoming the crisis and for restoring and ensuring democracy. The congress was marked by a lively discussion which proceeded at a sophisticated level during which diverse opinions were voiced. It was clear that the PCI had already come a long way from the monolithic parties of the East. Several speakers, Giorgio Amendola for one, regarded the "historic compromise" as a current problem which had to be solved as quickly as possible. Others emphasized that the "historic compromise" implied assistance for the progressive elements within the Christian Democratic Party. Therefore, one could not speak of a short-term realization of the "historic compromise."

Discussion centered not only around the domestic-policy aspects of the "historic compromise" but also around the effects on foreign policy. It was stressed that throughout Italy's entire history, its influence has always been the greatest when the government was based on the consent of a large part of the population. Moreover, new attitudes toward NATO were voiced at the congress. The PCI declared its willingness to support Soviet-American dialogue, insisting that it would not be hostile to either the Soviet Union or the United States. Berlinguer now spoke of overcoming the blocs, a feat which, in reality, could not be accomplished by unilateral withdrawal from NATO, but only by the promotion of international détente. He warned that discussion on Italy's withdrawal from NATO would lead to disunity among Italy's internal forces and consequently weaken the democratic forces of Italy.

The PCI since 1975

During the local and provincial elections on June 15, 1975—elections were held in fifteen of the twenty regions, in ninety-two of the ninety-three provinces, and in 7,727 of the 8,065 communities—the PCI received 33.5 percent of all votes cast as compared to 27.2 percent in May 1972. Thus, in merely three years, the influence of the PCI had increased tremendously. After the victory, several foreign and domestic policies, including positions on the EEC and NATO, were formulated more concretely. Giovanni Cervetti, a member of the Secretariat of the PCI, declared that the PCI not only rejected Italy's unilateral withdrawal from NATO, but would not question the present extent of military expenditures until a bilateral reduction of military forces of NATO and of the Warsaw Pact was achieved. In the event that the Italian Communists participated in the government, declared Cervetti, they would not demand the Ministry of Defense or that of Foreign Affairs.

In May 1976, Berlinguer declared that, in light of Italy's critical state, the PCI was ready, at least for a few years—for the period of time necessary to pull the country out of crisis—to participate in a coalition government as long as all democratic parties, including the PCI, were included in that coalition. This preparedness did not mean that the PCI was giving up the long-range "historic compromise," but rather, was offering a solution to the most pressing needs of the moment. The suggestion of cooperating in a coalition implied a government which was based on the widest consent of all democratic forces and which would be active for only a limited time.

During the elections for Parliament in June 1976, the PCI received 34.4 percent—the most votes ever. The Christian Democrats remained the strongest party, but they could not form a majority government. The number of Communist Party deputies rose from 179 to 227. The PCI became the strongest party even in Rome, and the Communist Pietro Ingrao was elected President of the Parliament. In addition, the Communists received the chairmanship of seven parliamentary committees. With Communists at the head of the Finance Committee of the Chamber of Deputies and the Budget Committee of the Senate, the PCI wielded much influence in all budgetary policies of the country. During the vote of confidence of the Christian Democratic minority government under Andreotti, the Communist delegates abstained. "We are no longer in opposition, but we are not yet in the government," declared Berlinguer. "We merely support the measures which appear justified to us." The PCI declared its willingness to agree to certain economic measures if changes in political and social life followed. All austerity measures had to be fair and were to be coupled with measures against the flight of capital and against tax evasion. They could not be undertaken at the expense of the workers and were acceptable only if measures were taken to create and assure jobs.

As voices within the party were proclaiming that the PCI was on the way to becoming a Social Democratic Party, Berlinguer declared, on September 20, 1976, at the festival of *Unità* in Naples that the PCI would remain faithful to the principles which Togliatti had announced in 1944; namely, that the PCI would be a national mass party which would give up its obsolete principles but which is and would remain Communist. Among the daily problems, one could never forget the goal of the emancipation of both the workers and the society as a whole and the building of a new society. Loyalty to these principles could not, however, be expressed through proclamations. The Communists faced the task of gradually implementing concrete changes within the economic and social structure until a change in the leading class of the country could be realized. The transformation of society in Italy would be carried out in a completely free and democratic way within the framework of the republican constitution. It would proceed through respect and extension of regional autonomy and plurality as well as with the continual cooperation of the popular forces.

In early May 1977, as a result of the changing realities in Italy, the first official meeting of the leaders of the Christian Democrats and the PCI took place. For the first time in thirty years, declared the PCI organ *Rinascità*, an attempt was being made to reach an agreement as the basis for governmental action. Through regular cooperation of the parties "within the framework of the constitution" (a term which includes all political parties of Italy with the exception of the neofascist *Movimento Sociale Italiano*), all political actions are now determined in advance. Thus the PCI has actually helped determine governmental policies since May 1977.

CP Italy—Election Results and Parliamentary Representation

The Communist Party of Italy is the only Communist Party whose share of votes proportional to the total population has increased in each election from 1945 to 1976 and particularly since its increasing autonomy from the Soviet Union as of the early 1960s.

Date	PCI votes	% of total	Deputies	Out of
June 1946	4,356,686	19	104	556
June 1953	6,120,809	22.6	143	590
May 1958	6,704,454	22.7	140	596
April 1963	7,763,854	25.3	166	630
May 1968	8,557,404	26.9	177	630
May 1972	9,085,927	27.2	179	630
June 1976	12,620,000	34.4	227	630

Reasons for the Success of the PCI

The increasing influence of the PCI has resulted, above all, from the party's growing popularity as well as the decline of popular anti-Communist feelings.

Of the many opinion polls regarding attitudes toward the PCI, the following seems to me of particular importance. In 1970, 45 percent of all those questioned were still of the opinion that the PCI posed a serious threat to freedom and that no coalition with it was possible. In 1974, this negative attitude had decreased to 25 percent. The Italian people's view of the PCI from 1967 to 1976 is also apparent in the following table:[36]

Communists . . .	1967	1974	1975	1976
		(in percent [a])		
"are honest"	21	28	29	45
"have many good ideas"	21	34	45	60
"are nice people"	15	24	27	34
"are against violence"	16	26	31	43
"are competent"	—	43	44	65

[a] Figures represent percentage of respondents in a nationwide sample agreeing with the statements.

The success of the PCI can be attributed to the following trends: *(a)* During the fifties, sixties, and early seventies, Italy underwent intensive modernization and urbanization, resulting in a break with traditional and often conservative outlooks and an increasing openness toward new ideas and goals. *(b)* The corruption, fragmentation, and internal struggles within the ruling Christian Democratic Party were the cause of increasing dissatisfaction. *(c)* The inability of the center-left coalition to cope successfully with the decisive problems of the country convinced an increasing number of Italians that successes could only be scored through active cooperation with the strong Communist Party. *(d)* As a result of the increasing secularization of Italian society and the decline of clericalism, fewer and fewer Italians were willing to let the church dictate political policies. The church's influence on election results diminished and, within the church itself, anti-Communism was weakened. *(e)* Finally, one must consider the increasing importance of young voters who no longer remembered the cold war and the confrontation between the Christian Democrats and the Communists in the late forties and fifties.

These objective facts alone do not suffice to explain the Communists' success completely. The ability of the Italian Communists to address themselves to the new problems was decisive for the PCI's success.

1. The PCI has for many years, and in several cases for even more than two decades, successfully managed the communities, cities, and regions under its control especially in Bologna, where the PCI has ruled uninterruptedly since 1946. Moreover, the Italian Communists developed realistic policies and constructive suggestions which enabled them to extend their influence to employees and members of the middle class and even to people who run small and middle-sized businesses. What is more, the PCI exhibits relatively little internal unrest and almost no tendency to form factional groups, common in

many other Italian political parties, and can count on rather strong support from intellectuals as well as influential people and groups.

2. The PCI strives for a constructive relationship with the Catholic church. In 1953, according to public polls, just over 20 percent of all Italians considered Communism and Catholicism compatible; in the mid-seventies, over 60 percent were of that opinion.

3. The clearly stated independence and critical attitude of the PCI vis-à-vis the Soviet Union and the Soviet bloc made it practically impossible to link the Italian Communists with negative events in Eastern Europe. Moreover, the PCI pursued a realistic foreign policy exemplified in its attitude toward the European Economic Community (EEC) and NATO.

4. The PCI rejected the term "Marxism-Leninism," criticized some of Lenin's theses, and relied on many of the ideas of Antonio Gramsci. There was a wide variety of party literature which included many works by authors who are forbidden in the Soviet bloc countries. Among them are the writings of Robert Havemann, Ernst Bloch, Roy Medvedev, Santiago Carrillo, the Yugoslav philosophers, and even, although with critical commentary, works of Leon Trotsky.

5. The PCI is willing to participate in a large democratic coalition without insisting on the leading role. Through a "historic compromise," it wishes to transform society with the consent of the majority of the population.

6. The PCI advocates a new model of socialism with all democratic freedoms, including the right to an organized political opposition, and asserts its willingness to step down from the government in the event of defeat at the polls. In addition, the PCI pursued an extremely successful media campaign not only with its own party publications, which are presented intelligently and in a lively manner, but also with commentaries, interviews, and articles in publications of other groups, even in conservative party organs. Similarly, most leaders and party officials of the PCI have superior qualifications.

7. The PCI deals concretely with specific Italian problems, acts as an Italian party, and clearly attempts to represent the national interests of the country without lapsing into nationalism. Moreover, it strives for joint solutions with the other industrialized countries of Western Europe.

The French Communist Party (PCF): Delayed "Socialism in French Colors"

Next to the Italian Communist Party, the French Communist Party is the strongest Communist Party of Western Europe. Of all Eurocommunist parties, however, the French Communist Party has followed a pro-Soviet course for the longest time. Only in the last few years has a new course become apparent. The difference between the French and Italian Communist parties is, however, still very great. In August 1977, Willy Brandt had this to say about the French Communists: "In general, I value the word of the Italian Communist leaders more so than that of the French Communist leader Marchais. I can't help but suspect that the tactical element plays a larger role in connection with the French Communist Party leaders than with a considerable part of the Italian Communist Party leaders."[1] The conduct of the PCF within the leftist coalition with which it has been hopelessly at odds since September 1977, and especially its rejection of a common governmental program of the left shortly before the elections early in 1978, make such doubt appear more justified.

Pro-Soviet Development (1945–1967)

Immediately after World War II, the PCF had a significant influence in the political life of France. It had been very actively involved in the resistance. At the time of the liberation of France, the PCF had almost a million members. Its leader, Maurice Thorez, had returned from the

184

Soviet Union in October 1944. During the first postwar elections on October 21, 1945, the PCF received over five million votes, i.e., 26 percent of all votes cast, and sent 155 (out of 545) deputies to the French Parliament. Maurice Thorez became Secretary of State without portfolio, and Charles Tillon took over the Ministry of Arms Production. In addition, Communist politicians directed the ministries of Industrial Production, of Labor, and of the Economy. In 1945, the PCF was considerably stronger than the PCI.

After the election of November 10, 1946, with 28.2 percent of all votes cast and 166 deputies, the PCF was the strongest party in France. Although the President and Premier were not Communists, the PCF participated in a few other governments, including, from January 1947 on, the government of the Socialist Ramadier.

With the onset of the cold war, on May 5, 1947, Premier Ramadier expelled all Communist Party functionaries from the government. With the founding of the Cominform in September 1947 and the subsequent harsh criticism of the PCF by the Kremlin, the line of the French Communist Party suddenly changed. A period of political strikes and unrest began, provoking countermeasures on the part of the government. Domestic problems, however, fell into the background and, in their place, anti-Americanism in the interest of the Soviet Union became the main keynote of the PCF's policies. The differences between the PCF and the PCI were already becoming apparent. After the official declaration of the PCF's loyalty to the Soviet Union on February 25, 1949, the party experienced a period of drastic decline in membership. In 1946, the party had 800,000 members; in 1953, membership numbered less than 300,000.

After Stalin's death, the PCF tried for the first time to maneuver itself out of isolation by changing its attitude toward the Socialists. During the elections in January 1956, the PCF received 25.6 percent of the votes and sent 145 representatives to the Parliament where it supported the government of the Socialist Guy Mollet.

In contrast to Togliatti, after the Twentieth Party Congress of the CPSU, Thorez tried to minimize the consequences of de-Stalinization; however, after the defeat of the Hungarian Revolution, the first significant voices of protest were heard in the PCF. Several prominent Communists, including Henri Lefèvre and Anni Kriegel, were ousted from the party. The official party maintained its unconditional loyalty to the Soviet Union and unreservedly welcomed the Soviet intervention.

After de Gaulle's return to power in 1958, heading a government which also included the Socialists, the isolation of the Communists began. In the elections in November 1958, the PCF received only 18.9 percent of the vote and, according to a new election law, could send only ten representatives to the Parliament. By early 1959, membership had dropped to 225,000. Moreover, during the Fifth Republic of the de Gaulle era, the PCF's policies proved somewhat inconsistent. Domestically, the PCF struggled against the President and condemned his regime as one of personal power and monopoly. In the realm of foreign policy, however, the PCF supported de Gaulle, obviously in agreement with the Soviet Union, since de Gaulle's national policies and critical attitude toward NATO and the USA were in the foreign-policy interests of the Soviet Union.

The PCF remained absolutely pro-Soviet both in the Sino-Soviet conflict and in the polemics against Togliatti and the Italian Communists in late autumn 1961. In 1962−1963, there were, however, several trends within the PCF advocating an "Italian road," which were expressed at a congress of French Communist students in April 1963, but they were promptly quelled by the party leaders. At the Seventeenth Party Congress in May 1964, the PCF leadership unambiguously acknowledged the "dictatorship of the proletariat" as the most important goal of the PCF. At the same time, Waldeck-Rochet took over the secretary generalship from the ailing Thorez. Thorez died on July 11, 1964, while on vacation in the Soviet Union.

Only since the end of 1965, when the PCF supported the Socialist Mitterand in the national election, the political line of the party has undergone certain changes. At that time, the PCF declared that one must consider the problem of the transition from capitalism to socialism in a new light. In France, the French Communists insisted, one should strive for a peaceful road to socialism. In addition, the PCF advocated a lasting coalition with the Socialists.[2] It was against this backdrop that the first "election coalition of the French left" was formed on September 20, 1966. According to this agreement, in the next election the parties with their own candidates and their own programs would appear on the first ballot. For the second ballot, the leftists of all parties would be urged to vote for the leftist candidates who had received the most votes during the first ballot.

The main goal of the election coalition was the removal of the Gaullist government. In addition, however, it strove for a constitutional reform, eliminating all articles which served the personal power of the President. It called for the independence of the Department of Justice, freedom of information, a democratic statute for radio and television, local autonomy, the right to strike, and the recognition of factory trade-union organizations. In the economic realm, the common election program of the French Socialists and Communists included nationalization of the armaments industry and of the banks, the democratic direction of nationalized industries, an increase in social legislation, and a tax reform and an agricultural policy which would be based on a cooperative system and a modernization of agriculture.[3] At the Eighteenth Party Congress of the PCF in January 1967, the resolutions were passed and Waldeck-Rochet officially became Secretary General.

In spite of the fact that the Communists and Socialists called themselves the first "election coalition of the French left," their willingness to cooperate was diminished immediately when, at the Eighteenth Congress, Waldeck-Rochet explicitly praised the Communists for being true Marxists and revolutionaries and reproached the Socialists for letting themselves be directed by reformist ideology. In accordance with past practice, Waldeck-Rochet again referred to the great example of the Soviet Union, which had demonstrated the way to overcome capitalism and establish a socialist society. According to Waldeck-Rochet, the social democratic leaders in power in different countries were always contented with "serving capitalism."[4] Such an attitude toward Social Democracy clearly disrupted the coalition with the Socialist Mitterand.

Beginning Domestic Political Flexibility (1967–1970)

In 1968, the PCF faced both the revolutionary events of the month of May and the extended period of the "Prague Spring" in Czechoslovakia.

At first, from May 3 to 11, 1968, the PCF was very critical of the student unrest. In official declarations, the PCF spoke of "irresponsible agitation" and "political adventuring." Only after the revolutionary movement started gaining momentum did the party try to approach it. On May 11, 1968, the leading trade unions, including the Communist-oriented Confédération Générale de Travailleurs, all called a twenty-four-hour general strike for May 13. The Politburo of the PCF agreed to the strike but at the same time experienced some reservations toward the workers' takeover of the factories, which was occurring in certain areas.

The more the unrest of the students incited the working class, the harder the PCF tried to establish itself as the leader of the movement. The PCF's main goal was to overthrow de Gaulle and to establish a "popular government of democratic unity." During the mass demonstrations on May 29, 1968, the party leadership demanded the formation of a popular government with Communist participation.

As de Gaulle's severe actions held the revolutionary movement more and more in check, the PCF once again underwent a complete turnabout. Now it announced that it was a party of order and would participate in the upcoming elections in order to effect a program of social progress, freedom, and the unity of all democratic forces. But during the elections on June 23 and 30, 1968, de Gaulle received 43.65 percent of the vote of the frightened citizens. The Communists suffered considerable losses, receiving only 20.14 percent of the vote and maintained only thirty-four representatives in the new French Parliament.

The PCF was most reserved toward the "Prague Spring" and, in mid-July, Secretary General Waldeck-Rochet played a particularly double-faced role in formulating the PCF's attitude. After speaking with Suslov in Moscow, on July 17, 1968, Waldeck-Rochet and the PCF leadership suddenly called for an immediate meeting of all European Communist parties in order to "deal with the Czechoslovak question." Then on July 19, Waldeck-Rochet, accompanied by the Central Committee associate on foreign affairs, Jean Kanapa, flew to Prague to inform Dubček and the other "Prague Spring" leaders of their objection to the reform course and the possible consequences which could result. Although they had not initiated it, the Soviets clearly approved of the PCF representatives' trip to Prague. The foreign-policy goal of the Soviets at that time was to prevent the need for a military intervention by increasing the pressure on the leaders of the "Prague Spring." Waldeck-Rochet's talks in Prague did not proceed as he had intended, however, and after his return the PCF reversed its declaration of July 17. It now stated that a conference of European Communists would not be advisable. The record of the Waldeck-Rochet/Dubček talks were later used by Husak to discredit Prague's reform leaders.[5]

The PCF expressed very mild disapproval of the occupation of Czechoslovakia on August 21, 1968. It declared that problems which arose among Communist parties should be solved through discussions and through bilateral or multilateral meetings. At such meetings the sovereignty of each country and each party's freedom of decision, as well as the spirit of international proletarianism, had to be respected. For Jeanette Thorez-Vermeersch, Maurice Thorez's widow, a previous proponent of an absolutely pro-Soviet course, even this disapproval was too severe, and on October 21, 1968, she gave up her seat in the Politburo of the PCF out of protest. On the same day, Plissonier, another member of the Politburo of the PCF, expressed his astonishment at the fact that printed statements from the Soviet Union and East Germany justifying the occupation in Czechoslovakia were being widely distributed throughout the French Communist Party. Nonetheless, such critical voices remained the exception rather than the rule. The PCF soon welcomed the "normalization" (i.e. re-Stalinization) in Czechoslovakia.

Starting in autumn 1968, the PCF tried implementing a two-sided policy. On the one hand, it wanted to maintain unconditional loyalty to the Soviet leadership and not to reform the extremely centralized organizational apparatus. On the other hand, it pursued a "policy of openness" with the goal of winning as many allies as possible. This "policy of openness" was the main focus of the programmatic Manifesto of Champigny ("For an Advanced Democracy—For a Socialist France"), which was adopted in December 1968 and published early in 1969 and to which the PCF has since continually referred. In this manifesto, Georges Marchais, who had taken over the leadership from the ailing Waldeck-Rochet, demanded a union of the French people in order to create a majority and thus the prerequisite for a socialist transformation of society. Marchais declared that the first stage toward socialism was "advanced democracy," marked by the sovereignty of a parliament chosen by a general election, by the guarantee of freedom of thought and of opinion, freedom of assembly and coalition, freedom to form trade unions and the right to strike as well as acknowledgment of the freedom to practice one's own religion. In light of the reaffirmation of an absolute pro-Soviet party line, however, the manifesto had relatively little effect. Maintenance of the pro-Soviet line went so far that the PCF did not even dare to send a delegation to the Congress of the League of Communists of Yugoslavia in March 1969. Only a single delegate was sent, and when he arrived in Belgrade he suddenly declared that he was not a delegate, merely an observer.

In keeping with the pro-Soviet line, the PCF supported the Kremlin's preparations of the Third World Communist Conference (June 1969). At the conference itself, the PCF remained absolutely pro-Soviet and signed all resolutions without hesitation. Above all, the PCF supported the re-Stalinization of Czechoslovakia. On the occasion of the first anniversary of the occupation, on August 21, 1969, the Stalinist French Politburo member Etienne Fajon held talks with the

Czechoslovak Politburo member and Stalinist Vasil Bilak in Prague. During these talks, Fajon submitted the record of the Waldeck-Rochet/Dubček meetings of July 19, 1968, to the Husak leadership By providing them with the record, the French Communists were giving the Czechoslovak Stalinists a means with which to apply even more pressure on the already overpowered reformers and on Dubček himself.

The actions of the PCF elicited considerable objection from many Communist parties and even from many French Communists themselves. As of early 1970, the PCF leadership was faced with increasing pressure from two sides. On the one hand, many party members advocated a new party line, the democratization of the party structure, a more critical appraisal of the situation in the East, and new concepts along the line of an "Italian road." On the other hand, they realized the necessity of becoming true partners with the Socialists despite the old pro-Soviet line. Under pressure from both these sides, the PCF leadership began to react inconsistently to new conditions.

The Influence of Critical Communists

The independent critical Communist newspaper *Unir Débat* (a merger of *Unir pour le Socialisme,* which had existed since October 1952, and *Le Débat Communiste,* which first appeared in March 1962) was first published in January 1967. The newspaper was established as a forum for free debate about the policies of the PCF and the international Communist movement and as an outlet for free discussion within the party. In January 1969, another new independent Communist newspaper, entitled *Politique Aujourd'hui,* appeared. Its editor was the former Central Committee member Paul Noirot. In addition, Roger Garaudy published many essays and books critical of the PCF and of Soviet Communism.

Roger Garaudy joined the PCF in 1933. During World War II, he was active in the then illegal French Communist Party and became a Central Committee member in 1945. From 1945 to 1951, he was a representative of the PCF in Parliament and from 1951 to 1955, he lived in the Soviet Union as a foreign correspondent for the party newspaper *L'Humanité.* He received a degree from the Sorbonne in 1953 and later from the University of Moscow and, in 1956, became a member of the Politburo of the PCF. A founder and director of the Marxist research center of the PCF, Garaudy was also repeatedly editor-in-chief of the theoretical Communist Party publication *Cahiers du Communisme*.

In 1964, Garaudy published his book *From Anathema to Dialogue*, in which he advocated dialogue between Communists and Christians. At the Conference of the Society of Saint Paul (1965–1967), he spoke out for a pluralistic model of socialism and an "opening up" of Marxism. Although his book was sharply criticized at a meeting of the Central Committee of the PCF in March 1966, Garaudy did not give up. Several months later, in October 1966, he published a second book, *Marxism of the Twentieth Century*, in which he criticized the Stalinist development in the Soviet Union. The PCF leadership also criticized this book. The same thing happened with the book Garaudy published in 1967, *The Chinese Problem*, in which he advocated an examination of the causes of Maoism and the Chinese Revolution. After the occupation of Czechoslovakia, Garaudy published an anthology of the most important declarations of the "Prague Spring." His introduction clearly demonstrated his sympathies to the cause of this "movement."

A year later his book *For a French Model of Socialism* appeared. In it, Garaudy discussed the significance of the scientific and technical revolution for the Communist parties. According to Garaudy, the results of this revolution had not been adequately considered in the Soviet bloc countries. The attempt to draw the appropriate conclusions from the scientific technical revolution had been prevented by administrative means. Moreover, Garaudy claimed that the industrial gap between the Soviet Union and the West was becoming greater. The Soviet Union, declared Garaudy, had the option of either developing into reactionary neo-Bonapartism, military dictatorship, or of striving for a democratization which would give socialism its true character— the liberation of human beings from alienation.

Garaudy summoned the Communist parties of the industrially developed countries to open their eyes to current problems or else risk degenerating into small sects which obstinately stick to propagandizing the Soviet model as the only model of socialism.

According to Garaudy, the PCF had to recognize and consider the lessons and experiences of socialist self-management as it was being practiced in Yugoslavia. The organizational structure of the party had to be fundamentally altered. Bureaucratic centralism was obsolete in light of the scientific technical revolution. Garaudy claimed that the most important duty of the party was to develop initiative and to create new directions. Furthermore, the apparatus was to be reduced to a minimum, a rotation system was to guarantee the continual change of officials, and inner-party democracy was to be established through open and public discussions. It was most important for the PCF to declare that the socialism which it wanted to establish in France was not the same as the socialism which Brezhnev was (and is) forcing upon Czechoslovakia.[6]

During a stay in Yugoslavia in autumn 1969, Garaudy declared that both the "Prague Spring" of 1968 and Yugoslavia's experiences with self-management were of great significance for the French Communists.[7]

Garaudy's writings and the activities of his supporters as well as the new critical newspapers began to have an effect upon the French Communist Party. Just before the Nineteenth Party Congress, in December 1968, and January 1969, "party discussions" took place focusing on the conflict with Garaudy. These discussions, of course, had been planned by the party leadership, for the Politburo had already condemned Garaudy's ideas as "revisionist" and "anti-Soviet." At the Nineteenth Congress which was held in Nanterre from February 4 to 9, 1970, Garaudy was treated with hostility. In the assembly hall, he was expelled from the seats reserved for members of the Politburo and was declared to have followed a road of opportunism. Garaudy was permitted to speak at the party congress for the last time. He said: "I reject the thesis that any effort to institute open discussion or political inquiry is to be considered a call for factionalism. The methods must be changed and the problems solved. And this will be the case."[8] But his plea was in vain, for Garaudy was removed from all party positions and on May 5, 1970, expelled from the party itself.

But Garaudy had supporters in the PCF. In early January 1970, a committee was formed of former and present critical party members who called for the liberation of Czechoslovakia and who demanded that the PCF publicly denounce the suppressive measures of the Husak regime. In May 1970, a conference of the so-called "Centers of Communist initiative" took place, consisting of one-third current PCF members and two-thirds former party members. The committee gathered thousands of signatures, more than half of which came from Communist Party members. The opposition in the PCF became even stronger when Charles Tillon was expelled from the party in July 1970. Tillon had been one of the most famous pioneers of the French Communist movement. In 1919, together with André Marty he built up a revolutionary organization for the defense of the Soviet Union. After six years of hard labor in Africa, Tillon returned to France and became a Central Committee member in 1932 and a Politburo member in 1936. He worked with the International Brigades in Spain, was later a leader of the resistance during World War II, and belonged to the first French government after the war. After the occupation of Czechoslovakia and the subsequent "normalization," he appealed to his comrades: "If one has accepted compulsory labor in order to defend freedom, one cannot permit Czechoslovakia to lose its freedom in the name of some principle, I was once a Stalinist, but it is not wrong to have been a Stalinist. It is wrong when one remains a Stalinist, knowing what Stalinism is."[9]

Besides the publications already mentioned, the Communist Party cultural journal, *Les Lettres Françaises*, under Editor-in-Chief Louis Aragon, began to develop in a critical direction. In January 1971, Aragon published "New Year's Wishes" to the Jews imprisoned in the Soviet Union and to the suppressed people in Czechoslovakia and in Poland. Socialism, according to Aragon, makes sense in the positive struggle against the suppression of capitalism only if current promises of humanity are kept after the accession to power.[10] From then on, representatives of the growing opposition and of the "centers of Communist initiative" met regularly, and finally, in May 1971, elected a leadership of sixty people. In addition, Louis Aragon repeated his protest of the occupation in Czechoslovakia. *Unir Débat* published a French edition of the socialist Czechoslovak newspaper in exile, *Listý*, and declared that it was the duty of truly independent Communist newspapers to support the victims of the "Prague Spring." In the beginning of October 1972, the PCF's cultural journal *Les Lettres Françaises* was suspended. Distribution of the journal in the Soviet Union and in Czechoslovakia had already been forbidden. Upon suspension of the publication, the Italian Communist Party declared that it had been of valuable assistance in the great intellectual struggle and had repeatedly indicated to the leadership of the PCF that it was necessary to fight against a conceited and uncritical optimism and against dogmatism and conformism.[11]

The Common Program of the French Communists and Socialists

After the defeat of the Socialists in the election in May 1969, when they received only 5 percent of the vote for their candidate, Defferre, the Socialist Party Congress decided in July 1969 to resume negotiations with the Communists. In December 1969, the first talks were carried out and in June 1971, Mitterand was elected Secretary General of the French Socialist Party.

By that time, the Communists had also made several attempts to reopen negotiations with the Socialist Party. Nevertheless, the PCF still did not want to discontinue its pro-Soviet policies. It hoped to be able to direct a united front in any coalition with the Socialists. As a result, there were considerable difficulties during the negotiations in May 1970. The worst disagreement was over pluralism, to which the French Communist Party leaders were opposed. The French Socialists declared that they could not rule with a political party which was not ready to submit the government to the permanent control of the Parliament and which would neither at present nor in the future respect pluralism and independence of the trade unions.

On June 22, 1970, Georges Marchais finally declared for the first time that the policies of the PCF were not made in London or Washington or Moscow, but in Paris. In July 1971, during further negotiations with the Communist Party, the Socialists demanded that the PCF dissociate itself completely from the political processes within Czechoslovakia. The PCF leadership disregarded such demands. In January 1972, the two discussion partners argued over the problem of the economy. The Socialists advocated self-management, while the PCF suggested nationalization according to Eastern European design. They also expressed different attitudes toward Europe and toward NATO.[12]

After more than two years of talks, negotiations began between the Socialists and Communists over a common program of government, on March 22, 1972. By the early morning hours of June 27, 1972, some progress had been made: the negotiators of the PCF and the French Socialist Party signed the text of a common program. Georges Marchais spoke of a "political event of primary importance," declaring that it was not a program for the building of socialism but that it should "provide opportunities for the road to socialism" whereby both parties would retain their independence.

The program was clearly a compromise. The PCF agreed to a positive attitude toward the EEC, and the French Socialists agreed to the nationalization of a larger number of factories and institutions. The Socialists were somewhat more open to ideas of a direct democracy and self-management while the Communists insisted upon nationalization. The common program was an arduous compromise after long negotiations between two leading political bodies. Several days later, a wing of the so-called Radical Socialists—in reality a moderate leftist liberal party—under the direction of Robert Fabre joined the government program of the leftists.[13]

The Main Points of the Common Program of Government

The preamble to the common program of government declared that profound changes in the political, economic, and social life of France were necessary in order to clear the way toward socialism.

The main theses of the program of government signed in June 1972 can be summarized as follows:

Nationalization in the Economy: The fundamental principle of capitalist economy, profit maximization, leads to an unequal rate of growth and does not satisfy the principal needs of the population, but rather, aggravates social inequalities. Instead, equal growth in favor of the majority of the population should occur. This growth should lead to a comparable increase in the standard of living and, more importantly, should be of the most benefit to the most disadvantaged classes of the population. Natural resources, the armaments industry, the space and aircraft industry, the atomic industry, and the pharmaceutical industry should be nationalized in their entirety as well as commercial banks and private insurance companies. The electronics industry (computers) and the chemical industry should be nationalized to a large extent. The state should also participate financially, until it owns a majority of shares in each of the iron, steel, and petroleum industries as well as in air and sea transportation. The public sector should be broadened, democratized, and restructured, but there should still be a considerably important private sector. The stockholders of nationalized industries would be compensated, whereby a distinction would be made between owners of small and middle-sized industries living on their acquired savings, on the one hand, and owners of large industries on the other.

Direction of the Nationalized Industries: The nationalized sector of the economy should be directed and controlled by enterprise committees which determine and implement investment and production procedures according to a democratic plan. The employees should be more closely involved in the direction of the enterprise and continually informed about all problems. The economy should be subject to democratic planning.

Agriculture: On the regional and departmental level, land offices should be established and run by elected farmers together with state representatives and representatives of the district councils. These land offices have purchase options on all land used for agriculture. The cooperative alliances in the areas of production, manufacture, and distribution of agricultural products should be supported, extended, and democratized.

Foreign Trade, Currency, and Financial Policies: In order to protect the economy against speculation, the government should exercise stronger control over the exchange of foreign currency and especially over the movement of capital by multinational corporations between France and all foreign countries. The extent of foreign direct investment in France as well as French investment abroad should be determined and controlled according to state planning and the state economic policy. The National Bank for Investment should be entrusted with the financing of a large part of industrial investments, and the French issuing bank should exercise a stricter control over foreign trade credit.

Salaries, Jobs, and Working Conditions: A new national minimum wage should be established for all professions and should be regularly revised according to a reasonable price index with the consent of the trade unions. A sliding wage scale should be created on the basis of this price index. The retirement age for men should be lowered to sixty and that of women to fifty-five, and working time should be reduced to forty hours a week for a five-day week with full pay. Free medical care should also gradually be established.

Education: Primary educational institutions, which are run on a private or parochial basis and which receive public financing, should be nationalized in order to create a single lay educational service. Throughout the entire school system democratic administrative councils should be formed, consisting of representatives of the state, faculty members, and students and should cooperate on different levels. Nevertheless, the main responsibility and decision-making authority should remain in the hands of the government. University students should participate in decision-making on all levels. In the realm of research, scientists, economic representatives, consumers, and state representatives should work together on state committees. University students as well as older secondary students should participate on all committees.

Freedoms and Rights: Freedom of thought, freedom of expression, the inviolability of privacy and secrecy of private correspondence and telephone conversation must be guaranteed. Each citizen should be protected against all attacks on his private life and religious freedom, and freedom of conscience must be guaranteed by the separation of church and state. The spread of racist and anti-Semitic discrimination should be prosecuted by law. All rules and regulations which restrict free practice of the right to strike should be eliminated. In addition, every three years the Parliament should elect a parliamentary commissioner responsible for the protection of rights, who would carry out inquiries into reported areas of violations of rights and who would present his findings to the Parliament.

Decentralization and Democratization of the State Apparatus: A far-reaching decentralization must be undertaken; planning, decision-making, administrative duties, and the means of financing should be transferred to autonomous regional and local institutions. Democracy must be further developed on the local level in order to afford the citizens more opportunities to participate in the development of their communities. Moreover, the prevalent controlling influence of the prefects over the local self-government must be eliminated. Private enterprises may not employ leading public servants who are responsible for overseeing those private enterprises unless a period of four years has elapsed since the individual had left the private firm.

Press and Information Services: Mass media should no longer be dependent on capital. An assistance fund should be established for press enterprises: tax exemptions, extra allowances for the high cost of paper, and a preferential staff should be established to benefit newspapers and magazines. All publications which are issued by private corporations or which are connected with financial, industrial, or commercial companies should be excluded from these privileges. The state radio and television must control all stations in French territory and must be directed by an administrative council which is comprised of representatives from the Parliament, of employees of radio and television, and of qualified radio listeners and television viewers. Private radio and television companies which broadcast into France from abroad must pay both a commercial tax and an added tax.

Foreign Policy and the Attitude Toward NATO: In the interests of disarmament, all forms of strategic atomic weapons must be halted immediately, the sale of weapons and armaments to racist, fascist, or imperialist governments must cease. Moreover, arms sale abroad must be well regulated. A government comprised of Communists and Socialists would advocate simultaneous dissolution of the North Atlantic Treaty Organization and the Warsaw Pact and would support all measures leading to an eventual attainment of this goal. France must refuse to reintegrate itself into NATO but would not hesitate, in case of emergencies, to conclude defensive alliances and nonaggression pacts. A government of the unified left would strive to lead the country to independence from political-military blocs but would respect France's responsibilities within the Atlantic alliance.

The Attitude Toward the EEC: France would take part in the construction of the EEC and its institutions with the goal of "freeing it from the domination of big capital, democratizing its institutions, supporting the demands of the workers and directing the community's achievements toward their interests." In addition, France will be careful to preserve within the EEC its freedom of action to carry out its own political, economic, and social program.[14]

If this program was carried out, the public sector of France would comprise 14 percent of domestic production, 13 percent of the labor force, and 40 to 50 percent of all industrial investment. The extent and limitations of the necessary nationalization measures are still being discussed. Meanwhile, the question of nationalization has become a test of the longevity of the coalition of the French left. At the time of the writing of this book, a reconciliation in the near future is unlikely.

The Transition to Autonomy (1972–1975)

With the adoption of the common program, the contradiction between the proclaimed solidarity to the Soviet Union, on one hand, and the democratic principles of the program, on the other, became more apparent than ever. "It would be easier to believe the PCF's

insistence that it professes loyalty to the existing institutions," wrote
Le Monde after the signing on June 30, 1972, "if they dissociated themselves from that regime in which doubtless only very few Frenchmen
see the model of socialism which they desire."

The PCF leadership found it difficult to do just that. At first, it
tried to announce both its solidarity with the Soviet Union and its
autonomy. With this intention, Roland Leroy, a member of the Politburo of the PCF, declared in mid-November 1972 that there was no
one model of socialism for the French Communists, but rather, only
universal principles which must be suited to the peculiarities and
traditions of each country.[15] Georges Marchais went further when,
on November 17, 1972, he declared: "We think that though there are
certainly general principles for the construction of a socialist society,
there is no 'model' of socialism which can be transported from one
country to another."[16]

The PCF held its Twentieth Party Congress from December 13 to
17, 1972. At this conference Waldeck-Rochet was officially replaced
by Georges Marchais as the Secretary General of the PCF. The congress advocated collaboration with the Socialists and the liberals. Of
even greater significance, however, was the apparent rejuvenation
within the PCF, in support of a new course of the party. The average
age of the delegates at the Twentieth Congress was thirty-three.

In his report to the congress, Marchais referred to the ideas of the
PCI, declaring that a pluralism of autonomous political parties was
necessary for the building of socialism. Future socialism, claimed
Marchais, would include the freedom to organize trade unions, the
right to strike, personal freedom, and freedom of cultural and creative
activity. There would be no official state ideology, and the organizational principle of democratic centralism could not be applied to society as a whole.

During the elections on March 4, 1973, the PCF received 21.3
percent of the votes cast and was entitled to send 73 (out of 490)
representatives to the Parliament. The Socialists received 19 percent
of all votes, which was the most they had received since 1946. François Mitterand proudly declared that he had achieved his goal, that
the PCF and the Socialists were equally strong, and that as a result
"internal balance of the leftist forces had been accomplished."[17]

In light of the success of the Socialists, the PCF began expressing
its independence more and more clearly. Before a crowd of 5,000 at a
gathering of the PCF in Toulouse at the end of April 1973, Marchais
declared: "The Soviet Union is the Soviet Union, Hungary is Hun-

gary, Czechoslovakia is Czechoslovakia, France is France. The road which we have chosen is different, just as our country, our people and our habits are different—this is 1973, not 1917. The surest road to socialism is the broadening of democracy."[18]

In May 1973, Marchais and Berlinguer appeared together at a mass rally in Bologna and declared that relations between the two parties had entered a "new phase." Several days later, Marchais advocated common initiatives of Communists, socialists, and the Catholic forces of all the capitalist countries of Europe.[19] In July 1973, the Communist faction of the European Parliament in Strassburg was formed after the three French Communist representatives finally agreed to join. And in September 1973, Georges Marchais's book *Le Défi Democratique* (The Democratic Challenge) appeared, in which he (and the PCF) openly advocated a pluralistic model of Socialism. Marchais wrote that it was unthinkable that socialism in France could possibly find its expression in a one-party system. These declarations lost some of their impact, however, with the contention that in Poland, East Germany, and Bulgaria "influential, non-Communist parties worked together with the Communists in ruling the country," and that in the Soviet Union, "the importance of elected bodies was increasing on all levels."[20]

But the justification of the Soviet system contained in Marchais's book did not reflect the opinion of the majority of the French population, nor of the CP sympathizers. The central organ of the PCF, *L'Humanité*, published a questionnaire in which readers were requested to submit their definitions of socialism. Only 1 percent of all those asked linked socialism with the system in the Soviet Union and the East European countries. All the others gave their own conceptions, which differed greatly from the system in the Soviet bloc.[21]

The decisive test of the left coalition's strength was the presidential elections in May 1974. In the preliminary elections François Mitterand, the leftists' candidate, received 43.3 percent; Giscard d'Estaing, 32.9 percent; and the Gaullists' candidate, 14.6 percent. Attention was then focused on the run-off, which was to take place on May 19, 1974, and in which only Mitterand and Giscard would compete. Shortly before May 19, in an extremely tense domestic situation, the Soviet Ambassador paid an official visit to Giscard d'Estaing. The PCF characterized this visit as "inopportune." In the run-off, Mitterand received 49.33 percent of the votes and Giscard 50.67 percent. It was an extremely close victory for Giscard.

Nevertheless, the fact that despite all this the left still did not win was obviously a result of the PCF's failure to dissociate itself completely from the Soviet Union. Although it made some efforts, they were clearly not sufficient. It was up to the French Communists to offer a democratic socialism as an alternative—a democratic socialism which corresponds to the conditions and traditions of West European countries and which is characterized by true inner-party democracy and is free from any form of paternalistic bureaucracy.[22]

The party leadership gradually decided to try to comply with the changing conditions. At the end of June 1974, the PCF started a membership drive with the unusual slogan, "The Communist Party with an open heart." During the drive, any person could participate in any of the deliberations of the party, including the higher party bodies. Beginning in summer 1974, *L'Humanité* supported the action with a much wider scope of opinion in its commentaries.

An opinion poll in October 1974 showed that 50 percent of all French people foresaw Communist participation in the government within the following five years. Fifty-nine percent advocated the participation of Communist ministers in a leftist government. And while 38 percent said that the PCF was still a revolutionary party, 49 percent declared that it was not.[23]

The main concern of the party leadership in October 1974 was once again the PCF's relationship with the Socialists. During the by-elections in five election districts in late September/early October 1974, the Socialists were considerably more successful than the Communists. Consequently, the party leadership decided on the unusual step of convening an extraordinary Twenty-first Party Congress (October 26 to 28, 1974) to concentrate on relations with the Socialist Party. Several delegates declared that they feared that the Socialists intended to take over the PCF and become the leading party of the left.

The reasons for the Socialists' strong success as compared with the Communists were clear: first of all, they were considered more serious, more moderate, and more independent. Second, they attracted the leftist votes more strongly because freer discussion took place within the party. Moreover, the Socialists were at least somewhat more open to the idea of direct democracy and self-management, while the Communists still insisted on nationalization and state ownership.[24]

At the extraordinary party congress, Marchais demanded that the PCF had to receive 25 percent of the votes. The contradiction was obvious. On the one hand, the PCF avowed its unity with the Socialists; on the other, it wanted to strengthen its own role within the left coalition at all costs.

Further Progress in 1975

On May 17, 1975, the Central Committee of the PCF published a "Declaration of Freedom," which was distributed throughout the country and which was to serve as the basis for discussion. This "catalogue of freedom" clearly served to dissociate the PCF from the Communist regimes of the East. Below are several of the freedoms proclaimed in the catalogue:

a) There may be no coalescence of parties and the state.

b) The members of a political party may not enjoy any special privileges.

c) Everyone may speak, write, print, publish, distribute, and act freely.

d) It is the duty of every government to subordinate itself to the will of the voting public.

e) The death penalty shall be abolished.

f) Conscientious objectors shall render substitute services in institutions of public welfare and may be neither discriminated against nor given preference over other young people.

g) Everyone shall have the right to freedom of conscience and of religion; religious places of worship are sacred and inviolable.

h) No French citizen may be exiled or expatriated.

i) Every citizen shall have the right to examine his or her personal file, to question its contents, and to be informed about any use made of it.

j) There shall be legal protection against arbitrary committal to a mental institution. No one may be committed to such an institution against his or her will.[25]

This listing of these freedoms alone indicates that they are precisely those freedoms which are either denied or endangered in the Soviet bloc countries.

Nevertheless, the dissociation from the East was still somewhat inconsistent. The party leadership recognized its responsibility, but did not want to go "too far." The PCF did not express its independence clearly until August 1975. On August 9, after the already mentioned Saradov article had been published in *Pravda* on August 6, Marchais announced at a press conference: "The policies of the PCF are made in Paris and not in Moscow. The strategy of the French Communists is concerned solely with achieving socialism along a democratic path reflecting the will of the people. It is based on the unanimity of the left as expressed in its common program."

The death of two Stalinist Communist Party leaders facilitated the shift in conceptions. Jacques Duclos died at the end of April 1975 and Benoit Frachon died in August of the same year. In October 1975, the PCF supported the case of the Soviet Marxist mathematician Leonid Plyushch, who had been arrested and held prisoner in a psychiatric clinic for two years. And on November 15, Mrs. Tatyana Plyushch gave a foreign press correspondent her letter to Secretary General Marchais thanking him for supporting her husband.

The most decisive turn in the direction of a new course occurred in November 1975 with the famous mutual declaration of the PCF and the PCI. In this declaration, numerous similarities between the two Communist parties became apparent.

The declaration emphasized the common goal of the two parties in the further development of freedoms under socialism, as well as the plurality of political parties and the right of opposition parties to exist and be active.

According to the declaration, the common goals of the two parties arose from an analysis of objective and specific historical circumstances in both France and Italy. For the first time, the PCF declared its willingness to participate in the European Common Market and to support initiatives for its democratization as well as to work for a democratic, peace-loving, and independent Europe.[26]

With the signing of this common declaration, the PCF stood—at least insofar as official declarations are concerned—in the Eurocommunist camp. Shortly thereafter, the leadership of the PCF made its independence from the Soviet Union even more clear. On December 11, 1975, French television broadcast a film of a Soviet camp taken secretly with a hidden telescopic camera. It showed the prisoners' rollcall at the forced-labor camp OZ 78 in Soviet Latvia. On December 12, the Politburo of the PCF declared that this film revealed "an intolerable picture of the living and working conditions in this labor camp," and criticized the fact that in the Soviet Union, people were arrested and convicted solely on the basis of their political beliefs. Such unjustifiable acts could only harm socialism, claimed the Politburo. Several days later, on December 19, *Pravda* declared that the film was a "crude anti-Soviet forgery" and reproached the PCF for having defended the cause of anti-Communism with this "provocation." On the following day, *L'Humanité* replied that the PCF always fought and would always fight against anti-Communism, but that it could not approve of replacing the political struggle by repression. One week later, on December 28, the PCF again declared itself for unrestricted freedom under socialism. Ideas must be fought with ideas, it claimed, not with repression. Lies must be refuted with facts, and slander with proof, not with administrative measures. The PCF found it intolerable that political prisoners were confined to work camps in a socialist country.

The Twenty-second Party Congress of the PCF

The controversy with the Soviet Union took place during the preparations for the Twenty-second Party Congress of the PCF which was finally convened from February 4 to 8, 1976. The preparations clearly demonstrated that the party leadership was preparing an important change. The draft resolution for the forthcoming congress, entitled "What the Communists Want for France" stressed the democratic freedoms, the rejection of the dictatorship of the proletariat, and the aim of "socialism in French colors."

The motto of the Twenty-second Congress, which met in a suburb of Paris, was "A democratic road to socialism, a socialism for France." Delegates numbering 1,522 represented a half-million party members, 93,000 of which had joined in 1975. Young people were in the majority; the average age of the delegates was thirty-two and a half, and 48.5 percent were under thirty. Approximately 46.5 percent of the delegates were classified as workers. Thus the PCF appeared as a youthful, dynamic, worker-oriented party. Many foreign Communist Party delegations participated in the congress, including a Soviet delegation under the direction of Politburo member Andrei Kirilenko. The foreign delegates, however, were not permitted to speak at the congress.

Secretary General Georges Marchais gave an opening speech entitled "The French Road to Socialism" and introduced three themes: the rejection of the dictatorship of the proletariat, the critical dissociation from certain characteristics of the Soviet Union, and the assertion of a French road to socialism based on the union of the left.

Marchais declared that the dictatorship of the proletariat did not "correspond to the reality of our policies." Socialist transformation of society is dependent upon the will of the majority and on free elections, and includes a far-reaching democratization of all economic, dictatorship of the proletariat because "dictatorship automatically reminds one of fascist regimes of Hitler, Mussolini, Salazar, and Franco—i.e., of the negation of democracy. That is not what we want."

It is interesting that Marchais mentioned the fascist dictatorships, but not Stalinism. Moreover, the reasons for the rejection of the dictatorship of the proletariat were indeed vague.

Marchais's dissociation from the Soviet Union proceeded with the utmost caution. Apparently, Marchais considered this caution necessary, since there were still many pro-Soviet illusions within the party. As the eighty-eight delegations were welcomed, the Soviet delegation with Politburo member Kirilenko received by far the loudest applause.[27] Marchais declared that the PCF and the Soviet bloc countries had common doctrines, a common enemy, and an equal zeal for socialism. According to the Secretary General, in the Soviet Union socialism had made tremendous historical progress, ended the exploitation of people by people and established an economic system which had developed without economic crises, without unemployment, and without galloping price increases. To this description, Marchais added that the PCF would combat anti-Sovietism, lies, and slander. Only afterward did he declare that it was necessary to resist the temptation to replace democratic persuasiveness, discussions, and intellectual debate with authoritative repression. Consequently, declared Marchais, the PCF did not agree with certain repressive measures within the socialist countries, and one could not allow the Communist ideal "to be defiled by unjust and unjustified acts."

As for the third aspect, the independent democratic road to socialism for France, Marchais claimed: "The world Communist movement is neither a church nor a centralized organization which subordinates itself to any obligatory directives or unified law." The transition to socialism, according to Marchais, would necessarily proceed in many different forms. "There is and can be no model of socialism that can be transported from one country to another or that can be copied. Therefore, we suggest a democratic road to our people in order to create a socialism in French colors."

Marchais strongly emphasized national identity and French sovereignty. An essential goal in the struggle of the PCF, he claimed, was to do everything "to assure France of its independence and sovereignty, i.e., to guarantee its people free decision and effective international action." Furthermore, "national independence is in no way an obsolete conception. It is an important demand of our time." There is nothing, claimed the leader of the PCF, more current or more modern than the struggle for the independence, the sovereignty, and the prosperity of France. As a result, the Communist Party implores all democrats and patriots of the country to "make his contribution to the national struggle."[28]

The Twenty-second Party Congress was unquestionably a great step forward for the PCF. Nevertheless, by comparison with other Eurocommunist parties, such as the Italian, Spanish, Japan, Australian, and Swedish Communist parties, the PCF still had far to go. Its criticism of the Soviet Union was limited to a few negative remarks and, accompanied by euphemisms about the general situation, lacked any overall critical analysis. The coalition policy with other leftist parties was stressed but not as emphatically as by PCI at its congresses. The Pan-European aspects and the similarities of the Communist parties in the industrially developed countries was hardly mentioned; instead, the PCF glorified national tendencies. The rejection of the dictatorship of the proletariat lacked detailed Marxist analysis and any justification for the new position. Moreover, there was no self-criticism of the position supporting the dictatorship of the proletariat which the PCF had taken at the Seventeenth Party Congress in 1964.

For many observers the change in course at the Twenty-second Congress appeared rather as a decree from above than a result of the conviction of a large majority.[29]

After the party congress, tension between the French and the Soviet Communists mounted. In its report on the party congress, *Pravda* did not mention the resolution rejecting the concept of the dictatorship of the proletariat.[30] Several days later, the leading Soviet organ expressed its discontent that for the benefit of the unity of the left, dubious arguments had been raised which could mean an ideological "Social Democratization" of the Communist parties.[31]

Instead of Secretary General Marchais, Politburo member Plissonier attended the Twenty-fifth Party Congress of the CPSU, from February to March 1976, announcing the new theses of the PCF which were recorded by citizens of the Soviet Union critical of its policies. After the Soviet Party Congress, the human rights advocate and Nobel Prize-winner Andrei Sakharov declared that it was difficult to say anything about the PCF, for the change had been so sudden and had occurred so recently that it could not yet be regarded as definitive. In the event that the new line was retained and developed, Sakharov added, the French phenomena would be of great significance, even revolutionary, with respect to the entire world Communist movement.[32] The French Communists themselves analyzed the Twenty-fifth Soviet Party Congress critically. According to the publication *La Nouvelle Critique,* which is connected to the PCF, the congress dealt with no important political problems and no new questions. Everything had proceeded as if the political debate had been consciously frozen. The desire to leave things as they were prevailed.[33]

The change announced at the Twenty-second Congress of the PCF played an important role in the local elections on March 7 and 14, 1976. A landslide occurred. Of the thirty-nine French cities with over 100,000 inhabitants, the leftist union had won 12 during the elections of 1971; in 1976 the number rose to 22. In 1971, the leftists had received majorities in 86 of the 182 towns numbering between 30,000 and 100,000. In 1976, that number increased to 133. Even France's most conservative strongholds, including Brest, Cherbourg, Nantes, and Rennes, fell into the hands of the leftists.

In the second election on March 14, the PCF faced alarming developments. During the run-off, 85 percent of all Communists voted for the favored Socialist candidate, but almost a third of the Socialists refused to vote for the favored Communist candidate. Under these circumstances, after the election the Communists advocated offering a common candidate on the first ballot in all future elections. But the Socialists rejected this suggestion.[34]

The local elections had shown that a victory of the leftist union was possible in the spring of 1978. But in such a victory, the Socialists would far surpass the Communists, who would thus be at best a junior partner in a future government of the left. Realizing this, the PCF stressed two new moves in its policies shortly after the election: a clearer dissociation from Soviet Communism in order to appeal to a

CP France—Election Results and Parliamentary Representation since 1945

Date	Votes	% of total	Deputies	Out of
October 1945	5,005,336	26	161	586
June 1946	5,199,111	26.1	153	586
November 1946	5,489,288	28.6	169	621
June 1951	4,910,547	25.6	99	627
January 1956	5,532,631	25.7	144	596
November 1958	3,882,204	18.9	10	465
November 1962	3,992,431	21.7	41	485
March 1967	5,039,032	22.5	73	485
June 1968	4,435,357	20	34	585
March 1973	5,026,417	21.2	73	490
March 1978	5,870,340	20.56	86	491

broader spectrum of voters, and an increasingly independent policy within the leftist union in order to stand out in the coalition. These policies soon led to a dispute with the Socialists.

The PCF's Increasing Criticism of the Soviet Union

The growing independence of the PCF became more obvious after a French Communist Party delegation's trip to Japan in April 1976 and a common declaration of the PCF and the Japan Communist Party, while the latter was in the midst of bitter controversy with the Soviet Union. Moreover, at the East Berlin Conference of European Communist parties in June 1976, Marchais took a clearly critical position toward the Soviet Union. His remarks were so harsh that all Soviet bloc newspapers, with the exception of *Neues Deutschland*, published a highly censored version of Marchais's speech.

Since the summer of 1976, the PCF has made open attempts at solidarity with Soviet dissidents. After his expatriation, the mathematician and critical Marxist Leonid Plyushch was received by the PCF, and in mid-October 1976, Central Committee member Pierre Juquin participated at a mass meeting of a committee protesting against political injustice (including in the USSR) where he voiced the PCF's point of view. Immediately thereafter, the Soviet news agency TASS expressed its displeasure at the fact that the French Communists had participated in such a "dirty event." The PCF stuck to its position and later published six million copies of the text of Juquin's speech.

In December 1976, the party organ *L'Humanité* objected to the expatriation of Wolf Biermann from East Germany: "We consider it inadmissible that a man fighting for an idea which he believes is right is given the horrible choice between prison and exile."[35] Still more important was the replay of the film *The Confession* in mid-December. The movie was based on the autobiography of Arthur London, one of the three accused who were not sentenced to death in the Slansky trial in Czechoslovakia in December 1952. The first time the film was shown in Paris, in 1970, *L'Humanité* sharply criticized it. This time, however, a television interview took place with Arthur London himself, his wife Lise, the PCF Politburo member Jean Kanapa, and Jiří Pelikan, the former director of Czechoslovak television during the "Prague Spring." During the interview, Kanapa declared that the film was a work of complete authenticity and supported all those fighting for socialism.[36] Afterward, the Czechoslovak Party newspaper *Rudé*

Právo attacked the PCF, declaring that the film was "trash from the anti-Communist arsenal," and an "anti-Communist provocation."[37]

The campaign continued and, in January 1977, the PCF intervened on the part of Charter 77 against the repressive measures in Czechoslovakia.[38] With his books *The History of Stalinism* and *The History of the French Communist Party*, Jean Elleinstein, Assistant Director of the Marxist Study Center of the PCF, finally took the first step toward a fundamental dispute with the Soviet bloc. At the end of January 1977, the Soviet weekly paper *New Times* accused Elleinstein of having grossly exaggerated the difficulties and violations of socialist legality. According to the publication, Elleinstein's description of refugees and emigrants, of the ineffective democracy, the lack of freedom, and the persecution of dissidents in the Soviet Union had been "derived from anti-Communist propaganda."[39] *L'Humanité* responded with a quotation from the resolution of the European Communist Party Congress of June 1976: "The Communists do not consider all those who do not agree with or who are critical of their actions as anti-Communist."

On February 22, 1977, Secretary General Georges Marchais appeared with the Soviet historian and dissident Andrei Amalrik in a discussion on French television. Although there were many obvious differences between the points of view of the two men, it was nevertheless remarkable when Marchais declared that for French Communists freedom was "indivisible" and that, as a result, "we cannot agree with any kind of arrests and persecutions for reasons of conscience in any country, including the Soviet Union." Furthermore, according to Marchais, freedom had to be protected not only in capitalist countries but in socialist countries too.[40]

In an interview at the beginning of March 1977, Jean Elleinstein mentioned a very sensitive topic—possible future changes in the Soviet Union and the role of human rights movements. Elleinstein insisted that Soviet policy was to avoid another "Prague Spring." Moscow's position is a difficult one, he claims, because the oppositional movements in Eastern Europe such as the Charter 77 in Czechoslovakia and the movements in Poland are obviously not against socialism but want only to democratize the system.

On possible future changes in the Soviet Union, Elleinstein declared that such changes could not occur on an international level, but had to be achieved by internal modification that depended on the individual development in each of the respective countries. Détente could possibly influence these developments, but only to a limited extent. Moreover, democratic socialism in France could very well become a model for all those in the Soviet Union and Eastern European countries who sought greater democracy in existing socialism.[41]

At the beginning of June 1977, when the forthcoming visit of Secretary General Brezhnev was announced, Marchais declared that by no means would the French Communists enter into a discussion with the Soviet Secretary General about France's current political principles. There was no longer a unified center for all questions about Communism. He finally declared that it was not necessary that the leadership of the PCF meet with the Soviet party chief during every visit to Paris.[42] When Brezhnev visited France at the end of June 1977, he did not, in fact, meet with the French Communists.

The Conflict with the Socialists

After the local elections in March 1976, the PCF began making noticeable attempts at playing up its national role. One of the first actions in this direction was the decision of the Central Committee of the PCF to support the French supersonic transport, the Concorde. The PCF urged not only the workers of the airlines industry but all workers to "defend our national property." The Communists, declared Marchais at a meeting of the Central Committee, "are committed to national independence."[43] Everything must be done in order to further develop the Concorde. Furthermore, he claimed, the PCF had decided to lead the fight against "the policy of liquidation and sell-out of the interests of the nation."[44]

Furthermore, on November 12, 1976, the PCF suggested that the left wing of the Gaullist UDR join the leftist union. Marchais declared that all those who advocated the independence of France, its economic prosperity and social progress, but who were not yet ready to join the Communists, Socialists, or leftist Liberals, could form a fourth component within the framework of the union of the left. However, the Socialists rejected this suggestion.

Early in 1977, there were several indications that the PCF had decided to comply with several Socialist suggestions in order to strengthen the leftist union. This became clear when, in a radio interview on April 19, 1977, Georges Marchais announced the PCF's new stand in favor of direct election of the French representatives to the European Parliament. The Socialists had always favored the direct election to the European Parliament, but the Communists had always objected, considering this a restriction of national sovereignty. Marchais declared that if the election law contained clear obligatory provisions limiting the power of those elected to the European Parliament and thus ensured that the French Parliament and the French Constitution would enjoy full effectiveness, the Communists would reconsider their attitude toward direct elections.[45] Marchais's declaration was heartily welcomed by the Socialists. It appeared that the two great leftist parties' differences over European politics had been overcome. But this soon proved to be an illusion for, as of May 1977, the many differences between the Communists and the Socialists could no longer be overlooked.

These differences began in May 1977, when Georges Marchais stressed the fact that a new situation had arisen—since nuclear arms were the only effective means of protection, they were indispensable. According to Marchais, a government of the united left would do anything to defend France's independence. He declared: "We want no power to doubt our commitment to protect by all possible means the sovereignty of our country, the inviolability of its territory, and the assurance of the peaceful work of its people," While nuclear arms were an element of NATO strategy for the Giscard regime, declared Marchais, for the PCF they would be a deterrent which would protect France against any threat, regardless of its origin.[46] With that statement, the PCF had clearly broken away from the common program of government of June 1972, which had stated, "We renounce all forms of strategic nuclear arms and advocate the suspension of the build-up of French nuclear weaponry."

Against this background the so-called Summit Conference of the Union of the Left took place from May 17 to 18, 1977. At this conference, the three participating parties agreed to bring the common program of June 1972 up to date. A working group comprised of five representatives from each party was to adapt the program to the present economic and social conditions.[47]

In the course of the summer of 1977, the Communists and Socialists disagreed on the number of and extent to which factories and enterprises should be nationalized. The common program of 1972 had specified nationalization of nine industrial groups, including banks and insurance companies, but there was no precise agreement over branches of the enterprises. Now the Communists demanded the nationalization of the iron industry as well as all enterprises in which the nine above-mentioned industrial groups (including the state) owned more than half of all stocks. In contrast, the Socialists advocated nationalizing only those enterprises in which the nine industrial groups, including the state, possessed at least 94 percent of the stocks. According to the Socialists, the possible nationalization of the iron industry, as well as the Peugeot and Citroën companies, could be dealt with only after formation of the government.

According to the PCF's recommendation, 729 French enterprises with a total of 600,000-650,000 workers and employees should be nationalized, while the Socialists' recommendation affected 227 factories with approximately 500,000 workers. Moreover, there was a disagreement over the minimum wage. The common program of 1962 had set a minimum wage of 2,200 francs a month. In light of inflation, the PCF now suggested a monthly minimum wage of 2,400 francs, while the Socialists stayed with the previous 2,200-franc mark and wanted to discuss possible wage increases with trade unions only after the government had been formed.

The actual reason for the sudden intensification of differences between the two parties was clearly the fear that the Communists would no longer keep up with the increasingly strong Socialist coalition partner. As a result, after the break-off of negotiations, the Communists no longer stressed the unity of the left but, rather, the strength of their own party. The PCF feared that the advantages of a successful leftist union—the PCF's emerging from the ghetto, the proof of its ability to govern, and the entrusting of large economic and social ministries to the PCF—would not compensate for the disadvantages the party would face, namely its loss of ideological entity, militancy, and a threatening "Social Democratization" of the party. On the other hand, the Socialists clearly hoped for a break in order to be able to approach the center of the voting population and possibly pass the 40 percent vote mark. It would then become the strongest party in France and, in accordance with French elective procedures, would claim an absolute majority in the National Assembly.

The conflicts within the Union of the Left caused great confusion and disillusionment among the leftist voters. According to a public-opinion poll conducted in October 1977 as to whether Mitterand would remain in the leftist union, 47 percent answered "yes," 29 percent answered "no," and 24 percent claimed they did not know.[48]

Today almost all commentators agree that the PCF has not yet progressed as far as the Communists in Spain and Italy have. Indeed, the PCF partly leans toward Eurocommunism, but primarily stresses the importance of national interests. Some experts regard the PCF as the embodiment of a "Gaullist Communism." In the long run, however, the Union of the Left is the only solution for the PCF. Nevertheless, the PCF leadership still expresses both the hope that it would receive a large share of the power in the event of a victory of the left and the fear that it would be double-crossed by its coalition partners after an election.[49] Further development of the French Communists depends on the depth and credibility of the incipient transformation. This transformation is occurring in the spotlight of an alert French press and, of course, before the critical eyes of the 600,000 members of the PCF and the almost six million people voting for it.

13

The Spanish Communist Party (PCE): New Roads and New Goals

Along with the PCI, the Communist Party of Spain portrays the new conceptions of Eurocommunism more clearly than any other Communist Party. At times, the PCE has even gone further than the PCI. The Spanish Communist Party's zeal is all the more significant since the rejection of the Soviet model occurred not under the conditions of a parliamentary democracy, as in Italy, but rather, during the illegal struggle under the dying Franco regime.

Santiago Carrillo, Secretary General of the Communist Party of Spain since 1960, summarized the development of Spanish Communism in the following manner:

> From 1939 to 1975 our history consisted of thirty-six years of illegality and persecution, including thirty years of activity in a dark tunnel, saving persecuted organizations, working with old groups who were tired or who had given up by emigrating and with young groups who were born abroad and who had no connection to the country, no relation to history. It was a difficult task to hold a party together under such conditions, especially since there were so many mistakes and so many defeats. . . . it was Sisyphean labor which offered too little compensation. It is only in the last year or two that we have caught a glimpse of the light at the end of the tunnel and we have since been like a plant after the winter. Today the party is a factor, a protagonist, a major force.[1]

214

The Communist Party of Spain in the Early Postwar Years (1945–1949)

The Spanish Communists' hope that the defeat of fascism in World War II would also bring the Allies to eliminate the Franco regime proved a fallacy. Even before the end of the war, the Spanish Communists had begun training guerrilla groups in Algeria for a later rebellion. During World War II more than 12,000 Spanish Communists had participated in the armed-resistance fight in France. Most belonged to the organization of the Agrupación de Guerrilleros Españoles. At the same time, in the illegal resistance movement in Spain itself, the Communists fought together with Socialists, Social Democrats, Republicans, and other Franco adversaries. In May 1945, the leadership of the Spanish Communist Party was comprised of different centers. In Moscow, the Secretary General of the Communist Party, Dolores Ibarruri ("La Pasionaria") directed the party. She was the successor to Secretary General José Díaz, who died in the Soviet Union in March 1942 under circumstances which have yet to be fully clarified. A second center of the party was located in Mexico under the direction of Vicente Uribe who had been Minister of Agriculture in the Popular Front government during the Civil War. Finally, there was a third center of the PCE in Argentina under the leadership of Politburo member Fernando Claudin.

Even before the war's end there were internal conflicts among these centers. In May 1943, Jesús Hernandez—General Commissar for the troops of the central and southern front, Minister of Education in the Popular Front government, and a Politburo member of the PCE—was sent from Moscow to Mexico where, in 1945, he broke from the party, advocating an independent socialist course and expounding ideas which today, almost thirty-five years later, belong to the Eurocommunist heritage of the Spanish Communist Party.

In Spain itself at the end of the war, the illegal Communist Party was preparing a national revolt with the help of Spanish guerrillas living in France who concentrated themselves on the Spanish border in order to assure the liberation of Spain by force. They wanted to invade Spain in small groups and incite an uprising. The individual guerrilla groups were linked by radio. For more than three years, from 1945 to 1948, these guerrilla groups were active and continued to receive the support of the illegal Spanish Communist Party. The Yugoslav struggle under Tito was their model. In May 1948—just one month before Yugoslavia's break with Moscow—a delegation of the

Spanish Communist Party under the direction of Santiago Carrillo called on Tito with the unusual request that the Yugoslavs help organize parachute raids over Spain. At that time, Tito suggested first discussing it with the Soviet Union. Several months later the leadership of the PCE, including Dolores Ibarruri and Santiago Carrillo, were invited to meet with Stalin in the Kremlin.

Besides Stalin, both Suslov and Molotov participated in the consultation. Stalin suggested to the Spanish Communist Party leaders that they concentrate more on legal mass organizations. Moreover, he advised them to infiltrate the fascist trade unions and mass organizations and there effectively expound their ideas. The guerrillas should only be used for the protection of the political leadership, to guarantee their safety.[2] But at that time, the guerrilla fighters were already showing signs of increasing demoralization. Their only goal was sheer survival. Moreover, the Spanish police were able to infiltrate the guerrilla groups with agents and instigators. Nonetheless, the guerrilla war was continued until 1949, resulting in the loss of about 15,000 Spanish Communists in the underground war. The party leaders' decision to give up the guerrilla struggle was therefore welcomed—it marked a new phase in the development of the Spanish Communist Party.

During the Soviet-Yugoslav break, the Spanish Communist Party leadership supported the Cominform's condemnation of Yugoslavia. Later, Santiago Carrillo called this support an "unforgivable error."[3] As a result of Yugoslavia's break with Moscow, hundreds of members left the party and advocated an independent socialist development according to the Yugoslav model. Among those who left were Felix Montiel, the long-time editor-in-chief of the party newspaper, *Mundo Obrero*, and José del Barrio, who had been one of the leaders of the United Socialist Party of Catalonia as well as of the Communist International. In 1950, Jesús Hernandez, who had already broken with the party in 1945, went to Belgrade to give a lecture at the Yugoslav party university. In an official announcement, Hernandez declared that he was a Titoist: "Although the Cominformists want to belittle us by calling us Titoists, we graciously accept the term because it enables us to differentiate ourselves from those Communists who dance to Moscow's tune."[4] The Spanish Communists who left or who were expelled from the party in 1948 formed a group called "Acción Socialista," whose concepts and ideas resembled those being expounded at the same time by Aldo Cucchi and Valdo Magnani in Italy.

The Policy of "National Appeasement"

After 1949, the PCE, following Stalin's advice, tried to legalize its illegal activity and to increase its cooperation with other political forces, especially in the trade unions. In addition, the party began trying to influence forces outside itself, such as students and intellectuals. The first success of this new concept was the general strike in Barcelona in 1951.

At the Fifth Party Congress, which was held in Prague, Dolores Ibarruri was officially made Secretary General, and several younger officials—including Santiago Carrillo, Fernando Claudin, and Enrico Lister—were made Politburo members. The party still considered itself the representative of the Spanish Republic, and leading Spanish Communists belonged to the Spanish government-in-exile. Such was the case of Vicente Uribe, who belonged to the Negrin government and, later, Santiago Carrillo, who belonged to the exiled Giral government. But it became increasingly difficult to maintain the fiction of a Spanish Republic-in-exile, for Spain itself had changed greatly since 1945. The Civil War generation had suffered much, was tired, and was growing older. New forces which were gaining strength within the legal organizations of Spain had to be approached. After long debate, the new policy of national appeasement was adopted at a Plenum of the Spanish Party leadership at the end of April 1956. The goal of this new policy was to open the party up to younger members and to unite all forces in the struggle against Franco, regardless of their position during the Civil War.

During this internal political discussion of the Spanish Communist Party, Khrushchev gave his secret speech at the Twentieth Party Congress of the CPSU. Carrillo later wrote about his reaction at that time: "At first the ideological reverence for Stalin crumbled, but at the same time, I was happy that we would now be in a position to carry out the changes which I so desired." In addition, Carrillo admitted self-critically that he had not examined and analyzed the problem as Togliatti had done. For Carrillo, the Twentieth Party Congress and Khrushchev's secret speech in February 1956 were a signal "that we had to start thinking with our own heads."[5] In his speech at the Plenum of the Spanish Communist Party Central Committee in August 1956, Carrillo admitted that at times the Spanish Communists had made the mistake of indiscriminately accepting Soviet experiences.

In September 1957, the policy of "national appeasement" was confirmed, and it was decided to name May 5, 1958, "National Appeasement Day" with the slogan, "Against the rise in the cost of living, against the economic policies of the dictatorship, for amnesty for political prisoners and emigrants, for political rights." On the twentieth anniversary of the end of the Civil War, in March 1959, the PCE announced its willingness to form an agreement with other opposition parties for a program of government in the transition period after the fall of the dictatorship. It declared that it was ready and willing to participate in such a government, as long as it guaranteed democratic rights and as long as the PCE could work as an equal partner. The Spanish Communist Party would also tolerate a royal ruler if the people later had the opportunity to chose their own political order—republic or monarchy.[6]

The first, although somewhat careful, dissociation from the CPSU occurred at the Sixth Party Congress of the PCE, held from January 28 to 31, 1960. For the first time, it was declared that, in a favorable international situation, Spain could achieve socialism along a peaceful parliamentary road. The possible existence of a wide coalition would result in less grievous forms of the transition to socialism than those which "had to be grasped at in other countries." Moreover, a majority of the population could help build a new society without serious upset or harsh conflict.[7] At the same time, the party congress decided upon changes in the party structure, declaring that, in contrast to what Bolshevik party doctrines prescribed, a party member did not necessarily have to be a member of a basic organization but could cooperate individually with the party. The term "Politburo" was replaced with "Executive Committee," since the new term better corresponded to Spanish political traditions. Besides the position of secretary general, the position of chairman was introduced: Carrillo was named Secretary General and Dolores Ibarruri became Chairman of the party.

The biography of the new Secretary General, Santiago Carrillo, born in 1916, is much like Tito's, although Carrillo is almost a quarter-century younger than the Yugoslav leader, who was born in 1892. Just as Tito represented the Yugoslav Revolution, the break with Moscow, and an individual Yugoslav road, the independence of the Spanish Communist Party is inseparably connected with Santiago Carrillo. Both leaders were born into the working class, both worked at first in the Social Democratic parties, both had solid international revolutionary experience in very different countries, and both participated in great revolutionary movements.

Santiago Carrillo is the son of a foundry worker. His father played an important role in the Social Democratic Party, was later a representative in Parliament, and even became Deputy Minister in the Republic. At first, Carrillo worked in a print shop and later was an editor's apprentice at the socialist newspaper *El Socialista*. In 1930, at the age of fourteen, he joined the Socialist Youths and was soon elected to the Madrid committee. By the time he was eighteen, Carrillo had already been imprisoned twice and was then named Secretary General of the Socialist Youth Union of Spain. From 1934 to 1936, the Socialist Youth Union grew from 20,000 to 50,000 members. Carrillo belonged to the left wing, was negotiating with the Communist Youth organizations, and prepared the merger of the two youth organizations. The unification of the Socialist and Communist Youth groups of Spain followed the victory of the Popular Front in February of 1936. During a short visit to Moscow at that time, Carrillo met the old Bulgarian Communist Dimitrov, who, as he wrote later, greatly impressed the young Spanish Communist.[8]

On July 18, 1936, as the Franco coup began, Carrillo was in Paris, having just returned from Moscow. From Paris, Carrillo made his way to Madrid, where, on November 6, 1936, he became a member of the defense junta. At that time, Madrid was practically surrounded and, as Carrillo claimed, "we had almost nothing with which we could protect the city." As the situation in Madrid settled, Carrillo again directed the youth organization, the so-called Union of Socialist Youth, first in Madrid and then, from late 1936 until January 1938, in Valencia. It was in Valencia that Carrillo officially joined the Communist Party.

The Moscow show trials of 1936 and 1938 did not shock Carrillo: "I must say that at that time I was convinced that they were in accordance with the truth." He could not imagine that the confessions had been forced from the accused. "I am one of those who actually believed that these people were counter-revolutionary and enemy agents." During the Civil War, Carrillo often met with Togliatti, whom he later described as an extraordinary person and as the most educated and intelligent leader of the entire world Communist movement.

At the end of the Spanish Civil War, Carrillo was in Barcelona. The same day Franco's troops marched into the city, he fled with Togliatti to Paris. He remained in the French capital until September 1939, but, since he possessed no papers, he could not work legally. Carrillo went to Belgium, than he was summoned by Moscow to go to the Soviet Union immediately. In December 1939, he arrived in the Soviet capital where he stayed for six months, acting as Secretary of the Communist Youth International and participating at sessions of the Executive Committee of the Comintern. In addition, while in Moscow, Carrillo repeatedly met with Chou En-lai.

In 1940, by order of the Comintern leadership, Carrillo traveled to the United States, then went to Cuba for six months, and finally to Mexico, where he published a periodical for Latin American youth entitled *Struggle of Youth*. More importantly, however, in Mexico, Carrillo was acting for the Spanish Communist Party and maintained connections with the illegal party organizations in Spain. With a Uruguayan passport, Carrillo then flew to Lisbon, where he met Alvaro Cunhal, the Portuguese Communist Party leader. From Portugal, Carrillo finally went to Algeria illegally.

During this time, Carrillo was for all practical purposes a Comintern representative. Looking back, Carrillo later said he thought that at the very beginning the Communist International had played an important positive role, but with the death of Lenin and the rise of Stalin, the International gradually became an instrument of Soviet politics. Carrillo also later said the predominant centralism was especially harmful to the Comintern. In addition, he claimed that the danger of fascism had been recognized much too late and even once it was recognized, no serious fight against the fascist danger was undertaken. On the other hand, Carrillo approved of the Seventh Congress of the Communist International, in the summer of 1935, because, he claimed, dogmatic positions had been eliminated at that time and an idea for the struggle against fascism had been formulated.

Carrillo remained in Algeria until 1944, and then went to Toulon illegally. He subsequently spent most of his time helping Spanish Communist Party leaders emigrate, until he was named Secretary General at the Sixth Party Congress in 1960.

The First Steps Toward Independence (1961–1967)

One of Carrillo's first steps as the new Secretary General—and at the same time the first sign in the direction of independence—was to publish a self-critical essay in April 1961 in which he candidly admitted that the Spanish Communist Party had made mistakes after the Civil War and that it had maintained false concepts. The necessary interconnection between legal and illegal work had at first been underestimated. It was not until the policy of "national appeasement" that the party began playing a larger role.[9]

Until then, the general policies of the Spanish Communist Party were for the most part in complete agreement with those of the Soviet Union. After Khrushchev's fall in October 1964, however, the party newspaper *Mundo Obrero* did not limit itself to the short reference in *Pravda*, but added its own positive commentary on the overthrown party leader. Moreover, in January 1966, on the occasion of the trial against the Soviet writers Daniel and Sinyavsky, the Spanish Communist Party did not hesitate to express its critical attitude.[10]

More intensive contacts between the PCE and the PCI began in 1966, and in the early part of that year, a Spanish Communist Party delegation under the leadership of Carrillo visited Romania, carried out extensive negotiations with Ceauşescu, and finally produced a common declaration with the Romanian Communist Party leader.

The "Prague Spring": The "Straw which Broke the Camel's Back"

The "Prague Spring of 1968," which the PCE immediately welcomed, had an enormous effect on the independence of the party. Carrillo had been impressed by the great demonstration in Prague on May 1, 1968, which convinced him of the sincerity of the people's enthusiasm. In an article on the same day, Santiago Alvarez, who held the fourth highest position in the party leadership after Dolores Ibarruri, Carrillo, and Lister expressed the Spanish Communists' acceptance of the "Prague Spring" and their desire to make it the model for the future of Spanish development.

In summer 1968, leading Spanish Communists started discussing the danger of a possible military intervention in Czechoslovakia. In Paris, the Spanish Communist Party leaders said to Soviet representatives: "If you attack Czechoslovakia, then for the first time in the history of our relations, we will openly condemn you. It would be better if you helped the Czechoslovak leaders. Let them have their own experience."[11]

On the day of the invasion of Czechoslovakia by Soviet troops, August 21, 1968, Dolores Ibarruri, Santiago Carrillo, and some other Spanish Communist Party leaders were in the Crimea. They immediately went to Moscow, where they held discussions with the Soviet leaders for two days. Carrillo later reported the fear at that time that the Soviet leaders would also order their troops to invade Romania and Yugoslavia. After consultation with the Soviet leaders, Carrillo immediately went to Bucharest where he conferred with the Romanian Communist Party leaders.[12]

In his book *Eurocommunism and the State,* first published in April 1977, Carrillo says that the occupation of Czechoslovakia was very important to the development of the PCE: "For us, for the Communist Party of Spain, the culminating point in winning our independence was the occupation of Czechoslovakia in 1968. The preparations for that operation had been carried out with methods similar to those employed in the famous trials of 1936 which had been exposed at the Twentieth Congress of the Communist Party of the Soviet Union, or similar to those used in the denunciation of Yugoslavia in 1948. That is to say, an unfounded statement was made in this case that Czechoslovakia was on the verge of falling into the hands of capitalism—and with that statement as the starting point, stories were concocted that were light-years away from the truth. This was far more than we could be expected to swallow. Czechoslovakia was the straw which broke the camel's back and which led our parties to say, 'No.' That kind of 'internationalism' had come to an end as far as we were concerned."[13]

After August 21, 1968, the Spanish Communist Party leadership harshly rejected the intervention. Czechoslovakia's problems, they insisted, were to be solved by the Czechoslovak Party and the Czechoslovak people. Carrillo had previously instructed officials of his party in Paris and later wrote: "I was still shaken by what I had experienced. I began my report with: 'I ask that you neither applaud nor protest if you do not agree with me—just listen.' Then I got off the subject and explained how we had reacted. Finally, I said, 'If we were in power and the troops of a socialist country crossed our borders, I would doubtless mobilize the army in order to protect us.' To say something like that right out in the open was something horrible. Many comrades said: 'Aren't we going too far? Aren't you afraid that we'll suddenly wind up in the minority?' I was willing to take that risk. But after a long and detailed discussion our party understood and supported us. And today I can say that as far as the principle of independence is concerned, there is an absolute consensus within our party. But it has cost us an ideological and political war."[14]

The Struggle Against the Pro-Soviet Splinter Group

In contrast to the PCI and to the PCF, the Spanish Communist Party had to undergo a harsh inner-party conflict in order to proceed along its course of independence. An enlarged meeting of the Central Committee of the PCE-in-exile in Paris in October 1968 passed a resolution condemning the occupation of Czechoslovakia by a vote of 66 to 5. After that the opponents took a stand. One of these five officials was Eduardo García, a member of the Party Secretariat. Juan Gómez, elected to the Executive Committee (Politburo) at the Sixth Party Congress in January 1960 and Chairman of the Basque section of the Spanish Communist Party, was also an opponent. Both men were living in the Soviet Union, and, immediately after the meeting, they organized a pro-Soviet faction. As the PCE made more and more progress in the direction of independence, the pro-Soviet faction made greater and greater efforts to combat this tendency.

In the meantime, Carrillo had appeared at the Twelfth Party Congress of the Italian Communist Party in February 1969, speaking out for the autonomy and sovereignty of Czechoslovakia. In March of that same year, with other Spanish Communist Party leaders, Carrillo participated in the Ninth Congress of the League of Communists of Yugoslavia. Then, at the Third World Communist Conference in Moscow in June 1969, the Spanish Communist Party rejected the concept of a unified center of the Communist movement, and mentioned the fact that several important Communist parties, particularly the Chinese Communist Party, had not participated in the world conference. Finally, the PCE was one of the few parties which hesitated in signing the resolution of the world conference.

In July 1969, Juan Gómez was expelled from the party leadership and Eduardo García resigned from his post. Several months later, in an "open letter" to all party members, they demanded that the resolution against the occupation of Czechoslovakia be repealed. After long disputes, at the end of December 1969, both men were expelled from the party as leaders of a factional group. At the beginning of 1970, they distributed a brochure entitled "On the Deformation of the Spanish Communist Party," reproached the PCE leadership for being extremely anti-Soviet and revisionist in domestic policies, and demanded that a new party congress convene at once.

In June and July 1960, several conferences of Spanish Communist emigrants took place throughout Europe, most notably in Moscow and in Prague. The party leadership was supported by an overwhelming majority, which condemned the activities of García and Gómez. In September 1960, at an enlarged Plenum of the Central Committee, it was announced that the pro-Soviet opposition had the support of only one hundred out of 1,000 Spanish Communists in the Soviet Union and sixty out of 10,000 Spanish Communists in France. Moreover, in Mexico and Cuba there was said to be no supporters of the García-Gómez faction whatsoever. At this Plenum, five pro-

Soviet party members, including Enrico Lister, were expelled from the party. Lister had been one of the leading members of the party and, as a former general in the Civil War, he enjoyed much prestige. In October 1978, the pro-Soviet opposition started publishing its own newspaper. Like the official party newspaper, it appeared under the name *Mundo Obrero*, its title was printed in red. It was clear that preparations for the formation of a new pro-Soviet party had started.

In mid-May 1971, at a world peace congress in Budapest, a confrontation erupted between the two invited delegations of the Spanish Communist Party—one representing the official party and the other representing the Lister faction. The delegation of the official Spanish Communist Party left the congress in protest. The seats for the Spanish delegates remained unoccupied, however, since the World Peace Council did not dare to recognize the mini-faction under Lister as the delegation from the Spanish Communist Party.

Lister's mini-faction played a very small role in the further development of Spanish Communism. Its minimal influence was due to its obvious pro-Soviet position. The publication of the Lister faction had declared: "We Spanish Communists emphasize today more strongly than ever before that a positive attitude toward the CPSU and the Soviet Union is the key to proletarian internationalism."[15]

The group received the support of only a very small minority in the Central Committee; what was most important of all was that Dolores Ibarruri clearly supported the road toward independence. Furthermore, the Spanish Communist Party was supported by the Italian, Yugoslav, and Romanian Communist parties, as well as other parties which are today known as Eurocommunist.

Dolores Ibarruri's position was particularly surprising since she had spent almost the entire time since the end of the Civil War in Moscow and had worked closely with Soviet functionaries. Her son was killed during the Battle of Stalingrad and her daughter, Amaya, who attended the Comintern school with me, was married to a Soviet general. In Moscow, it was clearly very difficult for Dolores Ibarruri to decide on this fundamental question according to her own conscience.

The New Course (1969–1973)

During the last decade of the Franco regime, the Spanish Communists had their most important strongholds in the heavily populated industrial centers of Madrid, Barcelona, and Valencia, in the industrial provinces of Catalonia, Asturia, and the Basque region. In these centers, the illegal labor commissions were most active. Besides the labor commissions, the Spanish Communist Party was well represented in many other oppositional bodies in Spain. There were about 600,000 Spaniards living abroad, 25,000 of whom were party members. Most of them (about 10,000) were living in France. The changes in the social structure of the party influenced its programmatic conceptions, and, at the same time, the new conceptions strongly attracted both workers and intellectuals.[16]

Besides the changes within Spain, increasing international contacts also played an important role in the new course of the party. Spanish Communist Party delegations under Carrillo visited the Italian Communist Party in January 1970, the Romanian Communist Party leadership and Ceauşescu in September 1970 and September 1971, and the Swedish Communist Party in April 1971, where they held long discussions with Carl Henrik Hermansson. These contacts encouraged the Spanish Communist leaders to continue an independent road, and often resulted in critical declarations about the Soviet bloc. In July 1970, the Spanish Communists protested Dubček's expulsion from the party and in August 1970 it again criticized the antisocialist character of the occupation. In December 1970, the Spanish Communists commented on the events in Poland, declaring that the uprising was a result of bureaucratic distortion of the building of socialism. The Spanish Communist Party also refused to take part in the Fourteenth Party Congress of the Czechoslovak Communist Party in June 1971.

During a second visit to Romania, at a friendship meeting in the presence of the Romanian Party leader Ceauşescu, Carrillo said, "The Communist movement is not a religion with its own apostles and Popes, its dogma and its unmistakable centers. It is a revolutionary class movement, which has to solve a lot of historically different problems in the fight for socialism, depending on the development and conditions within each country. The desire to reduce this diversity by intervention would be like trying to keep the sun from setting."[17]

During both trips to Romania, as Carrillo described them, contacts with the Chinese Communist Party were apparently also planned. At the end of November 1971 the central organ of the Spanish Communist Party reported that Carrillo and the Secretary of the Catalonian Socialist Unity Party, Lopez Raimundo, signed an agreement in Peking[18] until then the only agreement between a Eurocommunist party and China. In December 1971, the Spanish Party newspaper published Carrillo's detailed report on the Spanish Communist Party delegation's trip to China. This report openly assessed China's development, the role of the Chinese Communist Party, and the significance of the Cultural Revolution. The Chinese Communist leaders had mentioned to Carrillo that their Cultural Revolution was a development peculiar to China and not a universal prescription for Communism.

The Spanish Communist Party delegation was very open-minded about events in China, but at the same time did criticize certain aspects. The Spanish Communist Party delegation rejected, for example, the Chinese thesis that capitalism and fascism had developed in the Soviet Union. The Chinese Communist Party officials responded, "Very well. It is not worth discussing that any further. We do not agree. History will show who is right. But this is no obstacle to our relations." The Spanish delegation was under the impression that the Chinese Communists had difficulty understanding European reality. Nevertheless, Carrillo reported, the Chinese Communist Party leaders always listened carefully, analyzed what they had heard, and took great pains to understand the problems.[19]

In October 1962, the Eighth Party Congress, at which the new course was affirmed, took place. It cited the increasing strength of the inner-Spanish opposition, hailed the significance of the labor commissions, and confirmed the so-called Freedom Pact. An alliance of all opposition forces including Communists, Socialists, Catholics, and bourgeois groups, the Freedom Pact had as its goal the overthrow of Franco. The party congress advocated the autonomy of Catalonia, the Basque region, and Galicia. It stressed the importance of both détente and peaceful coexistence, but also pointed out that these conditions did not presuppose support of the status quo, since the revolutionary process would continue. The European Economic Community was criticized at the congress for being capitalistic and monopolistic, but the Spanish Communists did declare that after the Franco government, Spain's association with the EEC would be entirely possible. In the event of Spanish participation in the EEC, the Spanish Communist Party together with other progressive forces would try to democratize the EEC and turn the Europe of monopoly into a Europe of socialism. Furthermore, Dolores Ibarruri officially became party Chairman, and Santiago Carrillo was named Secretary General of the party.

Foreign policy differences with the Soviet bloc and China played an important role in the further development of the new course. Since the beginning of 1973, some East European countries had been trying to improve their relations with the Franco regime. In February 1973,

East Germany recognized the Franco regime, and in March of the same year the People's Republic of China did as well. The Spanish Communist Party protested against both recognitions because they implied new support for the Franco regime at a time when evidence of decay was clearly emerging. Moreover, the Spanish Communist Party considered it an incomprehensible break in solidarity that they were not consulted about these steps.[20]

In addition, 1973 witnessed a number of significant ideological disputes in which Carrillo and the party theoretician Manuel Azcarate played a decisive role. Along with the usual concepts of Euro-communism—the rejection of a world Communist center, the right to an individual road to socialism, support of a democratic process of transformation and of a pluralistic model of socialism—the Spanish Communist Party added several national features, the most important of which were the Comisiones Obreras. According to Azcarate, these Comisiones Obreras were not simply trade unions, but entirely new forms of a socialist democracy.

In contrast to other Eurocommunist parties, the Spanish Communist Party placed great emphasis on an accurate analysis of the Soviet state. The leading Spanish Communist theoretician Manuel Azcarate declared that as a result of historical developments, the state in the Soviet Union contained strong residual bourgeois and even, at times, feudal characteristics. If a true democracy, a true power of the people were not created there, then there could be danger. Azcarate declared: "We feel that in some aspects of the policy of the socialist states there is a conservative tendency which is the expression of this state interest. . . . That is why we support the socialist states against imperialism but, at the same time, make open and clear criticism when their policy reflects attitudes contrary to the interest of our revolution or the general movement."[21]

These discussions prepared the way for the Spanish Communist Party's draft of a new program in December 1973, which soon became one of the most important documents of Eurocommunism. The draft of the program was transmitted by the Spanish opposition station Radio Independent Spain between December 11 and 18 and, later, on December 26, 1973.

The Spanish Party Program

The Program Manifesto, as it was officially called, comprises about sixty printed pages and is without a doubt the most detailed program of any Western Communist Party. It can be considered, to a certain extent, a counterpart of the Action Program of the Communist Party of Czechoslovakia of April 1968. While the Czechoslovak Action Program outlines the transition from a bureaucratic, dictatorial system to a "socialism with a human face" and describes the aims of this new socialism, the Spanish Communist Party Program proceeds from the situation of a country with developed capitalism and illustrates the necessary forms and stages of transition up to the realization of a pluralistic socialism.

The following aspects of the Program of the Spanish Communist Party are the most important ones for the development of Eurocommunism.

1. The Experiences of the Socialist Development in the East: The Spanish Communist Party Program proceeded from the conviction that the socialist revolution has been successful only in those countries which did not meet the necessary economic prerequirements for a successful social transformation. For this reason, the first successful revolutions faced the task of industrializing a country in a relatively short period while at the same time carrying out the necessary political, social, and cultural revolutionary changes. All this occurred in a situation in which, especially in the Soviet Union, considerable means were necessary for defense. On the basis of these difficult conditions the amalgamation of party and state which took place resulted in authoritarianism, bureaucracy, and the strangulation of democracy. The experiences of these countries are, therefore, certainly of value for all revolutions, but cannot be regarded as a universal model.

2. Socialism in the Industrially Developed Countries: Marxism knows no obligatory model of socialism. Lenin had always stressed the diversity of forms for the transition to socialism in different countries. In light of present reality, it is clear that "the socialism which will succeed in the developed countries will be different in many ways from the socialism which has succeeded in the backward countries." In the developed countries, a successful revolution, by making proper use of the existing means of production and service equipment, would be in a position to guarantee an immediate distribution of goods which meet the needs of the people and which overcomes social inequalities. Besides a high level of material development, democratic traditions, cultural development, and the adherence to individual freedoms are also of decisive importance for the development of socialism. As long as these concerns are upheld, the victory of socialism in the developed countries need not result in the misguided developments which appeared in the Soviet bloc countries. The victory of socialism in the developed countries, with their higher level of production, enables the government to satisfy the needs of the entire population and to reduce underdevelopment in the third world, to fight against pollution, and to support the development of science and culture. Such a situation would meet the preconditions for minimizing the state apparatus as well as for eliminating bureaucracy and the barriers that prevent the population from participating in the administration of society.

The rejection of one-party rule and of a compulsory state philosophy in the Program of the Spanish Communists is based on Marxism and is expressed in the following important declaration:

"None of the masters of Marxism has theoretically propagated the existence of a one party system, still less the concept of a Communist party privileged by law over other parties; nor have they insisted on elevating Marxism to an official state philosophy, of subjugating culture and art to administrative rules, and of the state's monopoly on information. It is also true of the existence of a single model of socialism."

3. The Spanish Communist Party and Internationalism: The PCE declares that specific new forms of socialism must develop. The victory of socialism in one or more capitalist countries will bring more highly developed forms of socialism with it and, by so doing, will raise the existing socialist systems to a "higher, more developed level." Socialism cannot be forced upon other countries from without—it is based on the solution of internal problems of each country. For this reason it is necessary that the Communist Party be closely linked with the population in the concrete situation of that particular country. Moreover, the Communist Party has to be completely independent from every other state, even from those which are socialist.

A new form of internationalism, a "unity in diversity," is necessary for the world Communist movement. This includes the respect for existing differences of opinion, the acceptance of the diversity of the forms and models of socialism, the elimination of pressure or intervention from outside as well as the broadest possible democracy within the world Communist movement.

4. The Spanish Communist Party and Europe: The countries of Europe have to find a common answer to many economic and political problems. Therefore, a better coordination on the European level must be established in order to democratize the European Economic Community. The PCE favors a Europe which makes its own contribution to freedom, which overcomes the division of the continent into military blocs, and which eliminates the military bases of foreign blocs. This Europe must be capable of developing equal relations with both the USA and the USSR. Spain's foreign policy must be peaceful, independent, and sovereign—Spain should not belong to any military blocs.

The PCE advocates coordination among the Communist parties of Europe as well as cooperation among Communist and socialist parties and the Christian and other democratic organizations of Europe. This is especially important because in the developed countries of Europe a form of socialism will prevail which respects the value of individual and collective freedoms and which strives for a democratic and decentralized socialism with party pluralism, trade-union autonomy, and religious freedom.

5. The Transitional Phase: The transitional phase from capitalism to socialism is considered a "period of political and social democracy." According to the Spanish Communists, this stage must introduce political, economic, social, and cultural transformations which create the preconditions for a later transition to socialism. The program summarizes in thirty-one points the problems which should be solved in this transitional phase.

In the economic sphere, the PCE strives for the nationalization of large monopolistic enterprises, private banks, and insurance companies, division of large landholdings and the transfer of land among those who work on it—partially for individual farmers and partially for agricultural cooperatives. Nationalization limits the power of monopolistic capital and the large landowner, while protecting the interests of the small stockholders and small proprietors of the non-monopolistic middle class. Democratic planning is foreseen as the economic basis of this transitional phase. On one hand, it should guarantee the amount of centralization which is necessary for the overall goals of economic development and, on the other hand, it should, through broad economic regionalization, make allowances for local conditions. The management of the nationalized enterprises is controlled and directly influenced by commissions democratically elected by the employees.

Besides guaranteeing democratic freedoms, universal suffrage, the independence of the judicial process, and a reform of the penal code, the transitional phase should especially emphasize the realization of the right of self-determination of Catalonia, the Basque region, and Galicia. This transitional phase should also democratize education, raise the general level of education, and interconnect theoretical and vocational education. The faculty, students, and parents should participate in the administration of educational institutions and help implement new teaching methods suited to the demands of a modern society.

6. The Significance of the Transitional Period: In the stage of "political and social democracy," the large majority of today's middle-class proprietors will remain; this middle class with its social, political, and ideological characteristics, will have a considerable influence on the society. Within the framework of political and social democracy there is a very broad alliance between the working class and the middle classes. Any such alliance would require mutual concessions. The working class would be required to respect nonmonopolistic ownership and in exchange would receive the support of other social forces in eliminating monopolistic property. The transition to socialism can be undertaken only to the extent that productive forces have developed and the supply of goods and services has increased.

Thus the preliminary political and social democratization should create the most favorable economic preconditions for socialism. The democratic character of this transformation, expected to prevent the danger of bureaucratization, is politically significant.

Without such a transitional period, during the changeover to socialism, scarcity and supply problems or even political resistance could cause the new power "to employ stricter compulsory measures, to reduce democratic freedom and to establish a bureaucratic apparatus," all of which could result in crises and a dangerous development. It is therefore of fundamental importance that the development toward socialism be carried out in forms which are comprehensible to the large majority of people, which receive the largest possible societal consent and rely on the participation and responsibility of the majority of the people.

7. A Democratic Multiparty Model of Socialism: A democratic model of socialism should correspond to the democratic character of the transformation. In contrast to backward countries, in which the socialist revolutions took place, in industrialized countries a great number of other political forces—Social Democracy, the Catholic movement, and other democratic organizations—rightly demand to participate in the building of a new socialist society. All these forces and trends striving toward socialism from different ideological positions cannot possibly be united in a single party. As a result, it is inevitable that different parties should exist and collaborate as such in a socialist society. "One must strive for the model of a democratic multiparty socialism which not only maintains all preceding levels of acquired personal and political freedoms, but which elevates them to an even higher level." Moreover, there will also be differing philosophical and ideological currents; consequently, a socialist society cannot have an official philosophy. In socialism, the ideological struggles even among different socialist forces with similar viewpoints will be carried out freely and openly.

8. The Change in the Communist Party: Proceeding from the transitional stage and the pluralistic multiparty system, the program finally conceives of a change in the Communist Party. The party's main task is to prevent obsolete theses from hardening into paralyzing dogma and to overcome whatever rigidity and dogmatism remain from the past. It has to eliminate the concept of Communism as a type of church with its gods and its dogma, a type of closed sect, protectress of static and inflexible truths. The Communists must be rooted with their own people and not be isolated in enclaves.

The program prescribes striving for a new political group beyond the party, a group which could include all socialist factions. However, these factions would not have to give up their respective ideological characteristics, their particular outward forms, their independence and activity. Such a "new political formation" could be a true alternative to capitalist society and a guarantee for the sustained democratic multiparty character of a future socialist society, a political reality, as it were, of the alliance of labor and cultural forces.

Significantly, the Spanish Communist Party[22] not only proclaims transitional forms and models, but also explains them historically and ideologically. This has been especially true of the differences between the transition toward socialism in the backward countries and in highly developed capitalist countries and for the period of "political and social democracy." Moreover, it is the first document of its kind to warn that undertaking the transition to socialism too rashly could cause specific difficulties and dangers. The references to the party and to a future "new political formation" are also significant.

The Legalization of the Spanish Communist Party

As the Franco regime gradually dissolved, the PCE developed from an illegal to a legally active party and engaged in more and more disputes with the Soviet bloc.

The Spanish Communist Party program of December 1973 was neither mentioned nor criticized in the Soviet bloc. Instead, the Soviet leadership attacked the Spanish Politburo member Manuel Azcarate in a ten-page article in the publication *Party Life* in February 1974. Of course, the attack was not directed at Azcarate but at the Spanish Communist Party and its new party program. By attacking Azcarate, Moscow was hoping to split or at least to sow discord within the party. Under the title "In Response to an Article of the Leading Representative of the Spanish Communist Party, M. Azcarate" (the word "Comrade" was missing), the Soviet Party publication accused the co-author of the party program of the PCE of having debased the essence of Soviet foreign policy and of having "arbitrarily" declared that there was a difference between the interests of the socialist states and those of the revolutionary movement. The party publication also objected to the demand for a democratic socialist Europe without connection to the existing "world socialist system," i.e. the Warsaw Pact. Finally, Azcarate was accused of having incorrectly portrayed Soviet democracy.[23]

Only the weakness of the Lister group, which had since become a party, led the Soviet leadership to yield. Thus, in October 1974, negotiations again took place between a delegation of the PCE under the direction of Dolores Ibarruri and Santiago Carrillo, Soviet Politburo members Suslov and Pelsche, and Central Committee Secretariat member and Politburo candidate Ponomaryov. The resulting communiqué declared that both sides based their relations on "respect for equality and independence as well as nonintervention in internal affairs." In addition, both sides condemned all "schismatic activity aimed at undermining the unity of the fraternal party's ranks."[24] However, this declaration did not clarify all differences.

The PCE's increasing independence was expressed not only in relation to the East but also in relation to the pro-Soviet Communist parties in the West, especially the Portuguese Communist Party under the leadership of Alvaro Cunhal. After the fall of the Caetano regime in April 1974, the Portuguese Communist Party had entered upon a course increasingly inconsistent with that of the PCI and even more so with that of the PCE. Carrillo repeatedly took advantage of the opportunity to refer to the differences between the developments in Portugal and in Spain. As early as June 1974, Carrillo declared that the Spanish Communists were striving for a restoration of democracy, not a military rebellion, as in Portugal.[25] In April 1975, he added that in Portugal the army had taken over power in the country, whereas in Spain the political forces would be decisive. Moreover, a future democratic regime in Spain would be civil and not military. In Spain, all parties would be represented, and in the future, general elections would decide Spain's further development. "If the Spanish Communist Party receives 10 percent of the vote we will be ready to enter the government just as we will be ready to struggle in the opposition."[26]

The New Attitude Toward Europe and the United States

In 1975 and 1976, as the decay of the Franco regime accelerated and the PCE anticipated legitimacy, it frequently referred to new aspects of foreign policy. During these two years, it repeatedly stressed that Europe's growing interdependence was an irreversible process and, consequently, it was important not to oppose the European Economic Community, but to democratize it—especially now that 60 percent of Spain's foreign trade was with the EEC.

Aside from the European commitment, in July 1975 the Spanish Communists announced that they did not want "to make an enemy of such a strong country as the United States." The PCE, declared Carrillo, was still against NATO membership, and was acting on the assumption that one day the American military bases in Spain would be given up. But this could only happen as a result of détente policy and simultaneous dissolution of military blocs in both East and West. The United States withdrawal of its strongholds in Spain, for example, would be conceivable only when "the Soviets withdraw from Czechoslovakia."[27]

The new foreign policy positions were confirmed by Manuel Azcarate at the end of 1975. In a detailed essay, he declared that the Spanish Communists did support a great number of the USSR's foreign-policy positions, but at the same time he insisted on an individual political line which on several points did not correspond with Soviet policies. The Spanish Communists, he claimed, advocated Spain's participation, as a democratic state, in the EEC as well as the political unity of Western Europe, if, as a result, the strength of the masses and of the working class could be enhanced. These declarations are all the more important in light of the fact that the Soviet Union later accused Carrillo of having advocated Spain's incorporation into NATO. There is not a single declaration of any Spanish Communist to that effect.

In July 1976, Carrillo further clarified his position on the United States bases in Spain: "The Communists are against the existence of foreign military strongholds in Spain, just as they are against the existence of foreign strongholds in all countries of the world, including the socialist countries. Foreign military bases must disappear simultaneously from the East and the West and this should be achieved by means of international negotiations." For that reason, declared Carrillo, the PCE was not totally against the presence of American military bases in Spain. "We find it intolerable," added Carrillo, "when Kissinger takes advantage of this presence in order to have the last say in our country." Moreover, Carrillo declared that the PCE was in favor of Spain's entering the European Economic Community if democratic rules prevailed. Until then, according to Carrillo, Spain would always be at a disadvantage when trying to cooperate in the European Economic Community. The European left would have to fight constantly to transform the European Economic Community from multinational bodies and governments into a true community of the people.[28] At his first, still illegal, press conference in Madrid in December 1976, Carrillo declared: "We are for nonalignment and against Spain's entrance into NATO as well as into the Warsaw Pact."[29]

The Spanish Communist Party after Legalization

By the beginning of 1977, the transition from dictatorship to democracy could no longer be stopped. At his first press conference in Madrid in December 1976, Carrillo already talked about the forthcoming elections. The Communist Party, he declared, would prefer a wide alliance of the left in the form of a democratic front. Nevertheless, should this not succeed, it would run as an individual party.[30]

Despite the fact that it was technically still illegal, the Spanish Communist Party appeared in public more and more often. The PCE made it clear that it advocated a federalist state with a structure not unlike its own. Besides the Spanish Communist Party there were the United Socialist Party of Catalonia (PUSC), along with the Communist parties in Galicia, the Basque region, Valencia, and even in the Canary Islands.[31] After the illegal Madrid press conference in December 1976, Carrillo was arrested along with seven prominent officials of the Spanish Communist Party. A week later all those arrested were released. Apparently surprised, Carrillo stated: "I must admit that the Spanish government showed a great deal of understanding for the realities of that time and for the fundamental tendencies of the political development in Spain." His release, claimed Carrillo, had been a step along the road to the eventual legalization of the Spanish Communist Party. Moreover, he declared that the Spanish Communist Party was planning to convene a plenary session of its Central Committee in Madrid.[32]

On February 11, 1977, the Spanish Communist Party formally requested legal recognition as a party. Two days later, it was announced that Dolores Ibarruri, known as "La Pasionaria," was returning to Spain from the Soviet Union. Two thousand Spanish Communists living in the Soviet Union had already returned to their country since Franco's death and another two thousand were waiting for their entry visas.[33]

The Madrid meeting of Eurocommunists Marchais, Berlinguer, and Carrillo in early March 1977 provided the final impetus for legalizing the Spanish Communist Party. And in March 1977, the Spanish Communist Party—although still not officially legalized—started putting up lists of candidates in many provinces. Dolores Ibarruri headed the list of candidates for the mining provinces in Asturia, and Santiago Carrillo and Marcelino Camachio, the leader of the Comisiones Obreras (the pro-Communist trade unions) occupied the first and second positions, respectively, on the Communist lists of candidates in Madrid. On April 12, 1977, the Spanish Communist Party was finally legalized. Carrillo declared it had been a decision of elementary justice which was long overdue. From then on in Spain, it was no longer a crime to be a Communist. No one, said Carrillo, will be able to threaten us or to attempt to terrorize those who demonstrate for our party. Carrillo favored a new constitution, but admitted that a long struggle would be necessary before "democracy becomes a tree so strong that no bolt of lightning can destroy it."[34]

The legalization of the Communist Party was welcomed by a majority of the population. The Socialists declared that without the legalization of the Communist Party, Spain's democratization would have been very difficult. The Christian Democrats described the decision as completely just and correct. Only the rightist parties objected. A public-opinion poll in Spain showed that 55 percent of those polled were in favor of legalization and only 12 percent were opposed, while 22 percent were undecided and 11 percent gave no answer.[35]

In May 1977, Dolores Ibarruri returned from Moscow. On June 15, 1977, the Spanish Communist Party received 9.4 percent of the vote in the first free elections and, as a result, was represented by nineteen deputies in the Spanish Parliament. Then, at the beginning of July 1977, the secret station Radio Independent Spain was closed down. In the beginning of November 1977, the founding congresses of the Communist Party of the Basque region (Euzkadi) and of the United Socialist Party of Catalonia (PSUC) took place. For the first time in the history of Communism in Spain, the leading functionary was elected not by a show of hands but by secret ballot. Lerchundi was elected Secretary General of the Communist Party of the Basque region, and the former leader and resistance fighter of long standing, Ormazabal, received the position of Chairman of the party. In the United Socialist Party of Catalonia (PSUC), whose membership already at that time numbered more than 40,000, making it the strongest party in Catalonia, Gutiérrez became the new Secretary General, while the former leader, Lopez Raimundo, became the new Chairman. The Eurocommunist course of both groups was confirmed at their respective party congresses.

In contrast to the other Eurocommunist parties, the Spanish Communist Party's road to a new course is marked by the following peculiarities:

1. The Spanish Communist Party underwent its transformation while still illegal and thus did not have the legal possibilities that all the other Eurocommunist parties (with the exception of the Greek Communist Party) had for their new courses.

2. During the transition, the PCE had to contend for years with a pro-Soviet faction. This meant some difficulties but at the same time, with all the pro-Soviet elements excluded from the party, its development was somewhat facilitated.

3. The independence and new course of the Spanish Communist Party occurred later than in the Italian Communist Party. The first signs were apparent in the mid-sixties and the decisive event for the new road was the "Prague Spring" and the military intervention of the Warsaw Pact countries in Czechoslovakia.

4. During the process of setting a new course, the Spanish Communists were able to formulate a detailed Party Program, which is one of the most important documents of Eurocommunism.

5. In the course of acquiring independence, the Spanish Com-

munists dealt more with theoretical problems than did most other Eurocommunists. In contrast to the Italian Communists, however, the Spanish Communists had no special forerunner (such as Gramsci in Italy) on whom to rely.

6. The process of acquiring independence progressed more thoroughly than in almost any other Eurocommunist party. In one respect, the Spanish Communist Party stands at the head of Eurocommunism.

The Spanish Communist Party has however scarcely begun a self-critical examination of its history, which is essential to any growth in a Eurocommunist direction.

14

Eurocommunist Tendencies in Other European Countries

In addition to the three most important Eurocommunist parties in Western Europe—the Italian, Spanish, and French Communist parties—there are several other Communist parties which can be considered Eurocommunist, some of which are divided into a Eurocommunist and a pro-Soviet wing. These parties usually have little influence in their own countries. But since this book is not meant to concentrate on powerful influences in politics but, rather, attempts to consider Eurocommunism as a trend, a brief discussion on Eurocommunist tendencies in the smaller Communist parties seems justified.

Denmark: The Eurocommunist "Socialist People's Party" and the Pro-Soviet Communists

The majority of Danish Communists favored independence as early as 1957–1958. They left the existing Danish Communist Party and, with the formation of the Socialist People's Party, introduced a political direction which can today be considered Eurocommunist. The Socialist People's Party founded at that time was the first Eurocommunist attempt in Northern Europe. Today it has one representative in the European Parliament in the faction of "Communists and Sympathizers."

As was the case with other European Communist parties, the experiences of Stalinism and the hope of de-Stalinization after the

239

Twentieth Party Congress of the CPSU (1956) were the starting points for independent development in the Danish party. The active participation of Danish Communists in the resistance during the German occupation—in which the party Chairman, Aksel Larsen, played an important role—led to a considerable increase in popularity for the Danish Communist Party after the war. In 1945, the Danish Communist Party received 12.5 percent of the votes cast, and two Danish Communists, Aksel Larsen and Alfred Jensen, entered the government, Larsen as a minister without a portfolio in the cabinet and Jensen as Minister of Transportation.

The period of the cold war during which Communists in the West had to justify all developments in the Soviet Union and in Eastern Europe resulted in a drastic reduction in the influence of the Danish Communist Party. In 1947, it received only 6.8 percent of the vote; in 1953, the number fell to 4.3 percent and, finally, after the defeat of the Hungarian Revolution, the Communists in Denmark received only 3.1 percent of the vote in 1957.

After the Twentieth Party Congress of the CPSU and Khrushchev's secret speech, more and more members favored an independent road in accordance with the Italian model. At an extraordinary party congress of the Danish Communist Party in January 1957, a new course seemed to be developing. For the first time the party congress advocated the building of socialism on the basis of Danish democratic traditions. Nevertheless, there was considerable dispute over the realization of the party resolutions of January 1957. The reformers, led by the party Chairman, Aksel Larsen, were confronted by strong Stalinist forces. As a result, Larsen could no longer write freely for the party organ *Land og Folk*. On one occasion, the Stalinist forces refused to allow Larsen to publish an article in which he criticized the arrest of Imre Nagy. The conflict between the reformers and the Stalinists grew stronger after Larsen participated in the Congress of the League of Communists of Yugoslavia in March 1958. Aksel Larsen did criticize several aspects of the Yugoslav goals at a meeting of the Danish Central Committee at the end of May 1958, but strongly objected to condemning the Yugoslav Communists as Moscow had wanted.

Nevertheless, Larsen and his friends remained in the minority, for the majority of the party leadership condemned the Yugoslav Communists for being "revisionists." Larsen and his reform supporters' position on Yugoslavia became the test of their own political leanings. Declarations from Moscow, wrote Larsen in July 1958, were not "papal bulls of excommunication which all are to follow if they are not to be thrown into the darkness of hell."[1]

In the summer of 1958, Larsen formulated a detailed memorandum in which he described conceptions of the future development of the Danish Communist Party. Under the title "Where Do We Stand? What Is to Be Done?" Larsen declared that, despite the Twentieth Party Congress of the CPSU, uncritical traditions still prevailed and the Danish Communist Party habitually approved of everything originating in the Soviet Union. In his memorandum Larsen wrote, "We must free ourselves, without the slightest loss of international solidarity, from the tradition of mechanically or automatically saying amen to everything which comes from the socialist countries." Larsen claimed that Danish Communists were forgetting that they were fighting for socialism in Denmark. It was high time, he claimed, that the Danish Communist Party made democratic, independent policies in order to gain the trust of the Danish workers. According to Larsen, the tendency to rely on dogma instead of facing reality was still prevalent. The organization, working methods, and form of party leadership, claimed Larsen, had to be reanalyzed. The party was an active organism but not a military organization. Moreover, declared Larsen, one should not shun theoretical or political dispute in the name of "unity." For that reason, the party statutes had to be democratized; up to that time, the statutes were very similar to the Soviet Communist Party statutes. Furthermore, Larsen insisted that it was important to eliminate centralism and to see that the leading organs made regular reports to the members and that the leadership of the party be elected democratically. Most of all, in his memorandum, Larsen demanded greater independence from the Soviet Union: "We know that the most important propagandist weapon against us is the slogan that we are not a Danish, not an independent party, but that the Danish Communists receive their orders from Moscow. It is no use for us to insist in the most vehement way that we are a Danish and an independent party. Even the best contributions to Danish internal and foreign policy do not guarantee that we will earn the confidence of the Danish people, as long as most of them think and say: 'Yes, but even then—we cannot trust the Communists, for they fetch all their thoughts, ideas and politics from Moscow.' But we are responsible for that ourselves. Our own behavior makes it easier for our opponents to make us suspect."[2]

After long internal disputes in the Central Committee, on August 28, 1958, the party newspaper, *Land og Folk*, finally published Aksel

Larsen's memorandum, which played a role in the history of Eurocommunism similar to the one played by Togliatti's memorandum in June 1956. Soon thereafter, a majority of the party leadership organized a campaign against its own chairman. Although Larsen found more and more supporters, including well-known party officials such as the prominent Danish trade union leaders Willy Brauer and Carlo Hermansen, he was prevented from speaking to the party organizations of the three largest provincial towns.

At the extraordinary Twentieth Party Congress of the Danish Communist Party, which took place in Copenhagen-Christiansborg from October 31 to November 2, 1958, the Danish Stalinists received support from Moscow.

Piotr Pospelov, a member of the Soviet leadership in charge of international Communist matters, attended the congress. Larsen was removed from the party chairmanship and was succeeded by Knut Jespersen. Shortly thereafter, Larsen was expelled from the party, and in a major campaign, the Danish Communist Party lost some of its best trade-union officials, communal deputies, and representatives in other organizations. In contrast to what happened after the expulsion of officials from other parties in the world Communist movement, the members who left or who were expelled did not remain inactive. In many places they founded "socialist unions" as the basis for a new party, independent from Moscow.

In November 1958, seventy-six representatives of former Communist Party organizations were already meeting to prepare the founding of a new Socialist People's Party of Denmark. Leading trade-union officials called for support of the new party and Aksel Larsen was asked to represent the new party temporarily in the Danish Parliament. A central action committee was elected to found the new party. In its first announcement it declared that the Social Democratic Party had lost sight of its goal and that the Danish Communist Party was isolated and had no influence on the Danish population. It was important, the committee claimed, to strengthen the working people's trust in socialism and to make the transition to socialism in Denmark a task of the Danish people. According to the declaration, the one-party system was a product of the particular Soviet development, while in Denmark, on the other hand, the transition to socialism could and must be carried out with the cooperation of the Parliament and the maintenance of a multiparty system.

On February 15, 1959, in the presence of 174 delegates, the Socialist People's Party was founded in Hvidovre near Copenhagen. One day later, the new Danish party, since then referred to by its initials SF, introduced itself in a public assembly. Before almost 4,000 listeners, Mogens Fog gave a programmatic speech in which he once again clearly explained the founding and goals of the new party.

At the beginning, former Communists, especially those who had supported Larsen during the conflict with the Stalinists, formed the core of the Socialist People's Party (SF). But the party soon drew many members from the left wings of the Social Democratic Party and from pacifist circles. The first edition of the party newspaper, *SF Bladet*, with a circulation of 15,000, appeared on May 1, 1959. The first ordinary party congress took place from June 5 to 7, 1959, adopting new statutes and a new program. In the new party statutes an attempt was made to ensure inner-party democracy through a democratic organization. Of the twenty-five members of the National Committee, a maximum of six party functionaries could be directly or indirectly financially dependent upon the party. At the most, three of the nine members of the Executive Committee could be salaried party functionaries. The party program expressed the attitude that Denmark could achieve socialism in a peaceful way, with a multiparty system and based on the Parliament. It declared, however, that parliamentarianism was not enough, that it was necessary to have democratic activity outside the Parliament, and that workers and employees had to have decisive influence in factories and industries.

Despite its limited time to prepare, the newly founded SF was able to muster nearly 150,000 votes (6.1 percent) in the parliamentary election of November 1960, enabling it to send eleven deputies to the Parliament. The pro-Soviet Communist Party received only 1.1 percent of the vote and, as a result, it was no longer represented in Parliament. An analysis of the election showed that of the 150,000 votes for the SF, 52 percent came from former Social Democratic voters, almost 30 percent from Communists, and the rest from supporters of leftist democratic or pacifist organizations. A great number of those who voted for the SF were young people who belonged to the antinuclear-weapon movement.

After heated debate at its Third Party Congress in October 1963, the SF finally adopted a program expressing ideas which are today considered fundamental theses of Eurocommunism. The program declared, for example, that the social and welfare measures within a capitalist society were not solving Denmark's economic, political, and social problems. As a result, it declared, the SF advocated the establishment of a socialist society in Denmark, in which respect for "fundamental human rights," both during the process of transformation and in the future socialist society, had to be maintained. Socialism in Denmark had to be based on fundamental civil rights: freedom of opinion, freedom of speech, freedom of mobility, equality before the law, respect for personal integrity, protection against arbitrary arrest, economic security, and the right to education, to employment, and to lodgings. In order to counter the menace of bureaucratization, the program rejected the concepts of the dictatorship of the proletariat and the one-party system. Besides separating itself from Soviet Communism, the SF also rejected the social democratic ideas according to which the transformation of society could essentially be achieved through a legislative process. The program of the SF stressed that a popular majority had to participate actively in the socialist transformation of society. The socialist revolution could be carried out in a peaceful manner in accordance with the historical and social conditions and the parliamentary traditions of the country. According to the program, the success of the revolution depends upon an active participation of the overwhelming majority of the people involved in creating new institutions and democraticizing the old ones. For that reason it was necessary to extend current political democracy to include economic and industrial democracy and thus guarantee the people's right of economic decision-making and the employees' right to participate in determining management policies.

In an important article, Gert Petersen, a close associate of Aksel Larsen, spoke of the SP's position on Marxism. He claimed it was necessary "to view Marxism in light of the times and to apply its theoretical achievements to Danish reality on the basis of analysis." The Socialist People's Party, Petersen declared, rejected any sort of "holy idols" and favored the critical examination of all phenomena. Critical examination of both capitalist and socialist countries was valid, especially "since an analysis of the facts shows that socialism does not exist anywhere in a highly developed form."[3]

The interrelation between concrete reforms and long-term socialist goals had to be reexamined, declared Petersen. In striving for socialist goals, he claimed, one should not neglect the present task of improving the workers' standard of living. As a result, the SF advocated democratization of management in business enterprises and increased worker participation in the decision-making process. The SF rejected the idea of propagandistic declarations in Parliament and thus did not introduce any laws which might not be feasible. It pursued a practical policy to its outermost limits. Such a realistic policy, claimed the SF, was the starting point for new reasonable demands.

The opposition policies of the SF were by no means destructive, but rather were aimed at persuading the Social Democrats to end their cooperation with bourgeois or rightist parties. The SF's main goal was to enable a majority within the labor movement to pave the way for important internal political reforms.

These principles proved attractive to voters. During the election in autumn 1966, the SF received 10.9 percent of the votes and twenty seats in Parliament, while the old Danish Communist Party received barely 0.8 percent of the vote and remained without a representative in the Danish Parliament. In Copenhagen, the SF was even the second strongest party. In addition, after the elections of 1964, the Social Democrats could no longer rule without the support of Socialist People's Party representatives. As a result, the SF succeeded in implementing some of its aims. The left wing of the party, however, objected to the idea of sharing responsibility with the Social Democrats. Under pressure from these leftists, including Karl Moltke and Willy Brauer, an extraordinary party congress was convened for June 15 to 17, 1967.

Moscow and East Berlin regarded these difficulties as a favorable opportunity. The central organ of the SED, *Neues Deutschland*, wrote: "In light of the situation, the leftist forces must seize control!"[4] Despite the support it received from the Soviet bloc (the leftists in the SF should have wondered about the intentions behind the support offered), the leftists continued their factional activity and, on December 15, 1967, six of the twenty deputies of the Socialist People's Party in Parliament voted against a joint proposal of the SF and the Social Democrats. At the congress which followed immediately thereafter, the party was split. Of the 159 delegates, seventy-six leftists, including six of a total of twenty delegates to Parliament, left the assembly. On December 17, 1967, these six representatives founded the Left Socialist Party.

Although since 1968, the three parties to the left of the Social Democrats have no longer played essential roles in the political arena of Denmark. The split was a hard blow for Aksel Larsen, who resigned as Chairman at the congress in December 1968. His close associate, Sigurd Oemann, became his successor. At the end of January 1972, Aksel Larsen, who had often been compared with Tito, died. He had successfully resisted Soviet domination.

With its new independent program, the Socialist People's Party of Denmark became a model for the Communists of Europe striving for independence, especially those in the Scandinavian countries. In

1961, a Socialist People's Party was formed in Norway based on the Danish model and, as of 1964, similar independent tendencies could be seen among the Swedish Communists.

Denmark: Election Results and Parliamentary Representation since 1945

In 1958, the Communist Party of Denmark split, and in the spring of 1959 the Socialist People's Party was formed following a line independent of Moscow, close to Eurocommunism. In 1967, the Left Socialist Party, a third Marxist party, was founded.

Date	Party	Votes	% of total	Deputies	Out of
October 1945	CP	255,236	12.4	18	149
October 1947	CP	141,094	6.8	9	150
September 1950	CP	94,495	4.6	7	151
April 1953	CP	98,940	4.8	7	151
September 1953	CP	93,824	4.3	8	179
May 1957	CP	72,312	3.1	6	179
November 1960	CP	27,298	1.1	0	179
	SPP	149,440	6.1	11	179
September 1964	CP	32,290	1.3	0	179
	SPP	151,697	6	10	179
October 1966	CP	21,536	0.8	0	179
	SPP	304,243	10.9	20	179
January 1968	CP	29,824	1	0	179
	SPP	174,506	6.1	11	179
	LSP	56,897	2	4	179
September 1971	CP	39,564	1.4	0	179
	SPP	262,756	9.1	17	179
	LSP	45,979	1.6	0	179
December 1973	CP	110,715	3.6	6	179
	SPP	183,522	6	11	179
	LSP	44,843	1.5	0	179
January 1974	CP	127,952	4.2	7	179
	SPP	150,985	4.9	9	179
	LSP	62,806	2.1	4	179
February 1977	CP	114,022	3.7	7	179
	SPP	120,357	3.8	7	179
	LSP	83,667	2.7	5	179

CP—Communist Party (pro-Soviet)
SPP—Socialist People's Party
LSP—Left Socialist Party

Sweden: The Tensions Between Eurocommunists and Stalinists Lead to a Split

The Swedish Communist contribution to the development of Euro-communism is often underestimated. One cannot overlook the fact that in the early and mid-sixties, the Swedish Communists, together with the Italian Communists, were in the vanguard of the new, independent course.

The Swedish Communists had been experiencing a steady decline in influence since 1945. Although the Swedish Communist Party received 10.5 percent of the vote in the national election in 1944, in the following fifteen years, under the leadership of the Stalinist Hilding Hagberg, the rate fell to 6.3 percent in September 1948, 4.3 percent in 1952 and, finally, 3.8 percent in the fall of 1962. The iron hand of the Stalinist party leader Hilding Hagberg was so strong that the Swedish Communists hardly felt the effects of the Twentieth Party Congress of the CPSU and the beginning of de-Stalinization. The delayed reaction was due in part to the fact that the Swedish Communist Party, like several other Scandinavian parties, was under the tutelage of the East German SED; Swedish party functionaries were even trained at the SED party school at Bad Doberan in East Germany.

In the early sixties, criticism within the party became more pronounced. The Party newspaper, *Ny Dag*, was compelled to publish critical views. One reader complained: "We faithfully defend everything which happens in the socialist camp and only take one-sided positions on international affairs." Other readers disagreed that the Hungarian Revolution of 1956 had been called a "counter-revolution" and complained that in formulating its policies, the Swedish Communist Party overlooked the peculiarities of its own country. The dictatorial party structure and the authoritative methods of leadership were criticized with increased fervor. The erection of the Berlin wall in 1961 had stronger effects on Sweden than on any other Western European country. Even *Ny Dag* had to admit: "No event or measures in the socialist countries in recent years have evoked such a negative reaction among Swedish workers as the Berlin wall." The call for the complete renovation of the party grew stronger. In the middle of the ever increasing discussions Hilding Hagberg resigned as the leader of the Swedish Communist Party.[5]

The turning point for the Swedish Communists came at the Twentieth Party Congress of the Swedish Communist Party in January 1964. Carl-Henrik Hermansson, one of the most important forerunners of Eurocommunism in Europe, took over Hagberg's post as party leader. Although Stalinist dogmatists still sat in the Executive Committee of the party, Hermansson was soon able to implement his own popular ideas among party members. The Stalinists were increasingly put on the defensive. At his first press conference as new party Chairman, Hermansson protested the erection of the Berlin wall and called for an end to the training of Swedish Communist Party functionaries at Bad Doberan in East Germany. During the campaign in September 1964, Hermansson protested on radio and television against the Soviet invasion of Finland in 1939, the Prague coup in 1948, the suppression of the workers' uprising in East Germany in June 1953, and the Soviet intervention during the Hungarian Revolution in November 1956. He said: "We Swedish Communists do not consider the conditions in other countries such as the Soviet Union or the so-called people's democracies at all ideal for our party. We are not striving for that type of system. The state of affairs in those countries does not point the way for the Swedish Communists.[6]

In its critical comments on Khrushchev's downfall in mid-October 1964, the Swedish Communist Party went further than any other party, including the Italian Communist Party. Hermansson did not limit himself to a criticism of the methods of removal, but claimed outright that the removal itself was in defiance of the Soviet party statutes and the Soviet Constitution. Hermansson also suggested to the Soviet leadership that it follow the example of the democratic methods of the Scandinavian countries or of England in removing people of such great importance.[7]

Shortly thereafter, in January 1965, Carl-Henrik Hermansson became the first European Communist Party leader to reject the term "proletarian internationalism" (understood as subordination to the Soviet Union), favoring instead the term "international solidarity," which has become popular among Eurocommunists. He declared that international cooperation should not be limited to Communists: "We do not want to cooperate solely with Communist parties, but with national liberation movements, leftist Social Democratic and socialist parties or even social democratic parties, if possible.[8]

In an interview in April 1965, Hermansson clearly stated his ideas about the renovation of the party and its goals. According to the party Chairman, the Swedish Communists were to support social reform policies and, at the same time, demand structural reforms which would lead to changes in the economic and political system. This would only work, however, if the party itself underwent a socialist renovation. The party should be responsive to present-day reality. Communist parties could not be closed organizations, he insisted, but had to remain open to the entire labor movement and all true popular movements.[9]

Finally, on May 1, 1965, Hermansson became the first European Communist Party leader to proclaim a pluralistic model of socialism. He was also the first to declare that his Communist Party would honor the vote of the majority in a socialist society: "When we are asked if, after acceding to the government by parliamentary means, our party would comply with the rules and abdicate in the event of a vote of no confidence in the parliament or a defeat at the polls in a national election, we must answer with an emphatic 'yes.' Our position on this matter cannot be a tactical one, but must depend on the trust which all citizens are entitled to express."[10]

The rejection of the Leninist party doctrine was first proclaimed with the publication of the draft of a new party statute at the end of October 1965. While until then strict adherence to the party line was obligatory, the only imperative contained in the new party statute was the recognition of the program and the statute itself. Representatives of the Swedish Communist Party in parliamentary bodies were to receive only suggestions, and not directives, as to how they should vote on particular issues. The new statute also contained detailed regulations concerning election procedures and decision-making. Every party resolution was open to criticism from the entire party congress. All officials in the Executive Committee and in other offices had to be elected by secret ballot. Party representatives in the trade unions were to reserve suggestions and not orders. In the future, all party congresses were to be public and all records and documents accessible to the public.[11]

At the beginning of 1967, the Swedish Communist Party published a draft of the new party program. It was discussed between January and May 1967 and finally adopted at the Twenty-first Party Congress of the Swedish Communist Party, which was held from May 13 to 18, 1967. At the congress only representatives of the Communist and Left Socialist parties of Scandinavia participated. After a lively discussion, the thirty-seven-point program of "the socialist alternative" was adopted. The program contained no mention of the Soviet Union, of Lenin or Leninism or of the terms "dictatorship of the proletariat," "proletarian internationalism," or "democratic centralism," which were all so important to the Soviet Union.

The party program of 1967 proclaimed that the development of socialism should take place democratically, that democratic rights and freedoms had to be protected, and that democracy had to be expanded and developed. Nationalization according to the Soviet model was rejected. The raw-materials industry, banks, credit institutions, insurance companies, and large production enterprises were to be transferred to social ownership, whereby the employees themselves were to direct their own enterprises (point 21). The main goal was a socialist Sweden in which the people could openly and democratically determine their own living conditions and direct the development of their country. Swedish socialism did not imply a stagnant, apathetic society; the conflicting interests among different segments of the population, their ideas and their problems had to be freely discussed. Moreover, the basic principles of a socialist Sweden were a multiparty system as well as freedom of organization, of assembly, and of the press. [12]

At the Twenty-first Party Congress in May 1967, Hermansson and his supporters suggested changing the name of the Communist Party to the Left Party. The reason for this, Hermansson claimed, was that the Swedish Communists would recognize not only Communist parties but also socialist people's parties in the neighboring Nordic countries as fraternal parties. Communists as well as leftists and other socialists would feel at home in a Swedish Left Party. However, the suggestion met with considerable resistance, especially from the delegates of the northern Swedish industrial regions, where Stalinists had the upper hand. As a result, a compromise was reached and the party was to be called instead Left Party Communists. By the time they held their Twenty-first Party Congress in May 1967, the Swedish Communists had progressed the furthest, after the Italian Communists, along the road to a new course. [13]

Nevertheless, after this party congress the Stalinists' resistance strengthened. The greatest resistance was offered by the Stalinist bastions in northern Sweden centered in Kiruna, which published the newspaper *Norrskensflamman*. At the same time, Swedish reformers met with opposition from both the New Left and the Maoists, who accused the party leaders of being too reformist. The disputes within the party intensified after the occupation of Czechoslovakia was harshly condemned by the Left Party Communists. In a television interview, Hermansson demanded that the Swedish government break all relations with those countries participating in the occupation of Czechoslovakia. The Stalinist paper *Norrskensflamman* took the opposing view and defended the occupation.

During the national elections on September 20, 1970, the Swedish Left Party Communists received 4.8 percent of the vote. At the same time, the Swedish Social Democrats forfeited their majority and could only rule together with the Left Party Communists (the Social Democrats had 163 representatives, the Left Party 17, and the bourgeois parties 170), which increased the role of the Left Party.

In the summer of 1972, Carl-Henrik Hermansson made the unusual suggestion of summoning refugees and emigrants from the Soviet bloc to join his party: "We have harshly criticized the conditions during the Stalin cult in the Soviet Union and we will continue to criticize them. We know that these conditions also had and continue to have serious effects on other countries, particularly Poland, Czechoslovakia and Hungary. I am convinced that we must discuss openly with those Communists and Socialists who, out of protest against the development in their own countries, have chosen to emigrate to Sweden. We Swedish Communists are very much interested in such a dialogue.[14]

At the Twenty-second Party Congress held from October 26 to 29, 1972, disputes again arose among the different factions in the Swedish Communist Party. The resistance of the pro-Stalinist forces of the north was supported by Göteborg. Carl-Henrik Hermansson was confirmed as party Chairman but he was compelled to make concessions to the Stalinists. In comparison with the program of 1967, the declaration of 1972 was much less progressive.[15]

In his report to the party congress, Hermansson focused on the attitude toward Swedish social democracy. On the one hand, Hermansson criticized the Social Democratic government for administering a capitalist society without seriously striving for changes in the mode of production or the concentration of power. On the other hand, he declared that under no circumstances would the Communists help overthrow a Social Democratic government. This attitude of the Left Party Communists was particularly important for Sweden, since the Social Democratic government could not rule without the support of these reformist Communists.

The oppositional policies of the reform Communists became more important after the elections in September 1973, at which the Social Democratic share of the vote fell to 43.5 percent, while the Left Party received 5.3 percent of the vote as compared to 4.8 percent in 1970. In the Parliament, the 175 representatives of the Social Democrats and Left Party Communists faced 175 representatives of the three center and conservative parties. After the election, Hermansson again declared that his party would stand for far-reaching reforms but would not destroy a Social Democratic government. During an interview with a correspondent of the *Frankfurter Allgemeine Zeitung*, several leading representatives of the Swedish Left Party declared that, in Sweden, Social Democrats had been in power for forty years and that it was up to the Left Party Communists to strengthen the progressive and leftist forces within the Social Democratic Party.[16] The Swedish Communists wanted to have nothing to do with the SED's adage "The party is always right." Neither the party executive committee nor the party members were always right. The Swedish Communists placed a great emphasis on a free atmosphere in which different opinions were expressed openly. It would be nice, they said, if there were more freedom of opinion in the Soviet Union, too.[17]

At the Twenty-fourth Party Congress from March 12 to 16, 1975, Hermansson reproached the pro-Soviet minority with its newspaper *Norrskensflamman* for its factional activity and urged it to subordinate itself to the majority. In retaliation, the spokesman of the pro-Soviet minority accused the party leadership of being anti-Soviet and of refusing to support Moscow's policies against Maoism. The pro-Soviet minority bitterly opposed the party's increasing independence from the Soviet Union, the rejection of the occupation of Czechoslovakia, and the protests against the banishment of Solzhenitsyn.

Moreover, at this congress, Carl-Henrik Hermansson resigned from the party chairmanship. He had directed the party since 1964 and had instituted its reform course. The election of his successor was, however, not uncontested. Hermansson's deputy, Lars Werner, who also represented the reformist group, received 162 votes, compared to sixty-four votes for the pro-Soviet rival candidate, Rolf Hagel from Göteborg.

The new party Chairman, Lars Werner, was a laborer who eventually completed his studies as an engineer. He was a trade-union official and joined the party in 1953. Upon acceding to the chairmanship, he faced the impossible task of having to overcome the wide split in the party.[18] The party had adopted a resolution on unity which made compliance with all party decisions obligatory, but this only served to cover up temporarily the smoldering conflict. *Norrskensflamman* continued the campaign against the majority and demanded a return to the pro-Soviet course.

In the summer and autumn of 1975, the conflict reached its climax. The pro-Soviet functionaries in the north and in Göteborg refused to distribute the party newspaper *Ny Dag* and began publishing the local *Norrskensflamman* as the party newspaper throughout Sweden. The newspaper struggle became an important part of the conflict, especially when the question was raised as to who was financing the pro-Soviet *Norrskensflamman*. The situation rapidly grew worse as, in autumn 1975, the Stalinists formed their own rival organizations in many cities and several regions in Sweden.[19] Shortly before the national elections on September 19, 1976, three of the nineteen representatives of the Left Party Communists in the Swedish Parliament broke away from the party. They were members of the pro-Soviet group. Several pro-Soviet local groups and regional organizations put up their own lists of candidates for the election. With the elections of September 19, 1976, the Social Democrats were forced into the opposition for the first time in forty years. As a result of the inner-party conflicts between the Eurocommunist majority and the pro-Soviet minority, the Left Party Communists also lost ground; they received 4.8 percent of the vote, as compared to 5.3 percent in 1973.

In January 1977, the Eurocommunists of Sweden had welcomed the Charter 77 movement in Prague. The Stalinists, of course, had advocated its suppression. On March 1, 1977, there followed a final split among the Swedish Communists. Several pro-Soviet Communists who left the Left Party Communists founded a new party, called the Workers' Party (Communist). The fact that party Chairman, Lars Werner, had disapproved of the expatriation of Wolf Biermann played an important role in the split. There were now representatives of two Communist parties in the Swedish Parliament. The Left Party Communists still had sixteen representatives. The newly founded pro-Soviet Workers' Party (Communist), under the direction of Rolf Hagel, had three. The new situation became obvious to the Swedish public during the parliamentary debates of March 30, 1977. In the name of his new party, Rolf Hagel declared that democracy in the socialist countries was the highest form of democracy and that the criticism of the alleged lack of freedom was only an attempt to draw attention away from the undemocratic conditions in one's own country. At the same meeting, Lars Werner declared in the name of the Left Party Communists that his party felt it was aligned with the Eurocommunists: "We did not invent this name, but we are not ashamed of it either." He claimed that several parties in the industrialized capitalist countries of Europe as well as the Australian and Japan Communist parties professed similar ideas about socialism and democracy. "The Swedish Communists protect the democratic freedoms and rights for which the working people have fought. These rights and freedoms must be developed further into a pluralist socialist system in which democracy is prevalent in all realms of social life, in which trade unions remain an independent force with the right to strike and in which the opposition is guaranteed all democratic freedoms."[20]

As a result of the split in the party, the Left Party Communists lost about 1,500 members. Party officials declared, however, that the loss of membership had already been compensated for by new entries into the party. These new members had joined the party, they explained, precisely because it was now rid of the faction tied to Moscow.

The split among Swedish Communists may have serious effects on future elections. According to a public opinion poll in early 1977, only 3.5 percent of the population said they would vote for the Left Party Communists. This could mean that the Left Party Communists might lose their parliamentary representation in the near future, since, in Sweden, a party must receive at least 4 percent of the vote in order to be represented in Parliament.

The actions of the Stalinists in Sweden were obviously coordinated by Moscow. The Soviet leadership had recognized in 1977 that the possibility of "taming" the Eurocommunists in Sweden was minimal. Consequently, it decided to concentrate on a smaller group which, although completely sectarian and inactive, was faithfully pro-Soviet. It is unlikely that the pro-Soviet Workers' Party (Communist) will ever receive more than 1 percent of the vote in Sweden.

The split in the Swedish Communist Party can clearly be seen as a warning from Moscow to all Communist parties of the West: in the future, wherever Eurocommunist ideas win the upper hand, Moscow will strive to establish a pro-Soviet Communist group, even if it means weakening the Communist movement in individual countries and endangering their representation in Parliament.

The Soviet leadership invited two delegations from Sweden to the celebration of the sixtieth anniversary of the October Revolution in

CP Sweden—Election Results and Parliamentary Representation since 1945

In 1967, after its autonomy and new course, the Communist Party of Sweden changed its name to Left Party Communists.

Date	Votes	% of total	Deputies	Out of
September 1944	318,466	10.5	15	230
September 1948	244,826	6.3	8	230
September 1952	164,194	4.3	5	230
September 1956	194,016	5	6	231
June 1958	129,319	3.4	5	231
September 1960	190,560	4.5	5	232
September 1964	221,746	5.2	8	233
September 1968	145,172	3	3	233
September 1970	236,653	4.8	17	350
September 1973	274,929	5.3	19	350
September 1976	258,432	4.8	17	349

November 1977: one from the Left Party Communists with Lars Werner and Carl-Henrik Hermansson, and one from the newly founded pro-Soviet Workers' Party in order to increase its international recognition. Moscow had already made the same tactical maneuvers with the pro-Soviet splinter groups in Spain and in Australia.

Norway's Communists: Between a Moscow Course and Leftist Socialism

The conflicts in the Norwegian Communist Party had a very unusual result; one-third of the party officials and leaders, including the party Chairman, joined the Socialist Left Party, while the rest of the party remained pro-Soviet, with a negligible effect on the policies of the country.

Until 1962, the Norwegian Communist Party had followed a Soviet course with the usual disastrous effects. In October 1945, the Norges Kommunistiske Parti (NKP), received 11.8 percent of the vote and was even entitled to send two Communists as ministers in the government. In 1961, it mustered only 2.9 percent of the vote and was no longer represented in Parliament. Disputes between the resistance fighter Peder Furubotn, on the one hand, and the Stalinist Lövlien, on the other, characterized the decline of the NKP after World War II. Lövlien, party Chairman in the years after World War II, accused the Secretary General Furubotn, who had led the resistance against the German occupation in northern Norway, of being a Titoist and imperialist agent. In October 1949, Furubotn and a great many of his supporters were expelled from the party. As a result, the Lövlien leadership succeeded in regaining such a strong grip on the party that neither Stalin's death nor even the Twentieth Party Congress of the CPSU and Khrushchev's revelations about Stalin led to any significant change within the Party.

Certain changes finally became apparent as a result of the Sino-Soviet conflict. The leaders of the NKP took their own position on this conflict and, on December 20, 1962, published a commentary which went so far that it was even reprinted in the Chinese press. The widespread belief that the Norwegian Communist Party was already following a pro-Chinese course was, however, untrue. Rather, the NKP advocated a kind of Romanian line, stressing its own independence.

This first step in this direction soon spread to other realms, especially after Reidar Larsen took over direction of the party newspaper, *Friheden*. Larsen had a Stalinist past and until the sixties was faithful to Moscow. He was even promoted to the head of the Communist youth organization when Secretary General Furubotn and his supporters were expelled from the party as Titoists in 1949. Larsen was one of those "faithful Stalinists" who were truly shocked by later revelations. In any event, as of 1964, open discussion and even harsh criticisms appeared in the party newspaper which Larsen ran. Under the headline "Not Infallible," *Friheden* criticized the removal of Khrushchev and, in another article, declared that the Soviet methods and rules for changing leaders were highly unclear.[21] In a critical letter to the editor published in *Friheden*, a member of the NKP declared that most inhabitants of Norway were of the opinion "that we are a dead party, numbered by dogmatism." There were not many people in Norway, he claimed, who "believed a process of renovation was taking place in the Norwegian Communist Party."[22]

At the Thirteenth Party Congress of the Norwegian Communist Party, held from March 26 to 28, 1965, heated debate finally signaled the start of a real change. The Stalinist Lövlien was removed, and Reidar Larsen became party Chairman. At the party congress, it was declared that the Norwegian Communist Party would not follow any foreign directives. In addition, Larsen tried to give the party a new profile along the lines of the Swedish Communists under Hermansson, but he also had to contend with the Stalinist forces. The newly elected central body of the NKP was made up of representatives of Reidar Larsen's progressive group and the pro-Soviet group.

During the elections of September 12 and 13, 1965, the Socialist People's Party, which had been founded in 1961 and which was under the direction of the dynamic leftist Socialist, Finn Gustavsen, received 6 percent of the vote, far surpassing the Norwegian Communist Party, which only received 1.4 percent of the vote. The election victory of the leftist Socialists strengthened the reformist forces within the Communist Party under Reidar Larsen.

In the course of 1966 and 1967, the voices in the NKP critical of the Soviet Union grew louder. The party leadership now officially declared that the party would openly and freely discuss events in the socialist countries. The Norwegian Communist Party, it claimed, was not the provincial organization of a socialist country. That was a tradition from the outdated period of the Comintern. Moreover, the NKP also made positive comments on the Swedish and Romanian Communist parties.

As was the case in Sweden, bitter disputes dominated the internal atmosphere of the party. Under the leadership of Jörgen Vogt, the pro-Soviet minority faction tried helplessly to check the evolution toward independence and, finally, it withdrew from the party leadership out of protest.

In April 1967, the NKP announced that it was preparing a new party program which would be considered at the forthcoming Twelfth Party Congress in March 1968.[23] The new party program, it declared, would be free of the rhetoric of the past.[24] The party stressed its independent attitude toward the Sino-Soviet conflict and, on October 1, 1967, the Communist Party Chairman, Larsen, attended an official reception at the Chinese Embassy in Oslo commemorating the anniversary of the People's Republic of China—a first in the diplomatic practices of European Communist parties.

The struggle between the reformers and the pro-Soviet group continued at the Twelfth Party Congress of the Norwegian Communist Party, which was held from March 22 to 24, 1968. It was the first Communist Congress in Norway to be held in public. Reidar Larsen was reelected party Chairman and a resolution condemning the factional activities of the pro-Soviet minority was passed by a vote of seventy-one to twenty-two. Larsen advocated a "unity in diversity" of the world Communist movement in accordance with the Italian Communist principle.

On the domestic level, participants at the party congress decided to cooperate with the Socialist People's Party; on the international level, they advocated the neutrality of Norway, the dissolution of all military and economic blocs and, as a future goal, an alliance of neutral Nordic states.

The party congress once again protested against the occupation of Czechoslovakia and called for the withdrawal of all foreign troops. In addition, relations with the Romanian Communist Party were stepped up. The Norwegian Communist Party leadership conducted several talks with Ceauşescu in Bucharest, and Romanian party delegates repeatedly visited the Norwegian Communist Party leadership.

Even the Thirteenth Party Congress of the Norwegian Communist Party, which was held from April 23 to 25, 1971, stressed the NKP's neutral position on the Sino-Soviet conflict and asserted its right to comment critically on negative developments within socialist countries. During the unrest in Poland in December 1970, the Norwegian Communist Party vocally objected to the bureaucratic degeneration and the lack of democratization in that country. Such phenomena were not the result of socialism, they claimed, but resulted, on the contrary, from breaches of socialist principles.

In August 1972, the Norwegian Communist Party, together with several other Eurocommunist parties, protested the political show trials in Prague. The dispute over the question of Norway's joining the European Economic Community subsequently occupied the center of attention in the political arena. In a referendum in September 1972, the majority of the Norwegian population spoke out against Norway's joining the EEC. The Communists and other leftist forces, especially the Socialist People's Party, were very active in this referendum. After detailed negotiations, the campaign for the plebiscite against the EEC led to the formation of the Socialist Electoral Alliance under the direction of the Chairman of the Socialist People's Party, Finn Gustavsen. Besides the Socialist People's Party, two groups of Social Democrats opposed to the EEC, namely the Democratic Socialists and the Independent Socialists, as well as the Norwegian Communist Party, participated in the electoral alliance. The Socialist Electoral Alliance advocated national self-determination, a reduction in defense spending and economic democracy. Moreover, the electoral alliance proclaimed the long-term goal of a socialist Norway. Reidar Larsen considered the formation of this Socialist Electoral Alliance a breakthrough for the ideas "which we have always advocated."

During the elections on September 9 and 10, 1973, the Socialist Electoral Alliance received an amazing 11.6 percent of the votes and could thus send sixteen deputies to the Norwegian Parliament. Of these sixteen representatives, nine belonged to the Socialist People's Party, six belonged to the two groups of Social Democrats against the EEC, and one, Reidar Larsen, belonged to the Norwegian Communist Party. The victory of the Socialist Electoral Alliance was even more significant because Bratelli's Social Democratic government could no longer rule without the support of the alliance's representatives. From now on, the question of cooperation with the electoral alliance became a major preoccupation, especially for the Communists. At the Fourteenth Party Congress of the NKP, held from November 1 to 4, 1973, Reidar Larsen was confirmed as Chairman and the party congress advocated a strengthening of the Socialist Electoral Alliance.

After the victory at the polls, all four partners discussed the transition from an electoral alliance to a unified Left Party. For the first time in the history of Communism, a Communist party would voluntarily fuse with other parties to form a broader socialist grouping. It was clear from the beginning that in any such joint party, the Norwegian Communist Party would be only *one* partner among four and had no chance of playing a "leading role." Among the Norwegian Communists, Reidar Larsen in particular advocated the founding of a Left Party, while Deputy Party Chairman Gunnar Knutsen represented the wing opposed to such a measure. After the Central Committee adopted a resolution in favor of a new Socialist Left Party in January 1974, a majority of party members clearly backed Larsen.

On April 20 and 21, 1974, three hundred delegates of the four parties met in Trondheim and decided to create a new Left Socialist Party. Most difficulties seemed to have been already overcome. The joint Socialist Party was to be founded on March 15, 1975, and was to appear for the first time at the forthcoming communal elections in September 1975, while the individual parties were not to be dissolved until late in 1975.[25]

Within the Norwegian Communist Party, discussions intensified between the Larsen wing and the dogmatic Stalinist forces which opposed the new party. In the draft of a common program presented at a conference in Trondheim in mid-March 1975, the term "Leninism" was dropped. Instead, the term "Marxist-Revolutionary Socialist Party" was used. In the party program the Socialists wanted to condemn explicitly the lack of freedom in the Soviet Union as well as the occupation of Czechoslovakia. After the pro-Soviet wing objected, threatening to leave the congress, these critical passages were stricken from the draft of the program and included in a general resolution. Toward the end of the conference, the pro-Stalinist Communists under Knutsen declared that only the forthcoming congress of the Norwegian Communist Party could decide on dissolution.[26]

After *Pravda* reported critically on the Trondheim conference, the controversy continued. *Pravda* observed that the conference had not included the important fundamental principles of Marxism-Leninism in the party program. Moreover, the Soviet leadership made it clear that it opposed the formation of a new Left Party. Immediately after the *Pravda* article, Gunnar Knutsen declared that, for him, the resolution of Trondheim had been "null and void." The party Chairman, Reidar Larsen, however, said that he felt just as much a Communist as a member of the Left Socialist Party.

In June 1975, Knutsen headed a delegation of pro-Soviet officials to Moscow, where the Norwegians conferred with Suslov and Ponomaryov. A communiqué proclaimed that, in the future, the Norwegian Communist Party would act in accordance with Marxism-Leninism.

At the local elections in September 1975, the newly founded Left Socialist Party received 5.7 percent of the votes, only half the share of votes it had received in September 1973. The pro-Soviet Communists regarded this decline in popularity as a further argument for the rejection of the formation of a Left Party and the maintenance of the Communist Party.

The decisive dispute followed in November 1975 at the Fifteenth Party Congress of the NKP. At this congress, under pressure from Knutsen and a clear sign from Moscow, a majority of the delegates voted to uphold the Norwegian Communist Party as a separate organization. This, of course, led to a split in the party. A minority of about one-third, led by the former party Chairman, Reidar Larsen, left the NKP and joined the newly founded Left Socialist Party. From then on the remainder of the Communist Party under the leadership of its new pro-Soviet Chairman, Gunnar Knutsen, pursued a distinctly pro-Soviet course.[27]

Norway: Communist and Left Socialist Votes and Parliamentary Representation since 1945

Besides the pro-Soviet Communist Party, the Socialist People's Party emerged in 1961 and soon became much stronger than the pro-Soviet Communist Party. At the end of 1972, all the left-wing parties formed the successful but short-lived Socialist Electoral Alliance. After detailed negotiations, the Left Socialist Party, consisting of leftist Socialists and independent Communists, was formed in 1975. The pro-Soviet Communist Party still exists, but remains completely insignificant.

Date	Party	Votes	% of total	Deputies	Out of
October 1945	CP	167,704	11.4	11	150
October 1949	CP	102,722	5.8		150
October 1953	CP	90,422	5.08	3	150
October 1957	CP	60,375	3.38	1	150
September 1961	CP	53,678	2.9		150
	SPP	43,996	2.4	2	150
September 1965	CP	27,996	1.4		150
	SPP	122,721	6	2	150
September 1969	CP	22,494	1		150
	SPP	75,510	3.4		150
September 1973	SEA	242,000	11.2	16	155
September 1977	CP	8,355	0.4		155
	LSP	94,016	4.1	2	155

CP—Communist Party (pro-Soviet)

SPP—Socialist People's Party (1961–1975)

SEA—Socialist Electoral Alliance, 1972–73 (consisting of the SPP, the CP, and left-wing Social Democrats)

LSP—Left Socialist Party (founded 1975)

Reidar Larsen, now a member of the Left Socialist Party, did not participate at the conference of the European Communist parties in East Berlin in June 1976. Representing the Norwegian Communist Party, Gunnar Knutsen declared that the decision to continue the NKP's existence was the right one.

During the election in September 1977, the newly formed Left Socialist Party received 4 percent of the votes and could thus send two deputies to the Parliament. The pro-Soviet Norwegian Communist Party, under the direction of Gunnar Knutsen, received only 0.4 percent of the vote—the worst showing in the entire history of the party since its founding in November 1923. Even the majority of former Communist voters had thus decided against the NKP and for the Left Socialist Party. Today the Norwegian Communist Party exists only in order to cast a pro-Soviet vote at Moscow world conferences.

The Communists of Iceland: The Independent Role of the "People's Alliance"

After the Italian Communist Party, the Icelandic Communists are in proportion to the population the strongest Communist Party in Europe. (Of course, Iceland is a country of only 220,000 inhabitants.) The Icelandic Communist Party has participated in the government more frequently than any other Communist party. Moreover, the Icelandic Communists have broken off all contact with the Soviet-led world Communist movement.

The Communists of Iceland united with several groups from the left wing of the Social Democrats in October 1938, and since then have called themselves the Socialist Unity party, receiving 19.5 percent of the votes cast during the war in the elections of 1942. The first two leaders, Secretary General Brynjolfur Bjarnasson and the party Chairman Eeinar Olgeirsson, instituted the first steps toward an independent policy. Both party leaders had become Communists while studying in Berlin in the 1920s. In 1944, a coalition government of Social Democrats, Conservatives, and the Socialist Unity Party was formed in Iceland. The Socialist Unity Party was represented by two ministers: Bjarnsson was Minister of Education and Jakobsson was Minister of Labor. Communist participation in the government lasted until early 1947, when differences of opinion arose on the methods of fighting inflation and on the question of the American military base in Keflavik. The Socialist Unity Party was opposed to the American base, but at the same time it was the only Communist Party in the world which did not take part in the anti-Yugoslav campaign in 1948.[28]

The Socialist Unity Party formed an electoral alliance with the leftist Social Democrats which became known as the People's Alliance (Altydubandalagid). This People's Alliance participated in the Icelandic government between 1956 and 1958. As of the end of the fifties, the Icelandic Communists have clearly been evolving away from the world Communist movement. They attended the celebration of the fiftieth anniversary of the October Revolution in November 1967, but did not participate in the two official world Communist conferences of 1957 and 1960. They limited themselves to occasionally sending general greetings to party congresses of the Soviet bloc.

For the most part, the Icelandic Communists concentrated on their own internal problems. During the election in June 1963, the Icelandic People's Alliance received 16 percent of the vote and sent nine deputies out of a total of fifty-two to the Parliament. In the same year, it adopted a new party program proclaiming a peaceful transition to socialism.

In December 1967, after long internal dispute, it was decided to transform the People's Alliance from an electoral alliance to a political party. The Icelandic Communists sharply condemned the occupation of Czechoslovakia in August 1968, declaring that it considered relations with the ruling parties of the Soviet bloc countries which had participated in the occupation unacceptable to the membership of the People's Alliance. At the Sixteenth Party Congress in November 1961, Eeinar Olgeirsson, who had been Chairman of the party for thirty years, relinquished his post to the new leader of the People's Alliance, Ragnar Arnalds, who continued the independent policies of his predecessor. The new party statutes contained far-reaching proposals for democratization: from then on, the party congresses were to be public, the minority was to be allowed to express its opinion freely, even in the party leadership, and a rotation system was introduced, according to which no official could remain in the same position for more than three terms (i.e., nine years).

After the Icelandic Communists repeated their condemnation of the occupation of Czechoslovakia, a small pro-Soviet group also formed in Iceland. It called itself the Union of Icelandic Socialists and published its own newspaper, entitled *Ny Dagsbund*. This pro-Soviet group, however, was—and is—completely insignificant.

During the elections of June 1971, the People's Alliance received 17.2 percent of the vote, surpassing the Social Democrats who had received 10.5 percent. From June 1971 until the summer of 1974, the Icelandic Communists were again represented in the government: Ludvik Josefsson as Minister of Fishing and Commerce, and Magnus Kjartansson as Minister of Industry, Health, and Social Welfare. In 1971–1972, the Icelandic Communists again protested against the suppression of the opposition in Czechoslovakia and criticized the death sentence handed down to the alleged hijacker at the show trial in Leningrad.

At the party congress in mid-November 1971, Ragnar Arnalds was confirmed as party Chairman, and Mrs. Adda Bara Sigfusdottir, Deputy Minister of Health and Social Welfare, was elected Deputy Party Chairman.

The Icelandic Communists' participation in government ended after the elections on June 30, 1974. Although the People's Alliance did receive 18.4 percent of the vote, and although it was entitled to send eleven deputies to the Parliament, the election defeat of the Social Democrats, who received only 9.1 percent of the vote, led, in late August 1974, to the withdrawal of the center-left government.

Since 1974, the People's Alliance has continually emphasized its independence and, at the same time, has proved increasingly successful. Moreover, the Icelandic Communists no longer take part in any regional or international Communist conferences. The Icelandic People's Alliance, which considers itself a left-wing socialist party, did not even participate at the East Berlin Conference of European Communist parties, which took place in June 1976.

In the last years, the conservative Independence Party, beset with serious economic problems resulting from Iceland's absolute dependence on the export of fish, has lost much ground to the Icelandic People's Alliance. Consequently, the national elections of June 25, 1978, resulted in a landslide. The conservative Independence Party received only 32.4 percent of the vote, as compared to 42.7 percent four years earlier. The liberal Progressive Party fell from 24.9 to 16.9 percent, while the two left-wing parties were overwhelmingly successful. The Social Democratic Party received 22 percent of all votes cast (as compared to 9.1 percent in 1974), and the Icelandic People's Alliance share of the vote jumped from 18.4 to almost 23 percent.

The change in the party's strength led to long-term negotiations to form a new coalition government. Among the several attempts in August 1978 the sixty-four year old party Chairman of the People's Alliance, Ludvik Josefsson, was asked to form a coalition government. Both the Progressive Party (with 12 seats) and the Social Democratic Party (with 14 seats) demanded from the People's Alliance (also

14 seats) that neither Iceland's participation in NATO nor the maintenance of the American military bases in Keflavik be contested.[29] The
People's Alliance agreed. This led to a formation of a new Icelandic
government based upon a coalition of Progressive, Social Democrats
and Communists (People's Alliance). The new coalition is based on a
clear majority in the sixty seat Icelandic Parliament. The Communists
are represented in the Icelandic government by three Cabinet Ministers: Ragnar Arnalds, (Education, Culture, Transport); Hjorleifur
Guttormsson (Industry) and Svavar Gestsson (Commerce).

Thus, again, Communists are strongly represented in a Western
government. It is important to note however that the Icelandic
People's Alliance is the most independent Communist Party in the
world Communist movement.

**People's Alliance of Iceland—Election Results and
Parliamentary Representation since 1945**

*The Icelandic Communists were known from 1938 –1968 as the Socialist Unity Party,
and since 1968 as the People's Alliance.*

Date	Votes	% of total	Deputies	Out of
June 1946	13,049	19.5	10	52
October 1949	14,077	19.5	9	52
June 1953	12,422	16.1	7	52
June 1956	15,859	19.5	8	52
June 1959	12,929	15.3	7	52
October 1959	13,621	16	10	60
June 1963	14,274	16	9	60
June 1967	13,402	13.9	10	60
June 1971	18,055	17.1	10	60
June 1974	20,922	18.3	11	60
June 1978	27,962	22.9	14	60

The Greek Communist Party: Eurocommunist "Interior Party" and Pro-Soviet "Exterior Party"

The Communists of Greece are seldom mentioned in discussions on
Eurocommunism. This is unfortunate, since Eurocommunist tendencies play an important role in Greece. As a result of serious internal
disputes in early 1968, the Greek Communist Party split into a pro-
Soviet "exterior group" and a Eurocommunist "interior group." The
latter is closely linked with the United Democratic Left (EDA).

The origins of this development date back to the civil war between 1946 and 1949 in which over 50,000 people perished, 750,000 lost their homes, and huge parts of the country were destroyed. After three years of bitter warfare, the Greek Communist Party was finally defeated. The defeat was owing mainly to the lack of support by the Greek population, especially the working class, who had grown tired of war. Moreover, the resistance was openly supported by the Soviet Union and Bulgaria. In autumn 1949, the Greek Communist Party became illegal and tens of thousands of Greek Communists fled to countries of the Soviet bloc. About 25,000 refugees, including about 20,000 party members, have since been living in the Soviet Union and Eastern Europe.

The great majority of members and officials of the Greek Communist Party had joined the party under the German occupation. They practically knew only one form of struggle: armed resistance against the Germans. The meaning and significance of "political struggle" was unknown to most of them and the Communist party leadership often dealt with economic and social problems in the most primitive and dogmatic ways. Moreover, the dictatorial political structure of the Soviet bloc and the arbitrariness of Stalinism had negative effects on many Greek Communists living in exile in those countries. Within the exiled Communist Party, there were continual disputes among different cliques and factions. Many Greek Communist Party officials were arrested and some were even shot. Most important, however, was the fact that the Greek Communists in exile had no conception of the actual conditions in their native country. By the 1950s noticeable differences had already arisen between Greek Communists living in exile and those who remained in Greece.

In the mid-fifties the leftist forces could again be legally active in their own country but not as a Communist Party. A Party of the United Left (EDA) was formed. It consisted of Communist members and officials, but also included many sympathizers and non-Communist leftists. In elections, the EDA received a considerable share of the vote: 24.4 percent in 1958, 14.8 percent in 1961, 14.5 percent in 1963, and 11.8 percent in 1964.

The Greek Communists argued about the role of the EDA. Some Communists wanted the EDA to become an independent Marxist party and practically take on the role of a second Communist Party. Others wanted to retain the EDA as a legal leftist front organization, leaving the Communists to form their own illegal party organizations outside the EDA. There was also considerable debate as to whether the leadership of the Greek Communists should be stationed within the country or abroad.

The situation was intensified by the military coup in April 1967. Both the Communist Party and the EDA were now illegal: their members were considered conspirators and there were mass arrests. More than 6,500 Communists and sympathizers were either imprisoned or sent to the infamous camps on the islands.

Shortly after the military coup began, ten of the thirty-eight members of the Central Committee of the Greek Communist Party were already in prison. The party was being directed from abroad by the pro-Soviet and extremely Stalinist Secretary General, Kostas Koliyannis. A few weeks after the installation of the military dictatorship, Koliyannis tried to find scapegoats for the defeat which the party had faced. In November 1967, before the Politburo-in-exile, he declared that Polituro members Dimitrios Partsalides, Panos Dimitriou, and Zisis Zografos, who had worked closely together with the EDA, were responsible for the defeat of the party after the military coup. These progressive functionaries, he declared, should be demoted.

However, Koliyannis met with resistance from the majority of Greek Communists. He then convened the so-called Twelfth Enlarged Central Committee Plenum, without inviting any representatives of the CP members working illegally in Greece. At this Central Committee Plenum, which met from February 3 to 14, 1968—without Partsalides and his supporters—the three above-mentioned Politburo members were ousted from their positions by a vote of twelve to nine. In retaliation, the three ousted members and their supporters decided on February 17, 1968, to form a new Central Committee. They condemned the Twelfth Central Committee Plenum over the radio program "Voice of Truth," broadcasting from Bucharest, declaring that the resolutions of the Koliyannis group were obvious breaches of the party statutes and attacked this group for conservatism and dogmatism. Later, the Koliyannis group countered in a Moscow radio broadcast that the three Politburo members, Partsalides, Zografos, and Dimitriou, had not only been relieved of their duties but also expelled from the party. As a result, Partsalides, Zografos, and Dimitriou formed a new Central Committee of Unity with the goal of convening a representative party congress as soon as possible. The call for a new Central Committee was echoed by many Communists in Greece. And a letter from twenty-two high officials of the Greek Communist Party in Aegina prison was especially important. They protested sharply against Koliyannis:

"The Communists of Greece are no longer willing to tolerate this situation. The tragedy in which we find ourselves compels us to speak out: Comrades, you have been away from home for twenty years now, certainly by no fault of your own. You can no longer direct the movement in Greece. The leadership of the Greek Communist Party can only be made up of those members of the Central Committee who are at the head of the movement in Greece."

In March 1968, the Koliyannis group decided to transfer the party leadership and the program "Voice of Truth" and its entire editorial staff from Romania to East Germany. As a result, the party split into an interior group and an exterior group under the leadership of Koliyannis. The leadership of the EDA pledged its support to the interior group.

The situation was aggravated after the interior wing of the Greek Communist Party and the EDA condemned the Soviet intervention in Czechoslovakia. In addition, ninety well-known Communist prisoners confined on the island of Leros, including Manolis Glezos, condemned the Soviet invasion and demanded the withdrawal of the foreign troops so that the Czechoslovak people could decide their own fate. The pro-Soviet exterior leadership, on the other hand, supported the occupation of Czechoslovakia.

After 1969, the Koliyannis faction was active almost exclusively in East Berlin. It held several plenary sessions and published drafts of a program, but it was not able to establish a serious base for itself in Greece. In October 1971, Partsalides and Haralambos (Bambis) Drakopolous, the two leading representatives of the Communist Party (interior), were arrested by the military regime in Greece. They received no support from the Soviet bloc. However, in November 1971, the Romanian Party leader, Ceauşescu, received a delegation of the interior group of the Greek Communist Party and officially expressed the concern of the Romanian leadership about the arrest of Partsalides and Drakopolous. No other Soviet bloc state commented on the arrest of these Greek Communist leaders.

Although the leadership of the pro-Soviet faction changed at the so-called Seventeenth Central Committee Plenum in December 1972, the controversy between the two groups intensified. Koliyannis and many of his closest associates who had discredited themselves were removed. Harilaos Florakis, one of the few pro-Soviet officials who had been illegally active in Greece and who had spent many years in prison, became the new Secretary General. But Florakis also acted as a representative of the Soviet bloc. In January 1973, he held negotiations with Suslov and Ponomaryov in Moscow; in February he visited

Hungary; in March, Bulgaria; and finally, in May, he went to Czechoslovakia where he conferred with the Czechoslovak Stalinist, Bilak.

In the meantime, the interior group of the Greek Communist
Party increased its activities in Greece, where, at the end of January
1973, the leaders Partsalides and Drakopolous and fifteen other officials were sentenced to long prison terms. Before a special court of
law in Athens, Partsalides and Drakopolous declared that they were
striving for the unity of all democratic forces against the military regime. Greece needed a party, they said, closely connected to
the popular resistance movement which would provide a meeting
ground for all leftist forces. For that reason, the Communists of the
interior group were striving for the overthrow of the military regime
and the return to democracy and they advocated a government of
national unity which would free the country from all antidemocratic
laws and which would guarantee free elections. In Greece, they
claimed, the conditions existed for a peaceful road to socialism. During their trials, Partsalides and Drakopolous declared: "We are striving for a socialism which has its roots in Greek reality and which
expresses itself in a pluralistic society."

After increasing internal resistance and protests which, like the
student demonstration in November 1973, led to armed conflict, the
military regime was finally overthrown on July 23, 1974. On the following day, the Karamanlis government was formed. The bankruptcy
of the dictatorship as well as the popular revolt, which many middle-
class people had also joined, contributed to the wish to restore democracy. On August 4, 1974, the newspaper *Avgi*, the organ of the
United Democratic Left (EDA) and of the interior group of the Greek
Communist Party, could once again appear legally, and on August
21, 1974, the pro-Soviet Communist Party leadership under Florakis
returned to Athens. Shortly thereafter, the pro-Soviet Greek Communist Party opened its office in Athens and began publishing its
newspaper, *Rizospastis*.

Both the interior group and the EDA and the pro-Soviet Greek
Communist Party were now legal. Although the split persisted, on
October 11, 1974, both groups agreed to work together on the United
Democratic Left electoral platform for the coming national elections.
The United Democratic Left proclaimed its goal of protecting and
implementing national independence, the democratization of the
country, and the struggle for workers' rights. A committee comprised
of representatives of the pro-Soviet exterior group of the Communist
Party, the Eurocommunist interior group, and the EDA directed the

electoral alliance of the United Democratic Left. The first free campaign for the elections of November 17, 1974, was run under difficult conditions. Both Communist Party groups and the EDA had just been legalized. Moreover, there was no unity among the left since Andreas Papandreou and his own party, the Panhellenic Socialist Movement (PASOK), succeeded in mustering a majority of the leftist votes. In addition, the popularity of Karamanlis, who was regarded as a symbol of the liberation from the military dictatorship, played a decisive role. Finally, the electoral alliance suffered as a result of the split between the Communists, for despite the agreement and the common program, differences of opinion prevailed, and other parties in the election profited.[30] The elective alliance received only 9.45 percent of all votes cast during the first free Greek election, while the Panhellenic Socialist Movement (PASOK) received 13 percent.[31]

In the election partnership of the United Democratic Left, the exterior group of the Greek Communist Party had continued its factional activities and slander campaign against the EDA and the interior group. Of the eight representatives which the United Democratic Left sent to Parliament, five belonged to the pro-Soviet party (exterior) and only two belonged to the interior group; one represented the EDA. During the elections the exterior group had encouraged its members to vote only for their own candidates in the electoral alliance.

Thus, the Chairman of the EDA, Illias Iliou, received only 24,077 votes, although the United Democratic Left was able to muster 48,065 votes in all. The French newspaper *Le Monde* reported that there was much evidence that the parties would soon end this short-lived cooperation. On February 23, 1975, the Greek Communist Party (interior) declared that it was preparing its own congress for November and that it advocated a mass party and an end to the sectarian line of the past.

During the local elections on April 1, 1975, the opposition parties—the Greek Communist Party (interior) and Greek Communist Party (exterior), the EDA, the PASOK, and part of the Center Union—all opposed the government candidates. As a result, the opposition reached a majority in Athens, Saloniki, and other important cities of Greece. However, the alliance soon crumbled.

In 1975, the Greek Communist Party (interior) and the Spanish Communist Party issued a joint declaration which was important for the Greek party's Eurocommunist development. In the declaration, both parties advocated a pluralistic model of socialism, as well as respect for democratic, religious, and cultural freedoms and the rejection of an official state ideology. Both parties favored a union of the democratic forces of Europe, especially between Communists and Socialists, as well as a reform of the European Economic Community.

On July 6, 1976, the first party congress of the Greek Communist Party (interior) was convened in Athens. It occurred right after the East Berlin Conference of European Communist parties at the end of June 1976, in which the Greek Communist Party (interior) did not participate. Florakis, the leader of the exterior group, had appeared at the conference as a spokesman for all Greek Communists. At the interior group's party congress in Athens, a new line was announced, advocating the democratic road to socialism based on the particular conditions of the country. At the same time, the interior group declared that, despite the criticism it expressed about the negative aspects of the Karamanlis government, it wanted no political crisis which would only worsen Greece's situation. The documents of the party congress advocated political pluralism and the rights and freedoms of all citizens. In addition, the delegates from the Spanish, Yugoslav, and Romanian Communist parties as well as a delegation of the Norwegian left were warmly received. A number of other Communist parties, including those of Great Britain, Italy, Australia, and Switzerland, sent greetings. The pro-Soviet parties boycotted the party congress.

The party congress made it clear that the Greek Communist Party (interior) and the EDA wanted to pursue a constructive opposition. In September 1977, the head of the Greek government, Konstantin Karamanlis, decided to dissolve the Parliament and to hold elections in November 1977—one year before the scheduled date. In light of the serious domestic and foreign-policy issues—Cyprus, the EEC negotiations, the Turkish conflict, and the poor state of the economy—Karamanlis planned to achieve unlimited freedom of action and to prove that the majority of the nine million Greeks still had confidence in him.

The elections in November 1977 actually brought a confirmation of the Karamanlis policies. His party received 42 percent of the vote; on the other hand, the PASOK percentage rose from 13 to 25. The pro-Soviet Greek Communist Party received 9.4 percent of the vote and sent eleven deputies to the Parliament. The Eurocommunists received 2.7 percent of the vote and sent two representatives to the Parliament.

Greece is the only country in which the pro-Soviet Communists are considerably stronger than the Eurocommunists. This is obviously owing in part to the fact that the mood in Greece has been strongly anti-NATO and anti-EEC, and that the Eurocommunists have advocated a realistic relationship with the EEC. In addition, the extensive material support which the Soviet bloc gave to the pro-Soviet Communist Party clearly affected the electoral campaign.

The British Communist Party: Controversies about the "British Road to Socialism"

The British Communist Party, with its 26,000 members, is a relatively small party and plays a negligible role in elections. Because of British election laws, which do not favor small parties, the Communist Party has not been represented in Parliament for thirty years, and has very little chance of being represented in the future. Nevertheless, it does have an influence on the left in the labor movement, the factories, trade unions, and a part of British intelligentsia.

The leadership of the party is characterized by relative stability. Harry Pollitt directed the British Communist Party from 1929 until 1956, when John Gollan took over. Gollan remained at the head of the party until 1975, when Gordon McLennan took charge; he has been directing it ever since. The British Communist Party's road along a Eurocommunist course has been marked, since 1968, by continual disputes with a pro-Soviet minority.

The first signs of a change in a Eurocommunist direction became noticeable after the Twentieth Party Congress of the CPSU in February 1956. After 1956, the party, until then absolutely faithful to Moscow, indulged in free and open discussion; many British Communists supported Togliatti's concept of polycentrism in the Communist movement. The defeat of the Hungarian Revolution, though, came as a shock to the party. Over 7,000 members, almost a third of the total membership at that time, including many officials and intellectuals, left the party and began publishing their own newspaper, *The New Reasoner*.

Toward the end of the sixties, the British Communist Party gradually started following an "Italian line." The Thirtieth Party Congress (National Congress), in November 1967, stressed the necessity for each Communist Party to work out its own policies, corresponding to the conditions of the individual country. From then on, the British Communist Party rejected a leading center of world Communism, declaring that the policy of Communist parties could no longer be regulated by international Communist congresses. In foreign policy, however, the British Communist Party still advocated Britain's withdrawal from NATO, as well as a friendship treaty with the Soviet Union and recognition of East Germany.

The real change and the decisive disputes in the British Communist Party came, as in many other European Communist parties, as a result of the "Prague Spring" and the subsequent occupation of Czechoslovakia. The internal change was clearly marked by "The British Road to Socialism," a party program which had first appeared in 1947 and which was published in a revised form in early October 1968. Despite a dogmatic one-sided evaluation of the international situation, "The British Road to Socialism" of 1968 reflected some progressive thoughts about an independent road to socialism and a democratic socialist society. In the program, The British Communist Party considers itself a Marxist party (there is no reference to Leninism), which struggles for scientific socialism and for the unity of the working class. It has no intent of undermining or splitting the Labour Party. Acceptance of the Marxist standpoint can only come through personal conviction, as the fruit of experience, discussion, argument, and study. The British Communist Party insists that the most important way to change society is by increasing the nationalized sector of the economy. According to the program, the leading organs of the nationalized industries should be comprised of workers and technicians of the individual branches of the industry. Representatives of the trade unions should be included on all levels of administration and management. Newspapers and periodicals would be owned and controlled by political parties, social groups, trade unions, cooperatives, and professional associations. The British Communist Party calls for the introduction of the principle of proportional representation in local and national elections. The House of Lords, which, it claims, embodies no democratic principles, should be abolished. In addition, democratically constituted committees should guarantee the people's control over the police. Finally, the people of Scotland and Wales should be granted national self-determination and British troops should be withdrawn from Northern Ireland.

In the realm of foreign policy, the program of the British Communist Party proposes closer relations with the Soviet Union. It condemns American imperialism as the most aggressive opponent of democracy, of national liberation, and of socialism and for that reason insists that Great Britain free itself of American domination. NATO and other imperialistic alliances should be dissolved, it insists, and replaced by a European security system. Moreover, West German militarism has to be curbed, all British troops must be withdrawn from foreign countries, and all foreign troops withdrawn from Great Britain. The Common Market is portrayed as a concentration of the largest monopolies of capitalistic Europe, and poses a threat for democracy in Western Europe, for the working class, for the Soviet Union, and for all socialist countries.

The program of the British Communist Party, "The British Road to Socialism," describes the road to an independent socialism in the following manner: All democratic parties, including those which oppose socialism, can exist freely and participate in elections. The trade unions are independent of the state and represent the interests of their members. Moreover, they are to have an important function in economic planning. State planning and administration have to be decentralized and democratically elected regional councils should plan the economic, social and political development of their respective regions. In future socialism, all freedoms, including the right to strike, the right to choose a place of employment, freedom of faith, of travel, and of religious profession, will be guaranteed. Only racism must be forbidden. Furthermore, the judiciary should be independent of the executive.

In a socialist society, the Communist Party and the left wing of the Labour Party would be the most important political organizations of the working class and as such are responsible for the development of socialist society. In such a society, Marxism cannot be a state ideology, and Marxist ideas cannot be forced upon the members of the parties.

The British Communists, according to the closing words of the program, would never copy the experiences of other countries; they would pursue a British road to socialism.[32]

The program of autumn 1968 simultaneously expressed domestic Eurocommunism conceptions about the road to socialism and a pro-Soviet line in foreign policy. Nevertheless, on August 22, 1968, the party newspaper, *Morning Star*, did describe the invasion of Czechoslovakia as a "tragic mistake," claiming that the entire action was illegal. The British Communist Party, it said, advocates the immediate withdrawal of the troops of the Warsaw Pact countries from Czechoslovakia as well as the restoration of normal relations between the Warsaw Pact countries and Czechoslovakia. Two days later, the leaders of the British Communist Party repeated their condemnation of the military intervention.[33] In retaliation, *Pravda* published a criticism of the British Communists' point of view.[34]

The majority of the British Communist Party members shared the opinion of the party leadership, as revealed in the following statistics: In the London regional organization of the party, 152 voted for, and 72 voted against the condemnation (there were 7 abstentions). In Yorkshire, 64 voted for, 20 voted against, and there were 6 abstentions. In Middlesex, 50 were in favor, 25 against, and 3 abstained. In South Midlands, 24 were in favor, and 13 against. Only in the region of Surrey was the resolution of the party leadership defeated by a vote of 53 to 11.[35] Palme Dutt, a party veteran who had represented the British Communist Party in the Comintern in the thirties, was one of the most prominent advocates of Soviet intervention in Czechoslovakia. Dutt was supported by Sid French, the party Chairman in Surrey.

At the Third World Communist Conference in Moscow in June 1969, the British Communist Party was represented by John Gollan and Jack Woddis, the latter responsible for international affairs. At the conference, Gollan declared that it was not enough to base the relations between socialist countries and Communist parties on general theories; one had to discuss why the fundamental principles could not be converted into reality.[36] At the subsequent Thirty-first Party Congress of the British Communist Party, which took place from November 15 to 18, 1969, the resolution condemning the occupation of Czechoslovakia was accepted by 295 of the 413 delegates—more than 70 percent. In addition, Gollan's position at the Third World Conference was also approved by an overwhelming majority.

In June 1970, the British Communists protested against Dubček's expulsion from the Central Committee of the Czechoslovak Communist Party.[37] As a result, although party Chairman Gollan negotiated with the Soviet leaders Andrei Kirilenko and Boris Ponomaryov in August 1970, the tension between Moscow and the British Communist Party grew. The communiqué following the meeting mentioned the "open exchange of opinions" but said nothing of agreement.[38] Beginning in 1971 not only Communists, but supporters of the Labour Party, trade union leaders, and left-wing authors and journalists also participated in relatively open discussions in the party newspaper, *Morning Star,* which played an important role in the new course of the party.

Morning Star even printed some opinions critical of the British Communist Party. A leading official of the British coal miners' union, for example, asked why, in the fifty years of its existence, the British Communist Party had a certain influence on the trade unions but not at all in the political life. In his opinion thousands of faithful Communists were respected by the workers, and many even became trade union officials, yet there was still a deep mistrust of the Communist Party. The consistent defense of Stalinism lasting more than three decades, he declared, had led a majority of the British workers to believe that if the Communist Party ever came to power, it would set up a Stalinist-type regime in England. Consequently, the workers had to be convinced that the left advocated a socialist program which included the extension and not the restriction of democratic rights.[39]

During 1971, a delegation of the British Communist Party under the leadership of Jack Woddis visited Yugoslavia, where the two Communist parties agreed to increase contact. At the end of May 1971, the British Communist Party announced that since the Prague leadership refused to allow a British representative to speak out against the occupation, it would not attend the Fourteenth Party Congress of the Czechoslovak Communist Party.

In July 1971, Secretary General John Gollan went to the Soviet Union, where he conferred with Politburo member Arvid Pelshe. Once again, no agreement was announced in the resulting communiqué. Moreover, the resolution which Sid French introduced at the Thirteenth Party Congress of the British Communist Party, which was held from November 13 to 16, 1971, welcoming the occupation of Czechoslovakia, received the support of only 18 percent of the delegates.

In 1971, the party strengthened its campaign against Great Britain's entry into the European Economic Market, asserting that, as a result, the British Parliament would lose its sovereignty. Similar objections were raised in 1972. At the same time, the British Communist Party protested the trials which were being held in Czechoslovakia against the representatives of the "Prague Spring."

During a visit to England in February 1973, the Italian Communist Party Secretary General, Berlinguer, met with the leaders of both the Communist Party and the Labour Party. In the course of their talks, leading officials of the British Communist Party and Berlinguer agreed to increase cooperation between their respective parties. Almost simultaneously, a delegation of the British Communist Party, led by Gordon McLennan, was visiting the Soviet Union. At the Thirty-third Congress of the British Communist Party, which was held from November 10 to 12, 1973, it became clear that during the zigzag course, the Stalinist opposition had strengthened itself considerably. Sid French again demanded the repeal of the resolution against the occupation of Czechoslovakia. He was supported by John Tarver from South Midlands, who also suggested that the party congress invite a Soviet delegation to participate.

During the elections in October 1974, the British Communist Party put up candidates in twenty-nine election districts and received 0.1 percent of the vote. After John Gollan retired from the leadership of the party on March 11, 1975, fifty-year-old Gordon McLennan was elected to succeed him. McLennan continued the independent course of the British Communist Party. This was already evident at the Thirty-fourth Party Congress, which took place from November 15 to 18, 1975, when not only the Czechoslovak issue stood in the foreground, as had previously been the case, but the problem of the dissidents in the Soviet Union also received a great deal of attention. The document of the party congress declared that anti-Marxist ideas could only be fought with political discussions and not with administrative measures.

Despite the ongoing campaign of the Communist Party and numerous Labour Party politicians who were against Great Britain's entry into the EEC, 67.2 percent of the British voters favored Britain's staying in the EEC; they voted their opinion in a referendum on July 15, 1975.

In his brochure, "Socialism in Great Britain," published in February 1976, former Secretary General Gollan intensified his criticism of the Soviet Union. He quoted Brezhnev as saying that every writer who slandered Soviet reality deserved public condemnation. Gollan noted that, in order for the public to condemn a work, it must first become acquainted with it. In his brochure, Gollan emphasized the program of 1968 which proclaimed the goal of a future democratic socialism.

In 1976, in anticipation of the Thirty-fifth Party Congress planned for November 1977, the inner-party discussions intensified. A revised program was prepared which was to consider the events of the last decade. The Stalinists launched an offensive against the entire party, led by the Chairman of Surrey, Sid French. In the meanwhile, the opposition continually threatened an open break.

In the summer of 1977, the Stalinists decided to establish their own organization, justifying this move with the contention that they disagreed with parts of the draft of the party program. Since the Stalinists had had the opportunity to voice their opinions during the open discussions on the draft of the program, however, this contention was clearly only a pretense. The Stalinists obviously knew that they would face certain defeat at the Thirty-fifth Congress and were thus not willing to engage in political discussion.

There followed, in mid-July 1977, the political and organizational split of the British Communist Party. A party, called the New Communist Party, was formed under the leadership of Sid French. The number of people who actually joined the new party was not announced, but it is estimated that membership now numbers only several hundred.[40]

When the time seems right, the Kremlin will presumably want to establish this splinter group internationally as the "true British Communist Party."

At the Thirty-fifth Party Congress in mid-November 1977, the Eurocommunist program, "The British Road to Socialism," in its new version was adopted by a vote of 330 to 40. The acknowledgment of democratic freedoms, was clearly expressed and the program declared that even within the framework of a socialist society, a future British government would be willing to abdicate without resistance if it were to lose the consent of the majority of the voting public. In the presence of Soviet Politburo member Kunayev, Secretary General Gordon McLennan declared that the British Communist Party was independent, and agreed with the Eurocommunist parties on many issues. With reference to policies of the Soviet bloc, he declared that one could not simply forbid political parties. In a socialist society, he insisted, the people had to be granted the right to choose among different ideas.

CP Great Britain—Election Results			
CP Great Britain has not been represented in the Parliament since 1950.			
Date	Number of Communist candidates	CPGB votes	%
July 1945	21	102,780	0.4
February 1950	100	91,765	0.3
October 1951	10	21,640	0.08
May 1955	17	33,144	0.1
October 1959	18	30,896	0.1
October 1964	36	46,422	0.2
November 1966	57	62,092	0.2
June 1970	58	33,970	0.1
March 1974	43	32,741	0.1
October 1974	29	17,426	0.06
May 1979	38	15,958	0.05

Finland's Communists: The Struggle Between Reformers and Stalinists

The new orientation of the Finnish Communists was and is proceeding under difficult conditions. Tendencies toward independence vis-à-vis the Soviet Union played a small role for obvious geographical and political reasons. The disputes between reformers and Stalinists centered mainly on internal matters, including the participation in the government. Those disputes, however, are not confined to the Finnish Communist Party alone but also include the relationship of the Finnish Communist Party, with its approximately 50,000 members, to the Finnish People's Democratic League, with its 150,000 members.

In contrast to most European Communist parties, the Finnish Communist Party did not experience a noticeable loss of influence during the period of late Stalinism from 1945 to 1953. The Finnish Communists, who appear to their voters in parliamentary elections as part of a front organization, the Finnish People's Democratic League (Suomen Kansan Demokraattinen Liitto, known by its abbreviation SKDL) maintained its large share of the vote during the crucial postwar years. In July 1948, it had received 20 percent of the vote and a decade later, in July 1958, it received 23.1 percent of the vote. The death of Stalin, the Twentieth Party Congress in February 1956, the subsequent de-Stalinization and the suppression of the Hungarian Revolution had relatively little effect on the Finnish Communist Party.

Criticism was voiced for the first time at the beginning of the 1960s, and the publication *Tilanne* (The Situation) was instrumental in that criticism. *Tilanne* was published by a group of Communist intellectuals led by the writer and former antifascist resistance fighter Jarno Pennenen, who had either left or been expelled from the party. The publication, with the subtitle "Independent, Socialist, Humanist," criticized the Communists in capitalist countries for mechanically copying the development of the East European people's democracies. It was essential, *Tilanne* claimed, to strive for individual initiatives and independence and to form one's own ideas about socialism and the future socialist society. And it was necessary to conduct open discussions. As a result, the publication approved of the Socialist People's Party in Denmark.[41]

Discussions of these theses soon followed in the Finnish Communist Party and the Democratic League. In the party newspaper, *Kansan Uutiset* (Voice of the People), party members complained that the Finnish Communist Party was "controlled from abroad" and "dependent." The members' fear of not appearing faithful enough to the party made open discussion impossible. Moreover, members declared that the party should also take an independent stand on the problems of the Soviet Union. Its working methods were outmoded, they protested, and no longer corresponded to the changing society.[42]

In the mid-sixties, Finnish Communism began to change in two ways: on the one hand, the Democratic League began to separate itself from the Finnish Communist Party and, on the other, the Finnish Communist Party began to experience a distinct split between a progressive reformist majority and a Stalinist minority.

At the end of 1964, the Democratic League began striving to free itself from Finnish Communist Party regimentation. In February 1965, the Communist Secretary General of the Democratic League, Mauno Tamminen, was removed from his post. He was succeeded by the independent socialist Dr. Ele Alenius, who has directed the Democratic League ever since. From the very beginning, Alenius advocated a peaceful road to socialism which would correspond to the conditions of Finnish society. Although the Democratic League still remains the front organization for the Communists, it has developed more and more into a rather independent organization. At the party congress in May 1970, the Democratic League adopted new statutes which formally reflected the tendency toward independence. In his speech, Alenius advocated greater independence and freedom of opinion, simultaneously stressing the particularly important role of the Soviet Union for Finland. In his address to the congress, the Soviet guest, Leningrad Party Secretary Nikolai Romanov, declared that the Finnish Communists had to remain the leading political force in the Democratic League. Later that year, seventeen Communists and eight non-Communists were elected to the executive body of the Democratic League, but the majority of the elected Communists belonged to the reformist group. In April 1973, the Stalinists lost almost every position in the leadership of the Democratic League. The conflicts became so serious that run-off elections had to be held between individual candidates. In one such run-off, the independent Socialist Alenius was confirmed as Party Chairman, defeating the Stalinist candidate Enzio Laine by a vote of 185 to 48.

Since 1965, the Democratic League has succeeded in increasing its independence from the Communist Party.

At the same time, however, the Finnish Communist Party itself was beset by serious disputes. As of the mid-sixties, Communists themselves criticized the authoritative style of leadership and complained about the lack of inner-party democracy as well as the remnants of Stalinism in their own party.

The decisive turning point came at the Fourteenth Party Congress of the Finnish Communist Party held between January 29 and February 1, 1966. It was the first Finnish Communist Party Congress which was not completely regimented; serious discussions took place and different views surfaced. The congress resolved to formulate a new party program and the reformer Aarne Saarinen, who is still in office today, replaced Stalinist Party Chairman Aino Aaltonen, who had led the party for two decades. Stalinist Ville Pessi was endorsed as Secretary General of the party, but another reformer, Erkki Salomää, became Deputy Party Chairman.

The success of the leftist forces during the Finnish elections in March 1966—the Social Democrats received 27.2 percent of the vote and the Democratic League received 21.2 percent—resulted in the formation of a coalition government in Finland which included the Communists. Communists took over the ministries of Social Welfare and Transportation, and Dr. Alenius became Deputy Minister of Finance. The Stalinists opposed the participation of the Democratic League in the government and waged a campaign against Deputy Communist Party Chairman Erkki Salomää, who early in June 1966 had declared that the working-class road to power in Finland would be different from the one in Russia in 1917.

A draft of the Finnish Communist Party program adopted at the Fourteenth Party Congress was published in autumn 1967, and the subsequent period was marked by bitter confrontation between the reformers and the Stalinists. The program can be summarized in the following main points:

1. The material prerequisites for socialism in Finland have already been met to such a great extent that any significant reform is also a step toward socialism.

2. The Finnish Communist Party strives to achieve socialism in a free and democratic way.

3. The transition to socialism can be accomplished only with the support of the overwhelming majority of Finnish people, and the implementation of socialist measures necessitates a strong majority in Parliament.

4. The transition to socialism is possible only if the political and social organizations of the workers and other large organizations actively cooperate.

5. Besides previous experiences in the socialist countries, the indi-

vidual Finnish experiences, the national traditions, characteristics, norms, and customs must be considered.

6. A socialist democracy does not mean that the democratic institutions are eliminated, but rather, that they are expanded.

7. Decisions in a socialist society depend on the will of the majority. Any dissident group which observes the constitution of the socialist state and the prevailing rules of order has the right to its own activity.

8. Besides public ownership, communal and cooperative ownership according to Finnish conditions should play a greater role in socialist society.

9. In order to achieve its goals, the Finnish Communist Party advocates close and constructive cooperation among all democratic parties, both in capitalism as well as in the transition to socialism and in the socialist society itself.[43]

The term "Dictatorship of the Proletariat" was not used in the draft of the Finnish Communist Party program of autumn 1967, and in place of the usual term "Marxism-Leninism," the terms "Marxist theory" or "theoretical principles of Marx, Engels, and Lenin" appeared. A large majority of party members welcomed the draft, while a Stalinist minority bitterly opposed it. The Stalinists, led by Aaltonen (who had been removed in February 1966), were represented in the southwestern harbor town of Turku and in the eastern part of central Finland, Kuopio.

The Stalinist opposition continually demanded the repeal of the resolution of the Fourteenth Party Congress and the revision of the draft of the program, which it criticized as "revisionist." The opposition was becoming so pronounced that at an extraordinary session of the Central Committee, in December 1967, discussion centered around ways to overcome the threatening split. The Central Committee decided to form a commission for the restoration of unity of the party.

But even this commission could not bridge the gap, especially since the activity of the Stalinist opposition increased rapidly after the spring of 1968. As a result, the party leadership summoned all party members to an open discussion in April 1968 in order to bring the factional struggle to light.

As a result of the occupation of Czechoslovakia, the disputes within the party intensified. The Politburo opposed the occupation by a vote of nine to four and the Central Committee also by a vote of twenty-four to one. Afterward, the leadership of the Finnish Communist Party protested, although in mild form, against the occupation of Czechoslovakia. Only the regional organization of Turku, under the control of the Stalinists, supported the occupation. *Pravda* published only the Turku declaration, an action which party Chairman Saarinen called "deplorable and tactless."

The Fifteenth Party Congress of the Finnish Communist Party, at which the draft of the program announced in October 1967 was to be adopted, was scheduled for April 1969. During the preparations for the congress, the controversy worsened between the reformers under the direction of Saarinen and Salomää and the Stalinist minority, led by Aaltonen and Sinisalo. At the end of March 1969, the Stalinists organized their own conference. One hundred and sixty-five functionaries participated and declared that the forthcoming Fifteenth Party Congress had to put an end to revisionism and that the reformer Erkki Salomää had to be expelled from the party leadership.

The Fifteenth Party Congress, which took place from April 3 to 6, 1969, ran a stormy course. Differences between the two groups were obvious right at the very outset with the welcoming of foreign delegates. The Stalinists applauded the mention of pro-Soviet foreign party delegations only, and not those which they considered revisionist. The party program was finally adopted by a wide margin, setting the party on a free and democratic road to socialism and ending the "dictatorship of the proletariat." At the same time, the congress adopted a new statute which guaranteed the freedom of religious beliefs, lessened the party obligations, and somewhat limited the power of the Central Committee.

The elections for the leading party bodies were marked by such strong disagreement that a run-off election was necessary, a rarity for Communist party congresses. The Stalinist opposition demanded a stronger representation in the Central Committee and ran Enzio Laine as their candidate for party chairman. Saarinen, however, defeated him by a vote of 263 to 214. The thirty-seven-year-old party Secretary of Lapland, Arvo Aalto, became Secretary General, barely defeating Ville Pessi. Despite the resistance of the Stalinists, Erkki Salomää remained Deputy Party Chairman. The party congress resolved that the Stalinist regional party newspaper *Tiedonantaya* (The Reporter) could only be distributed in its traditional region and no longer throughout Finland as the rival publication to the official party newspaper, *Kansan Uutiset.*

When the Stalinists convened a counterparty congress at the end of April 1969 and, combined with other organizational measures (such as establishment of their own party district officers, etc.), made a split in the party seem inevitable, the Soviet leadership intervened.

The Soviet party official sent to Finland, A. S. Belyakov, tried to mediate between the two Finnish party factions, but the negotiations became increasingly difficult, particularly since the Stalinist opposition put up additional demands and claimed the post of Deputy Party Chairman for Taisto Sinasalo. In mid-September 1969, the Stalinists threatened to put up their own list of candidates at the forthcoming national elections in March 1970. At the end of 1969, a temporary compromise was finally reached. The leadership of the Finnish Communist Party declared its willingness to accept Aino Aaltonen, one of the two leaders of the Stalinist faction, into the Central Committee. They could not agree, however, on the Deputy Party Chairman. The pressure from the Stalinists remained so strong that the party leadership convened an extraordinary party congress for mid-February 1970, which divided the most important leading bodies of the Finnish Communist Party proportionally between reformers and Stalinists. According to the breakdown, the thirty-five-member Central Committee was to be composed of twenty representatives from the reformist group of Saarinen and fifteen representatives from the Stalinist group under Sinisalo. Saarinen was confirmed as party Chairman, but he received two deputies having equal rights—the reformer Salomää and the Stalinist Sinisalo. The Politburo was increased from twelve to sixteen members; ten seats went to the reform group and six to the Stalinists. Five reformers and three Stalinists made up the Secretariat of the Central Committee. The party congress further resolved that although the members of the Central Committee could express differing opinions in public, they had to comply with the decisions of the majority.

These serious internal disputes led, at election time in March 1970, to a reduction in the Communist share of the vote. In the March 1970 elections, the Communists received only 16.6 percent of the vote as compared to 21.2 percent in 1966. Instead of the forty-one representatives to which they were entitled after the elections of 1966, the Finnish People's Democratic League now had only thirty-six deputies in the Finnish Parliament. Eighteen of these representatives belonged to the reformist group, fifteen belonged to the Stalinists, and three were independent socialists. Nevertheless, the new participation in the government (the Communists controlled three ministries) did not last very long. In March 1971, under the increasing pressure of the Stalinists, the Democratic League renounced its participation in the government. Within the Finnish Communist Party, the confrontation between reformers and Stalinists began to escalate again. At the Sixteenth Party Congress of the Finnish Communist Party, held from

March 31 to April 2, 1972, party Chairman Saarinen declared that indeed the party was split. This congress confirmed the proportion system between reformers and Stalinists in the party leadership. In August 1972, the Stalinist newspaper *Tiedonantaya* described the occupation of Czechoslovakia as "the day of victory for proletarian internationalism" and welcomed the trials which were taking place in Czechoslovakia.

The proportion system was strictly observed during the subsequent negotiations with the Soviet leadership. Both Saarinen, representing the reformists, and Sinisalo, representing the Stalinists, were included in the Finnish Communist Party delegation in Moscow in June and October 1973 and again in February 1974.

The differences between the reformers and the Stalinists became so strong that at the fiftieth anniversary celebration of the Finnish Communist Party in summer 1974, the supporters of Saarinen showed up wearing red shirts, while the supporters of Sinisalo wore blue ones. In the presence of the Soviet Central Committee Secretary, Kapitonov, Saarinen declared that the Communists desired to cooperate with other parties during the transition to socialism as well as after its establishment. The Stalinist Sinisalo, on the other hand, directed harsh attacks against the Social Democrats and accused the Social Democratic government of "greasing the machinery of capitalism" and claimed that its policies were aimed at stifling the struggle of the working class.[44]

Although in mid-March 1975, a ten-member Finnish Communist Party delegation (six reformers and four Stalinists) again conferred with the Soviet leadership in Moscow, the internal split of the Finnish Communist Party could not be overcome. At the Seventeenth Party Congress of the Finnish Communist Party, which took place from May 16 to 18, 1975, the possible future Communist participation in government was again the center of discussion. In the domestic sphere, as a stipulation for participation in government, delegates to the congress demanded stronger price and rent controls and nationalization of the banks and large industrial enterprises. In the foreign-policy sphere, the congress elected to reduce Finland's imports from the West, to increase economic cooperation with the socialist countries, and to call off the trade agreement with the EEC. One unusual resolution of the party congress, intended to promote party unity, forbade the Stalinist minority to accuse the majority of being "rightist revisionists," and the reformist majority in turn to call the minority "leftist sectarians." Moreover, the congress reconfirmed the 1970 proportion system in the main bodies of the party.

After the Democratic League received 19 percent of the vote in the elections in September 1975 and sent forty representatives to the Parliament, participation in government again became the main topic of discussion. In the Central Committee of the Communist Party, twenty reformers voted for participation in the government and fourteen Stalinists voted against it. During the formation of the government at the end of November 1975, three representatives of the Democratic League, all of whom belonged to the reformist wing, were accepted into the government. Nevertheless, participation remained very difficult, since the parliamentary faction was split. Although it was agreed upon by the Democratic League (which included the Communists), the Stalinist minority faction voted against the government's resolutions in February 1976. In the course of 1976, the split in the parliamentary faction together with the continuing inner-party disputes affected the trade unions. Soon the Social Democrats and reform Communists were at odds with Stalinists in the trade unions.

The proportion system still exists in the Finnish Communist Party today. The peculiarity of Finnish Communism is the fact that the split between a reformist majority and a Stalinist minority has been institutionalized for almost ten years by a meticulously observed proportion system. To a certain extent, the reformist majority can be considered Eurocommunist, especially in its ideological goal, its party structure and its pluralistic model of socialism, but due to Finnish conditions not in the realm of foreign policy.

The Soviet leadership seems up till now to be interested in retaining the proportion system in the Communist Party of Finland—which

---

**CP Finland—Election Results and
Parliamentary Representation since 1945**

The Communist Party of Finland participates in elections through the Finnish People's Democratic League (Suomen Kansan Demokraattinen Liito, SKDL).

Date	SKP votes	% of total	Deputies out of 200
March 1945	398,618	23.5	49
July 1948	375,820	20	38
July 1951	391,362	21.5	43
March 1954	433,528	21.6	43
July 1958	450,506	23.2	50
February 1962	507,124	22	47
March 1966	502,713	21.2	41
March 1970	420,894	16.6	36
March 1972	438,387	17	37
September 1975	438,757	19	40

is unique in the history of Communism—and in preventing an overt split. Moscow values Finland's good conduct in the realm of foreign policy and the Finnish Communist Party's participation in government more than it values the implementation of its own concepts within the Finnish Communist Party. In the event that the interests of the Soviet Union change, a split will be unavoidable and Finland will have both a reformist Communist Party on the one hand, and a Stalinist party, on the other.

15

Eurocommunism Outside Europe: The Japan Communist Party (JCP), the Communist Party of Australia (CPA), and the Movement Toward Socialism (MAS) in Venezuela

The Japan Communist Party: A Eurocommunist Mass Party in the Far East

The Eurocommunists themselves have repeatedly stressed the special significance of the Japan Communist Party (JCP). Santiago Carrillo declared that the term "Eurocommunism" was incorrect, especially because such an important party as the Japan Communist Party fell outside its scope. In addition, the party Chairman of the Left Party of Sweden, Lars Werner, declared in his speech in the Swedish Parliament in March 1977, that the Japan and Australian Communist parties must definitely be considered Eurocommunist.

The Japan Communist Party has more than 370,000 members and, during the last national election in Japan, received over 10 percent of the vote. It is represented in the Parliament, and the mayors of many Japanese cities were elected by coalitions of which the Communist Party was a member. With a daily circulation of over a half-million and a Sunday circulation of more than two million, the Japan Communist Party newspaper, *Akahata* (Red Flag), is one of the most widely circulated Communist Party newspapers in the world.

In contrast to other parties, the process of independence and a new course took place in three steps. From 1963 until 1965, the party successfully freed itself from Soviet trusteeship. Over the next few years, it separated from the Chinese Communists. And since 1968, the Japanese Communists have been approaching the Western Eurocommunists, a fact which has led to a Eurocommunist policy in the Japan Communist Party since 1970.

After World War II, the Japan Communist Party was legalized and refounded by a group of veterans, in October 1945. Two members of this group were Kyuichi Tokuda, who was released after many years' imprisonment, and Sanzo Nosaka, who had spent many years with the Chinese Communists in Yenan, their partisan capital at that time, and who returned to Japan in January 1946. Today Nosaka is the Chairman of the Politburo of the Japan Communist Party.

From 1946 until the beginning of 1950, the Japan Communist Party pursued relatively moderate policies. The official line consisted of carrying out the bourgeois-democratic revolution. Advocacy of land reform, the improvement of working conditions, and activity within the framework of the democratic constitution were linked with a commitment to a peaceful road to socialism. During the elections of 1946, the Japan Communist Party received barely 4 percent of the vote and, in 1949, this number rose to almost 10 percent, enabling the Japan Communist Party to send thirty-five deputies to Parliament. However, shortly before the Korean War, this evolution was suddenly interrupted. In January 1950, Stalin personally initiated sharp criticism of the Japan Communist Party in the Cominform and forced it to introduce a harder line.[1] The Japanese Communists were compelled to sharpen the party line drastically—especially through a harsh anti-American course and open commitment to a revolutionary overthrow of the government. As a result, the Japan Communist Party lost half of its membership, the party organ *Akahata* ceased appearing between the years 1950 and 1952 and, during the elections of 1952, the percentage of votes the party received fell from 10 to 2.5 percent. It also lost its representation in Parliament.

This ultrarevolutionary course was not softened until 1955-1956. At the Seventh Party Congress, in 1958, Nosaka was elected party Chairman and Kenyi Miyamoto was elected Secretary General. Miyamoto was later to play an important role in the formation of the new course. Born in 1908, Miyamoto graduated from the University of Tokyo and became a member of the JCP in 1931. In 1933, he was already in control of the propaganda department. Miyamoto was imprisoned from 1933 to 1945 and, after his liberation in 1946, he became a member of the Central Committee; in 1947, he also became a member of the Politburo.

The increasing Sino-Soviet conflict proved to be the decisive impetus for the new course of the Japan Communist Party. At the beginning, the JCP, much like the Romanian Communist Party, tried to steer a neutral course between Moscow and Peking. But Khrushchev's demand, in October 1961, that the Japanese Communists finally join the Soviet line and clearly align themselves against China and Albania increased the resistance of the Japanese. In 1963, the JCP began taking a pro-Chinese line. Although it published Chinese and Albanian articles, it never fully identified itself with Maoism. Under these circumstances, the Soviet Union started intervening in the internal affairs of the JCP through its diplomatic representatives, party officials, and journalists, establishing contacts with pro-Soviet functionaries within the JCP. As early as 1963, the JCP repeatedly complained to Moscow. An article in *Pravda* by the Soviet journalist Zhukov finally alerted the public to the dispute between Moscow and the JCP for the first time.[2]

Negotiations between the leadership of the JCP and Brezhnev, Suslov, and Ponomaryov took place in Moscow from March 2 to 11, 1964. The Japan Communist Party representatives, according to later Soviet publications, complained about "intervention in the internal affairs of the JCP" and threatened to break off relations between the two parties. The dispute continued primarily through a new exchange of letters between Moscow and the JCP, with the JCP publishing all the letters and the Soviet newspapers publishing only the Soviet letters.[3]

In an official letter to the Kremlin leadership, dated July 15, 1964, the Japanese Communists protested the Soviet leadership's continued unfounded accusations and charged the Soviet leaders with having established contact with antiparty groups under the direction of Yoshio Shiga and Ichizo Suzuki during the negotiations between the Soviet and Japan Communist Party delegations in Moscow. Moreover, the Soviet population was completely misinformed about the JCP, for only the Soviet accusations, and not the replies of the JCP, were being published in the USSR. The letter from the Japanese Communists contains the first reference to the independence of the Japan Communist Party: "As an independent political party which follows the principles of Marxism-Leninism, our party emphatically rejects your unjust and unprincipled demands."[4] In a second letter to the Kremlin leadership in August 1964, the JCP documented its independence for the first time. "Our party does not defend another party without criticism, nor does it obey another party blindly. Instead, it views all matters, including the polemics within the world Communist movement independently and in accordance with Marxist-Leninist principles."[5]

In the course of these press polemics, Yoshio Shiga and Ichizo Suzuki, who were conducting their own relations with the Soviet leadership, were expelled from the Presidium of the Central Committee of the Japan Communist Party, in May 1964, and, in June and October 1964, other well-known pro-Soviet party activists followed. In mid-July, the pro-Soviet group published the first issue of its newspaper *Nippon Koe* (The Voice of Japan), of which *Pravda*, in its July 16 issue, thoroughly approved.

The Ninth Party Congress of the now autonomous Japan Communist Party met in Tokyo from November 24 to 30, 1964. Shortly thereafter the pro-Soviet splinter group, which called itself the "Communist Party of Japan/The Voice of Japan," was founded, but until today it has remained a small, relatively insignificant faction.

After the Cultural Revolution broke out in China, the JCP began to dissociate itself also from Peking. This incited the Soviet leaders to try reestablishing relations with the JCP in the hope of attracting it to the Soviet side. As a result, in June 1966, a member of the Soviet Politburo, Victor Grischin, spoke with the leaders of the JCP in Tokyo and, several months later, in May 1967, discussions were held with a member of the Central Committee of the CPSU, Ivan Kovalenko. However, discussions were broken off without result. It became clear that the JCP had not separated itself from Peking in order to become dependent on Moscow again.

At the Tenth Party Congress of the JCP, which was held from October 24 to 30, 1966, the goals of a wide unity front with the socialists, the Komeito (a middle of the road Buddhist party), and the Social Democrats were announced. During the elections in January 1967, the Japan Communist Party raised its share of the vote slightly from 4.01 percent (in 1963) to 4.76 percent. In 1968, Moscow's hopes grew after the JCP had expressed even sharper criticism of the Chinese development, of the Mao personality cult, and rejected Mao's theses about the violent revolution and about the people's war.

At the beginning of January and the end of February 1968, talks were again held (in Tokyo) between a delegation of the Japan Communist Party headed by Miyamoto and a Soviet party delegation headed by Suslov. For the first time, the communiqué proclaimed the principles of autonomy, equality, and nonintervention in internal affairs.[6] Suslov promised to refrain from any further support of the Shiga splinter party. However, the Soviet leadership's hope that, after these talks, the JCP would participate in the Third World Conference in June 1969 was not realized—the Japan Communist Party did not participate at either the preparatory conference or the world conference itself.

During and after the "Prague Spring" of 1968, tension between the JCP and the Soviet Communist Party increased. In July 1968, the Japan Communist Party sent a letter of support to the leading representatives of the "Prague Spring" and published reports praising the Prague model. In August 1968, a serious controversy developed between Hakamada, the head of a Japan Communist Party delegation, and the Soviet party ideologue Suslov over the situation in Czechoslovakia. In these Moscow negotiations Hakamada strongly protested the intervention in the internal affairs of another socialist state. The Shiga splinter group welcomed the occupation of Czechoslovakia; the Japan Communist Party published a clear and harsh condemnation of the occupation.[7] Later, the JCP consistently rejected all attempts by the Soviet leadership to justify the occupation. As a result, intense press polemics arose between Moscow and Tokyo.[8]

After liberation from Soviet and Chinese domination, the Japan Communist Party was now, in 1968, seriously interested in improving its relations with the West European Communist parties. In autumn 1968, a delegation under the leadership of Hakamada first visited the French Communist Party, then the Italian Communist Party, and finally the Romanian, where it was received by Ceauşescu. In all countries, the Japanese Communists stressed that they advocated relations in the world Communist movement based on the principles of equality, independence, and mutual nonintervention.

Further controversies with Moscow broke out during the occasion of the celebration of Lenin's one hundredth birthday in April 1970. The official representative of the Japan Communist Party in Moscow was forbidden to speak on Lenin and Leninism at the official international conference. He was allowed to speak only at a small local meeting at which no foreign delegation was present. Moreover, the Japanese spokesman's references to the independence of his party and his demands for nonintervention in the internal affairs of other Communist parties were not published in full in *Pravda*. At the same time, however, Soviet diplomats officially participated in Lenin memorials of the pro-Soviet Shiga group which took place in Tokyo,

Osaka, and Kyoto. The Japan Communist Party again protested against the one-sided interference of the Soviet Communist Party.[9]

The controversy over the Kuril Islands also played an important role in the disputes between the two Communist parties. Already, ten years earlier, at the Twenty-first Extraordinary Party Congress of the CPSU, which took place in Moscow at the end of January 1959, Khrushchev had discussed this matter with the Japanese Communists and declared that the Kuril Islands, which had become part of the Soviet Union after 1945, would be returned to Japan as soon as Japan became an independent, peaceful, and neutral country. Eleven years later, in the summer of 1970, the Soviet publication *Party Life* printed an article harshly attacking the JCP under the headline, "On a Dangerous Road."[10] In over 900,000 copies of the Soviet publication, the Japan Communist Party was accused of having departed from proletarian internationalism. Its demand for the return of the Kuril Islands, according to the publication, was vindictive and anti-Soviet. The Japan party newspaper, *Akahata*, published the full text of the Soviet accusation and, alongside it, the JCP's rejection of the charges one by one. The JCP accused the Soviet Union of intervening in the internal affairs of the Japan Communist Party (the support of the Shiga group despite the Soviet's promise against it), of conducting a policy of superpower chauvinism (the intervention in Czechoslovakia and the retention of the Kuril Islands), and of disregarding Leninist principles.[11]

The JCP's new, clearly Eurocommunist course began with the Eleventh Party Congress, held from July 1 to 7, 1970, the first congress ever to be held in public. From abroad only a delegation from the Italian Communist Party and one from the Australian Communist Party participated; representatives of the Soviet and Chinese Communist parties had not been invited. The new course was expressed in the programmatic document "Perspectives for the 1970s and the Tasks of the Japan Communist Party." The main goal, according to the document, was the formation of a democratic coalition government—a wide unity front based on peace, neutrality, and democracy. The Japan Communist Party, it proclaimed, would attempt to achieve its goals legally through elections and through parliamentary activity. A coalition government would not be a one-party government, but would facilitate the activity of all parties, including the opposition parties. The idea that Marxism-Leninism was a "guide to action" was stricken from the party statutes at the congress. The activity of the party, according to the new statutes, would serve the interests of the population and would be in accordance with morality.

It was the first time that the concept of morality had been mentioned in Communist Party statutes.

After the Eleventh Party Congress, the relations with the parties of Europe which are today regarded as Eurocommunist were intensified. A final attempt by the JCP to achieve a normalization of relations with the Soviet Union took place in Moscow in September 1971. In the communiqué following the meeting, both parties stressed their independence, equality, and respect for nonintervention in internal affairs. Despite the differences of opinion over a great many issues, it claimed, the two parties would strive for normalization.[12] However, on the occasion of the fiftieth anniversary of the founding of the Japan Communist Party in July 1972, the two parties again voiced their differences of opinion. The JCP adopted a new symbol—Mount Fuji replaced the hammer and sickle—which corresponded more closely to Japan's individuality. Moreover, at the anniversary celebration, the parliamentary road to socialism, the condemnation of violence, and the goal of a democratic coalition government were reaffirmed. On July 15, 1972, *Pravda*, and especially the Soviet periodical *Problems of the History of the CPSU*, took advantage of the celebration to publish a negatively biased picture of the Japan Communist Party. It portrayed the Comintern as especially important and even Stalin's ominous instructions advocating the adventurous leftist course of the Japan Communist Party in January 1950 were justified as "constructive criticism." The road to independence of the JCP since 1964, however, was greatly distorted.[13] In a lengthy article, the Japan Communist Party newspaper *Akahata* rejected the Soviet publication's distortion of the history of the JCP.

Because of its independent attitude and increasingly Eurocommunist policies, JCP's influence on the Japanese people grew. During the elections on December 10, 1972, the Communist Party received 5.7 million votes (as compared to 3.2 million in 1969) and could now send thirty-eight deputies to the Japanese Parliament. The Japan Communist Party was now the third strongest political party after the Liberal Democrats and the oppositional Socialists. In light of the new conditions, the oppositional parties—the Socialists, Communists, Komeito and Social Democrats—strove to work more closely with each other.

Early in 1973, the four oppositional parties decided to unite to oppose the economic policies of the government, which were seen as serving the interests of big business, and to fight corruption, speculation, and rearmament. At the same time, they demanded the protection of the population's standard of living, to oppose any reduction of social security, and to increase pensions and social measures. The Italian Communist Party praised this as an important step in the formation of an alternative to the ruling conservative government.[14] These activities of the oppositional parties had an effect on the local elections in which common candidates of the four parties were having more and more successful results. In 1973, the candidates of the opposition parties were successful in Nagoya in April, in Osaka in June, in Tokyo in July (where the Communist Party even received more than 20 percent of the vote), and finally in Kobe in October.

This wave of success also characterized the Twelfth Party Congress of the JCP, which took place from November 14 to 21, 1973. During the period of autonomy and independence of the Japan Communist Party, the number of party members increased from 140,000 in 1964 to 300,000 in 1970, and finally to 330,000 at the time of the Twelfth Party Congress. With the founding of an Institute for Social Sciences comprised of renowned political scientists and sociologists, including nonparty members, the party increased its image in public affairs. At the Twelfth Congress, Miyamoto was confirmed as Chairman of the Presidium and Nosaka was confirmed as party Chairman. Representatives of the Italian, French, Spanish, and Australian Communist parties were among the foreign representatives, but no delegates representing the Soviet or Chinese Communist parties were present.

The "Platform for a Democratic Coalition Government" adopted at the Congress stressed respect for and defense of the Constitution. The Communist Party still wanted to dissolve the security pact with the United States, but, at the same time, advocated equal relations with the United States and emphasized the positive aspects of Japanese-American economic relations. A democratic coalition government, according to the platform, would respect all election results and would withdraw in the event of a defeat at the polls. In the economic realm, the platform called for nationalization of the energy sector (electricity, coal, gas, oil, nuclear energy); it did not advocate a planned economy, but rather, democratic control. In the platform, the Soviet Union was no longer regarded as the "front line of the world Communist movement" and the term "dictatorship of the proletariat" was replaced by "rule of the working class." Moreover, the political demands on the party members were reduced, and the platform stressed the democratic parliamentarian road to an independent, peaceful, and neutral Japan.

The reactions to the Twelfth Party Congress of the JCP were diverse. While the Italian Communists praised the new line,[15] *Pravda* complained that the Japanese Communists had portrayed the Soviet foreign policy in a "distorted way" and also criticized the JCP's attitude on the subject of the Kuril Islands.[16] In May 1974, the Soviet periodical *Party Life* once again published a harsh attack on the Japan Communist Party in the context of the Twelfth Party Congress. Officially the article was by the Secretary of the Central Committee of the Argentine Communist Party, Athos Faya, but it obviously expressed the Soviet leadership's opinion. The Japan Communist Party's advocacy of the return of the Kuril Islands was described as a unique case in the history of the world Communist movement. It was inconceivable, claimed Faya, that a Communist Party congress should make territorial demands of a socialist state. In addition, he accused the Japan Communist Party leadership of putting the Soviet leadership on the same level with China, in order to emphasize Japan's own independence.[17] After its publication, Faya's article was reprinted in many other publications of pro-Soviet parties in order to spread the one-sided information to the world Communist movement. The Japan party newspaper *Akahata* responded that the article, supposedly written by an Argentine Communist Party member, was obviously inspired or even written by the Soviets, for the Japanese names were reproduced in Russian transcription. *Akahata* defended the legitimate demand for the Kuril Islands, demanding that the Soviet Union finally conclude a peace treaty with Japan and that after the establishment of a democratic coalition government the Kuril Islands be returned to Japan. In addition, *Akahata* published the text of the 1959 agreement between the Soviet and Japan Communist parties, made during the Twenty-first Party Congress of the CPSU, which had been reconfirmed at the Moscow talks in 1971.[18]

European Communists watched the transition of the Japan Communist Party very closely. In the summer of 1974, *Le Monde* declared in a detailed analysis that the Japan Communist Party had succeeded in creating a new balance of power in the political life of the island state. As a result, the beginning of a possible alternative to the conservative government of Japan was clearly in sight. The fact that the JCP had dissociated itself from Moscow and Peking, claimed *Le Monde*, and that it had pursued an independent national course was instrumental in this development. According to the French newspaper, the Japan Communist Party, with its greater structural flexibility, power of persuasion, and realistic and moderate policies, had become more and more popular with the people and had attracted many

Japanese who wanted a change. Moreover, its strength was based not only on numbers, for with its new policies it created new possibilities for cooperation among opposition parties. [19]

During the local elections in 1975, the Japan Communist Party also succeeded in putting up lists of candidates in common with other opposition parties and in enjoying elective victories, such as in Osaka, the second largest city in Japan, with a population of over eight million, which has since been ruled by a representative of the left. Even in Tokyo, the capital, the opposition party candidates were elected.

The Japan Communist Party did not accept the Soviet invitation to the Twenty-fifth Party Congress of the CPSU, which took place at the end of February 1976. Instead, it improved relations with the Eurocommunists. Of particular importance in this context was the visit to Tokyo of a Spanish Communist Party delegation under the leadership of Santiago Carrillo in March 1976. It ended in a mutual acknowledgment of a socialist society according to the historical and social conditions of the individual countries. [20] Several weeks later, in April 1976, a delegation of the French Communist Party under the leadership of Secretary General Marchais also visited Tokyo. Both parties stressed their common ideas. Still more important was the manifesto of the Japan Communist Party of June 1976. This manifesto expressed more clearly than ever before the need for party pluralism, and respect of possible defeat at the polls; it emphasized freedom of the press, speech, religion, and art and promised not only to allow, but to support, private ownership of small and medium-sized enterprises and to nationalize only large key industries. The term "nationalization," however, was avoided. Instead, the manifesto spoke of democratic control. In addition, since 1976 the JCP has been conducting a campaign against moral and cultural decadence (the increase in criminal activity and violence, especially among young people), against drugs and alcohol, against idleness and compulsive gambling, and against sexual promiscuity and pornography in films and on television. The struggle for moral integrity of Japanese daily life thus became an important part of the Japan Communist Party line.

During the last national elections in December 1976, the JCP received 10.38 percent of the vote, as compared with 10.49 percent in December 1972, but because of new election laws, instead of the thirty-eight representatives it had, the JCP could now send only seventeen representatives to Parliament. The Liberal Democratic government party, however, lost its absolute majority. It received barely

42 percent of the vote and was faced with opposition from the Socialists, who received 20.7 percent; the Komeito, with 10.9 percent; the Communists, with 10.3 percent; and the Social Democrats, with 6.3 percent; while the remaining votes went to a splinter group of neoliberals (4.2 percent) or to other groups.

The latest evolution of the Japan Communist Party is marked by an intensification of the polemics between the Soviet Union and the Japanese Communists. On June 11, 1977, *Pravda* published an essay entitled "Against the Interests of Peace and of Good Neighborliness" with probably the strongest criticism yet of the JCP. The alleged "unjustified claims" of the Japan Communist Party to the Kuril Islands was the center of these polemics. The JCP's declaration entitled "On the Basis of International Law," was rejected by *Pravda*, which declared that one should not forget that the concept of law has a class character and that there is no abstract law. The Japan Communist Party's position, claimed *Pravda*, was also in opposition to international détente. But the JCP stood firm.

One of the leading representatives of the JCP declared that, at the Yalta Conference, Stalin had demanded southern Sachalin and the Kuril Islands—a part of Japan's traditional territory. This, claimed the representative, was the price for the Soviet Union's entry into the war against Japan. *Pravda*'s present position, he declared, was a repeat of Stalin's earlier mistakes.[21]

The JCP's development has much in common with Eurocommunism in the industrialized Western European nations. In Japan,

CP Japan—Election Results and Parliamentary Representation since 1945				
Date	CP votes	% of total	Deputies	Out of
April 1946	2,135,757	3.8	5	464
April 1947	1,002,903	3.7	4	466
January 1949	2,984,780	9.7	35	466
October 1952	896,765	2.6	0	466
April 1953	655,990	1.9	1	466
February 1955	733,122	2.0	2	467
May 1958	1,012,036	2.6	1	467
November 1960	1,156,723	2.9	3	467
November 1963	1,646,477	4.01	5	467
January 1967	2,190,564	4.76	5	486
December 1969	3,199,032	6.81	14	486
December 1972	5,496,827	10.49	38	491
December 1976	5,878,192	10.38	17	491

similarities in economic development, social problems, and the internal balance of power led to processes similar to those in Western Europe.

The Japan Communist Party was exposed to more press polemics with the Soviet Union than any other Eurocommunist Party. As in other countries, the Soviet leadership did not succeed in organizing a pro-Soviet counterparty.

Australia: Eurocommunists and the Pro-Soviet "Socialist Party"

The starting point for the new course of the Communists of Australia was the strong unrest after the Twentieth Party Congress of the CPSU in February 1956. Nevertheless, not much changed at first, partly because the party was directed by the absolutely pro-Soviet Secretary General Laurence Sharkey and partly because many Communist Party members at the time still hoped that the revelations at the Moscow Party Congress would help overcome the Australian party's own problems and make possible a completely new general course.

The Sino-Soviet conflict in the sixties, however, very much affected the Australian Communist Party (CPA). In the fifties, the Chinese and Australian Communists were in close contact and Australian Communist Party officials at that time were trained at the International Party Academy in Peking. In 1963, pro-Maoist trends began to form within the party, and in 1964, under the direction of E. F. Hill, the Maoist Communist Party (Marxist-Leninist) was formed, but it did not play a significant role in Australia's political left. The disputes before and after this split, however, led to far-reaching repercussions in the Australian Communist Party. Since 1963 more and more supporters of an "Italian direction" were making themselves heard within the CPA. This became even more important when, in June 1964, Sharkey was replaced by Laurence Aarons as new Secretary General. In October 1964, the CPA published its own declaration about Khrushchev's downfall. In 1965 after Khrushchev's downfall, de-Stalinization in the Soviet Union came to a halt and the effects of re-Stalinization began to be felt. Hopes for reforms in the Soviet Union died and the need for independence and reorientation in the CPA grew stronger.

In April 1965, Isi Leibler, a political scientist from Melbourne, published a book entitled *Soviet Jewry and Human Rights*. At first, the Political Committee (as the Politburo of the CPA was called) rejected the author's assertions that an officially inspired anti-Semitism prevailed in the Soviet Union. Leibler, however, wrote to Secretary General Aarons that he would gladly discuss the issues raised in his book with representatives of the Australian Communist Party. As a result, the political scientist engaged in talks with the leaders of the CPA, convincing them of the validity of his arguments. Finally, Aarons declared his intention to discuss the problem of anti-Semitism with the Kremlin leaders during his coming visit to the Soviet Union.

In Moscow, in December 1965, the Soviet leadership assured the leading representatives of the Australian Communist Party that some of the anti-Semitic articles in the Soviet press did not reflect the official attitude. Toward the end of his stay in Moscow, Eric Aarons, the brother of the Secretary General of the CPA, was approached with the demand that the Australian Communist Party publish a detailed official article against the Chinese Communist Party. The Soviet Communist Party leadership would provide the article. Later, Eric Aarons reported: "The way the whole affair was conducted made it clear that this was not the first time that Soviet articles had been printed in the foreign press."[22]

In 1966, during the preparation for the Twenty-first Party Congress of the Australian Communist Party, there was considerable debate over the documents to be adopted at the congress which would establish the Communist Party as an equal partner in the coalition of the left. During the discussion, those who participated realized and accepted the need for free discussions among the leftist parties and within the CPA itself. Since that time, the term "democratic centralism" has never been mentioned, and the names of the leading offices and bodies of the CPA have been changed to better suit Australian conditions: the Secretary General became the National Secretary and the Central Committee was renamed the National Committee. The decisive turn, however, came at the Twenty-first Party Congress of the Australian Communist Party, held in June 1967, which supported a coalition of the left and a democratization of the party structure. Furthermore, the leftist coalition was to become much more than a popular front. It was needed, claimed the CPA, because of the complex nature of modern society, the diversity of activity of social forces, and the variety of problems arising. The negative experiences in the past were discussed in detail, as were overcentralization and ideological conformism. The coalition of the left was to proceed from the assumption that there were several groups in Australia which agreed to a socialist transformation of society in general but which expressed different opinions on important points of ideology, program, and organization. The growing leftist trend in the Labour Party as well as trends within the trade unions, among students, intellectuals, and members of the middle class were all seen as indications of the coalition of the left. This coalition—a sort of Australian "historic compromise"—was to carry out the most varying forms of common actions and to enable different groups to cooperate. Even forces which limited themselves unilaterally to the solution of a single problem, such as civil rights, social and health care reform, and school reform, were to be included in such a coalition. Finally, the coalition of the left was also supposed to lead to discussions on theoretical, programmatic, and organizational matters and to contribute to a challenge of opinions based on "mutual respect, tolerance and candour among the different groups and parties." This was to be an important guarantee "for a true democracy in future socialist society."[23]

During the discussions at the Twenty-first Party Congress, several participants suggested eliminating the term "Communist" from the name of the party. Others suggested dissolving the party and to work as an individual organization within the Labour Party. Nevertheless, the majority rejected these suggestions.

At the same time the Twenty-first Party Congress of the Australian Communist Party advocated a "Charter of Democratic Freedoms" affirming democracy. All this occurred in June 1967, before the "Prague Spring." Moreover, at the party congress, the CPA already rejected the principle of "democratic centralism" and the theses of a leading role of a monolithic Communist Party. The conditions in Australia, it was claimed, could not be compared to previous socialist revolutions which were accompanied by violence and civil war. In Australia, the congress insisted, a socialist society could be established without the use of force. Liberation from Stalinism and restoration of a moral position would be a precondition of such a development. The Twenty-first Party Congress also effected democratic changes in the organizational structure of the party. From then on, all elections to party positions were conducted in secret. Special commissions were formed to discuss questions of personnel and inner-party conflicts. Only party members who did not belong to the local or regional party leadership could be elected to these commissions. The National Committee (previously called the Central Committee) was charged with informing the entire party of any political questions which were unclear or in which there were differences of opinion. Richard Dixon was elected new Chairman of the party, Laurence Aarons became National Secretary, and Claude Jones and John Allen Sendy were elected Deputy Chairmen.

The Twenty-first Party Congress, in June 1967, marked the beginning of the Communist Party of Australia's independent course. In January 1968, the CPA protested against the trials of four young Soviet writers taking place in Moscow. The Australian Communist Party newspaper *Tribune* declared that it was deplorable that the facts of the case were not published and that the Soviet reports were unclear, even contradictory. As a result, the National Committee decided to send a delegation to the Budapest consultation meeting planned for February to March 1968. The delegation was to discuss supposed anti-Soviet activity of Soviet dissidents with the representatives of the CPSU. In Budapest, Bernard Taft, representing the CPA along with Claude Jones, met with the Hungarian philosopher Georg Lukács, who had very definite opinions about the Soviet Union, Stalinism, and the "Prague Spring." Lukács admitted to the Australian Communists for the first time that he had spent some time in prison in the Soviet Union himself. Lukács asked Taft not to publish the transcript of the meeting until after his death, and Taft complied with his wishes. In 1968, Taft traveled to Czechoslovakia, where he was an eyewitness to the "Prague Spring"; he wrote an enthusiastic report about it in the Australian Communist Party newspaper. [24] Consequently the Australian Communist Party welcomed the development in Czechoslovakia during the "Prague Spring" more clearly and emphatically than any other Communist Party. In July 1968, it also organized mass meetings for the "Prague Spring" in all large cities of Australia.

After the occupation of Czechoslovakia in August 1968, the CPA not only protested in its party newspaper but also sent protest delegations to the embassies of the Warsaw Pact countries in Sydney. In addition, the CPA spoke out for a common initiative of all Communist parties which had taken a stand against the occupation of Czechoslovakia. The CPA coupled the criticism of the occupation of Czechoslovakia with an analysis of the situation in the Soviet Union, declaring that the overconcentration of power in the hands of the Soviet bureaucracy had restricted democracy there to such an extent that every attempt at democratic reforms in the Soviet Union was regarded as a rejection of the principles of socialism. [25]

Under these circumstances, it was not surprising that the pro-Soviet forces suffered quite a setback during the elections for delegates to the Twenty-second Party Congress, receiving, on the average, only one-fourth of all votes cast. The Twenty-second Congress of the Australian Communist Party, held at Eastertime 1970, confirmed the independent course of the party. At the party congress, discussion focused on the development in the socialist countries. Participants decided it was necessary to formulate an objective analysis of socialist development, especially in the Soviet Union. During the course of the discussion, they determined that the Soviet Union would no longer be called a "socialist country" but, rather, a country "with a socialist economic basis."[26]

Shortly after the Twenty-second Party Congress, the Soviet leadership in Moscow began its counteroffensive. *Pravda* had published only excerpts of the suggestions made by the small pro-Soviet minority of the CPA.[27] The Czechoslovak Party newspaper *Rudé Právo* published an article which strongly condemned the course of the Australian Communist Party.[28] The Australian Communist Party newspaper *Tribune* reprinted the full text of the article, adding its own response in which it suggested that *Rudé Právo* might also print, in Czechoslovakia, the response of the CPA. In *Tribune*, the Australian Communist Party declared: "Socialism cannot win trade unions if trade union representatives who are elected by the workers are discharged by resolutions of smaller party bodies. Socialism cannot win democrats if representatives of the parliament are dismissed by a higher party body which does not give the people the opportunity to express its will through new elections. Socialism cannot win Communists if the party record depends on the approval of foreign intervention, or if a policy established by the leaders is implemented without approval of the party congress and if half of the members of the party are thereby excluded."

Rudé Právo, of course, did not publish the Australian response, and the Soviet weekly *New Times* took over *Rudé Právo*'s attack of the Australian Communist Party without even mentioning the CPA's reply. During the disturbance caused by the press campaign, a pro-Soviet splinter group formed in Australia. In June 1970, two former leading Australian Communist Party officials, Edgar Ross and Alf Watt, founded the pro-Soviet publishing house Socialist Publications and began publishing the periodical *The Australian Socialist*. In autumn 1971, the pro-Soviet minority formed a Standing Committee and at the beginning of December 1971, the founding conference of the Australian pro-Soviet Communists finally took place. Ironically, the new party called itself the Socialist Party of Australia.

At the Twenty-third Party Congress of the Australian Communist Party, held from March 31 to April 4, 1972, there were no longer any protests from the pro-Soviet forces, for the congress was boycotted by all pro-Soviet Communist parties. Only the Japan and Spanish Communist parties sent delegations. The Eurocommunist parties of

Italy, Romania, Yugoslavia, Great Britain, and Greece (interior) sent greetings. The party congress confirmed the aim of a coalition of the left. National Secretary Aarons declared that, rather than denouncing one another, Communists should talk among themselves. Charges of mutual "revisionism," "Stalinism," "Maoism," or "bureaucratism" were to remain part of the past, he said. The Australian Communist Party, he declared, was an open and democratic party. The congress decided on further democratization of the party structure (the National Secretary would be elected for only six years). It also proclaimed the goal of "socialism with a human face" after the model of the "Prague Spring" and stressed more emphatically than any other Eurocommunist party workers' control and self-management in both economy and society.[29] After the party congress, a delegation of the CPA visited the Eurocommunist parties in Spain, Italy, France, Romania, and Yugoslavia.

In boycotting the Twenty-third Party Congress of the Australian Communist Party and forming a rival pro-Soviet socialist party, the Soviet leadership went further than it had done with any other Eurocommunist Party. In December 1972, representatives of both the Communist Party of Australia and the pro-Soviet Socialist Party of Australia were invited to Moscow to attend the celebration of the fiftieth anniversary of the founding of the USSR. Pat Clancy, the pro-Soviet SPA representative, was given preferential treatment on radio and on television. *Pravda* also spoke only of Clancy as the representative of the Australian Communists. When two seats were reserved for the main event in the Kremlin, John Sendy, Chairman of the Eurocommunist CPA, left the room in protest and then informed Ponomaryov that the Australian Communists would not tolerate putting the newly founded SPA on the same level as the CPA.

The last negotiations between the Australian Communist Party and the Soviet leadership took place in Moscow from September 28 until October 3, 1973. National Secretary Laurence Aarons participated on the Australian side and Ponomaryov and several of his closest advisers participated on the Soviet side. Aarons repeatedly declared that it was absolutely legitimate for Communist parties to discuss the policies and actions of the socialist countries in a friendly manner. A new relation between democracy and socialism, he claimed, was necessary in the struggle for socialism in the industrially developed capitalist countries such as Italy, France, Great Britain, and Australia. Furthermore, it was necessary to show that the goals of socialism also meant liberation for all people. Therefore, Aarons insisted, ideological conflicts in socialist countries could never be settled by administrative measures. According to the Australian Communist, the actions of the Soviet authorities against people like Andrei Sakharov and Major General Piotr Grigorenko would harm both the Soviet Union and the socialist cause in general. Aarons added that in the future, the CPA would also take it upon itself to criticize the mistakes of the CPSU. Finally, Aarons demanded that the CPSU withdraw its support of the SPA in order to clear the way for the normalization of relations with the CPA. Speaking for the Soviets, Ponomaryov declared that the issue of normalization depended upon the Australian Communist Party and its "anti-Soviet attitude." The Soviet Union, he insisted, would be ready for normalization when the *Tribune* no longer published anti-Soviet articles. Ponomaryov finally demanded that the CPA no longer call the Soviet Union a country "with a socialist economic basis" but that it again officially recognize the Soviet Union as a "socialist country." (*Tribune*, November 20–26, 1973). The insistence on this distinction in terms had serious ramifications, for if the Soviet Union were considered a socialist country, the term "socialism" would refer to an already existing political and social form which was becoming more and more intolerable for the Eurocommunists.

After the Australian Communists refused to comply with the Soviet demand (a majority of the National Committee had voted to refuse), the press campaign intensified. In November 1973, the Soviet journal *Questions of Philosophy* published an attack on the Australian Communist Party; in February 1974, *Party Life* followed with another attack, and, finally, Moscow arranged to have the pro-Soviet Communist Party in the United States issue a criticism of the Australian Communist Party.[30]

Today the Australian Communist Party is boycotted by all pro-Soviet Communist parties. It has connections only with the Eurocommunists, favoring the social self-management system of Yugoslavia. Therefore, in November 1973, the CPA published an official apology for its declaration against Yugoslavia in the summer of 1948, in which it had harshly attacked President Tito and other Yugoslav Communists.[31] The Australian Communist Party sent a particularly warm greeting to the League of Communists of Yugoslavia during its Tenth Congress, praising the development of self-management and the struggle against the corruption of democracy as the Yugoslav Communists' decisive contribution to revolutionary theory and the international movement.[32] Early in 1975, an Australian Communist Party delegation visited Romania and then Yugoslavia and Italy. In November 1975, it held friendly talks with leading representatives of the Spanish Communist Party.

Nevertheless, the membership of the Australian Communist Party is relatively small, varying between 3,000 and 5,000 in the last few years. In addition, the CPA has no representatives in Parliament. However, the Australian Communist Party plays an important role in the theoretical and political development of Eurocommunism.

The Communists of Venezuela: The Independent MAS and the Pro-Soviet Communist Party

In his report at the Twenty-fourth Party Congress of the CPSU on March 30, 1971, Secretary General Brezhnev warned the 5,000 delegates about renegades like Garaudy in France, Fischer in Austria, and Petkov in Venezuela. . . .[33] His listeners grew attentive. Petkov? Venezuela? Were there "deviants" in Venezuela also? Yes, there were and there still are today in the Movimiento al Socialismo (Movement toward Socialism). The MAS was formed in January 1971, after two years of conflict within the Communist Party of Venezuela. Like the Socialist People's Party of Denmark, the MAS was formed when a group of leaders and a majority of the members left the Communist Party, proclaiming new roads and goals and even creating a completely new type of organization in the world Communist movement.

The Communist Party of Venezuela, founded in May 1931, existed for the most part either illegally or semilegally. Only after the downfall of dictator Perez Jiménez in 1958 did it begin to play a role in the country's political and social arena, quickly gaining considerable influence in the organized labor movement. During the elections in December 1958, the Communist Party of Venezuela received 6.3 percent of the vote. In Caracas, the capital, it even became the second strongest party. But this legal period was short-lived. After Castro's takeover in Cuba in the beginning of 1959, revolutionary forces to the left of the Communist Party appeared in Venezuela. At the same time, many within the Communist Party were disappointed with the legal forms of struggle and, late in 1960, started talking about joining in the armed struggle of the leftist revolutionary movement MIR, which had been inspired by Castro. From 1962 to 1965, the party concentrated predominantly on armed guerrilla warfare, although unlike the MIR, it also continued the political struggle. Only at the beginning of 1966 did the Communist Party of Venezuela return to legal methods of struggle, and in March 1967, a bitter conflict with Castro ensued. At that time, the party was being led by Secretary General Jesús Faria, but since he spent most of his time in Moscow,

Acting Secretary General Pompeyo Marquez wielded most of the authority. In June 1968, during the "Prague Spring," three representatives of the Communist Party of Venezuela, including Secretary General Faria, conferred with Suslov and Ponomaryov in Moscow. In August 1968, Faria returned to Venezuela. In March 1969, the Communist Party was again legalized and the political prisoners, including many Communists, were released.

Under the direction of its pro-Soviet Secretary General, Jesús Faria, the Communist Party of Venezuela approved of the occupation of Czechoslovakia. Critical voices were first heard during the preparation for the next party congress (which had been planned for December 4, 1970) after the party press had become more open and allowed free discussion. One of the most prominent critics was Teodoro Petkov, who wrote articles in which he objected to the intervention in Czechoslovakia. Petkov, who was born in 1932, joined the party in 1948 at the age of sixteen, studied economics, and became a professional revolutionary. Petkov was imprisoned for the first time at age eighteen, and from 1951 to 1953, he was arrested repeatedly. In 1960, after the collapse of the dictatorial regime, at the age of twenty-eight he entered the Parliament as a Communist Party deputy. During a period of armed struggle, Petkov lost his political immunity and was again imprisoned. He escaped, however, and participated in the conflict. Arrested once more, he spent two-and-a-half years in prison until he was able to arrange his escape. In 1964, Petkov became a member of the Politburo of the Communist Party of Venezuela.

In July 1969, Petkov published a series of interviews in the Venezuelan weekly *Semana* and some time later, his book *Czechoslovakia—the Problem of Socialism* appeared. In his book, Petkov declared that the Soviet model of socialism could not be obligatory for all countries. Czechoslovakia, he pointed out, had tried to develop a new model, and it was tragic that this new model was destroyed by the troops of the Warsaw Pact countries. In response to the Soviet arguments, Petkov declared that there had been no danger of either an invasion by West Germany or a return to capitalism in Czechoslovakia. The bureaucratic and authoritarian character of the Soviet Communist Party, according to Petkov, had ruined an important experiment of socialism. The Soviet Union, he claimed, was still enslaved by Stalinism and "proletarian internationalism" was simply another term for Soviet nationalism. Czechoslovakia had raised issues, continued Petkov, which were also significant for socialism in Venezuela. Petkov concluded the following for Venezuelan Communists: (a) they had to end the dependency on the Soviet Union and become a real Venezuelan Communist Party; *(b)* the party had to be democratized and the authoritarian party structure abolished; *(c)* the main struggle was to be directed not only against American imperialism, but against the capitalists of Venezuela.

Petkov's book, which also deals to a certain extent with the development of the Spanish, Italian, and Japan Communist parties, received much attention. In October 1969, Secretary General Faria drew up an open letter, bitterly reproaching Petkov. Then the party newspaper *Tribuna Popular* published articles accusing Petkov of an "anti-Communist" attitude. In response, Petkov asked in the same newspaper whether any criticism of the Soviet Union was automatically "anti-Communist." If so, he declared, then maybe Comrades Mao Tse-tung, Fidel Castro, Nicolae Ceauşescu, Kim Il Sung, and Luigi Longo were also "anti-Communist."[34]

In February and March 1970, the Central Committee convened an important meeting. Of the nine members of the Politburo, Secretary General Faria along with three others advocated taking disciplinary measures against Petkov. They accused him of being a Trotskyite, anti-Soviet, and against the party. However, Petkov received the support of two other Politburo members. Furthermore, between the Stalinists and the supporters of Petkov there were the so-called centrists, including the respected Politburo member Pompeyo Marquez. This middle group wanted to reduce the dependency of the Venezuelan Communist Party on the Soviet Union and did not want to deny Petkov the right to speak. Nevertheless, it wanted to mediate between the two extremes in order to prevent a split in the party.

While the youth organization of the party and many intellectuals sided with Petkov, the Stalinists under Faria continually lost support. Petkov was very popular and affected not only members of his own party but many other leftists. Discussion intensified in late autumn 1970, when Petkov's second book, *Socialism for Venezuela,* appeared. In this book, Petkov criticized the leadership of the Communist Party of Venezuela for suppressing all independent criticism. In addition, he advocated a coalition of leftist forces without the hegemony of one party and as a pluralistic socialist society aimed at putting an end to a monolithic dictatorship in political and cultural life. Shortly thereafter, at the end of October 1970, the Soviet journal *Questions of Philosophy* published a sharp criticism of Petkov's book, which was signed by S. S. Romanov and M. I. Mopshnalchev. Even more important for further development, however, was an article in *Pravda* by Mosinov,[35] accusing Petkov of having slandered the Leninist organizational principle of "democratic centralism" and of having corrupted

the process of building socialism. The article ended with a direct call
to the members of the Communist Party of Venezuela to restore the
unity of the party by rejecting Petkov's "anti-party activities." The
Stalinists in the party leadership regarded this article as a directive
from Moscow, and the *Tribuna Popular* published the Mosinov article
at the end of October.

In November 1970, in addition to the articles against Petkov,
Tribuna Popular also published articles which supported him and, finally, even an article by Petkov himself. The conflict intensified during the elections for delegates to the next party congress. The overwhelming majority supported the Petkov group, now known as "Los
Renovadores" (the Renewers). Under pressure of the Stalinists, the
middle faction, led by Pompeyo Marquez, also started approaching
the reformers. As a result, the emphasis was clearly beginning to
shift. At the Plenum session of the Central Committee of the Communist Party of Venezuela, held from November 23 until December 4,
1970, the opposing sides clashed. The Stalinists wanted to postpone
the next party congress, which was scheduled for December 4, for as
long as possible in order to convert the Stalinist minority in the meantime into a majority with the help of the party apparatus. The reformers, supported by the centrists, rejected this plan. However, the party
congress was postponed, but only until January 23, 1971.

Both sides began forming their own ranks. On December 10, 1970,
Tribuna Popular published a biting attack against the Renewers in
which Secretary General Faria claimed that they represented only a
small minority of the party. On the same day, the Renewers held a
press conference at which both Petkov and his supporters, and Pompeyo Marquez and the centrists participated. At the conference,
Faria's autocratic party leadership was sharply criticized and Faria
himself was accused of preparing a purge in order to change the tide
in his favor, fearing that the Fourth Party Congress would end with
his defeat.

On December 14, 1970, the die was cast. The Stalinist members of
the Central Committee held a meeting and decided to discharge five
members from the Politburo and twenty-two of the sixty-eight Central Committee members. But the plan was thwarted when, immediately thereafter, the officially "discharged members" formed a
Preparatory Committee for the Fourth Congress. It issued a declaration about socialism in Venezuela, advocating a wide coalition of all
anti-imperialist forces in which no party would dogmatically claim
the leading role, and later convened the party congress on January 14,
1971. Several days later, in the Venezuelan newspaper *Ultimas*

Noticias, Petkov published an article against the "mothball Marxists" who canonized Marxism and who wanted to reduce it to pompous perorations.

On January 14, 1971, the founding congress of the Movement toward Socialism (MAS) took place in Caracas. Pompeyo Marquez was elected Secretary General and Teodoro Petkov and the other Renewers and centrists of the former Politburo were given leading positions. The party newspaper *Deslinde* sided with the newly founded MAS. The founding congress spoke out for a coalition with all leftist forces. Thereafter, from January 23 to 28, 1971, the Stalinist forces of the Venezuelan Communist Party could only hold a party congress among themselves, using the meeting to declare their unshakable loyalty to the Soviet Union and to elect a new Central Committee and a new Politburo under the direction of the pro-Soviet Secretary General, Jesús Faria.

The manifesto for the founding of the MAS contained the following paragraph:

"There exist two different ideas of the party of Venezuelan economic and social reality and of the revolution. We have found ourselves in increasing disagreement with those who treat Marxism as a dogma or catechism and who turn the party into a sect with their backs to the masses. We consider those the worst forms of Stalinist degeneration."[36]

At the beginning of February 1971, in its newspaper *Deslinde,* the MAS announced the importance of developing clear political suggestions, to be ready for different forms of struggle, to develop an individual Venezuelan road to socialism, and to avoid mechanically transferring the experiences of other countries to Venezuela. The party, according to the MAS, had to be considered a force which facilitated the formation of an anti-imperialist, socialist people's government, which would enjoy the trust of the people and in which the working class would not be a spectator but the creator of a new society. The MAS was neither pro- nor anti-Soviet, it declared, neither pro- nor anti-Chinese, and neither pro- nor anti-Cuban.[37] Early in 1971, Secretary General Pompeyo Marquez, heading a delegation of the MAS, visited Romania and Yugoslavia as well as the Communist parties of Italy, France, and Spain. Upon his return, he declared that the Eurocommunists welcomed the formation of the MAS.

The MAS completely rejects the Leninist party structure. Moreover, it considers itself a movement and not a party. "We prefer horizontal structure and want to put an end to the pyramidal type of organization which existed under Stalinism," declared Teodoro Petkov. The MAS holds no closed party meetings and members are free to act in factories, enterprises, or neighborhoods "without being accountable to any particular party organization." According to Petkov, the MAS has been "excommunicated by the leadership of the CPSU," but is accepted as a revolutionary movement by many Communists. "Our main concern is not to condemn others but moderately to find and tread a road to socialism which corresponds to the specific conditions in Venezuela."

Thus, since 1971, there have been two Marxist trends in Venezuela: the Eurocommunist MAS and the pro-Soviet Communist Party under the direction of Jesús Faria. During the national elections on December 9, 1973, the MAS received 216,473 votes, or 5.2 percent of all votes cast. It was entitled to send nine deputies to the Parliament as well as one representative to the Senate. The MAS had become the third strongest party in Venezuela. The pro-Soviet Communists received only 1.1 percent of the vote and were entitled to send only two deputies to the Parliament and no representative at all to the Senate.

The situation has endured during the last several years. In the last election in December 1978, the Eurocommunist MAS received just under 6 percent of the vote and was entitled to send eleven deputies to the Parliament and two to the Senate. The pro-Soviet Communists received less than 1 percent of the vote and sent only one deputy to the Parliament. It is a miniature party serving only to enable the USSR to have an additional pro-Soviet voice at world conferences.

Part IV

Eurocommunism as a Challenge for East and West

The Challenge
for the East

16

Eurocommunism is a challenge for the bureaucratic dictatorial system in the Soviet Union and in Eastern Europe because Eurocommunists reject Soviet domination, advocate their own road to socialism, and consequently threaten Moscow's monopolistic position. Of even greater significance, however, is the fact that the Eurocommunist model of socialism has proved increasingly attractive to many critically thinking people of the East European countries. It supports the process of reform, gives new impulse to the human rights movement, and threatens the powerful bureaucratic structure of Eastern European regimes.

In the Western parliamentary capitalist systems many fear a negative Eurocommunist influence on the economic and political integration of Europe (i.e., on the EEC). Likewise, they fear a weakening of NATO and a change in the economic and social order along the lines of Marxism, especially in the countries in which the Eurocommunists stand a chance of participating in the government.

Consequently, it is no coincidence that leading representatives of the bureaucratic systems in the East as well as some politicians (primarily conservative) in the democratic capitalist countries of the West are very suspicious of Eurocommunism. They consider Eurocommunism, as mentioned before, "camouflaged Stalinism or disguised tyranny," a sort of "Trojan Horse" which will result in the destruction of the free world. Similar views, however, are also aired in Eastern Europe. Vasil Bilak, for example, the Stalinist Secretary of the Communist Party of Czechoslovakia, claimed that Eurocommunism is a conscious effort on the part of Western capitalists "to split up international Communism according to regional groups." Although the propagandists of capitalism "hide these revolutionary products in sheep's clothing," he claims, "a wolf in sheep's clothing is still a wolf."[1] Herbert Mies, Chairman of the pro-Soviet German Communist Party (DKP) in West Germany called Eurocommunism "a weapon of Western rightist Social Democrats . . . hoping to weaken the Communist movement" by setting the Western Communists "against the countries of real socialism."[2]

It is interesting to note that both sides have the same conception. The Stalinist bureaucrats in the East as well as some conservative politicians in the West regard Eurocommunism as a clever ploy or diversion initiated by the other side.

Many renowned experts on the Soviet Union and Communism stress that Eurocommunism is having a spreading effect on Eastern Europe. George F. Kennan has declared that the more independent the Western European Communist parties became, the more political choices the Eastern European parties would have. This new situation, he claims, could be very significant for world Communism.[3] The British scholar Hugh Seton Watson, who is in general skeptical of Eurocommunism, agrees with Kennan on this issue. According to Watson, West European Communists who act in accordance with their own constitutions would certainly make it easier for the Czechoslovak and Hungarian Communists to ask the question "Why can't our system be freer too?"[4] The British expert on Communism Victor Zorza believes that "the Kremlin knows that the greatest danger to its rule is posed by the discussion and dissemination of political ideas which would challenge its interpretation of the Marxist dogma."[5] And as early as 1970, the German expert on the Soviet Union and Eastern Europe Boris Meissner referred to the widespread effect of reform Communist ideas on the Soviet bloc countries, pointing out that the military intervention in Czechoslovakia was obviously a reaction to these ideas.[6]

Recently, several well-known West German commentators have referred to Eurocommunism's effect on the East. They stress that "the Eurocommunist model of socialism is becoming increasingly attractive to the socialist countries and, as a result, is threatening the power base of the Soviet Union in Eastern Europe, the basis upon which the Soviet Union's status as a world power rests." The Eurocommunists' theses and criticisms, they claim, have become "a thorn in the flesh of Soviet Communism." And in Poland especially, Eurocommunism is becoming an object of tremendous appeal not only outside the party, but also within the circle of officials.[7]

Similar views have been aired in the United States. The political scientist Charles Gati, for example, claims that having gone beyond criticism of single events in the East—such as the Soviet-led invasion of Czechoslovakia and the harassment of dissenters in several of the ruling-party states—Eurocommunists now press for the emulation of their own concepts and hence for systematic political change in Eastern Europe and eventually the Soviet Union itself. Moreover, claims Gati, East Europeans see Eurocommunism as "a promising source of ideological justification and political leverage in their search for more independence from Moscow. It tends to reinforce the image East Europeans have always had of their historic role in Europe as a bridge between East and West and more recently, as a kind of ideological potting shed for the introduction of Western ideas into the Soviet Union."[8]

The British commentator R. E. M. Irving declared that "independent Communism has a momentum of its own: the more the Western parties emphasize the importance of civil liberties, the more they are bound to come into conflict with the Soviet Union, whose system of government is in the last analysis based on a denial of certain human rights."[9]

But there have also been some skeptical voices among Soviet experts. The Italian commentator Pietro Sormani, in discussing the effects of Eurocommunism in Eastern Europe with various experts, says that "many shake their heads, affirming that nothing would change, or worse that the Soviet Union would tighten its controls on the Socialist countries."[10]

Michael Ledeen, a foreign affairs specialist, for example, is also skeptical about Eurocommunism's effect on Eastern Europe. "The Italian Communists," he claimed, "have been severely shaken by the phenomenon of East European dissidence, and they are caught between a rock and a hard place. They dare not attack Amalrik, Bukovsky and company for fear of presenting a Stalinist image to the West. Yet they are equally incapable of embracing the cause of human rights within the Soviet bloc, because their own rank and file will not tolerate such an 'anti-Soviet' position."[11]

Most Soviet experts, however, recognize the importance of Eurocommunism. Milovan Djilas, for example, declared that the Eurocommunist parties had nothing to do with the Leninism of the Soviet Union. "One cannot say that Eurocommunism will turn out to be a 'Trojan Horse' of the Soviet Union. It has nothing to do with

Soviet tactics and policies toward Western Europe. Indeed, the Soviet Union is very unhappy with Eurocommunism." If the Eurocommunists succeed, Russia will gradually lose its leading role in the progressive West, and a development will follow which "sooner or later will also turn against state capitalism in Russia."[12]

The Trotskyite theoretician Ernest Mandel appraised the situation in the following manner: "In Eastern Europe and the Soviet Union, the declarations of the Eurocommunists are greedily seized upon to defend political pluralism and democratic freedoms because these declarations are accepted as an alternative to the present form of political rule of the East European countries and as an alternative model of worker states. It is for that reason that Eurocommunism is a potential danger as far as the Kremlin is concerned."[13]

Eurocommunism has several different effects on the Soviet bloc:

a) The Eurocommunists' rejection of Moscow as the "center" and their emphasis of an individual road to socialism weakens Moscow's monopolistic power in the world Communist movement. Moreover, the emphasis on the individual road to socialism encourages the autonomy of similar forces within the Soviet bloc.

b) The Eurocommunists' criticism of Stalinism and of the present system in the Soviet Union adds validity to criticisms circulating within the country itself. The advocacy of a pluralistic multiparty model of socialism strengthens the moral and political forces which advocate reforms along the lines of democratization and liberalization.

c) The new Eurocommunist interpretation of Marxism offers critical and thoughtful citizens in the East ideological alternatives.

The new concepts and goals of the Eurocommunists serve as encouragement for the dissident reformers, especially critical Marxists in the Soviet Union and East European countries. They provide the dissidents with moral support and the opportunity to appeal to the new ideas of the West European Communists. In several cases, there has already emerged a solidarity between Eurocommunists in the West and critical Marxists in the East.

The Challenge of Moscow's Leading Role

The Eurocommunists' rejection of a "center" in the world Communist movement, their denial of the Soviet Communist Party's leading role, and their demand for complete equality and nonintervention in the internal affairs of individual parties all represent a considerable challenge to the bureaucratic dictatorial apparatus of Moscow. The Eurocommunists do not accept the most important theses of the Soviet Communist Party, whereby the world Communist movement acts as a unified instrument based on common goals and whereby all Communist parties of the world must accept "proletarian internationalism," which they understand as subordination to the CPSU and the Soviet Union. [14]

Eurocommunism entails more than just the rejection of important Soviet concepts. It denies the Soviet leadership the opportunity to manipulate Communist parties in important Western countries for its own foreign-policy goals. The Soviet leadership must renounce its hope of exercising any controlling influence over the Communist parties of Western Europe and through them extending its sphere of influence to Western Europe.

Moreover, the Eurocommunists' challenge threatens Moscow's interest in legitimizing its own power. The more the bureaucratic dictatorial system departs from Lenin's original revolutionary goals, the more important it is for Soviet leaders to refer to the revolutionary internationalist traditions of the past and thereby portray their own policies as embodiments of the goals of the world Communist movement. World Communist conferences therefore serve not only the practical policies, but also the legitimation of revolutionary internationalism. The Eurocommunists' rejection of the Soviet leaders' claim that they control the world Communist movement and their objection to regularly held world conferences endangers the internationalist legitimization of the Soviet leader.

Still more serious for Moscow is the Eurocommunists' rejection of the thesis of "general laws" in the development of socialism, their demand that policies be based on the conditions of individual countries, and their desire for autonomy and "unity in diversity" within the world Communist movement. The fact that the Soviet leadership felt compelled to accept this principle at the East Berlin Conference in June 1976 is not only significant for the Communist parties outside the Soviet sphere of influence but is also an incentive to the autonomous forces in Eastern Europe, for now the Communist parties in Poland, Czechoslovakia, Hungary, and East Germany can eventually demand more autonomy. Even within the Soviet Union itself, demands can now be made for the institution of pluralistic principles.

The Criticism of the Present System of the USSR and East Europe

Eurocommunism's second challenge for the East lies in its criticism of the contradictions in the present system of the Soviet bloc countries and its protest against the repressive measures which are so much a part of these systems.

This challenge is especially serious since the bureaucratic dictatorial system in the Soviet bloc is presently in a state of crisis.

Even many Soviet officials are realizing that the system which was created by Stalin in the late 1920s and which still exists today cannot meet the needs of a modern, industrialized Soviet society. The contradictions between the complex problems of a modern, industrially developing Soviet society and a completely obsolete, bureaucratic, dictatorial, hierarchical system can no longer be overlooked. The Soviet Union lags behind in scientific and technical progress. Its neglect of consumer-goods production and its frequent food shortages, the increasing conflict between the nationalities, and especially the suppressive nature of the regime all promote the tendency to develop an alternative and to advocate reforms and new roads to Soviet development.

Against the backdrop of these inconsistencies, the independent and often critical analyses of the Eurocommunists play an important role. As a rule, the Eurocommunists acknowledge the October Revolution of 1917 without reservation. Furthermore, they recognize the socialist character of the Soviet Union and the East European countries, the Soviet Union's decisive role in the defeat of fascism in World War II, and the principal features of Soviet foreign policy. Nevertheless, Eurocommunists condemn the repressive measures of the Kremlin, including the overthrow of Khrushchev in October 1964, the show trials against the Soviet writers Daniel and Sinyavsky in August 1966, the occupation of Czechoslovakia in August 1968, the suppression of the Polish workers' rebellion in January 1971, the expulsion of Solzhenitsyn early in 1974, the continual subjugation of intellectuals in the Soviet Union, the retaliations against the supporters of Charter 77 in Czechoslovakia, the expatriation of Wolf Biermann, the house arrest of Robert Havemann, as well as the anti-Semitic outbreaks in the Soviet Union and in other Soviet bloc countries.

Many East European and Soviet citizens share the Eurocommunist criticisms of such measures within the Soviet bloc. Several Eurocommunists have even begun to analyze critically the whole of Soviet development. As mentioned above, Togliatti declared, as in his memorandum of August 1964, that the problems of the Soviet Union and the East European countries could not be attributed to the personal characteristics of Stalin; rather, that Soviet development was a far-reaching process of bureaucratic degeneration. As a result, Togliatti claimed, it was important to overcome Stalinism as a system and to struggle for democratization.

Eurocommunists repeatedly blame the bureaucratic degeneration of the Soviet Union on the unfavorable conditions and the lack of democratic traditions of that country. Enrico Berlinguer, for example, declared that socialist development had taken place in countries "in which there were hardly any liberal or democratic traditions."[15]

Manuel Azcarate spoke of a Soviet development which was the result of a historic period that was bourgeois, and at times even feudal.[16] The Spanish Communist Party program of 1975 referred to the backwardness of Russia in 1917 and the influence of Soviet absolutism. In addition, it spoke of a negative development, especially the tendency to fuse the party with the state, a tendency which led to authoritarianism and bureaucracy.[17]

The Eurocommunist declarations about bureaucratization pose the most obvious challenge to Soviet leaders. In several cases, Eurocommunists even came close to questioning, at least partially, the true socialist character of the Soviet Union. In his book *Eurocommunism and the State*, Santiago Carrillo, after a detailed analysis concluded that the October Revolution of 1917 did in fact destroy the bourgeois state, but that the further development of the Soviet Union had led to the establishment of a state which repressed not only the former ruling classes, but also a large part of the working people. Complemented by acute societal contradictions, a bureaucratic stratum which acted in accordance with its own specific mechanisms and objective laws developed in the Soviet Union, claimed Carrillo. It was not a capitalist class, to be sure, but it commanded a limitless and practically uncontrolled political power with which it made decisions for the working class, and even for the party.[18] In addition, the French party theoretician Jean Elleinstein declared that in the course of Stalinism, a new bureaucratic stratum had arisen which could not be considered a ruling class but which represented socialism based on underdevelopment and from which Stalinism had not yet been eliminated.[19]

The Australian Communist Party, which dealt quite extensively with the system in the Soviet Union, refuses to consider the USSR as the realization of a socialist society but prefers to characterize the Soviet Union as a country "with a socialist economic basis." In late 1976, Lucio Lombardo-Radice, a member of the Central Committee of the Italian Communist Party, declared that the Italian Communists should study Soviet development systematically and theoretically, since all studies undertaken until then had been inadequate. Moreover, Lombardo-Radice suggested defining the system in the USSR as "state socialism."[20]

As a rule, however, Eurocommunists do not deny the socialist character of the USSR and are not ready to come to an overall critical analysis of the systems in that country. Indeed, the Western Eurocommunists' criticism does not go nearly as far as that of the dissident Marxists in Eastern Europe and the Soviet Union. The analyses of Robert Havemann and Roy Medvedev, for example, are certainly more comprehensive than any Eurocommunist analysis. This is also true of Jacek Kuron and Karol Modzelewski's analytically comprehensive conception of "monopolistic bureaucracy" and of Svetozar Stojanović's theory of "Oligarchic Statism." Both Stojanović and the dissident Soviet Marxist, P. Jegerov, defined "Oligarchic Statism" as a system based on state ownership of the means of production and state control over production and all social activities.[21]

Obviously, Western Eurocommunists believe that their primary task is not to formulate analyses of the Soviet Union. However, the fact that the books of Medvedev and Havemann have appeared (although in limited quantity) in the Italian Communist Party publishing house indicates that some Eurocommunists in the Western countries are dealing with the problem of analyzing the Soviet Union to some extent.

The Demand for Reforms in the USSR and Eastern Europe

Eurocommunists' criticisms of the system in the Soviet bloc are closely connected to their advocacy of democratic reforms. This is especially significant because in the Soviet Union and countries of Eastern Europe more and more groups are calling for an end to the bureaucratic centralist system. Even within the party apparatus, members and officials are beginning to favor granting economic managers, engineers, and scientists greater freedom of action, freeing economy and science from the restraints of bureaucratic and ideological tutelage, and encouraging the transition to a more modern, more rational, and more liberal government. This implies, of course, an end to the all-embracing dictatorship of the party; it also means that terrorism must be replaced by rule of law. Nevertheless, all attempts to carry out reforms run up against unyielding resistance on the part of the bureaucratic authoritarian forces which cling to their positions of power and privileges and whose sole political goal is to retain as much Stalinism as possible.

In addition to the vocal dissidents, other forces also advocate reform. In the scientific and technological realm, demands continue to grow for a modernization of the economic system, a greater delegation of authority and greater freedom of decision—demands which cannot be met without liberalization in the political realm. A self-assured Soviet working class in its third generation is now making its own demands, which the Kremlin cannot simply disregard. The non-Russian nationalities continue to object to Russification and are constantly pushing for autonomy. In many sectors of the population, opposition to the restrictive regimentation, to the inadequate freedom of mobility, and the almost nonexistent opportunity to travel abroad is growing rapidly. In addition, a modern faction within the party, state, and economic apparatus is beginning to realize that reforms are inevitable, and this group sympathizes at least in part with the reform tendencies.

In light of the situation, it is understandable that events such as the Helsinki Declaration of 1975, President Carter's human rights campaign, and the Eurocommunists' advocacy of reforms in the East play an important role. Already in the early sixties, Togliatti had favored reforms and democratization of the Soviet Union and Eastern Europe. The party program of the Spanish Communists, adopted in autumn 1975, declared that the progress of Eurocommunists in the West "would help raise the present socialist countries to a higher, more developed level."[22] In his book *Eurocommunism and the State*, Santiago Carrillo declared that through constructive criticism, one could help the Soviet Union "make progress in transforming itself into a real working people's democracy."[23]

Berlinguer's declaration at the East Berlin Conference of European Communist parties in June 1976, in which he explicitly advocated "a broader and freer exchange of ideas, of cultural currents and men, both in Europe and in the world,"[24] was a strong encouragement for the dissident forces in Eastern Europe. Several months later, Lucio Lombardo-Radice, a member of the Central Committee of the PCI, claimed that the new Italian, French, and Spanish models would pose a serious problem for the ruling Communist regimes in Eastern Europe. The Eurocommunists concentrated mainly on problems in Italy and Western Europe but their declarations "could become the voice of the opposition if they are translated and distributed in Moscow, East Berlin and Warsaw."[25]

In February 1977, Lombardo-Radice expressed this hope, claiming that in Eastern Europe "the outdated political structures must change now, too. They no longer correspond to present reality."[26] Jean Elleinstein even hoped that "at some party congress in the not too distant future people will appear who will demand progress out of economic need and democratic hope for the people of the Soviet Union."[27]

The Impact of the Pluralistic Model of Socialism on Eastern Europe.

The concept of a future pluralistic model of socialism also represents an important challenge. It is certainly no coincidence that the Soviet bloc newspapers censor almost all declarations of the Eurocommunists about political freedoms in a future socialist society.

The Eurocommunists advocate many democratic freedoms, including the inviolability of private life, the opportunity for unrestricted travel at home and abroad, the affirmation of a multiparty system together with the right for all opposition parties to exist and to be active as well as the opportunity for a democratic change of government in the event that the majority is no longer satisfied. These conceptions are inconsistent not only with the reality of the bureaucratic and dictatorial one-party system in the Soviet bloc but also with officially declared principles. According to Soviet ideology, a socialist society is characterized by its socio-political and ideological unity and, for that reason, there is no basis for conflict. This socio-political, ideological unity supposedly gives to all groups the opportunity to achieve their common goals. Consequently, there can be only one party—the Communist Party. It alone is the political leader and organizer of the people.[28]

The Eurocommunists reject the concept of a one-party system. Moreover, many critical Marxists in the Soviet Union and in the East European countries also advocate a multiparty model of socialism.

The demand for a multiparty system appeared in the middle sixties in an underground *Samizdat* publication "On the Multi-Party System," which an underground opposition group distributed in Leningrad. In 1970, the work of the critical Soviet Marxist Ilya Glumov, "On the Touchstone of Leninism," which also advocated a multiparty system in the Soviet Union, was distributed in dissident Soviet circles. Both publications declared that the Soviet one-party system was necessitated by and served the needs of the dominating bureaucratic class. According to critical Soviet Marxists, the official argument, which claims that a one-party system is necessary because it reflects the unified goal of Soviet society, is wrong because in reality such a moral-political unity does not exist. Even if it did exist, however, they claim, it would be entirely possible to have different parties striving for the same goal but suggesting different roads. One dissident Marxist group declared: "There are no justifiable arguments for the defense of the one-party system which can hold up to criticism; moreover, they are not consistent with Marxist portrayal of a socialist society."[29]

The demand for a multiparty system can also be found in later works by Soviet dissidents. Roy Medvedev, for example, has on several occasions advocated the need for a multiparty system. A multiparty system is necessary, he claims, because of the considerable social and political differences between city dwellers and the rural population in the USSR, between workers and intelligentsia, and between all of these and the bureaucratic elements that still exist in the state and party apparatus. The development of a multiparty system and the existence of opposition parties, according to Medvedev, would also create a new climate and new conditions for the ruling party. Under such circumstances, the party would have to be open to free discussion and appoint people with the most diverse qualifications to leading posts. Moreover, the mass media, and especially the press, would have to take on new characteristics. Only in conditions of overt political struggle will it be possible for genuine political figures to emerge, people who are capable of guiding the construction of a developed socialist and Communist society. A multiparty system characterized by true openness would be the best method of curing Soviet society from the evils of bureaucracy and corruption, and would serve as a guarantee against arbitrariness and unlawfulness.[30]

Three years later, Medvedev summarized his ideas about a multiparty system: "Although many people have different conceptions of socialism, the overwhelming majority of the Soviet citizens unconditionally favor the socialist road of development in our society. For that reason, there is no realistic development for the Soviet Union other than that of perfecting socialist society—the transition from the primitive bureaucratic variations of socialism and pseudo-socialism to socialism with a human face."[31]

The New Interpretation of Marxism as a Challenge for the Soviet Bloc

An especially important challenge of the Eurocommunists lies in their new interpretation of Marxism. The concept that Eurocommunists and Soviet Communists have "the same ideology" is simply no longer true.

Soviet Marxism-Leninism is marked by an unrestricted claim to universality and totality. It is officially "the only scientific ideology." Only the recognition of these doctrines enables one "to maintain a true scientific picture of the development of human society."[32] The existence of any supernatural force is rejected. Moreover, atheism is an inseparable part of the ideology, and the party statutes require all members not only to be atheists themselves, but to fight against "religious remnants." Marxism-Leninism explains all changes in nature, in society, and in human thought. The Soviet ideologues declare that, armed with this ideology, "man becomes strong, politically resolute and principled."[33]

The present claim to complete universality of Marxism-Leninism has led to a one-sided schematic ideology which allows only one correct Soviet interpretation. There is no room for either Trotsky's or Bucharin's ideas or for those of the Yugoslav theoreticians or the Maoists; there is also no room for the concepts of the "Prague Spring" or those of Eurocommunism. Although this compulsory and narrow-minded ideology today produces only disinterest and boredom—and many party officials of the Soviet Union have themselves admitted this—all independent thought is still considered deviationist. In this way, all further discussion is prevented.

The Soviet ideology clearly serves the legitimization of the regime, the ex-post-facto justification of the leadership's resolutions and measures, as well as forced models of thought, whereby what one must believe is not so important as what one must reject. Finally, Soviet ideology requires that an "ideological struggle" be conducted against all "deviations."

The Eurocommunists reject this decayed form of Marxism. For

that reason, the Italian, Spanish, French, Japanese, Swedish, and Australian Communists no longer employ the term "Marxism-Leninism." Even Lenin's theses are no longer sacrosanct and are criticized. Since the sixties, Eurocommunists no longer use Soviet ideological textbooks.

The Eurocommunists' new interpretation of Marxism can be summarized in the following main points:

1. The Eurocommunists reject some of the most important doctrines of Soviet ideology, such as "proletarian internationalism," "the general laws of the development toward socialism," the universal validity of the "dictatorship of the proletariat," the concept of a "moral and political unity" in socialist society, the doctrine of "socialist realism" as an obligatory general line for literature and art, the doctrine of "limited sovereignty," and especially the doctrine of the "leading role of the party" both during the struggle for socialism and after the establishment of a socialist society.

2. In addition, the Eurocommunists reject the Soviet ideology's restriction of Marxism to the works of Marx, Engels, and Lenin as interpreted in the official Soviet textbooks and party congress resolutions. Instead, they advocate an "opening up of Marxism." Eurocommunists stress the complexity of Marxism and accept the most diverse interpretations. The Italian Communists have published books by Marxists who have been expelled from their own parties, such as the Austrian Marxists Ernst Fischer and Franz Marek, the Polish writer Stefan Morawski, and the Czechoslovak writers Karl Kosik and Eduard Goldstücker.[34] All Eurocommunists refer to the writings of Antonio Gramsci, Rosa Luxemburg, Karl Korsch, Palmiro Togliatti, Tito, Georg Lukács, and Ernst Bloch. Even Leon Trotsky, who was (and is) ostracized by the entire Soviet bloc, is published and objectively discussed by the Eurocommunists.[35]

3. Eurocommunists in no way consider Marx, Engels, and Lenin as "sacrosanct." As mentioned above, Lenin's theories were and are criticized. In 1964, Luciano Gruppi, a leading theoretician of the Italian Communist Party, declared that some of Lenin's theses about the state and the dictatorship of the proletariat did not correspond to present reality. In his book *Eurocommunism and the State*, Santiago Carrillo opposes Lenin's "restrictive conception of democracy" which led disciples of Lenin to underestimate the value of democracy and which, as a result, contributed to the monstrous aberrations of Stalinism. Lenin's conceptions about the dictatorship of the proletariat are outdated, declares Carrillo, and no longer correspond to

present reality since today there are other ways of altering society.[36]

The Eurocommunists also make their own judgments about Marx and Engels. Enrico Berlinguer, for example, declared that, in contrast to what Marxist classics forecast, industries, artisan enterprises, merchants and peasant farms have continued to exist.[37]

4. Above all, Eurocommunists reject the Marxist-Leninist claim to universality. The reference in the Spanish Communist Party program is typical of the rejection: "The socialist state will have no official philosophy; the ideological struggle will be able to develop freely and openly even among socialist forces with similar conceptions."[38] These conceptions have since been adopted by all Eurocommunist parties. Enrico Berlinguer no longer considers Marxism an infallible scientific ideology, but rather, an instrument "which enables one to understand the happenings of today's world, an instrument which can give a solid theoretical foundation to the struggle for socialism."[39]

5. The Eurocommunists advocate a more serious attitude toward religion in general and toward Christianity in particular. Carrillo stressed the significance of those theologians who followed Teilhard de Chardin and who tried to bridge the gap between official Catholicism and science. According to Carrillo, the Second Vatican Council and the readiness to have open dialogue with science has brought a further amenability to the social currents of change and toward socialism. Therefore, argues Carrillo, it is not the simple repetition of doctrinal formulas valid in other periods, or, even less, an unpleasant after-taste of anti-clericalism that can help . . . advance and integrate Christians into the revolutionary forces. New forces have emerged which Marx, Engels, and Lenin could not have foreseen in their own time.[40]

Similar thoughts have also originated recently in Eastern Europe. The East German Marxist Rudolf Bahro, a critic of the regime who was arrested in November 1977, emphasized the need for Communists to consider the new developments within Christianity. On the one hand, claimed Bahro, many reflective Christians see in Marx's historical materialism an indispensable instrument for the understanding of social changes. Marxists, on the other hand, had to comprehend the significance of that ethical challenge which is part of Jesus Christ's Sermon on the Mount.[41]

As a general rule, the Eurocommunists emphasize their willingness to learn from all other intellectual currents. Berlinguer, for example, referred to Gramsci's declaration "that one should reach for every bit of truth, however small, that might be contained in the arguments of the opposition."[42] As for Christianity, Berlinguer said:

"A Christian, for example, sees aspects of life and of human relations that may in part escape the Marxist. We are ready to recognize the values and truths of others."[43]

Eurocommunists and Critical Marxists in Eastern Europe

Robert Havemann recently advocated a close cooperation between the struggle for democratization in the East and the struggle of the socialist workers' movement in the West. The progress of the Eurocommunist parties in the West, he claimed, would support the struggle for democracy and political human rights in the countries of "real socialism." Havemann said about Eurocommunism: "For me, the new road which the Communist parties of Italy, France, Spain and other parties of Western Europe have introduced and which is somewhat imprecisely called Eurocommunism is an extraordinarily encouraging sign."[44]

Rudolf Bahro sees the position of the bureaucratic apparatus in the East weakened as a result of the new developments in European Communist Parties: "The truth of the matter is that this so-called Eurocommunism brings the spirit of discord into the East European parties from the lower ranks of party officials all the way up to the Politburo." A successful Western European road to socialism along the lines of Eurocommunism, according to Bahro, would facilitate the institutional reforms in Eastern Europe, for "the peoples of Eastern Europe certainly favor political ideas along the lines of what Berlinguer, Marchais, Carrillo, et al. presented at the Berlin Conference."[45] In Hungary, the critical Marxist sociologist Agnes Heller, who belongs to the so-called Budapest School, declared that, as a representative of Eastern Europe, she would like to thank the PCI for filling "so many hearts with hope and for saving from desperation so many people who believe in the ideas of socialism."[46]

Edward Lipinski, a Polish Marxist economist, is another East European who holds similar views. In an open letter to the First Party Secretary in Poland, Edward Gierek, Lipinski wrote that he had long been following the development of socialist thought in the West, especially in Italy, for this line of thinking was completely stagnant in the Soviet Union or Poland. The violent introduction of the Soviet system in Poland, he said, had had devastating effects on the social, political, and moral life. This had occurred, claimed Lipinski, at a time when many Communist parties were freeing themselves from the

Soviet Union and realizing the importance of political democracy. Lipinski praised the Communists in Italy, France, Spain, and other countries for advocating political pluralism and for stressing the importance of political freedoms. "These ideological changes and transformations are of great historic significance," claimed Lipinski; "they represent an important step toward authentic socialism." Socialism, according to Lipinski, was only conceivable as the result of a change in the hierarchical, social, and political structures of society. "That is why I side with the Communist Berlinguer, with the Communist Marchais and with the Spanish Communists but not with the Communist Brezhnev."[47]

In June 1978, a Communist dissident group in East Germany called the League of Democratic Communists urged its followers "to propagate our criticism, popularize the ideas of the European and Japanese reform Communists and demand the basic documents of fraternal West European and Japanese parties.[48]

Critical Marxists of Eastern Europe and the Soviet Union have repeatedly turned directly to the Eurocommunists for assistance and support. In an open letter to Western Communist parties, Communists arrested in the Soviet Union appealed to the Communists of the West to demand the formation of an international commission to examine the conditions of the political prisoners in different countries, including the Soviet Union.[49] The son of Jiří Lederer, an imprisoned Czechoslovak critic of the system, urged Georges Marchais to intervene on the part of his father, who had signed the Human Rights Manifesto, Charter 77.[50] In July 1976, Jacek Kuron, a leading defender of human rights in Poland, wrote to Enrico Berlinguer asking him to intervene on the part of Polish workers who had been arrested in June during the demonstration against price increases.[51]

There are also some dissidents who, although favorably inclined toward Eurocommunism, nevertheless have certain reservations about it. According to these dissidents, the Eurocommunists are not consistent enough in their criticism of the East. Jiří Pelikan, for example, the director of Czechoslovak television during the "Prague Spring," declared that he had found the Italian Communists sincerely compassionate, but that he had noted with some dismay that the Eurocommunists limited themselves to criticism of certain details of Soviet reality, they did not dare to "put into question the true character of the system."[52] He welcomed the Eurocommunists' critical judgment of the Soviet Union but he also said he would prefer it if "their criticism went even further. Until now it has definitely not gone far enough." The violations of human rights which the

Eurocommunists condemn, claimed Pelikan, were not individual cases, but were typical for regimes which could not survive without repression and censorship.[53]

In addition, Eugen Loebl, a long-time Czechoslovak Deputy Minister of Foreign Trade and active participant in the "Prague Spring," who now lives in the United States, declared that the Eurocommunists should push for the right of self-determination for the peoples of the Soviet bloc and criticize Soviet imperialism openly.[54]

The Soviet Bloc Leadership and Eurocommunism

There can be no doubt that the concepts and activities of the Eurocommunists have forced the leadership of the Soviet bloc onto the defensive.

Within the leadership of the Soviet bloc, there is no longer any common general line regarding Eurocommunism. Rather, the leadership of each individual country takes its own stand on this issue. Moreover, Romania's leaders take absolutely no part in the campaign against the Eurocommunists, indeed they even support them. The bureaucratic Stalinist forces in the Soviet Union, Czechoslovakia, and Bulgaria have attacked Eurocommunists most harshly. The Polish leadership, although in a somewhat milder form, has also participated in these attacks. The most hostile opponents of Eurocommunism are the Bulgarian Party leader Zhivkov, the Czechoslovak Central Committee Secretary Vasil Bilak, and a number of Soviet ideologues. While Zhivkov called Eurocommunism "the latest work of bourgeois propaganda, saturated with anti-Sovietism," the First Secretary of the Hungarian Communist Party, Janos Kádár, told journalists in Vienna that he did not share Zhivkov's views.[55] Later, the Hungarian press also expressed a more understanding attitude toward Eurocommunism.

With the exception of the Romanian press, Soviet bloc newspapers do not publish Eurocommunist points of view, obviously fearing that readers could draw their own conclusions for their own countries. Even ideological, or so-called theoretical publications of the Soviet Union and East European countries do not present the principal ideas of the Eurocommunists and do not include excerpts from Eurocommunist publications. As a result, the polemics against the Eurocommunists are weak, helpless, and unconvincing. The many new problems and concepts which the Eurocommunists raise are not analyzed, but rather, are "denounced" as works of the enemy. Soviet bloc publications speak of "sly forms of bourgeois intrusion," whereby the opponent is portrayed as "sly, clever and mysterious." They reject Eurocommunist concepts as "revisionist" and claim that they are "a sign of the growth of petty-bourgeois influence."[56] Other Soviet ideologues believe that as a result of détente, the Communists are faced with new and complicated problems, including having to cooperate with other forces, especially the Social Democrats. This, however, paves the "way for the revival of revisionist elements."[57] The Social Democrats, they contend, tried to force their conciliatory positions on others "by working out common platforms."[58] For Soviet ideologues, Eurocommunism is just a modern form of "rightist revisionism," socially embodied in the growth of petty-bourgeois influence, politically determined by détente. Détente makes Communist parties face difficult problems, cooperate with other forces, and inevitably submit to the danger of being influenced by them.

Proceeding from this "analysis," the Soviet ideologues suggest to their Eurocommunist comrades that they strengthen the ideological struggle, hold fast to the Soviet model, comply with proletarian internationalism, and increase the struggle against anti-Communism and anti-Sovietism. They simply ignore the Eurocommunists' concepts altogether.

Break with the Soviet Union?

Although the Eurocommunists criticize the East, why don't they openly break with the Soviet Union? Even some of the relatively sympathetic critics of Eurocommunism declare that the Eurocommunists would gain credibility if they were to break openly with the Soviet leadership[59] and that as a result, their ideological and political development would be accelerated.[60]

There are many Eurocommunists who want to intensify the criticism of the East. Until now, however, official representatives of the Eurocommunist parties have rejected a complete break with Moscow. Enrico Berlinguer spoke of an "absurd demand that Communists surrender their friendship and solidarity with countries which contributed the most to the defeat of fascism and Nazism, which fought against imperialism and which are protagonists in the struggle for the maintenance of world peace."[61] Even Santiago Carrillo wants to prevent an absolute break. In March 1977, he declared that the Spanish

Communist Party had "criticized that, which in the political system of several countries of the Soviet bloc was undemocratic and thus not socialist" but the Eurocommunists, he claimed, refused "to aggravate a situation where a critical attitude exists differentiating us from the ideas of certain Communist parties in power and turn it into a matter of our having been misused elements of the Cold War."[62]

There appear to be two main reasons why the Eurocommunists refuse to break completely with Moscow:

First, the Eurocommunists hope, through a "policy of presence," to have the opportunity to support the dissident and reform movements in the Soviet Union and other East European countries by maintaining contact with these forces and by giving them encouragement. A complete break would, of course, make such contact impossible and, as a result, the Eurocommunists' critical voice would no longer be heard in Eastern Europe.

Second, although they themselves rarely admit it, many members and even some officials of the Eurocommunist parties still believe in the Soviet Union and the myth of the CPSU. The Eurocommunist leaders must take into account these pro-Soviet trends which are still present in their parties. According to an opinion poll taken of the members of the PCI in autumn 1977, 93 percent of the Italian Communists still believed that all inhabitants of the Soviet Union received jobs, regardless of their political affiliation, 53 percent believed there was religious freedom within the Soviet Union and—I think this is of particular importance—even 28 percent of the members of the PCI really believed that Stalin was the man who did the most for the Soviet state.[63] Of course, this 28 percent figure can be interpreted in different ways. One could say in a positive sense that 72 percent of the PCI members had overcome the Stalin myth. Nevertheless, 28 percent is not an insignificant figure. Clearly, the leadership of the PCI and of other Eurocommunist parties must consider the existing pro-Soviet attitudes.

Several eye-witnesses have emphasized the existence of such pro-Soviet currents. Jiří Pelikan, who now lives in Rome and has considerable contact with the Italian Communists, said: "Besides Berlinguer and the other enlightened party leaders, there are numerous officials who remain prisoners of the past and who would be ready to return to a hard Soviet line."[64] Other commentators declared that pro-Soviet forces in the Communist parties of Italy, France, and Spain systematically build up resistance against the Eurocommunists.[65] Milovan Djilas stressed that in the Eurocommunist parties there were still "Stalinist groups" some of which "are very strong and which receive support from the Soviet Union but which have no hope of taking over the leadership of these parties."[66]

There are interesting precedents in the history of the world Communist movement when the consideration of existing pro-Soviet attitudes was important. For at least two years after their break with Moscow in summer 1948, the Yugoslav Party leaders had to take into account some remaining pro-Soviet sentiments within the party and create a foundation for independent policies over a two-year period of political education and discussion.

The problem of a possible break between the Eurocommunists and the Soviet leadership, however, has also to be looked at from Moscow's point of view. Currently, the Soviet leadership seems to be interested in preventing an open break with the more important Eurocommunist parties, such as those of Italy and France. However, one should not forget that in countries with smaller Communist parties, such as Australia, Great Britain, Sweden, and Spain, the Soviet leadership did not hesitate to establish pro-Soviet rival parties. The Soviet leadership's interest in such important parties as the Italian and French Communist parties is apparently different. A break with these parties could seriously endanger the Soviet claim that it embodies the world Communist movement. There are also foreign-policy reasons for which the Soviets try to prevent a break. In Italy and France, the Communists stand a certain chance of participating in the government in the near future. A break with these Communist parties would therefore also affect the Soviet Union's official relations with those two countries. For that reason, the Soviet leaders postpone a final decision about Eurocommunism, leaving itself open to all possibilities.

Consequently, a break between Moscow and the Eurocommunists is unlikely in the very near future. Later, however, such a break might be entirely possible. The situation could change—and here I agree with Heinz Timmermann—if the Eurocommunists took over direct responsibility in the government of their countries. In that event, they would have to decide once and for all to whom they owed allegiance—to their own country or to their still existing albeit critical connection to the world Communist movement. Tito and Mao also first faced the real problem of their relations to the Soviet Union only after they had taken over the leadership of their respective countries. If that were ever the case in Western Europe, one could certainly expect dramatic developments between the Kremlin and Eurocommunism.[67]

The Challenge
for the West

17

Eurocommunism's challenge to the Western industrialized nations lies in the formation of a new left-wing party which is clearly different from the Soviet-type Communist parties but which nonetheless openly proclaims the goal of a transformation of society. Currently, the Eurocommunists' possible participation in governments in Italy, France, and Spain is a major issue in many political discussions. Most often discussed and important are the effects that such participation would have not only on the internal development of these countries but also, and to a much greater extent, on the European Economic Community and the Western defense alliance, NATO.

Eurocommunism
and Social Democrats

Some observers interpret Eurocommunism as a development in a Social Democratic direction.[1] Communist commentators in Eastern Europe stress the danger of a "Social Democratization," and the Trotskyite theoretician Ernest Mandel compares the development of Eurocommunism with the changes which occurred in German Social Democracy between 1890 and the mid-1920s. But also non-Communist commentators consider the transitions of the Eurocommunists as approaches toward Social Democracy. In November 1977, Italy's Christian Democratic Prime Minister, Andreotti, declared that the

Italian Communist Party 'shares many of the ideas of the Social Democratic parties."[2]

Eurocommunists themselves, however, repeatedly declare that their independence and new course do not imply that their ways have become Social Democratic conceptions. According to their own appraisals, the main difference between Eurocommunists and Social Democrats lies in the fact that Social Democrats strive for and have even accomplished reforms within the framework of the system, but nowhere have they been able to change the capitalist system itself. In June 1976, Berlinguer declared that despite much social and material progress, "none of these Social Democratic experiments has actually been able to overcome capitalism," or even to overcome "the domination of large economic and financial corporations."[3]

According to Berlinguer, one could not forget that future socialism means the assertion of new human values. In the Social Democratic societies, despite progress made in material well-being, many negative aspects of capitalism, such as alienation, still remained.[4]

Carrillo declares that Eurocommunism cannot be confused with Social Democracy, at least not with Social Democracy as it has manifested itself up to now. What is commonly called Eurocommunism proposes to transform capitalist society, not merely to administer it.[5]

This clear distinction between the Eurocommunists and Social Democrats does not mean, however, that the Eurocommunists judge Social Democracy in the same way that the Soviet Communists judge it. In the Soviet ideology, a distinction is commonly made between the "class conscious Social Democratic workers" and the "reformist officials," between the "progressive" Social Democrats (a term which applies to all those willing to cooperate with the Soviet Union) and the "rightist" Social Democratic leaders (who reject cooperation with the Soviet Union). The Eurocommunists reject such statements and, moreover, even recognize Social Democratic successes. Berlinguer does not wish to "be contemptuous" of the fact that the Social Democratically ruled countries have reached a certain level of prosperity. But he adds that all this has still not resulted in the actual defeat of capitalism.[6]

Eurocommunists reject above all the primitive Soviet thesis that in history the Social Democrats have always been wrong and the Communists have always been right. Santiago Carrillo urges Communists to examine carefully the grounds which have enabled Social Democracy to enjoy such a strong position in developed countries. It is no longer enough, he claims, to declare that capitalism has made Social Democracy its tool. The Social Democrats have certainly administered capitalist societies for years, but on the other hand, the Communists were not in a position to recognize the strength and prospects of capitalism and to wield greater influence over the working class. One should not forget, warns Carrillo, that Social Democracy still plays an important role in the workers' movements of many countries. This was partly possible because for a long time the Communists had mistakenly pictured the takeover of power as the storming of the Winter Palace—a conception which no longer corresponds to reality in Western Europe.[7]

In some of their publications, Eurocommunists also admit that both Social Democrats and Communists could not realize their goals because one side had insisted too much on reforms and the other had relied too heavily on pure propaganda. In that context, French Communist Party theoretician Jean Elleinstein refers to the historical mistrust between Social Democrats and Communists, declaring that this mistrust was mutual and went back to the split of socialist forces some sixty years ago.[8]

The Eurocommunists explicitly stress the difference between themselves and the Social Democrats, but they also indicate their willingness to review objectively previous attitudes toward Social Democracy. With certain exceptions, the same is true about the Social Democrats and their attitudes toward Eurocommunism. On the one hand, the Social Democrats want to maintain their fundamental opposition to Communism, but on the other, they are willing to take into consideration certain changes within Communism, such as the evolution of Eurocommunism. According to Willy Brandt, the Italian Communists in particular are undergoing "interesting de-dogmatization processes," although it was hard to tell just how far they went. After everything that has happened, declared Brandt, the Communists would surely have to wait for a closer, more careful scrutiny of these processes. Even if it were only a tactical maneuver, declared Brandt, it would still gradually lead to changes. "When that which appears to be happening in Italy finally occurs, it will alter the situation in other countries considerably."[9]

The willingness to recognize the evolution of Eurocommunism is often coupled with statements that one must evaluate this evolution carefully (draft of the Austrian Socialist Party program) and should "remain a skeptical and critical observer of the development." With all skepticism, it is evident that these Communist parties are ready to give the democratic process a try (Horst Ehmke). In the future, Eurocommunist parties could develop in such a way that they would no longer be "Communists as we know them" (Richard Lowenthal).

In the event that such transformations turn out to be real changes of opinion, "new perspectives for the development of Social Democracy" would result, it is claimed in the draft of the program of the Socialist Party of Austria.[10]

Both sides—Social Democrats and Eurocommunists—clearly demonstrate great discretion in their statements. At the same time, however, there are also some first indications that the deep-rooted split of the past is no longer as pronounced as it used to be. Both sides strive for a more objective evaluation, even if both parties—Social Democrats and Eurocommunists—still insist on their own positions. The Social Democrats especially cannot simply forget the suppression which their party members in the Communist-ruled countries must endure.

A rapprochement between the two parties can proceed only gradually. Any change in attitude on the part of Social Democrats, however, would be limited exclusively to the Eurocommunists and would not affect their uncompromising attitude toward dictatorial forms of Soviet-type Communism.

The Eurocommunists made the first attempts to overcome the previous split—which originated in the early twenties—through a sober and critical examination of both sides. Santiago Carrillo declared that the split between the Social Democrats and Communists in 1921 was understandable and even a historical necessity. "But it does not have to be eternal. In light of the conditions of today's world . . . there is a real historical need to overcome the split of 1921." Several conditions, according to Carrillo, were already developing which would help overcome the split. Needless to say, "this would not be an easy or quick process." Carrillo sees a common understanding between Communists and Socialists in several countries as a first step.[11] In addition, in November 1977, Gian Carlo Pajetta, one of the top leaders of the PCI, spoke of a possible future Communist-Socialist unity for Europe which would have to be discussed with West European Social Democrats.[12]

Possible Participation in Government

The possibility of future Communist participation in government has led to widespread public discussion. Such discussion is centered around not only the possible domestic consequences for the West European countries but primarily to the relationship of these countries to the European Economic Community and to NATO. Many fear that Communist participation in government will endanger West European unity and NATO and that, as a result, Western Europe will fall into the hands of the Soviets. Others see such participation as the opportunity to fulfill necessary basic economic and social reforms in these countries and, with the inclusion of leftist forces, to accomplish a greater social consensus within the framework of European unity.

Any consideration of the possible Communist participation in government must begin with an examination of the differences among the countries in question: Italy, France, and Spain.

For Italy, the Communists' entry into the government would clearly mark the start of a new phase in that country's postwar history. Following the Christian Democratic and center-right coalition between 1947 and 1962, the center-left coalition of Christian Democrats, Social Democrats, Socialists, and Republicans governed Italy between 1962 and 1976. In the meantime the political influence of the PCI increased. In many provinces and regions the Communists form the executive, sometimes together with Socialists, sometimes with Christian Democrats. Moreover, one must consider the PCI's strong influence in trade unions, without whose approval no economic or socio-political measures can be undertaken. Finally, of particular importance is the fact that, as of the elections of June 1976 in which the PCI received 34.4 percent of the vote, the Christian Democratic government is dependent on the support of the Communists in Parliament.

Since that time, many different points of view have been aired concerning possible Communist participation in the Italian government.

George Ball was among the more pessimistic commentators and described the effects of Communist participation in government in gloomy terms:

> What, in fact, would happen if the Communists should join an Italian coalition government? Even the prospect of that event has already triggered a mass capital flight; its actual occurrence would mean the exodus not only of capital but of many of Italy's leading financial and industrial figures. Investment would dry up; multinational companies would try to extricate themselves from their Italian commitments, even at the cost of closing plants and increasing unemployment. The Italian government would be forced to impose tight defensive controls. If the EEC were to take no action under the "mutual help" provisions of the Rome Treaty, and if the EEC nations, together with the United States, failed to support a rescue operation through the International Monetary Fund,

Italy could quickly find herself in a severe financial panic, with mounting inflation, labor strife and increased unemployment. Faced with a financial panic, the Communists in government would almost certainly opt for repressive measures that would unequivocally disclose their antidemocratic instincts. Far from inducing other European states to follow Italy's lead, the resulting uproar might rather be expected to induce a sense of fear and revulsion. If it were clear that Italy was on the way to isolating itself from the rest of Europe, Communism for other European countries could rapidly lose its appeal. [13]

Most important for the further development is the agreement of July 1977, which seemed to put an end to thirty years of antagonism between Christian Democrats and the PCI. This agreement marked a significant change in the parliamentary system, since it virtually ensured that the representatives of the six parties of the Parliament (the Christian Democrats, the Socialists, the Social Democrats, the Republicans, the Liberals, and the Communists) confer on all decisions beforehand. This meant, however, that the terms of the policies were not determined by the Prime Minister, as the Constitution prescribes, but rather, by the highest party bodies. With the inclusion of Communists in the decision-making process, the PCI, the second strongest party, finally celebrated the end of its status as an opposition party.

Once the Italian Communists were to enter the government, they would first work to overcome the economic crisis. Therefore, the Communists would not immediately start heading in the direction of a socialist transformation of society.

The Italian Communists have repeatedly declared that they "do not propose to extend further the state-directed sector of the economy," but rather, to reorganize the public sector, which is already comprehensive enough. With the help of economic planning, which would be undertaken with every consideration for the mechanism of the market, new priorities could be established for economic development. All fundamental decisions concerning economic planning would have to be presented to the Parliament, which reserves all rights to direct control. The regional authorities should not only present their regional plans, but should also participate in the national planning process. Moreover, trade unions should also participate in the process of economic planning.

In the realm of politics, Italian Communists advocate placing a higher value on the Parliament as an essential forum for the democratic decision-making process. The structure and function of Parliament should be suited to the new conditions of society, and the activities of the two chambers should be coordinated in order to prevent pointless repetition of debate and to simplify and accelerate the law-making process. The state apparatus, according to the Italian Communists, should be decentralized, and the regional authorities should receive more important duties and responsibilities. Moreover, the political parties must become organizations which can fulfill their actual purpose. They are to be freed from external pressure and decay and are once again to become politically active forces. The investigative committee of Parliament is to be strengthened in order to raise the public morale. Moreover, a more effective democratic control must be applied to all appointments to public institutions. The old-time practice of "dividing the goods" among the different parties in the government must be stopped. Appointments must be made solely on the basis of competence.

The relations between church and state must be based on acknowledgment of the freedom of religion and of the autonomy of all religious organizations and churches, as well as on the unquestioned sovereignty and independence of the Italian state. The state may not become the representative of any one party's ideology and may not favor any cultural, philosophical, scientific, or artistic idea. The state must act to guarantee the free exchange of ideas.

The military forces must also be democratized; soldiers and officers must be allowed to enjoy the same rights as civilians. The military forces should not alienate themselves from society, but rather, must live in close community with the population and with the democratic institutions of society. The positive character of military service should be emphasized, and the service should not only be viewed as instruction on how to handle weapons, but also as an opportunity to acquire additional education and vocational preparation and to increase conscientious citizenship.

In order to fight terrorism effectively, the police must receive the necessary technical schooling and must be compelled to adhere to democratic, constitutional principles. Policemen must have the right to organize trade unions. Moreover, much of the manpower which is wasted in administrative and bureaucratic duties should be converted to help fight terrorism directly. The numerous bureaucratic responsibilities of the police force should be transferred to civil authorities, especially in provinces and communities. As a result, the number of forces directly fighting crime would double or even triple. [14]

There is much dispute over the possible effects on Italy's internal development of the PCI's participation in the government. Some fear that the Communists could force their allies into a corner and establish a one-party rule. The Bavarian Minister of Education, Hans Maier, declared that he did not deny that "there can be Eurocommunist currents in the West" but that he questioned their ability to do what they might want. Until now, he claimed, "there has not been a single ruling Communism which has been able to liberalize itself."[15] Furthermore, the renowned journalist François Bondy already sees dangerous effects in the realm of the mass media. The fault lies not so much with the Communist politicians themselves, but their supporters, who join the winning side, try to prevent everything from being publicized in the press, over radio and on television, which might not be favorable to the Communist Party line.[16] On the other hand, in November 1977 the Italian Christian Democratic Prime Minister, Andreotti, did not think democracy was being endangered. He stated: "I believe that our constitution is respected and supported by most of the population. I do not see how this fundamental support could be altered. As far as the PCI is concerned, it is a group which shares many of the Social Democratic parties' views."[17]

The PCI's participation in the government would not only result in a change in the political arena of Italy, but would also create certain problems for the Italian Communists themselves.

In such a case, the Italian Communists would be faced with the dilemma of either realizing its great goal of transforming society through structural reforms or of solving current practical problems and of sharing the responsibility for difficult and unpopular measures which are necessary to pull Italy out of its present state of crisis.

In this process many of the Eurocommunists' supporters could be disappointed, especially if these measures proved wearisome and difficult. On the one hand, the PCI would have to take into account the views of its members, many of whom fear a "Social Democratization of the Party." On the other hand, the PCI would constantly have to prove its ability to rule.[18]

Were the PCF to enter the government, the French situation would be completely different. After the parliamentary elections of March 1978, however, the chance of such an entry seems remote. Originally the chances of PCF participation in government as a result of victory during the elections of March 1978 seemed good. For a time, it appeared as if the PCF would finally, after thirty years, have the opportunity to participate in the government. According to the cantonal elections of March 1976 and the local elections of March 1977, the Union of the Left could have expected to receive about 53 percent of the vote. But, because of the intensified disputes between the Communists and the Socialists, which began in autumn 1977, the French left forfeited its opportunity to join the government. The French Communists' sudden campaign against the Socialists hurt the PCF's position significantly, and in the national elections of March 1978, the Socialists received 22.6 percent of the vote while the Communists received only 20.5 percent.

If the Union of the Left should be re-created and win an election, it would be by a very small margin. As a result, France would be politically and socially divided. A drastic polarization would result between the newly elected forces controlling the country and the economic, military, and administrative establishments which would oppose the new government. The Union of the Left would have to contend with a strong resistance by the conservative forces, especially since their aims include the nationalization of a considerable sector of the economy. A victorious left would also have to contend with the powerful French presidency. The President enjoys far-reaching control and veto power, and he would certainly not allow the Union of the Left to act with complete freedom. Most important, however, are the increasing conflicts between the French Socialists and Communists. With the PCF's constant attempts to make more of a name for itself, these tensions have increased and cause the Socialists to lean more toward the center. In 1977, Marchais claimed that the Socialists would "advocate an administrative policy for the financial crisis" and that they had already undergone a "swing to the right."[19] Since then, during 1978–1979 the Communists have waged many attacks against the Socialists.

The situation is quite different in Spain. Already in November 1977, the PCE had 215,000 members. But during the elections in June 1977, it only received 9.4 percent of the vote. The Spanish Communist Party has twenty deputies in the Parliament, as compared to the 118 representatives of the Socialists. As is the case in Italy, in Spain only a gradual inclusion of the Communist Party in political responsibility is conceivable but, with less than 10 percent of the vote, the PCE has relatively little influence.

An agreement was reached between the government and the political parties of Spain over the implementation of an economic program, at the end of October 1977, in the so-called Moncloa Pact. The program was to reduce unemployment, to create the necessary conditions for a revival of the market and an increase in investments, and to raise the number of jobs considerably. The Moncloa Pact was approved almost unanimously (there was only one opponent) but was still criticized by both the entrepreneurs and representatives of the extreme leftists. The entrepreneurs declared that they could not fulfill the Moncloa Pact, which, they claimed, restricted all initiative.[20] The radical left claimed that the Moncloa Pact represented "an attempt of the bourgeoisie to burden the workers with the costs of the capitalist crisis."[21]

The Spanish Communist Party had actively cooperated in the realization of the Moncloa Pact, and it continued to support it, claiming that the pact was the only possible way to secure democracy against the dangers of a reactionary coup d'état. Democracy, they insisted, was still too fragile and the danger of a political about-face too great. The most important task was first to secure democracy. They proposed a government of national concentration—in other words, a government in which all democratic parties participated. To a certain extent, this pact might represent a first step in the development of a Spanish-type "historic compromise." It is interesting to note that on some issues the Communists of Spain today advocate a more moderate policy than the Socialists. Carrillo highlighted the Moncloa Pact by declaring that the Communists were willing to cooperate constructively in order to help overcome the economic crisis. The Socialists (PSOE) were more reserved and declared that the pact was not a long-term obligatory agreement, but rather only a basis for understanding which did not exclude future differences of opinion.

In November 1977, the Spanish Communists came one step closer to a possible future working arrangement with the government. They participated in the seven-member preparatory committee consisting of three representatives of the government party (the Democratic Center) and one representative from each of the other parties to draw up the Spanish Constitution. In the Spanish elections of March 1, 1977, the Communist Party increased its share of popular votes from 9.4 percent to 10.7 percent, sending twenty-three (instead of twenty) deputies to parliament. In the following municipal elections in April the Spanish Communists received more than 13 percent.

Eurocommunists, the EEC, and NATO

In light of a possible future participation in the government, the Eurocommunists' attitude toward the EEC and NATO are of great significance. The Italian Communists were the first to change their position on the EEC. Already in 1962—in contrast to the Soviet anti-EEC position—the Italian Communists advocated realistically analyzing the process of European economic integration. This led, as of the mid-sixties, to the Italian Communists' clear readiness to cooperate in the European Economic Community, although they wanted to reform the structure of the EEC, to democratize the different branches of the EEC, to reevaluate the European Parliament, and strengthen the democratic forces and the trade unions under the EEC's authority. The Italian Communists do not consider the present European institutions in Brussels democratic, since all decisions are made from above. As a result for many years they have advocated direct election to the European Parliament. Giorgio Amendola declared before the European Parliament, in 1976, that the Italian Communists were in favor of direct elections because this would mean that the European Parliament would be "capable of becoming the working center of a real unity of Western Europe."[22]

The Italian Communists, according to Enrico Berlinguer, want a Europe which is capable of developing equal relations with both the United States and the Soviet Union and of establishing new relations with the countries of the Third World. "In this context, we stress the decisive importance of the problem of Europe: our essential goals are the achievement of agreements for disarmament measures and pan-European security and collaboration; democratization of the European Economic Community, its unity and autonomy vis-à-vis the United States and the Soviet Union and its active participation in the dialogue between the two biggest powers; the search for new relations of friendship and cooperation with the Third World countries, and particularly with those of the Mediterranean area. For this reason, a further development of democracy is necessary in Western Europe."[23]

After some initial hesitation, the Spanish Communists have also adopted similar positions. Santiago Carrillo speaks of a "Europe independent of the USSR and the United States, a Europe which is oriented toward socialism, a Europe in which Spain can preserve its individuality."[24]

The French Communist Party's attitude toward the EEC is considerably more reserved. It demands its own economic and social policies within the framework of the EEC, claiming that it is essential to free the EEC from the domination of big business, to democratize its institutions, and to meet the demands of its workers. Neither should membership in the EEC be an obstacle for economic and political cooperation with other countries.

Gaston Thorn, President of the Federation of Liberal Parties of

Europe, views the effects of Communist participation in government on the EEC with "concern." Communist participation in government could result in decisive changes in European politics.[25]

The British Foreign Minister, David Owen, declared that Communist participation in the government of a member state of the European Economic Community would only cause problems "if the Communists were to gain supremacy in that country," and then "possibly endanger a functioning democracy."[26]

George Ball indicated that the United States "should do everything possible to develop a concerted strategy with its western allies, while contenting itself, for once, "with a silent supporting role." The EEC members should make it known, he claimed, that they are closely watching the Italian Communists. "If it should once become clear that the Communists were systematically destroying democratic institutions and regimenting the Italian economy in violation of the principles of the Common Market, the question would assume a different aspect."[27] Other commentators, however, take a more moderate or even positive stand on the Eurocommunists' changing attitudes to European unification.[28]

On the even more important question of the relations to NATO, the PCI and the PCE differ substantially from the PCF.

For the Italian Communists the continuation of détente policy is extremely important. Since a strategic military balance between the USA and the USSR is essential for détente, the Italian Communists after they have achieved participation in the government would reject a unilateral withdrawal from NATO. They declare that they would tolerate American military bases in Italy.

The French Communist Party strongly emphasizes its national sovereignty when discussing its relations to NATO. It is against contributing any more French military forces, and claims that even if the PCF were to enter into the government, although it would not neglect France's alliance responsibilities, it would always conduct a policy of independence vis-à-vis the military blocs.

Spain does not belong to NATO, but since the United States does maintain military bases there, the situation of the Spanish Communist Party is slightly different from that of the PCI or the PCF. Many Spanish Communists believe that NATO has become an instrument of American political, economic, and military control over Europe and that Spain should remain outside the organization.[29]

The Spanish Communist Party's attitude toward the American military bases is more flexible. Carrillo pointed out that military bases in general, both in the East and in the West, should be discontinued gradually by means of international negotiations. Under the present conditions, however, the Spanish Communists, according to Carrillo, have nothing against the presence of American military bases in Spain as long as they are not used to interfere in Spain's internal affairs.[30] Moreover, Carrillo claims that the question of American military bases in Spain would only be considered by the Spanish Communists when "the Soviet troops withdraw from Czechoslovakia."[31]

Official statements issued so far clearly indicate that much more attention is being given to the effects that a Communist participation in government might have on NATO than to the possible effects such participation would have on the European Economic Community. Helmut Sonnenfeldt, a close associate of former Secretary of State Henry Kissinger, declared that Communist participation in European government would "certainly influence America's duty to defend Europe." Americans, he said, would not understand "why American troops are stationed in Europe in order to defend governments which were partially Communist." Moreover, a pro-Communist development in Italy could lead to a noticeable shift to the right in West Germany.[32] The Chairman of the Christian Democratic Union of West Germany, Helmut Kohl, declared that an accession to power by the Communists would "throw the Atlantic Alliance into a state of crisis."[33] Willy Brandt also claimed that "the question of loyalty in the defense of those NATO countries" whose Communist parties have controlled their own development is "still unclear." One would have to ask, he said, whether the development of these parties has gone so far that they "would uphold the Western Alliance." Brandt insisted that this was doubtful, for Eurocommunism was a process which, even if it were to continue in the same direction, still needed time to complete its development.[34]

Other specialists point out that "Communist participation in the government of a NATO ally would create problems and would not help Europe's relations with the United States.[35] Some observers, however, do not expect significant changes. "Italy will not withdraw from NATO, and the PCI will want to show that it is contributing to a more active pursuit of Italian interests internationally, but its chief concerns will be domestic." On European politics, the PCI is likely to press for more independence and a greater authority for European institutions. None of these policies, however, would be fundamentally damaging to US strategic interests.[36]

Within NATO itself there have of course already been thoughts on how to react to a possible Eurocommunist participation in the government of a NATO country. Many seem to think that NATO would and could not expel a particular country, but rather would react by taking appropriate measures to safeguard military priorities. It has already been said that Italian Communists' entry into the government could lead NATO to proclaim specific conditions for continued membership, such as the maintenance of defense contingents, contribution of a certain percentage of the gross national product for the defense of Europe, the unrestricted use of existing bases, and the exclusion of Communists from important command posts. This could, however, result in NATO's being divided up into various "classes," whereby, for example, Italy could no longer participate in some bodies, such as the nuclear planning group. In the same way, if the French Communists entered the government, France's potential contribution to defense might be ordered "lower" than before, which, however, would not be advantageous for the alliance as a whole.[37]

Eurocommunism — Tactical Maneuver or New Orientation?

18

Most discussion of the possible effects on the EEC and NATO of the Eurocommunists' entry into the government centers around the fundamental appraisal of Eurocommunism: Is it merely a tactical maneuver or does Eurocommunism represent a real change and an actual new orientation?

Many people consider Eurocommunism merely a tactical maneuver. Those skeptical of the movement claim that, although Eurocommunists promise to respect democratic institutions and principles and stress their independence, they actually maintain their old goals and are still directed and controlled by Moscow. As soon as they enter the government, it is believed, they will show their real face and, as in the countries of Eastern Europe after World War II, will erect their own dictatorship and break with the allies they had wooed. As a result, many feel Communist participation in governments of Western Europe would pose a serious threat to the EEC and NATO. "Communist remain Communists," declare the supporters of this position. They make promises, but history has shown that they cannot be trusted. In the past, Communists have repeatedly donned democratic apparel, they contend, only to show their real face as soon as they had established their own power apparatus. Many believe that, despite all their declarations of autonomy and independence, Eurocommunists are still a part of world Communism whose center is Moscow.

This view is shared not only by conservatives but by some follow-ers of different democratic parties in various Western countries. It reflects experiences which extend from the mass arrests and show trials in the Soviet Union to the Hitler-Stalin Pact in 1939 and the dictatorial "normalization" of the countries of Eastern Europe, the suppression of the popular revolt in East Germany in June 1953 and of the Hungarian Revolution of 1956, the erection of the Berlin wall, the occupation of Czechoslovakia, the shootings at the border be-tween East and West Germany, and the present repressive measures in East Germany and the entire Soviet bloc.

This picture of Communism is not limited to the Communist-ruled countries of the East, but rather is extended to all Communists, espe-cially since the Communists of Western countries defended, excused, and praised the events in East Germany, Eastern Europe, and the Soviet Union for many years.

A distrust which stems from a decade of historic events as well as a fear of once again falling victim to a tactical maneuver produces much of today's skepticism about Eurocommunism. Although much of this skepticism is understandable, I believe it is wrong to label all developments within Communism only as tactical maneuvers and to hold Communists of all countries and of all times responsible for the events in Eastern Europe and the Soviet Union.

The history of Communism contains much more than the above-mentioned tragic developments and is certainly not limited to tactical maneuvers—it also includes real, profound changes. In the history of Communism, the movement produced not only dictatorial Stalinists, but also reflective, searching, critical Communists, who honestly ad-vocated social justice and human freedom. There were, indeed, many Communists who were concerned that developments in the Soviet Union did not correspond to the original socialist principles and who continually expressed the hope that in the future other countries would develop a different and better system.

Even during the Stalin era, besides the dictatorial apparatchiks, there were many critical Communists who expressed their own hopes and ideas and who in many ways can be thought of as the forerun-ners of Eurocommunism. For a long time, however, they had little or no say, for the entire history of world Communism was being di-rected by the tremendous political apparatus under Moscow's direc-tion.

But in many ways this conception of Communism is already part of the past. For the last thirty years, since Yugoslavia's break with Moscow in the summer of 1948, world Communism has achieved a great diversity. The individual stages of this process have been described in this book. It seems important to realize that this diversity is characterized not only by the twenty-year-old Sino-Soviet conflict—China's independence is generally agreed upon today—but also by several West European and non-European Communist parties' emancipation from Soviet leadership.

Their emancipation led not only to autonomy and independence vis-à-vis Soviet domination and to an increasing dissociation from developments in the Soviet bloc, but also to the rejection of Soviet doctrines, practices, and strategies and the acceptance of new goals oriented toward freedom and democracy. The new trend, first called "Autonomism" and then "Reform Communism" clearly manifested itself before the world at the East Berlin Conference of European Communist Parties in June 1976. The new trend's independence, influence, and importance can no longer be overlooked. Now known as "Eurocommunism," a term first coined in June 1975, these ideas occupy the center of attention in most political discussions abroad.

What we consider Eurocommunism today has evolved in world Communism over a period of thirty years. Consequently, Eurocommunism, in my opinion, cannot be judged on the basis of analogies to the Stalinist past or, from a purely current political standpoint. Eurocommunism, rather, must be recognized and appraised as a political trend which has developed during the course of a long-term process of transformation and emancipation.

A number of factors played significant roles in the formation of the new Eurocommunist trend. To begin with, one should consider *experiences* during the period of the monolithic structure of world Communism. During that time the Communist parties, chained to Moscow, had to support all the changes in Soviet foreign policy without objection, even if such support destroyed that party's effectiveness in its own country. All Communist parties had to defend everything in the Soviet Union, even if such defense defied all common sense and resulted in serious doubts. The rejection of Soviet domination in world Communism and the establishment of autonomy and independence were the most important logical results of these experiences.

The *realizations* borne of *necessity* furthered this emancipation. Step by step, and not without internal dispute and difficulties, the Communists slowly began to realize that Soviet Communism's dogma, schemes, and strategies could not be applied to the new and different conditions and problems of a modern, industrialized, parliamentary, democratic society. Furthermore, Communists began to realize that they would have to develop new political concepts which corresponded to contemporary conditions, problems, and duties. This could obviously not be accomplished unless the Eurocommunists dissociated themselves to a great extent from the Soviet bloc systems.

Every step along a new course logically made another step necessary: the proclamation of an individual road to socialism, which corresponded to the historic traditions and the economic, political, and cultural conditions of the country in question were particularly important. They provided the impetus for the new concepts of a democratic transformation based on the will of the majority of the population, the constitution, and the parliamentary institutions. The new concepts then created the need for a completely new coalition policy, which could not be realized in the long run without renouncing the leading role of one's party. As a result the cornerstone has been laid for a complete rejection of the claim to universality, for a new interpretation of Marxist ideas—including a new attitude toward religion—and for a more open party structure. These changes have resulted in a new interpretation of the final goals of socialist society which logically could not be the "real socialism" of the Soviet bloc but which could be conceived as a multiparty system with all democratic rights and freedoms.

Tactical motives certainly played an important role in this transformation. Experience had all too plainly shown that the Communists could only be successful if they appeared as a truly independent force, if they based their policies on the realities of their countries, and if they attempted to reach their goals through open dialogue and a policy of broad coalition with other political forces and groups. It was also clear that the more strongly they were chained to the Soviet Union, the harder and more uncompromisingly they fought against and condemned other forces, including other leftist forces and even their own party members, the further they sank to the level of insignificant groupings. The independence and new course begun by different Eurocommunists at different times achieved greater and greater success. The Italian Communist Party continuously increased the percentage of votes at elections. In 1946, it received 18.9 percent of the vote and, in 1976, it reached 34.4 percent. Moreover, since 1970, the Japan Communist Party has also been able to raise its percentage of votes from 2.6 percent to over 10 percent. Such successes clearly accelerate the process of emancipation.

Clearly, the element of success played—and plays—a very important role. All Eurocommunists today realize that their new concepts are the only things which guaranteed their further successes, while every deviation from these concepts and every impairment of autonomy and a new course led to drastic setbacks.

This tactical character can certainly not be denied. But it would be wrong, or at least an oversimplification to regard the entire process of emancipation as merely a tactical maneuver. Even if tactical aspects played a role, especially at the beginning, the ten- to twenty-year development has since acquired its own characteristics which have shaped a serious transformation.

As a result of their emancipation thus far, the Eurocommunists already differ greatly from Soviet-type Communists. But the transformation is clearly not yet complete. The Eurocommunists are still in a transitional stage. Despite the many new and significant realizations, the scars of the past have not yet fully healed, and for that reason Eurocommunism does still manifest inconsistencies.

Eurocommunist denunciation of many repressive measures and its often biting criticism of the bureaucratic aspects of the Soviet bloc are clearly a welcome sign. Nevertheless, a critical and complete analysis is still lacking. Advocacy of a democratic road to socialism and of structural reforms, rejection of a complete nationalization of the economy, and emphasis on basic democratic planning, on decentralization, and on pluralism can certainly be viewed as encouraging new conceptions in world Communism. But some points still remain unclear.

What measures do the Eurocommunists foresee, for example, in case of possible difficulties or resistance in the process? The concept of a "historic compromise" without a claim to the "leading role" of the Communist Party, and the emphasis on dialogues and cooperation among different forces clearly represent a noticeable positive change from earlier tactical schemes of the Soviet-type Communists. It remains still unclear, however, how this development will proceed if a "historic compromise" is not reached and how parliamentary democracy will continue to function in the event that, through a long-term "historic compromise," all or most parties share in the responsibility for government and, as a result, a parliamentary opposition is virtually nonexistent. Finally, the avowal of a pluralistic, democratic multiparty system in socialism, the guarantee of the unhindered existence of opposition parties, and the respect for the will of the majority expressed in elections clearly represent the most pronounced rejection of the concepts of Soviet-type Communism. However, the precise interrelation between the public sector in the economic sphere and the desired pluralism in the political sphere still remains unclear.

These and other aspects which must still be clarified attest to the fact that, although the process of emancipation has progressed quite far, it is by no means complete. Indeed, the Eurocommunists face many new problems. Berlinguer himself repeatedly declared that the Eurocommunists' new roads "were at times unexplored," adding that we "do not hesitate to recognize them as such."

Eurocommunism is marked not only by unexplored roads but by different tendencies and currents within the individual parties. Not all Eurocommunist party members have entirely freed themselves from the burden of the Stalinist past; the process of independence is by no means complete. In addition, although they are numerically almost insignificant, the active counterforces must not be underestimated. In most Eurocommunist parties, especially the larger ones, the antagonistic forces cannot hope to turn back the tides. Nevertheless, they could clearly be reactivated by certain forces in the East, especially if the realization of structural reforms and the democratic road entails certain difficulties, setbacks, or disappointments for individual members.

Although the process of emancipation is indeed not yet complete, I think one can already safely say that Eurocommunists differ qualitatively from Communists of the Soviet type. In discussions of the Eurocommunists' possible entry into government and the effects on the EEC and NATO, one cannot proceed from the premise that these Communists are faithful to Moscow. Moreover, as this book has tried to demonstrate, the Eurocommunists represent a significant, even serious, challenge to the bureaucratic dictatorial regime of the East. This fact should also be considered in discussions about the foreign-policy aspects of Eurocommunism, especially since there are also Eurocommunist currents in the East European countries, currents which, under certain political conditions—remember the "Prague Spring"—could become influential or even decisively effective political forces.

There is something to be said for the idea that maybe in the long run, Eurocommunism implies nothing less than the formation of a new left-wing party in the European political spectrum which differs from both the pro-Soviet Communists and the Social Democrats. This emerging new left-wing party clearly proclaims the goal of the transformation of society, but in practice it also demonstrates a greater flexibility and willingness to concede and unite with other forces than most of the existing left-wing parties.

Needless to say, in many countries there is still a wide gap between the Eurocommunists and those parties with which they wish to form a coalition, especially the Socialists and Social Democrats. Much has happened in the sixty years since the split in the left in the 1920s. Many older Social Democrats can still remember the Communists' hateful campaigns against "Social Fascists," the brutal repression of Social Democrats in Eastern Europe, and the imprisonment of many thousands of Social Democrats.

The fact that Eurocommunists dissociate themselves from and even condemn the tragic and loathsome events of the Stalin era is uncontested. In the long run, this might even provide new perspectives, especially since the earlier conflicts which led to the split in the twenties have long since been reconciled. The Eurocommunists themselves have abandoned the old concepts of the violent overthrow of capitalism and the dictatorship of the proletariat, and no longer uncritically defend the Soviet Union. Instead, they now profess democracy and democratic freedoms. Surely the Social Democrats could today rightly declare that they have always regarded democracy and freedom as indispensable—but among Social Democrats there are some who feel that in light of the increasing danger of bureaucratization and a totally controlled society, their earlier goals of a welfare state should be reconsidered. Any new developments in the European left would doubtless be characterized by debate and disagreement and would compel all participants to consider seriously the new problems and perspectives. New aspects, such as the attitude toward the state and toward freedom of the individual, would take the place of outdated controversies of the twenties and thirties between the Social Democrats and Communists.

All this may sound like idealistic optimism, but it is indeed quite possible that the Eurocommunists' emancipation will affect not only the Eurocommunists themselves but other left-wing forces as well. New perspectives and goals would be of great significance not only to the left but to all groups, parties, and organizations in the European political sphere.

Eurocommunism, therefore, I think, cannot be thought of as a deceptive maneuver but, rather, as a significant and ongoing process of emancipation. Eurocommunism should be studied and analyzed seriously both to the extent and to the limits of its development in order to appraise accurately this new left-wing movement in the European political scene.

Notes

1 The Concepts of Eurocommunism

1. Manfred Steinkuhler, "Ursprung und Konzept des Eurokommunismus," interview with Frane Barbieri in *Deutschland-Archiv*, (a publication on East German politics), Cologne, no. 4 (April 1977).
2. See "What Is Euro-Communism?" *NIN* (Belgrade) December 26, 1976.
3. See Alfons Dalma, "Der Italo-Kommunismus," published in *Euro-Kommunismus*, Zürich, Interform Edition, 1977, p. 7.
4. Boris Meissner, "Moskauer Orthodoxie und Reformkommunismus," *Moderne Welt*, Düsseldorf-Vienna, no. 2 (1970).
5. Enrico Berlinguer in a speech at the conference of the Communist Parties of Europe in East Berlin on June 30, 1976.
6. Santiago Carrillo, *Eurocommunism and the State*, trans. Nan Green and A.M. Elliot (Westport, Conn.: Lawrence Hill and Co., 1978), pp. 8, 40.
7. *Unità* (Rome), December 31, 1976.
8. *Frankfurter Rundschau*, June 6, 1977.
9. Eduard Kardelj, "Revolutionaries in Their Visions and Realists in Respect to Possibilities," *Socialist Thought and Practice*, Belgrade, no. 5 (May 1977), p. 72.
10. See Zdeněk Hejzlar, "Linkssozialisten in Skandinavien," *Wiener Tagebuch*, no. 5 (1977).

2 The Debate over Eurocommunism in the West

1. "Ex-Präsident Ford: Euro-Kommunismus ist verkappte Tyrannei," *Die Welt* (Hamburg), October 31, 1977.
2. "Kissinger Sees NATO End if Europe Elects Red," *New York Times*, April 7, 1976.
3. "Kissinger Warns West on Its Reds," *New York Times*, April 14, 1976.
4. Henry Kissinger, "Communist Parties in Western Europe: Challenge to the West," *The Atlantic Community Quarterly*, Fall 1977, pp. 261-274.
5. Kai-Uwe von Hassel, "Was muss denn noch passieren?" *Weltbild*, January 3, 1977.
6. "Dialog um die Zukunft Italiens und Europas," *Vorwärts*, Bad Godesberg, no. 20 (May 19, 1977); see also *Encounter* (London), January 1978, pp. 20–22.
7. *Die Welt* (Hamburg), May 12, 1977.

8. Ingeborg Schawol, "Thorn: Die Neuen mussen erklären, wohin sie wollen," *Die Welt* (Hamburg), October 28, 1977.
9. Wilfried Hertz-Eichenrode and Manfred Schell, "Volksfront ist Sunde wider den Geist," interview with CSU Chairman Franz Josef Strauss in *Die Welt* (Hamburg), December 16, 1976.
10. Rolf Görtz, "Kohl: Eurokommunismus ist Teil des Weltkommunismus," *Die Welt* (Hamburg), May 25, 1977.
11. Walter Laquer, " 'Eurocommunism' and Its Friends," *Commentary*, April 1976, p. 27.
12. *International Herald Tribune* (Paris), November 5, 1976.
13. *New York Times*, April 19, 1977. Also published in *Unità* (Rome), April 20, 1977.
14. Interview with Jimmy Carter in the supplement, "Europa und die Welt," *Die Welt* (Hamburg), May 3, 1977.
15. "NATO auch mit Kommunisten, Carter: Regierungsbeteiligung nicht sofort Ausschlussgrund," *Frankfurter Rundschau*, September 21, 1977.
16. Theodor Leuenberger, "Was das politische Establishment in Washington über den Euro-kommunismus—und über die Macht im allgemeinen—denkt," *Tagesanzeiger*, Zurich, no. 46 (November 19, 1977).
17. *New York Times*, January 27, 1978.
18. "Wir Sozialdemokraten dürfen nicht so weinerlich sein," in an interview with Willy Brandt in *Stern*, Hamburg, August 11, 1977.
19. *Frankfurter Allgemeine Zeitung*, February 24, 1976.
20. From a speech at the National Congress of the Socialist Party of Austria in Vienna on March 12, 1976, quoted from Horst Ehmke, *Der demokratische Sozialismus als geistige und politische Kraft*, Friedrich-Ebert-Stiftung, Bonn-Bad Godesberg, 1976.
21. *Der Spiegel*, Hamburg, no. 11 (1977).
22. Quoted from Leopold Spira, "Zum Entwurf des SPÖ-Programms," *Wiener Tagebuch*, no. 11 (November 11, 1977), pp. 4–6.
23. "Dialog um die Zukunft Italiens und Europas: Verterter der sozialistischen, christdemokratischen und liberalen Parteien Italiens nehmen Stellung zum Problem des Eurokommunismus," *Vorwärts*, no. 20 (May 19, 1977).
24. *Ibid.*
25. Horst Ehmke, "Communism's New Face: A Historic Compromise," *Atlas*, New York, August 1976, pp. 33–34.
26. Richard Löwenthal, "Im Osten erstarkt, im Westen gescheitert," *Der Spiegel* (Hamburg), no. 18 (April 25, 1977).

3 European Communism During the Stalin Era

1. Joseph Stalin, *Works* (Moscow: Foreign Language Publishing House, 1954), 10: 53.
2. From the Program of the Communist International adopted at its Sixth

Congress, in Jane Degras, ed., *Documents of the Communist International* (London: Oxford University Press, 1965), 2 (1923–1928): 547; for a brief history of the Comintern, see also Witold S. Sworatowski, ed., *World Communism: A Handbook, 1918–1965* (Stanford, Calif.: Hoover Institution Press, 1973), pp. 78–91.

3. Vladimir Dedijer, *Tito Speaks* (London: Weidenfeld and Nicolson, 1953), p. 112.
4. Degras, *Communist International*, 3 (1929–1943): 261.
5. Julius Braunthal, *History of the International*, trans. John Clark (New York: Frederick A. Praeger, Inc., 1967), 2: 506.
6. Degras, *Communist International*, 3 (1929–1943): 477.
7. *Einheit*, East Berlin, no. 1, 1946.
8. *Ibid.*, see also Wolfgang Leonhard, *Child of the Revolution*, trans. C. M. Woodhouse (London: Collins, 1957), pp. 348–349.
9. *Kommunisten und Staatsmänner* (Vienna, 1947), p. 149.
10. *Ibid.*, pp. 59–60.
11. *Times* (London), November 18, 1946.
12. *Kommunisten und Staatsmänner* (Vienna, 1947), pp. 121–123.
13. Vladimir Dedijer, *The Battle Stalin Lost* (New York: Grosset and Dunlap, 1970), p. 101.

5 Yugoslavia – Cornerstone of Today's Eurocommunism

1. Santiago Carrillo, Regis Debray, Max Gallo, *Spanien nach Franco* (West Berlin, 1975), pp. 131–132.
2. Vladimir Dedijer, *Tito Speaks* (London: Weidenfeld and Nicolson, 1953), pp. 95–115.
3. *Ibid.*, p. 333.
4. Svetozar Vukmanović-Tempo, *Mein Weg mit Tito* (Zurich, 1972), p. 191.
5. Dedijer, *Tito Speaks*, pp. 359–360.
6. Robert V. Daniels, ed., *A Documentary History of Communism* (New York: Vintage Books, 1960), 2: 172.
7. *Ibid.*, p. 174.
8. Vladimir Dedijer, *The Battle Stalin Lost* (New York: Grosset and Dunlap, 1970), p. 138.
9. Erich W. Gniffke, *Jahre mit Ulbricht* (Cologne, 1966), p. 325.
10. See U.S. Congress, Senate Committee on the Judiciary, *Yugoslav Communism: A Critical Study*, 87th Cong., 1st sess., October 18, 1961, pp. 166–167.
11. See Wolfgang Leonhard, "Kominform und Jugoslawien: Über einige grundsätzliche Fragen des Kominform-Konflikts," (Belgrade: Jugoslovenska-Knjiga, 1949).
12. Milovan Djilas, *Lenin on Relations between Socialist States* (New York: Yugoslav Information Center, 1949), p. 48.
13. Eduard Kardelj, *Socialist Democracy, Its Effects on the Whole Development and*

Social Life of Yugoslavia (Belgrade: Federation of Yugoslav Jurists' Association, 1952), pp. 50–53.

14. Josip Broz Tito, *Workers Manage Factories in Yugoslavia* (Belgrade, 1950), pp. 29–30, 40–43.
15. *Tanjug Wochenbericht* (Bad Godesberg), June 7, 1951.
16. Der sechste Kongress der Kommunistischen Partei Jugoslaviens, 1952 (Bonn: Press and Information Bureau of the Yugoslav Embassy), pp. 139–140.
17. *Ibid.*, pp. 110–111.
18. *Ibid.*, p. 35.
19. "Political Emigrants in Yugoslavia," *Review of International Affairs*, Belgrade, December 1, 1952.
20. *Pravda* (Moscow), November 7, 1954.
21. Seweryn Bialer, *News from behind the Iron Curtain*, no. 10 (1956).
22. Robert Bass and Elizabeth Marbury, eds., *The Soviet-Yugoslav Controversy 1948–58: A Documentary Record* (New York: Prospect Books, Inc., 1959), p. 53.

6 The Effects of the Twentieth Party Congress of the CPSU on European Communism

1. Khrushchev, "Report to the Twentieth Congress of the CPSU," *Pravda* (Moscow), February 15, 1956; *Current Digest of the Soviet Press*, VIII, no. 4 (March 7, 1956), p. 11.
2. See Wolfgang Leonhard, *The Kremlin since Stalin*, trans. Elizabeth Wiskemann and Marian Jackson (New York: Frederick A. Praeger, Inc., 1962), pp. 160–161.
3. Strobe Talbott, ed., trans., *Khrushchev Remembers* (Boston: Little, Brown and Co., 1970), pp. 347–350.
4. See Wolfgang Leonhard, *Three Faces of Marxism*, trans. Ewald Osers (New York: Capricorn Books, 1974), pp. 148–154.
5. *Ibid.*, p. 154.
6. Ralph Giordano, *Die Partei hat immer recht* (Cologne, 1961), pp. 198–199.
7. *Unità* (Rome), March 15, 1956.
8. *Daily Worker* (London), June 22, 1956ff.
9. *For a Lasting Peace, for a People's Democracy*, Bucharest, April 17, 1956.
10. *Pravda* (Moscow), April 18, 1956; *Current Digest of the Soviet Press*, VIII, no. 16 (May 30, 1956), p. 7.
11. *Borba* (Belgrade), April 19, 1956.
12. *Unità* (Rome), April 18, 1956.
13. Interview with Togliatti in *Unità* (Rome), June 17, 1956; *The Anti-Stalin Campaign and International Communism*, edited by the Russian Institute, preface by Henry L. Roberts (New York: Columbia University Press, 1956), pp. 103–104, 108, 112, 120–121, 138–139.
14. *L'Humanité* (Paris), June 18, 1956.
15. *Daily Worker* (London), June 22, 1956.

16. *Friheten* (Oslo), June 1956; *Drapeau Rouge* (Brussels), June 19, 1956.
17. *Pravda* (Moscow), July 2, 1956.
18. See Tamas Aczel and Tibor Meray, *The Revolt of the Mind* (New York: Frederick A. Praeger, Inc., 1959).
19. Imre Nagy, *On Communism: In Defense of the New Course* (New York: Frederick A. Praeger, Inc., 1957).
20. Aczel and Meray, *The Revolt of the Mind*.
21. *Po prostu*, Warsaw, no. 45 (November, 1956); also in German in *Ostprobleme*, Bonn, no. 2 (January 11, 1957), pp. 52—54.
22. *Ostprobleme*, Bonn, no. 52 (1956), p. 1706.
23. *Neue Zürcher Zeitung*, November 13 and 15, 1956.
24. *Unità* (Rome), December 15, 1956.
25. *Neues Deutschland* (East Berlin), November 28, 1956.
26. *L'Humanité* (Paris), February 16, 1957.
27. *Unità* (Rome), December 15, 1956.
28. *Daily Worker* (London), April 20, 1957.
29. *Aus der Internationalen Arbeiterbewegung*, East Berlin, no. 10 (May 25, 1957).
30. *Kommunist*, Moscow, no. 12, 1957.
31. See Leonhard, *The Kremlin since Stalin*, pp. 260—264.
32. Günther Nollau, *Der Zerfall des Weltkommunismus* (Cologne, 1963), p. 35.
33. *Unità* (Rome), November 24, 1957; see also Nollau, *Der Zerfall des Weltkommunismus*, p. 38.

7 European Communism in the Shadow of the Emerging Sino-Soviet Conflict (1957—1967)

1 Strobe Talbott, ed., trans., *Khrushchev Remembers* (Boston: Little, Brown and Co., 1970), pp. 513—514.
2. See Wolfgang Leonhard, "Rumäniens Weg zur Selbstandigkeit," *Die Zeit* (Hamburg), July 10, 1964, and the essays by Victor Meier in *Neue Zürcher Zeitung*, May 9, 12, 15, 19, 22, and 25, 1964, as well as those by Harry Hamm in *Frankfurter Allgemeine Zeitung*, September 11, 1964; see also Stephen Fischer-Galati, *The Socialist Republic of Rumania* (Baltimore, Md.: Johns Hopkins Press, 1969).
3. *Neuer Weg* (Bucharest), May 7, 1966; *Europa-Archiv.*, Bonn, ser. 12, 1966, pp. 303—314.
4. Palmiro Togliatti's "Memorandum" first appeared in *Unità* (Rome), September 4, 1964, and in English on September 5, 1965, in the *New York Times*. Reprinted in full in W. E. Griffith, *Sino-Soviet Relations, 1964—1965* (Cambridge, Mass.: M.I.T. Press, 1967), pp. 373—383. Also quoted in part in an article by Luigi Longo, "The Italian Communist Party and Problems of the International Communist Movement," *World Marxist Review*, 7, no. 11 (November 1964): 3—10.
5. *Unità* (Rome), October 23, 1964.
6. *East Europe* (Munich), November 1964.
7. *Ny Dag* (Stockholm), October 21, 1964; see also Daniel Tarschys, "Unique

Role of the Swedish Communist Party," *Problems of Communism*, Washington, D.C., no. 3 (1974).

8. *Unità* (Rome), February 16, 1966, and *L'Humanité* (Paris), February 16, 1966.

8 European Communism and the "Prague Spring"

1. Zdeněk Mlynář, "Reflections on the Decisions of the January Plenum— Our Political System and the Division of Power," *Rudé Právo* (Prague), February 13, 1968, in Robin Alison Remington, ed., *Winter in Prague* (Cambridge, Mass.: M.I.T. Press, 1969), pp. 43–47.

2. Ivan Sviták, "Open Letter to the Workers and Technicians of the Dubrava Mines," March 29, 1968, *Literárný listý*, Prague, no. 8 (April 18, 1968).

3. Josef Smrkovský, *Rudé Právo* (Prague), February 9, 1968.

4. Jiří Pelikan, *Ein Frühling, der nie zu Ende geht* (Frankfurt am Main, 1976), pp. 224–225.

5. Smrkovský, *Pravda* (Bratislava), April 19, 1968.

6. "Resolution on the Political Situation Adopted by the Plenary Session of the Central Committee of the Communist Party of Czechoslovakia," *Rudé Právo* (Prague), April 6, 1968. For more detailed information on the Central Committee Plenum, see also Phillip Windsor and Adam Roberts, *Czechoslovakia, 1968* (New York: Columbia University Press, 1969), pp. 147–149; and H. Gordon Skilling, *Czechoslovakia's Interrupted Revolution* (Princeton, N.J.: Princeton University Press, 1976), pp. 217–221.

7. "The Action Program of the Communist Party of Czechoslovakia," April 5, 1968, *Rudé Právo* (Prague), April 10, 1968; reprinted in *Winter in Prague*, pp. 88–137; see also *Studies in Communism*, Los Angeles, July/October 1968, pp. 178–180.

8. *Pravda* (Moscow), April 17, 1968.

9. Luigi Longo in *Rinascità*; quoted from *Informations-Bulletin*, Vienna, 1968, nos. 23–24 (1968), p. 74.

10. Longo, Press Conference in Prague, May 7, 1968, *Informations-Bulletin*, Vienna, nos. 26–27 (1968), p. 72.

11. Longo, "Report on Czechoslovakia at the Gramsci Institute in Rome," May 8, 1968, quoted from *Weg und Ziel*, Vienna, nos. 7–8 (July–August 1968), p. 353.

12. *Tribune* (Sidney), April 24, 1968.

13. *Mundo Obrero*, Central Organ of the Spanish Communist Party, Madrid, May 1, 1968.

14. *Volksstimme* (Vienna), April 18, 1968; quoted from *Informations-Bulletin*, Vienna, nos. 23–24 (1968), p. 75.

15. *Informations-Bulletin*, Vienna, nos. 26–27 (1968), p. 64.

16. Andrei D. Sakharov, *Progress, Coexistence and Intellectual Freedom* (New York: W. W. Norton and Company, Inc., 1968), p. 67.

17. Robert Havemann, "Sozialismus und Demokratie—ein freisinniges Wort zu der Umwalzung in der Tschechoslowakei," *Die Zeit* (Hamburg), May 31, 1968.

18. Karel Kosík, "The Crisis in Our Time," *Literárný listý,* Prague, nos. 7–12 (April 1968); Robert Kalivoda, "Democracy and Critical Thought," *Literárný listý,* Prague, nos. 13, 14 (May 2 and 9, 1968).

19. Čestmír Císař, in an interview with the Hungarian newspaper *Elet es Irodalom* (Budapest), May 4, 1968; English translation in *Hungarian Press Survey,* Radio Free Europe, Munich, no. 1294 (May 11, 1968), p. 4.

20. V. Gorin, "In Whose Favor Is It?" in the Soviet trade-union newspaper *Trud,* May 15, 1968. This article was directed against the article by L. Sohor, "Marx and Our Times," in the Czech trade-union paper *Prace,* May 5, 1968. See also Lev Onikov, "Socialist Democracy," *Pravda* (Moscow), May 19, 1968.

21. *Pravda* (Moscow), June 14, 1968.

22. *Komsomolskaya Pravda* (Moscow), June 21, 1968.

23. *Pravda* (Moscow), July 5, 1968.

24. Pelikan, *Ein Frühling, der nie zu Ende Geht.*

25. "Resolution on the Present Situation and the Further Tasks of the Party," *Rudé Právo* (Prague), June 2, 1968, English translation in Paul Ello, *Czechoslovakia's Blueprint for Freedom* (Washington, D.C.: Acropolis Books, 1968), pp. 53–80.

26. Ludvík Vaculík. "Two Thousand Words to Workers, Farmers, Scientists, Artists and Everyone," *Literárný listý,* no. 18 (June 27, 1968); also in *Winter in Prague,* p. 201.

27. "To the Czechoslovak Communist Party Central Committee," *Pravda* (Moscow, July 18), 1968, in *Winter in Prague,* pp. 225–230. See also Windsor, Philip and Adam Roberts, *Czechoslovakia 1968: Reform, Repression and Restoration,* (London: Chatto & Windus, for the Institute for Strategic Studies, 1969), pp. 150–157; and Skilling, Harold Gordon, *Czechoslovakia's Interrupted Revolution,* (Princeton, N.J.: Princeton University Press, 1976), pp. 287–294.

28. Czech answer to the Warsaw Letter, "Statement of the Presidium of the Central Committee of the Communist Party of Czechoslovakia to the Letter of the Five Communist and Workers' Parties," *Rudé Právo* (Prague), July 19, 1968, in *Winter in Prague,* pp. 234–243.

29. Secret Arms Caches at the Border with FRG." *Pravda* (Moscow), July 19, 1968, in *Current Digest of the Soviet Press,* XX, no. 29 (August 7, 1968), p. 7.

30. "Adventurist Plans of the Pentagon and CIA," *Pravda* (Moscow), July 19, 1968, in *Current Digest of the Soviet Press,* XX, no. 29 (August 7, 1968), pp. 6–7.

31. "FRG Interference in Czechoslovakia," *Pravda* (Moscow), July 20, 1968, in *Current Digest of the Soviet Press,* XX, no. 29 (August 7, 1968), pp. 7–8.

32. Pelikan, *Ein Fruhling, der nie zu Ende Geht,* p. 235; (GUM is the abbreviation for *Gosudarstvennoye Universalnoye Magazin,* "State Department Store" in Russian).

33. "Statement of the Communist and Workers' Parties of Socialist Countries" (Declaration of the Bratislava Conference), *Pravda* (Moscow), August 2 and 4, 1968, in *Current Digest of the Soviet Press,* XX, no. 31 (August 21, 1968), p. 3.

34. *Unità* (Rome), August 6, 1968.
35. Radio Zagreb, August 25, 1968, 8:00 P.M.; see also *East Europe*, New York, 10 (1968): 47−51; for a further discussion of Communist parties' reactions to the occupation of Czechoslovakia, see Skilling, Czekoslavakia's Interrupted Revolution, pp. 710−712, 747−753.
36. Quoted from Wolfgang Leonhard, "Weltkommunismus nach der Prager Tragodie," *Tschechoslowakei Heute* (Zurich), August 1968.
37. Luigi Longo's Memorandum on Unity in Diversity, in *Rinascità* (Rome), October 20 and 27, November 3 and 20, 1967.
38. *Unità* (Rome), December 6, 1968.
39. Declaration of the Central Committee of the Communist Party of Great Britain, *Informations-Bulletin*, Vienna, no. 16 (July 1969), pp. 5−7.
40. *Informations-Bulletin*, Vienna, no. 17 (August 1969), pp. 8−9.

9 Eurocommunism Becomes an Independent Force (1970−1976)

1. See Roy A. Medvedev, *On Socialist Democracy*, trans. Ellen de Kadt (New York: W. W. Norton & Co., Inc. 1975).
2. 2. "On the Multi-party System," in *Kolokol*, quoted from Cornelia Gerstenmeier, *Die Stimmen der Stummen* (Stuttgart, 1971); see also Boris Levitsky, *Die linke Opposition in der Sowjetunion* (Hamburg, 1974), pp. 151−160.
3. *Unità* (Rome), December 27, 1970.
4. *L'Humanité* (Paris), December 25, 1970.
5. *Neuer Weg* (Bucharest), April 4, 1971; see also *Current Digest of the Soviet Press*, XXIII, no. 14, p. 34.
6. *Borba* (Belgrade), April 3, 1971; see also *Current Digest of the Soviet Press*, XXIII, no. 15, p. 31.
7. *Pravda* (Moscow), April 8, 1971.
8. Helmut König, "Dissidenten im Dilemma—Zum Auftreten einiger auslandischer Delegationen auf dem 24. Parteitag der KPdSU," in *Osteuropa*, Stuttgart, nos. 8, 9 (1971), pp. 722−737.
9. *Unità* (Rome), April 28, 1971.
10. *Izvestia* (Moscow), September 14, 1971, in *Current Digest of the Soviet Press*, XXIII, no. 37, p. 24.
11. *Borba* (Belgrade), September 12, 1971.
12. *Unità* (Rome), September 12, 1971.
13. *Unità* (Rome), October 6, 1971.
14. *L'Humanité* (Paris), January 11, 1971.
15. *Unità* (Rome), February 19, 1971.
16. *Politika* (Belgrade), February 23, 1971.
17. *Mundo Obrero* (Madrid), March 9, 1971.
18. *Unità* (Rome), January 6, 1971, June 20, 1971.
19. *Mundo Obrero* (Madrid), December 10, 1971.
20. "Manifesto of October 28, 1970," in Jiří Pelikan, *Sozialistische Opposition in der ČSSR* (Frankfurt/Cologne, 1973), pp. 126−132.

21. *Unità* (Rome), January 15, 1971.
22. *L'Humanité* (Paris), January 18, 1971.
23. *Comment* (London), February 6, 1971.
24. *NIN* (Belgrade), May 23, 1971.
25. *Vie Nuove* (Giorni), September 17, 1971.
26. *Tribune* (Sydney), August 12, 1972.
27. See Pelikan, *Sozialistische Opposition in der ČSSR*, pp. 160–162.
28. *Unità* (Rome), August 21, 1973.
29. See Heinz Timmermann, "Der Fall Solschenizyn als Herausforderung an die Westkommunisten," in *Osteuropa*, Stuttgart, no. 9 (1974), pp. 651–669.
30. See *Times* (London), February 14, 1974, and *Unità* (Rome), February 13, 1974.
31. *Akahata* (Tokyo), March 20, 1974.
32. *Le Monde* (Paris), February 15, 1975.
33. *Pravda* (Moscow), August 6, 1975.
34. *Unità* (Rome), August 9, 1975.
35. "Brezhnev's Report to the Congress," *Pravda* (Moscow), February 25, 1976, in *Current Digest of the Soviet Press*, XXVIII, no. 8 (March 24, 1976).
36. *Pravda* (Moscow), February 26, 1976, in *Current Digest of the Soviet Press*, XXVIII, no. 9 (March 31, 1976), pp. 2, 5.
37. *Ibid.*, p. 10.
38. *Ibid.*, p. 11.
39. *Ibid.*, p. 13.
40. Helmut König, "Brudergrüsse mit schrillem Nachhall," *Osteuropa*, Stuttgart, nos. 8–9 (1976), p. 838.
41. *Le Monde* (Paris), February 27, 1976.
42. *Corriere della Sera* (Rome), February 26, 1976.
43. *La Stampa* (Turin), March 5, 1976; *Times* (London), March 5, 1976.
44. *Pravda* (Moscow), March 18, 1976; and *Kommunist*, Moscow, no. 5 (March 1976).
45. *Le Monde* (Paris), March 20, 1976.
46. *Unità* (Rome), March 28, 1976.
47. *Ibid.*, March 19, 1976; see also, Kevin Devlin, "Italians, Yugoslavs, React Sharply to Soviet Attack on 'Revisionism,'" *Radio Free Europe Research*, no. 72 (March 25, 1976).
48. Radio Belgrade, March 23, 1976.
49. *Mundo Obrero* (Madrid), April 3, 1971.

10 Recent Developments of Eurocommunism

1. Warsaw Conference of European Communist and Labor Parties in *Informations-Bulletin*, Vienna, nos. 19/20 (1974); see also Heinz Timmermann, "Das Konsultativtreffen der Kommunistischen Parteis Europa in Warschau," *Berichte des Bundesinstitutes für ostwissenschaftliche und internationale Studien*, no. 55 (1974); see also *Radio Free Europe Research*, nos. 2116, 2126–2128 (September 30, 1974, October 17–19, 1974).

2. *Unità* (Rome), March 28, 1976; see also *Radio Free Europe Research*, no. 86 (May 22, 1975).

3. *NIN* (Belgrade), May 2, 1976; see also *Radio Free Europe Research*, nos. 66 and 75 (March 18 and 31, 1976).

4. See Kevin Devlin, "The Interparty Drama," *Problems of Communism*, Washington, D.C., 29, no. 4 (July-August 1975): 18–34.

5. All speeches of the East Berlin Summit Conference are reprinted in full in *Neues Deutschland*, East Berlin, June 30 and July 1, 1976. Excerpts from the document as well as from speeches by Brezhnev, Tito, Berlinguer, Marchais, Ceauşescu, and Carrillo are reprinted in the *New York Times*, July 1, 1976; for Enrico Berlinguer's speech in full, see *The Italian Communists, Foreign Bulletin of the PCI*, nos. 2–3 (March–April 1970), pp. 54–65.

6. See F. Stephen Larrabee, "Moscow and the 'Autonomous' Communist Parties after East Berlin: How Much Compromise?" *Radio Liberty Research*, no. 422/76, (September 27, 1976), and Kevin Devlin, "The Challenge of Eurocommunism," *Problems of Communism*, Washington, D.C., no. 1 (January/February 1977), pp. 1–20.

7. Botho Kirsch, Commentary on Deutsche Welle, Cologne, July 2, 1976.

8. Victor Zorza, "Breschnew stekt nicht auf. Beim Ostberliner Kommunistentreffen nur taktische Ruckzugsgefechte," *Vorwärts* (Bad Godesberg), July 5, 1976.

9. Robert Havemann, "Das sind schreckliche Wahrheiten," essay in *Der Spiegel*, Hamburg, no. 28 (July 5, 1976).

10. Declaration of the Politburo of the CPSU on the subject of the Berlin Conference, *Neues Deutschland* (East Berlin), July 3, 1976; Boris Ponomaryov, "The International Significance of the Berlin Conference," in *Kommunist*, Moscow, no. 12 (July 1976); *Partinaya Zhizn*, Moscow, no. 15 (1976), p. 63ff; see also Boris Levitsky, "Zur Auseinandersetzung mit dem Eurokommunismus in der UdSSR," in *Berichte des Bundesinstitutes für ostwissenschaftliche und international Studien*, no. 16 (1977).

11. W. Jegorov, "The Party of Proletarian Internationalism," in the army newspaper *Red Star* (Moscow), August 5, 1976.

12. S. Trapesnikov, "Social Sciences—Ideological Wealth of the Party and the People," *Kommunist* (Moscow), August 12, 1976, p. 28.

13. *L'Humanité* (Paris), November 17, November 22, 1976; *Rinascità* (Rome), November 26, 1976; *Mundo Obrero* (Madrid), early December 1976.

14. *Frankfurter Allgemeine Zeitung*, June 7, 1977.

15. *La Stampa* (Turin), December 8, 1976; see also Kevin Devlin, "Biermann and the Eurocommunist Comrades," *Radio Free Europe Research*, no. 241 (November 26, 1976).

16. See *Listy-Blätter*, Publication of the Czechoslovak Socialist Opposition, no. 12 (February 1977).

17. *Weltgeschenen*, October–December 1976, published by Hans Siegler, "Archiv der Gegenwart," Villigen-Schwenningen, 1977, p. 410.

18. *Unità* (Rome), January 16 and 21, 1977; *Drapeau Rouge* (Brussels), January 15, 1977; *Morning Star* (London), January 19, 1977; *Le Monde* (Paris),

January 25, 1977; see also Kevin Devlin, "Spanish CP Spokesman Backs East European Dissidents," *Radio Free Europe Research*, no. 26 (February 4, 1972).

19. *Le Monde* (Paris), March 19, 1977.

20. "Mlynár dankt der KPI für Hilfe gegen Moskau," in *Die Welt* (Hamburg), July 29, 1977.

21. *New York Times*, March 3, 1977. For more on Madrid communiqué, see *Radio Free Europe Research*, no. 59/77 (March 14, 1977).

22. Jürgen Rühle, "Eurokommunismus—Arzt an wessen Krankenbett?" in *Deutschland-Archiv*, Cologne, no. 4 (1977), p. 345.

23. *Unità* (Rome), May 10, 1977; *L'Humanité* (Paris), May 12, 1977; *Unità* (Rome), May 21, 1977.

24. See "Die Euros schicken die dritte Garnitur. Die Hintergrunde des Prager April-Treffens," *Frankfurter Rundschau*, May 27, 1977.

25. Santiago Carrillo, *Eurocommunism and the State*, trans. Nan Green and A M. Elliot (Westport, Conn.: Lawrence Hill and Co., 1978).

26. "Against the Interests of Freedom and Socialism in Europe," about the book by the Secretary General of the Spanish Communist Party, Santiago Carrillo, entitled *Eurocommunism and the State*, New Times, Moscow, no. 26 (June 1977); see also *International Herald Tribune* (Paris), June 24, 1977.

27. *Drapeau Rouge* (Brussels), June 24, 1977; see also Kevin Devlin, "Soviets Step Up Attack on Carrillo, Eurocommunism," *Radio Free Europe Research*, no. 125 (June 24, 1977).

28. *Frankfurter Allgemeine Zeitung*, June 27, 1977.

29. *Neue Zürcher Zeitung*, June 28, 1977.

30. *Frankfurter Allgemeine Zeitung*, June 29, 1977.

31. *Unità* (Rome), June 24, 26 and 29, 1977; *Politika* (Belgrade), June 28, 1977; *Kommunist* (Belgrade), June 27, 1977; *Drapeau Rouge* (Brussels), quoted from *Wiener Tagebuch*, June 30, 1977, p. 13; *Vorwärts*, organ of the Swiss Labor Party, June 30, 1977; *Morning Star* (London), July 4, 1977.

32. *Unità* (Rome), July 4, 1977.

33. *L'Humanité* (Paris), July 7, 1977.

34. *NIN* (Belgrade), July 3, 1977.

11 The Italian Communist Party (PCI): A Twenty-Year Period of Transition

1. *Beratung des Informationsburos kommunistischen Parteien*, East Berlin, 1971, pp. 51−67.

2. See Helmut König, "Der Konflikt zwischen Stalin und Togliatti um die Jahreswende 1950/51," *Osteuropa*, Stuttgart, no. 10 (1970), pp. 697−706.

3. See the brochure, "A Revolution Cannot Be Accomplished with the Guns of a Foreign Army," Bologna, 1951, and the reports in the *New York Times*, January 29, 1951, and in *Le Figaro* (Paris), February 10−11, 1951; see also *Ostprobleme*, Bonn, no. 6 (February 10, 1951), p. 160, and no. 11 (March 17, 1951), pp. 226−227, and Wolfgang Leonhard, "Valdo Magnani and

Aldo Cucchi," *Freie Tribüne,* Düsseldorf, no. 7 (February 17, 1951) as well as Leonhard, "Die Krise in der KP Italiens," *Freie Tribüne,* Düsseldorf, no. 10 (March 10, 1951).

4. Pietro Secchia, former Deputy Secretary of the Comintern, in *For a Lasting Peace, for a People's Democracy,* February 22–26, 1951; see also *Ostprobleme,* Bonn, no. 11 (March 17, 1951), pp. 327–328.

5. "The Problem of Unity," *Rinascità* (Rome), August/September 1953.

6. Togliatti's report to the Central Committee of the PCI on the events of the Twentieth Party Congress of the CPSU in *Unità* (Rome), March 15, 1956; see also Donald L. M. Blackmer, *Unity in Diversity: Italian Communists and the Communist World* (Cambridge, Mass.: M.I.T. Press, 1968), pp. 23–24, 61–66, 200–202.

7. Interview with Togliatti in *Unità* (Rome), June 17, 1956; in *The Anti-Stalin Campaign and International Communism,* ed. by the Russian Institute, preface by Henry L. Roberts (New York: Columbia University Press, 1956), pp. 103–104, 108, 112, 120–121, 138–139.

8. See *Ostprobleme,* Bonn, nos. 12, 22 (March 1957), pp. 422–424; and Aldo Mardelli, "The Crisis of the PCI and Its Intellectuals," *Aggioramenti Sociali* (Milan), March 1957.

9. Political Resolution of the Eighth Party Congress of the PCI in *Unità* (Rome), September 15, 1956.

10. Roger Garaudy, "Notes on the Italian Road to Socialism," *Cahiers du Communisme* (Paris), January 1957.

11. *Rinascità* (Rome), December 1956 (this issue did not appear until early February 1957).

12. See Franz Marek, "Antonio Gramsci—zu seinem 30. Todestag," *Weg und Ziel* (Vienna), April 1967, pp. 183–195, and Iring Fetscher, "Ein Marxist namens Gramsci," *Frankfurter Allgemeine Zeitung,* May 6, 1967.

13. A. Dormont, "The Ninth Party Congress of the PCI," *East & West* (Paris), April 1960.

14. Report by Comrade Togliatti on the Twenty-second Party Congress of the CPSU, in *Unità* (Rome), November 11, 1961.

15. Jacques Duclos, "Problems of Unity of the International Communist and Labor Movement," *World Marxist Review* (East Berlin), December 9, 1961.

16. *Neues Deutschland* (East Berlin), December 2, 1961; see also Helmut König, "Die italienischen Kommunisten und der Weltkommunismus," *Osteuropa,* Stuttgart, no. 8 (1965), p. 713.

17. *Pravda* (Moscow), August 26, 1962.

18. *Unità* (Rome), August 20 and September 4, 1962.

19. Luciano Gruppi, "Lenin's and Engel's Theories of the State," *Rinascità* (Rome), July 25, 1964.

20. Roland Leroy, *L'Humanité* (Paris), October 14, 1964.

21. Enrico Berlinguer, "Response to Comrade Leroy on the Yalta Memorandum," *Rinascità* (Rome), October 24, 1964.

22. "Genosse Luigi Longo," *Neues Deutschland* (East Berlin), August 27, 1964.

23. "Togliattis Nachfolger zum Wechsel in Moskau. Luigi Longos Rede in Mainland," *Die andere Zeitung* (Hamburg), November 12, 1964.

24. Peter Geller, "Parteitag der italienischen Kommunisten," *Weg und Ziel* (Vienna), March 1966, pp. 143–146.
25. Franz Marek, "Internationaler Gramsci Kongress in Cagliari," *Weg und Ziel* (Vienna), June 1967, pp. 309–311; Iring Fetscher, "Ein Marxist namens Gramsci," in *Frankfurter Allgemeine Zeitung*, May 6, 1967; see also Helmut König, "Die italienische kommunistische Partei nach der Krise," *Osteuropa*, Stuttgart, nos. 5–6 (1967), pp. 354–356.
26. Luigi Longo's Memorandum on Unity in Diversity, in *Rinascità* (Rome), October 20 and 27, November 3 and 10, 1967.
27. *Unità* (Rome), January 12, 1968; see also *Weg und Ziel* (Vienna), February 1968, p. 68.
28. *Voprosi Economiki* (Questions of the Economy), Moscow, no. 9 (1968), p. 153.
29. See Helmut König, "Bologna und das rote Weltkonzil," *Osteuropa*, Stuttgart, no. 7 (1969), p. 481.
30. See *Unità* (Rome), February 18, 1969.
31. *Pravda* (Moscow), April 2, 1971.
32. *Unità* (Rome), November 14, 1970, and June 20, 1971.
33. *Unità* (Rome), March 14, 1972; for more on Italy's attitude toward NATO see Sergio Segre, "The 'Communist Question' in Italy," *Foreign Affairs* (New York), July 1976, and *Rinascità* (Rome), March 17, 1972.
34. *Rinascità* (Rome), September 28, October 5 and 12, 1973.
35. Enrico Berlinguer, "Reflections after Events in Chile," *The Italian Communists, Foreign Bulletin of the PCI*, nos. 5–6 (1973), p. 27; see also *Radio Free Europe Research*, nos. 2108 and 2112 (September 11 and 20, 1974).
36. *Bolletino Doxa* (Milan), September 1, 1976, quoted from Giacomo Sani, "The PCI on the Threshhold," *Problems of Communism*, Washington, D.C., no. 6 (November/December 1976), pp. 27–51.

12 The French Communist Party (PCF): Delayed Socialism in French Colors

1. Willy Brandt, "Wir Sozialdemokraten dürfen nicht so weinerlich sein," in an interview in *Stern*, Hamburg, no. 34 (August 11, 1977), pp. 84–92.
2. Waldeck-Rochet before the Central Committee of the PCF in *Weg und Ziel* (Vienna), February 1966, pp. 91–93.
3. The Election Coalition of the French Left, see *Weg und Ziel* (Vienna), February 1966, pp. 91–93.
4. Waldeck-Rochet, "Discussions between Socialists and Communists," a speech at the Eighteenth Party Congress of the PCF on January 4, 1967, pp. 63–64; see also Jakob Ferner, "Tauziehen um die Einheit der Linken in Frankreich," *Weg und Ziel* (Vienna), November 1966, pp. 586–594.
5. See Heinz Timmermann, "Die Kontroverse um den Dialog von Prag. Zum Protokoll der Unterredung Rochet-Dubček vom Juli 1968," *Osteuropa*, Stuttgart, no. 2 (1971), pp. 107–116.
6. Roger Garaudy, *The Crisis in Communism: The Turningpoint of Socialism*, trans. Peter and Betty Ross (New York: Grove Press, 1970); *Marxism in the*

Twentieth Century, trans. René Hague (New York: Scribner, 1970); *Peut-on Etre Communiste Aujourd'hui?* (Paris: B. Grasset, 1968); *Pour un Modèle Français du Socialism* (Paris: Gallimard, 1968).

7. See Maurice Cranston, "Thought of Roger Garaudy," *Problems of Communism*, Washington, D.C., no. 5 (September–October 1970), pp. 11–17.
8. *Le Monde* (Paris), February 7, 1970; see also *ibid.*
9. *Wiener Tagebuch*, 1970, p. 16.
10. *Les Lettres Françaises* (Paris), January 6–12, 1971.
11. *Unità* (Rome), October 11, 1972.
12. *Le Monde* (Paris), January 15, 1972.
13. "Volksfront—2. Auflage?" *Wiener Tagebuch*, no. 9 (1972), p. 8.
14. "Le Programme Commun de Gouvernement Établi par les Delegations Communistes et Socialistes," *L'Humanité* (Paris), June 26, 1972, pp. 5–12.
15. *Le Monde* (Paris), January 15, 1972.
16. An interview in the *Times* (London), November 17, 1972.
17. "Die Franzosischen Wahlen," *Wiener Tagebuch*, no. 4 (1973), p. 8.
18. *Le Monde* (Paris), April 29/30, 1973.
19. *L'Humanité* (Paris), May 25/26, 1973.
20. Georges Marchais, *Le Défi Democratique* (Paris, 1973), p. 119.
21. *L'Humanité* (Paris), May 9, 1974.
22. "Mathematik des Unglücks," *Wiener Tagebuch*, nos. 7/8 (1974), pp. 8–9.
23. SORES Opinion Poll, published in *Le Figaro* (Paris), October 24, 1974, and in *Le Nouvel Observateur* (Paris), October 28, 1974. See also, *Europa-Archiv*, Bonn, ser. 2 (1975), p. 43.
24. Franz Marek, "Gemeinsames Programm, verschieden programmiert," *Wiener Tagebuch*, no. 12 (December 1974).
25. *L'Humanité* (Paris), May 17, 1975.
26. "Common Declaration of the PCI and the PCF," *Unità* (Rome), November 18, 1975; see also *Osteuropa*, Stuttgart, no. 2 (February 1976), pp. 69–74.
27. See Kevin Devlin, "The PCF's Turning Point Congress," *Radio Free Europe Research*, no. 33 (February 4, 1976), and Devlin, "The French CP's 'New Look' Congress," *Radio Free Europe Research*, no. 37 (February 10, 1976).
28. Georges Marchais, "The French Road to Socialism," *L'Humanité* (Paris), February 5, 1976.
29. For a detailed discussion of the French Communist Party's "transition," see Ronald Tiersky, "French Communism in 1976," *Problems of Communism*, Washington, D.C., January, February 1976, pp. 20–47.
30. *Pravda* (Moscow), February 10, 1976.
31. *Ibid.*, February 13, 1976.
32. *La Stampa* (Turin), March 5, 1976, and *Times* (London), March 5, 1976.
33. *Le Monde* (Paris), December 16, 1966.
34. Franz Marek, "Linksunion in Frankreich—Erfolge, Erwartungen," *Wiener Tagebuch*, no. 5 (May 1976), p. 9.
35. *L'Humanité* (Paris), December 17, 1976.
36. *Le Monde* (Paris), December 16, 1976.
37. See George Scheuer, "Das Geständnis der KPF," *Vorwärts*, Bonn, no. 1 (January 6, 1977).

38. *L'Humanité* (Paris), January 25, 1977.
39. *New Times*, Moscow, no. 5 (January 1977).
40. *Le Monde* (Paris), December 16, 1976.
41. *Ibid.*, March 9, 1977.
42. From *Süddeutsche Zeitung* (Munich), June 3, 1977.
43. *L'Humanité* (Paris), April 1, 1976.
44. *Ibid.*, April 2, 1975; see also Paul Branet, "Inwiewiet haben sich die franzosischen Kommunisten geandert?" *Die Zukunft*, Vienna, no. 11 (June 1976).
45. "Marchais Gives Up Hard Line against Direct European Elections," *Die Welt* (Hamburg), April 19, 1977; *Le Monde* (Paris), April 19, 1977.
46. *Le Monde* (Paris), May 13, 1977; see also "Frankreichs KP für Autommacht," *Frankfurter Rundschau*, May 13, 1977.
47. *Frankfurter Allgemeine Zeitung*, May 20, 1977.
48. *Vorwärts*, Bad Godesberg, no. 43 (October 27, 1977), p. 12.
49. See Jean Kanapa, "A 'New Policy' for the French Communists?" *Foreign Affairs* (New York), January 1978, pp. 280–294.

13 The Spanish Communist Party (PCE): New Roads and New Goals

1. "Das Konzept Santiago Carrillos," *Wiener Tagebuch*, no. 12 (December 1975), p. 4.
2. Regis Debray, Max Gallo, Santiago Carrillo, *Spanien nach Franco* (Hamburg, 1975), pp. 87–88.
3. Santiago Carrillo, *Eurocommunism and the State*, trans. Nan Green and A. M. Elliot (Westport, Conn.: Lawrence Hill and Co., 1978), p. 131.
4. Jesüs Hernandez, "What is Titoism?" *Freie Tribüne* (Düsseldorf), January 6, 1951.
5. Debray/Gallo/Carrillo, *Spanien nach Franco*, pp. 99 and 102.
6. "Program for the Cooperation of All Anti-fascist Forces," *World Marxist Review*, no. 7 (July 1959), pp. 59–62.
7. Fernando Claudin, "Unity—The Way to Victory," *World Marxist Review*, no. 4 (April 1960), pp. 39–45.
8. The dates and descriptions of Carrillo's biography appear in Debray/Gallo/Carrillo, *Spanien nach Franco*, in which Carrillo talks about his own life.
9. Carrillo in *World Marxist Review*, April 1961, pp. 11-21.
10. Debray/Gallo/Carrillo, *Spanien nach Franco*, p. 125.
11. *Ibid.*, p. 120.
12. *Ibid.*, p. 121.
13. Carrillo, *Eurocommunism and the State*, p. 132.
14. Debray/Gallo/Carrillo, *Spanien nach Franco*, p. 114.
15. *Mundo Obrero* (with red letters, organ of the Lister group), July 1972 and September 1972; see also Kevin Devlin, *Radio Free Europe Research*, no. 1664 (January 9), 1973.
16. See Eusebio M. Mujal-Leon, "Spanish Communism in the 1970's," *Prob-

lems of Communism, Washington, D.C., March–April 1975, pp. 43–55; and Fernando Claudin, "The Split in the Spanish Communist Party," *New Left Review* (London), November–December 1971.

17. Quoted from *Neuer Weg* (Bucharest), September 5, 1971.
18. *Mundo Obrero* (Madrid), November 26, 1971.
19. Debray/Gallo/Carrillo, *Spanien nach Franco*, p. 114.
20. An interview with Carrillo in the Slovenian newspaper *Djelo* (Ljubljana), May 26, 1973.
21. See "Interview with Manuel Azcarate" in *Australian Left Review*, Sydney, no. 40 (May 1973), p. 14.
22. From *Beiträgen zum wissenschaftlichen Sozialismus*, Hamburg-West Berlin, no. 2 (1976), pp. 115–173.
23. *Party Life*, Moscow, no. 4 (February 1974).
24. *Pravda* (Moscow), October 16, 1974.
25. An interview with Carrillo in *Le Monde* (Paris), June 23, 1974.
26. Press conference with Carrillo in Paris, April 21, 1975.
27. Carrillo's interview in *Time* (New York), July 28, 1975; see also Heinz Timmermann, "Spaniens Kommunisten auf dem Weg in die Legalität," *Osteuropa*, Stuttgart, no. 2 (1976), pp. 125–145.
28. *Unità* (Rome), August 1, 1976.
29. See *Le Monde* (Paris), December 12/13, 1976.
30. *Le Monde* (Paris), December 12/13, 1976.
31. *Neue Zürcher Zeitung*, December 9, 1976.
32. *Frankfurter Rundschau*, January 3, 1977.
33. *Frankfurter Allgemeine Zeitung*, February 14, 1977.
34. *Il Manifesto* (Rome), April 12, 1977.
35. *Cambio* (Madrid), late April 1977.

14 Eurocommunist Tendencies in Other European Countries

1. Aksel Larsen in *Frit Danmark*, Copenhagen, July 1958; as quoted in Ursula Schmiederer, *Die Sozialistische Volkspartei Dänemarks* (Frankfurt am Main, 1969), p. 33.
2. Aksel Larsen, "Where Do We Stand? What Is to Be Done?" *Land og Folk*, Copenhagen, August 28, 1958; quoted from Peter P. Rohde, "The Communist Party of Denmark," in A. F. Upton, *Communism in Scandinavia and Finland* (Garden City, N.Y.: Anchor Books/Doubleday, 1973), p. 28.
3. Gert Peterson, "The Socialist People's Party in Denmark," *Review of International Affairs*, Belgrade, no. 388 (June 1966).
4. *Neues Deutschland* (East Berlin), August 30, 1967.
5. See William E. Griffith, ed., *Communism in Europe* (Cambridge, Mass.: M.I.T. Press, 1966), 2, chap. 15, "Sweden,": 287–319.
6. "Die Kommunisten Skandinaviens suchen eine Linie," *Die Welt* (Hamburg), September 18, 1964; see also A. Sparring, "The Communist Party of Sweden," in Upton, *Communism in Scandinavia and Finland*, pp. 88–91.
7. *Ny Dag* (Stockholm), October 21, 1964.

8. Carl Henrik Hermansson on Swedish radio, January 28, 1965; quoted from A. Sparring, ed., *Kommunisten im Norden* (Cologne, 1966), p. 48; see also Sparring's article on Sweden in Griffith, *Communism in Europe*.

9. Hermansson, "Zur Strategie und Taktik der Schweischen Kommunisten," *Vorwärts* (Basle), April 29, 1965.

10. From Sparring, ed., *Kommunisten im Norden*, p. 4.

11. *Ibid.*, p. 47.

12. *Norrskensflamman*, February 4–11, 1967; see also *Ostprobleme* (Bonn), 1967, pp. 396–402.

13. Irma Trevi, "The Strategy of the Swedish Communists," *Rinascità* (Rome), May 26, 1967.

14. *Vart Ny Land*, Stockholm, no. 5 (1972); see also *Internationale Presseschau*, Vienna, no. 122 (May 17, 1973).

15. *Partiprogram für Vänsterpartiet Kommunisterna*, Göteborg, 1972.

16. "Schwedens Kommunisten grenzen sich ab," *Frankfurter Allgemeine Zeitung*, December 14, 1973.

17. D. Cramer, "Bei den schwedischen Kommunisten ist die Moskauer Richtung noch schwach," *Frankfurter Allgemeine Zeitung*, December 15, 1973.

18. "Gemässigte Kommunisten setzen sich in Schweden durch," *Frankfurter Allgemeine Zeitung*, March 15, 1975; see also the analysis of Zdeněk Hejzlar, "Schweden—der vertagte Konflikt," *Wiener Tagebuch*, no. 5 (May 1975), pp. 18–19.

19. "Der schwedischen KP droht die Zersplitterung," *Die Welt* (Hamburg), November 11, 1975; and "Der Bruch der schwedischen Kommunisten vertieft sich," *Frankfurter Allgemeine Zeitung*, December 6, 1975.

20. Zdeněk Hejzlar, "Linkssozialisten in Skandinavien," *Wiener Tagebuch*, no. 5 (1977).

21. *Friheden* (Oslo), October 30, 1964.

22. *Ibid.*, January 8, 1964.

23. *Ibid.*, April 21, 1967.

24. *Ibid.*, January 4, 1968.

25. Zdeněk Hejzlar, "Gemeinsame Linkspartei in Norwegen," *Wiener Tagebuch*, no. 5 (1977); see also Per Egil Hegge, " 'Disunited' Front in Norway," *Problems of Communism*, Washington, D.C., May–June 1976, pp. 49–64.

26. "Zusammenschluss der Linken in Norwegen," *Frankfurter Allgemeine Zeitung*, March 18, 1975; see also Trond Gilberg, "Patterns of Nordic Communism," *Problems of Communism*, Washington, D.C., May–June 1975, pp. 20–35.

27. "Norwegens Linksparte lost sich auf," *Frankfurter Allgemeine Zeitung*, November 4, 1975.

28. Eeinar Olgeirsson, "Inselkommunisten: Island," *Wiener Tagebuch*, no. 7/8 (July–August 1976), pp. 24–27; for more discussion on the development of Communism in Iceland, see also *Problems of Communism*, Washington, D.C., May–June, 1975, pp. 32–35.

29. See *Frankfurter Allgemeine Zeitung*, August 19 and 23, 1978, and *Der Spiegel*, August 21, 1978.
30. See the report in *Unità* (Rome), October 26, 1974.
31. See also, Dimitri Kitsikis, "Greek Communists and the Karamanlis Government," *Problems of Communism*, Washington, D.C., January–February 1977, pp. 42–56.
32. *The British Road to Socialism: Program of the Communist Party* (London, October 1968).
33. *Morning Star* (London), August 26, 1968.
34. *Pravda* (Moscow), September 16, 1968.
35. *Morning Star* (London), September 16, 1968.
36. *Ibid.*, June 13, 1969.
37. *Ibid.*, June 29, 1970.
38. *Ibid.*, August 8, 1970.
39. "Erfrischende Diskussionen," *Wiener Tagebuch*, no. 11 (1971), p. 3.
40. "Brief Aus London: Zur Spaltung der KP Grossbritanniens," *Wiener Tagebuch*, no. 9 (September 1977), pp. 16–17; see also "Die britischen Kommunisten spalten sich," *Frankfurter Allgemeine Zeitung*, July 19, 1977, and *New York Times*, July 19, 1977.
41. *Tilanne*, Helsinki, no. 7/8 (autumn 1962), a special edition for the World Youth Festival in Helsinki, Autumn 1962, *Problems of Socialism in the 1960's*, Helsinki, pp. 301–304.
42. See William Griffith, ed., *Communism in Europe* (Cambridge, Mass.: M.I.T. Press, 1966), vol. 2, chap. 17, "Finland," by Bengt Matti.
43. From the program of the Finnish Communist Party, in *Weg und Ziel* (Vienna), May 1969, pp. 258–265.
44. *Frankfurter Allgemeine Zeitung*, June 7, 1974, and Zdeněk Hajzlar, "Die KP Finnlands: 'Die Rothemden und die blauhemden,' " *Wiener Tagebuch*, nos. 7/8 (1974), pp. 32–33; see also John H. Hodgson, "Finnish Communism and Electoral Politics," *Problems of Communism*, Washington, D.C., January–February 1974, pp. 34–45.

15 Eurocommunism Outside Europe: The Japan Communist Party (JCP), the Communist Party of Australia (CPA), and the Movement Toward Socialism (MAS) in Venezuela

1. *Partinaya Zhizn*, Moscow, no. 14 (1965); see also Paul F. Langer, "The New Posture of the CPJ," *Problems of Communism*, Washington, D.C., January–April 1971, p. 16.
2. *Pravda* (Moscow), August 25, 1963.
3. From the letter from the Central Committee of the CPSU to the Central Committee of the Japan Communist Party of April 18, 1964, *Osteuropa*, Bonn, no. 11 (June 4, 1965), pp. 337–344.
4. From the letter from the Central Committee of the Japan Communist

Party to the Central Committee of the CPSU of July 15, 1964, *Akahata* (Tokyo), June 20, 1964; see also *Ostprobleme,* no. 11 (June 4), 1965, pp. 345–347.

5. From the letter from the Central Committee of the Japan Communist Party to the Central Committee of the CPSU of August 26, 1964, *Akahata* (Tokyo), September 2, 1964; see also *Ostprobleme,* Bonn, no. 11 (June 4, 1965), pp. 347–351.

6. *Akahata* (Tokyo), February 8, 1968.

7. *Ibid.,* August 25, 1968.

8. *Ibid.,* October 19, 1968; *Pravda* (Moscow), October 25, 1968; *Akahata* (Tokyo), October 27, 1968.

9. "On the Subject of New Serious Interventions of the CPSU in the Affairs of Our Party," *Akahata* (Tokyo), May 5, 1970.

10. *Partinaya Zhizn,* Moscow, no. 13 (July 1970), pp. 76–79.

11. *Akahata* (Tokyo), August 5, 1970.

12. *Pravda* (Moscow), September 28, 1971.

13. *Problems of the History of the CPSU,* Moscow, no. 8 (1972), pp. 56–59.

14. *Unità* (Rome), March 22, 1973.

15. *Ibid.,* December 9, 1973.

16. *Pravda,* November 16, 1973, p. 4.

17. Athos Faya, "The Twelfth Party Congress of the Japan Communist Party and Several of Its Positions with which We Do Not Agree," *Party Life,* Moscow, no. 10 (May 1975), pp. 54–58.

18. *Akahata* (Tokyo), September 17, 1974.

19. *Le Monde* (Paris), July 10, 1974; see also Hong N. Kim, "The JCP's Parliamentary Road," *Problems of Communism,* Washington, D.C., March–April 1977, pp. 19–35.

20. *Unità* (Rome), April 3, 1976.

21. *International Herald Tribune* (Paris), June 13, 1977; see also Uwe Engelbrecht, "Auch Japans Kommunisten geraten in Moskaus Schusslinie," *Stuttgarter Nachrichten,* July 26, 1977.

22. Eric Aarons, "Australien: Eine Autonome KP," *Wiener Tagebuch,* no. 10 (1970), pp. 18–20.

23. *Ibid.*

24. *Tribune* (Sydney), April 24, 1968.

25. *Ibid.,* September 4, 1968.

26. *Ibid.,* November 24, 1968; see also *Radio Free Europe Research,* April 28, 1972.

27. *Pravda* (Moscow), March 29, 1970.

28. *Rudé Právo* (Prague), July 15, 1970; See also "Deviations from the Principles of Marxism-Leninism," *New Times,* Moscow, no. 36 (September 1970).

29. *Tribune* (Sydney), April 11 to 17, 1972.

30. *Daily World* (organ of the Communist Party of the United States), New York, July 8, 1974.

31. *Tribune* (Sydney), November 1973.
32. *Ibid.*, May 21—27, 1974.
33. "The Twenty-fourth Congress of the CPSU, March 20 to April 9, 1971" (English edition), (Moscow: Novosti Press Agency Publishing House, 1971), 9, nos. 7—8:27.
34. *Tribuna Popular* (Caracas), November 14, 1969.
35. "On the Eve of the Venezuelan Communists' Fourth Congress," *Pravda* (Moscow), October 20, 1970. English, "Current Digest of the Soviet Press," XXII, no. 42, p. 16.
36. Quoted from *Wiener Tagebuch,* no. 4 (1972), p. 8.
37. *Deslinde* (Caracas), February 9, 1971; for a detailed background on the split in the Venezuelan Communist Party see Benedict Cross, "Marxism in Venezuela," *Problems of Communism,* Washington, D.C., November—December 1973, pp. 51—70.

16 The Challenge for the East

1. Quoted from *Frankfurter Allgemeine Zeitung,* June 20, 1977.
2. Herbert Mies, "Die Deutsche Bourgeoisie und der Eurokommunismus," *Unsere Zeit* (Düsseldorf), organ of the German Communist Party (DKP), February 25, 1977.
3. George F. Kennan, "Kann der Westen bestehen?" *Europäische Rundschau,* Vienna, no. 1 (1977), pp. 3—32; for a detailed discussion of Eurocommunism's effect on Eastern Europe see Jiří Valenta, "Eurocommunism and Eastern Europe," *Problems of Communism,* Washington, D.C., March—April 1978, pp. 42—54.
4. Hugh Seton Watson, "George F. Kennans Illusionen. Eine Antwort," *Europäische Rundschau,* Vienna, no. 1 (1977), pp. 33—48.
5. Victor Zorza, "Eurocommunism and the Soviet System," *International Herald Tribune* (Paris), April 27, 1977.
6. Boris Meissner, "Moskauer Orthodoxie und Reformkommunismus," *Moderne Welt,* Düsseldorf, vol. 2, 1970.
7. Wolf Ruthardt Born, "Der Eurokommunismus," *Informationen für die Truppe,* no. 5, 1977; Harry Schleicher, "Immer Aerger mit dem Westen," *Frankfurter Rundschau,* November 8, 1977; Eduard Neumeier, "Spaltpilz im Ostblock," *Die Zeit,* July 22, 1977; Theo Sommer, "Ein Weisser Kommunismus," *Die Zeit,* November 28, 1975; Harry Hamm, "Moskau in Bedrängnis," *Frankfurter Allgemeine Zeitung,* July 2, 1977; Georg Scheuer, "Vom Umgang mit Kommunisten," *Vorwärts,* June 29, 1976.
8. Charles Gati, "The Europeanization of Communism," *Foreign Affairs* (New York), April 1977, pp. 540, 546.
9. R. E. M. Irving, "The European Policy of the French and Italian Communists," *International Affairs,* July 1977, p. 421.
10. Pietro Sormani, "The View from the East," *Atlas* (New York), August 1975, p. 40, adapted from *Corriere della Sera.*

11. Michael Ledeen, "Eurocommunists Exposed," *New Republic* (New York), March 26, 1977, p. 13.
12. Milovan Djilas, "Auf dem demokratischen Weg," *Die Zeit*, March 11, 1977. *Der Spiegel*, no. 26 (June 23), 1975.
13. Ernest Mandel, "Die Drei Gesichter des Eurokommunismus," *Was tun?* Frankfurt am Main, no. 156 (April 28, 1977).
14. See V. Afansayev, *Scientific Communism* (Moscow: Progress Publishers, 1967), pp. 314–315.
15. Enrico Berlinguer, "The New and Different Roads to Overcoming Capitalism in the Developed Countries of Western Europe," speech at the youth rally at the Palazzo dello Sport in Milan, June 6, 1976.
16. *Australian Left Review*, Sydney, no. 40 (May 1973).
17. See *La Conferencia nacional del Partido Communista de España. Manifiesto-Programa del Partido Communista de España*, Paris, 1975.
18. Santiago Carrillo, *Eurocommunism and the State*, trans. Nan Green and A. M. Elliot (Westport, Conn.: Lawrence Hill and Co., 1978), pp. 160–165.
19. Jean Elleinstein, "Ich mochte in der Sowjetunion nicht leben," *Der Spiegel*, no. 21 (May 16, 1977).
20. *La Stampa* (Turin), December 8, 1976; see also Victor Zorza, "Eurocommunism and the Soviet System," *International Herald Tribune* (Paris), April 27, 1977.
21. P. Yegerov, "Was ist demokratischer Kommunismus?" *Aufzeichnungen aus den sowjetischen Untergrund* (Hamburg, 1977), pp. 131–160, and Rudolf Bahro, *Die Alternative* (Cologne, 1977).
22. Quoted from Heinz Timmermann, "Eurokommunismus, eine Herausforderung für Ost und West," *Deutschland Archiv*, Cologne, no. 12 (1976), pp. 1283–1284.
23. Carrillo, *Eurocommunism and the State*, p. 172.
24. Enrico Berlinguer, "For New Roads to Socialism in Italy and Europe," *The Italian Communists, Foreign Bulletin of the PCI*, Rome, no. 2–3 (1976), p. 57.
25. Lucio Lombardo Radice in an interview in *La Stampa* (Turin), December 8, 1976.
26. Lucio Lombardo Radice, "Havemann ist ein sehr treuer Kommunist," *Der Spiegel*, no. 10 (February 28, 1977), pp. 41–44.
27. *Der Spiegel*, no. 21 (May 19), 1977.
28. Afanasyev, *Scientific Communism*, pp. 183–184, 287–288.
29. *On the Multi-party System*, Leningrad, 1965, quoted from Cornelia Gerstenmayer, *Die Stimmen der Stummen* (Stuttgart, 1971), pp. 323–327.
30. Roy A. Medvedev, *On Socialist Democracy* (New York: Alfred Knopf, 1975), pp. 98–99, 101, 137, 311–312.
31. Roy Medvedev, "Wir brauchen eine zweite Partei," *Der Spiegel*, no. 37 (1974), pp. 98–105.
32. See Rosenthal, M. and P. Yudin, eds., *A Dictionary of Philosophy* (Moscows Progress Publishers, 1967), p. 270.
33. *Fundamentals of Marxism-Leninism* (Moscow: Foreign Languages Publishing House, 1963); see the introduction, pp. 7–13.

34. See the article by Lucio Lombardo Radice, "Philosophie et politique dans la pensée Marxiste italienne," *Praxis,* edition internationale, Zagreb, no. 1–2 (1974), pp. 69–80.
35. See *NIN* (Belgrade), February 12, 1972 and *Unità* (Rome), May 20, 1971.
36. Carrillo, *Eurocommunism and the State,* pp. 88–90, 52–54.
37. Enrico Berlinguer in an interview in *Corriere della Sera* (Rome), June 15, 1976; for the English translation, see *The Italian Communists, Foreign Bulletin of the PCI,* nos. 2–3 (1976), p. 50.
38. See *La Conferencia nacional del Partido Communista de España. Manifiesto-Programa del Partido Communista de España,* Paris, 1975.
39. Enrico Berlinguer, *Report at the Fourteenth Party Congress of the Italian Communist Party,* Rome, March 18, 1975.
40. Carrillo, *Eurocommunism and the State,* pp. 28–33.
41. Rudolf Bahro, *Die Alternative: Eine Dokumentation* (Cologne, Frankfurt am Main, 1977).
42. Enrico Berlinguer's speech at the Fourteenth Party Congress of the Italian Communist Party, March 23, 1975.
43. Enrico Berlinguer in an interview in *Corriere della Sera,* Rome, June 15, 1974; for the English edition, see *The Italian Communists, Foreign Bulletin of the PCI,* Rome, no. 2–3 (1976), p. 46.
44. Robert Havemann, "Eine neue Internationale auf dem Marsch?" *Frankfurter Allgemeine Zeitung,* November 3, 1977.
45. Rudolf Bahro, *Die Alternative: Eine Dokumentation;* see also. Jiří Valenta, "Eurocommunism and Eastern Europe," *Problems of Communism,* Washington, D.C., March–April 1978, pp. 52–53.
46. *Unità* (Rome), May 26, 1977.
47. Edward Lipinski, "Offener Brief an den Genossen Eduard Gierek," *Wiener Tagebuch,* nos. 7/8 (July 1976), pp. 17–20.
48. *Der Spiegel,* January 2, 1978 and January 9, 1978 quoted from Jiří Valenta, "Eurocommunism and Eastern Europe," *Problems of Communism,* Washington, D.C., March–April 1978, p. 53.
49. "Offener Brief russischer Kommunisten aus dem Gefängnis," *Wiener Tagebuch,* no. 9 (September 1972), p. 24.
50. From *Frankfurter Rundschau,* November 8, 1977.
51. From *Le Monde* (Paris), July 21, 1976.
52. Jiří Pelikan, *Ein Frühling der nie zu Ende geht* (Cologne, Frankfurt am Main, 1976), p. 317.
53. Jiří Pelikan in an interview in *Die Neue Welt,* Frankfurt am Main, no. 3 (May 1977).
54. Eugen Loebl, "Eurokommunismus und Demokratie," *Die Welt,* December 1, 1977.
55. "Kádár wiederspricht Shiwkoffs Urteil über Eurokommunismus," *Frankfurter Allgemeine Zeitung,* December 8, 1976.
56. Sergei Trapeznikov in *Kommunist,* Moscow, no. 12 (August 1976), p. 28.
57. A. Koslov, B. Pushkov, "The Twenty-fifth Party Congress and the Inter-

national Communist Movement," *Politicheskaye Samoobrazovanie*, Moscow, no. 8 (1976), p. 23.

58. V. Katshanov, "In the Vanguard of the Class Struggle in Capitalist Countries," *Communist of the Armed Forces*, Moscow, no. 18 (September 1976), p. 82; see also Boris Levitsky, "Zur Auseinandersetzung mit dem Eurokommunismus in der UdSSR," *Bundesinstitut für ostwissenschaftliche und internationale Studien*, no. 16 (1977).

59. Wolfgang Wagner, "Kommunisten im westlichen Bündnis," *Europa-Archiv*, Bonn, no. 10 (1976), pp. 319–320.

60. Hans Gunther Brauch, "Eurokommunismus und atlantische Allianz," *Frankfurter Hefte*, no. 5 (1977), p. 3.

61. Enrico Berlinguer, "The Basic Differences in the Roads to Socialism in Western Europe," a speech before the Central Committee of the Italian Communist Party, October 29, 1975.

62. *Cambio*, Madrid, March 20, 1977, quoted from Heinz Timmermann, "Die Entspannungskonzepte der Eurokommunisten," *Berichte des Instituts für ostwissenschaftliche und internationale Studien*, no. 48 (1977), p. 14.

63. From Johan Georg Reismüller, "Ein Wort vielleicht für später," *Frankfurter Allgemeine Zeitung*, November 8, 1977.

64. Pelikan, *Ein Frühling, der nie zu Ende geht*, p. 299.

65. Karl Grobe, "Das Gespenst des Eurokommunismus," *Frankfurter Rundschau*, March 8, 1977.

66. Milovan Djilas, "Auf dem demokratischen Wege," *Die Zeit*, March 11, 1977.

67. Jiří Pelikan in an interview in *Die Neue Welt*, Frankfurt am Main, no. 3 (May 1977).

17 The Challenge for the West

1. See, for example, Gunther Nenning, *Realisten oder Verräter? Die Zukunft der Sozialdemokratie* (Munich, 1976).

2. Andreotti, in an interview in *Deutsche Zeitung*, Stuttgart, no. 49 (November 25), 1977, p. 7.

3. Enrico Berlinguer, "The New and Different Roads to the Defeat of Capitalism in the Developed Countries of Western Europe," a speech at the youth rally in Milan, June 6, 1976.

4. Enrico Berlinguer, "Our Policies Are in Italy's Best Interests," an interview in *Corriere della Sera*, Rome, June 15, 1976; for the English translation, see Enrico Berlinguer, "Italy Cannot Be Governed without the PCI," *The Italian Communists, Foreign Bulletin of the PCI*, Rome, no. 2–3 (April–June 1976), p. 51.

5. Santiago Carrillo, *Eurocommunism and the State*, trans. Nan Green and A. M. Elliot (Westport, Conn.: Lawrence Hill and Co., 1978), p. 104.

6. Enrico Berlinguer, "The New and Different Roads to the Defeat of

Capitalism in the Developed Countries of Western Europe," a speech at the youth rally in Milan, June 6, 1974.

7. Santiago Carrillo, Regis Debray, Max Gallo, *Spanien nach Franco* (West Berlin, 1975), p. 79.

8. *Der Spiegel*, no. 21 (May 16, 1977).

9. *Ibid.*, no. 4 (January 26, 1976).

10. Horst Ehmke, *Atlas* (New York), August 1976, adapted from *Die Zeit;* Richard Löwenthal, "Im Osten erstarkt, im Westen gescheitert," *Der Spiegel*, no. 18 (April 25, 1977); draft of the party program of the Socialist Party of Austria, quoted from *Wiener Tagebuch*, no. 11 (November 1977), pp. 4–6.

11. Carrillo, Debray, Gallo, *Spanien nach Franco*, p. 175.

12. *Der Spiegel*, no. 51 (December 12, 1977).

13. George Ball, "Communism in Italy," *Washington Post*, May 30, 1976.

14. *Politika ed Economica*, Rome, vol. 1–2, 1976; see also Enrico Berlinguer, "The Country Demands a Change," report to the Central Committee, May 13–14, 1976, *The Italian Communists, Foreign Bulletin of the PCI*, Rome, nos. 2–3 (April–July 1976), pp. 3–4.

15. In the "Pro und Contra" broadcast of South German Radio Stuttgart, early December 1976.

16. François Bondy, *Merkur*, Stuttgart, no. 11 (1977).

17. Andreotti in an interview in *Deutsche Zeitung*, no. 49 (November 25, 1977), p. 7.

18. Franca Magnani, "Die italienische Krise und der historische Kompromiss," *Vorgänge*, vol. 1, 1977.

19. *Der Spiegel*, no. 51 (December 12, 1977), p. 128.

20. See Rolf Görz, "Ein Pakt für Funktionäre," *Frankfurter Allgemeine Zeitung*, November 15, 1977.

21. From *Was Tun?* Frankfurt am Main, no. 182 (November 3), 1977.

22. Georgio Amendola, "On the Elections for the European Parliament," *Unità* (Rome), September 22, 1976; see also *The Italian Communists, Foreign Bulletin of the PCI*, Rome, no. 4–5 (1976), p. 28.

23. See the political resolution approved by the Fourteenth National Congress of the PCI, *Unità* (Rome), March 25, 1975; see also *The Italian Communists, Foreign Bulletin of the PCI*, Rome, no. 2–3 (1975), p. 127.

24. Carrillo, *Eurocommunism and the State*, p. 105.

25. Thorn in an interview in *Die Welt*, October 28, 1977.

26. *Die Welt*, June 7, 1977.

27. George Ball, "Communism in Italy," *Washington Post*, May 30, 1976.

28. See R. E. M. Irving, "The European Policy of the French and Italian Communists," *International Affairs* (London), July 1977, pp. 405–421.

29. *Neue Zürcher Zeitung*, August 21, 1976.

30. *Unità* (Rome), August 1, 1976.

31. Santiago Carrillo in an interview in *Time* (New York), July 28, 1975.

32. Helmut Sonnenfeldt in an interview in *Stern*, no. 43 (October 13, 1977).

33. *Die Welt*, May 18, 1977.
34. Willy Brandt in an interview in *Der Spiegel*, no. 5 (January 26, 1976).
35. Horst Ehmke, *Atlas* (New York), August 1976, p. 34, adapted from *Die Zeit*.
36. Peter Lange, "What's To Be Done—About Italian Communism," *Foreign Policy*, Winter 1975–1976. For a more detailed discussion of the PCI and NATO, see also, Walter Laqueur, " 'Eurocommunism' and its Friends," *Commentary*, April 1976, pp. 25–30.
37. Wolfgang Wagner, "Kommunisten im westlichen Bündnis," *Europa-Archiv*, Bonn, no. 10 (1976), pp. 314–324.

Index